Robert K.
MERTON
& CONTEMPORARY
SOCIOLOGY

Robert K. **MERTON** & CONTEMPORARY **SOCIOLOGY**

Carlo Mongardini & Simonetta Tabboni
EDITORS

Transaction Publishers
New Brunswick (U.S.A.) and London (U.K.)

Library of Congress Catalog Number: 97–16720
ISBN: 1–56000–318-9
Printed in the United States of America

Library of Congress Cataloging-in-Publication Data

Opera di R.K. Merton e la sociologia contemporanea. English.
   Robert K. Merton and contemporary sociology / edited
by Carlo Mongardini & Simonetta Tabboni.
      p.   cm.
   Papers presented at an international conference held in Amalfi,
Italy, in 1987.
   Includes bibliographical references and index.
   ISBN 1-56000-318-9 (alk. paper)
   1. Merton, Robert King, 1910–   —Congresses. 2. Sociology—
Congresses. I. Merton, Robert King. 1910–   . II. Mongardini,
Carlo. III. Tabboni, Simonetta, 1937–   . IV. Title.
HM22.U6M3854   1997
301—dc21   97–16720
                                                       CIP

Contents

Foreword   ix
Carlo Mongardini

Foreword to the American Edition   xv
Carlo Mongardini

Preface   xvii
Robert K. Merton

Part 1: Robert K. Merton's Place in Contemporary Sociological Thought

Introduction   1
Simonetta Tabboni

1. Robert K. Merton's Structural Analysis:
   The Design of Modern Sociology   21
   Volker Meja and Nico Stehr

2. Robert K. Merton: The Relation between Theory
   and Research   45
   Paolo Ammassari

3. Merton and the Sociology of Science in Europe   61
   Gianni Statera

4. The Informative-Formative Reception of Robert K.
   Merton's Work in Italy   77
   Filippo Barbano

Part 2: Concepts of Sociological Analysis

5. Sociological Ambivalence in the Thought of R.K. Merton   101
   Pierpaolo Donati

6. Robert K. Merton's Concept of Sociological Ambivalence:
    The Florentine Case of the "Man-Ape"   121
    Birgitta Nedelmann

7. Accumulation of Advantage and Disadvantage:
    The Theory and Its Intellectual Biography   139
    Harriet Zuckerman

8. Robert K. Merton's Four Concepts of Anomie   163
    Piotr Sztompka

9. The Unanticipated Consequences of Action:
    Sociological and Ethical Aspects   177
    Arnold Zingerle

10. Some Reflections on Latent Functions   187
    Peter Gerlich

11. Patterns of Manifest and Latent Influence:
    A Double Case Study of Influences on and from Robert K.
    Merton   197
    Charles Crothers

Part 3: Short Papers

12. Conditioning or Conditionings? Revisiting an
    Old Criticism of Mannheim by Merton   213
    Alberto Izzo

13. Some Thoughts on Two Works by Robert K. Merton   221
    Paolo Almondo

14. Robert K. Merton, the Teacher: Episodic Recollections
    by an Enthusiastic Apprentice   239
    Rocco Caporale

15. Notes towards an Analysis of the Relationship between
    Ambivalence and Rationality   247
    Alessandro Cavalli

16. Robert K. Merton for an "Open Society" ? Or, a
    Concept of Society Beyond Functionalism   251
    Giuliano Giorio

17. Robert K. Merton's Contribution to Sociological
    Studies of Time   257
    Simonetta Tabboni

18. Serendipity in the Work of Robert K. Merton 273
Maria Luisa Maniscalco

19. R.K. Merton: The Model of Theory-Empirical Research
Circularity as a Way Out of the Micro-Macro Dichotomy 285
Elena Besozzi

20. Sztompka's Analysis of Merton's Writings:
A Description and Some Criticisms 289
Charles Crothers

Afterword 295

Unanticipated Consequences and Kindred Sociological Ideas:
A Personal Gloss
Robert K. Merton

Contributors 319

Index of Names 325

Foreword

Carlo Mongardini

Robert K. Merton and Contemporary Sociology offers scholars of sociology the fruits of an international conference which took place in Amalfi in 1987 under the auspices of the Sociological Theories and Social Transformations Section of the Italian Sociological Association and with the participation of Merton himself.

Anyone who keeps up with the most recent developments in sociology knows how many doubts and uncertainties there are to ensnare sociological theory nowadays. Dissatisfaction with the results produced by the discipline affects three types of sociologists equally. There are those who keep themselves strictly in line with the traditional sociological models, making efforts to gather up social life into tables and unitary systems after the model of the natural sciences, and taking the concept of society as the ideal point of reference; there are those who find social unity despite its complexity in a moral judgement more or less associated with a political project; and there are those, lastly, who reduce sociological understanding to an anarchical aestheticism which takes the experience of everyday life as its subject and which amounts to an abandonment of theory as well as a more or less conscious retreat into the realm of the present.

Faced with these diverse positions, none capable of furnishing adequate tools for the interpretation and measurement of contemporary social reality, the attention of scholars turns again to the classic sociologists of the twentieth century. In particular to R.K. Merton, perhaps the least "classic" among the classics. In Merton, in fact, we find no system or unitary interpretative construct and yet we find a coherent system of thinking and of analytical build-up that takes us back to the need for unity and conceptual organization expressed by the first theoretical school of thought. In Merton, we find no search for moral valuation and less than ever compromises with political positions; but this independence is sustained by a rigid morality in the conception of the science and in the application of scientific method. In Merton, finally, we find no surrenders or even concessions to aestheticism in the manner of the third theoretical school of thought in the list, but it is precisely his great aesthetic taste, his aesthetic intuition of the complexity that underlies the apparently unilinear appearance of facts, that allows him to identify the multiformity of sociality even before it has been expressed. Thus, there is something in Merton of all that contemporary sociological theory seeks to express but without falling into mere attitudes and simply radical interpretations. His strength as a classic writer lies in his balance, his unveiling of complexity rather than over-simplifying of it, and in his humanism which knows to look beyond the seeming simplicity and coherence of social reality.

These qualities make his position particularly relevant to the contemporary sociological scene. Dissatisfaction with the results of most recent sociological theory leads us to look with increasing admiration at the evolution of his work, at the significance of its gradual changes from 1936 to the present day. In this work we see clearly a love of reason and at the same time a mistrust of the frequent results of rationality; a sense of science and the scientist's constraining morality and at the same time a sense of the irony of the relatively modest results that the scientist can achieve.

This is the basis for "wisdom"—the "sociological wisdom"—of Merton. The great love for the facts which must be present in any good sociologist is connected with the awareness that the facts do not speak for themselves. I do not know the facts, said Nietzsche, but only interpretations of the facts. And Merton finds in irony and ambivalence the right tools for covering the unbridgeable distance between facts and interpretations, between unreachable objectivity and the inevitably personal standpoint of the researcher which is the basis for his reflections and scientific constructions.

Irony and ambivalence, which are much discussed in this book, impose on Merton a further distance from reality. His great love for facts does not turn into a fetishism of factuality. Truth needs time. But time is distance. Thus, at the same time that Merton does not deny himself a strict observation of facts, he does impose an enlarged distance from them. That enlarged distance allows him to see the complexity of play and counterplay in the processes of social interaction; in other words, it allows him to raise his gaze from naked facts and to include the "significant little facts" in the vision of the person who represents them or who observes them. That is the meaning of Merton's humanism, where facts and viewpoints, observations and interpretations merge into an uncommon capacity to describe social processes.

Merton's irony and ambivalence represent the experience, even the drama, of his intellectual development based on a deep awareness of humanity. They represent the irreconcilable confrontation of *"undivided" holistic thinking* to which human beings are drawn in order to deal with practical daily needs and which are expressed in the tendency to control reality not according to its real nature but by reducing it to standard formulae and explanations, and *"reflected" thinking* so weak, sometimes so useless, often so difficult to reach, yet upon which all the possibilities for the construction of a science of man ultimately rest. Irony and ambivalence represent the drama of Merton, caught as he is between the European spirit of knowledge which he has cultivated from his earliest years and which can carry one down tortuous, labyrinthine paths of meditation, and the American spirit directed to factuality and discovery. It is a meeting of two continents and two ways of looking at reality and history. Irony and ambivalence also represent the drama of Merton in the confrontation of the natural and the social sciences. While he refers to the former all that tradition has handed down to us of the ideals and ideas of science, he recognizes in the latter a peculiarity that distinguishes them and distances them from what has been the interpretation of positivism. Positivist and antipositivist precisely because of his irony and ambivalence, insofar as he wants to forgo mere tables and mere systems, Merton is obliged to perform a continual conceptual readjustment; in short, he is obliged to develop the processuality of his thinking. Unwilling to bring reality down to tables and systems, he is obliged to follow reality in the many and diverse experiences in which it is manifested to him and to demonstrate how his thinking is modified (in a coherent framework, of course), as a result of each of those experiences. In this sense, Merton "lets himself go" with reality: he controls it by allowing himself be dominated by it, he tries to extract an experience from every occasion, not to develop an interpretative plan, but more simply to extend the range of his powers of thinking about reality.

The outcome is, as is obvious from most of the contributions gathered here, that Merton is a humanist first and only then a sociologist. He does not offer us schemata, he invites us to discover the ability of the mind to represent sociality, by putting its various aspects together and by taking them apart. He leads us not only to the discovery of uniformity, but to discovery of those differences of form that the cleverness of our reason tends to hide or cancel out in order that we to have the illusion of controlling reality.

We need the work of Merton because it offers us today that weight and consistency which is necessary to authentic sociological knowledge; because it does not try to fence in reality but takes us down many paths that bring reality closer; finally, because it does not deny the multiplicity of needs that have emerged in contemporary sociological theory. Rather it gives sociological theory that place, that dimension which arises from a humanistic vision of social relationships and processes. I do not think that either with Simmel or with Merton we have the feeling of climbing on the shoulders of a giant; we have the less dramatic, but perhaps more useful sense, of having a good guide and good advice in exploring the multiple and often contradictory aspects of social life.

The Amalfi Conference on the works of R. K. Merton took place in a very special atmosphere, not alone for its abiding academic commitment. The contributions gathered together in this volume can only partly convey what it was like: they do not tell the story or recreate the very special tone which having the presence of Merton in person imparted. Merton left a deep impression on me in what was, after all, a brief encounter: a few hours in Rome, a journey to Amalfi, a few minutes here and there between sessions. In total a few talks, the occasional anecdote and exchange of intellectual tastes, preferences and antipathies. Too little for a few days packed with so much activity and all this against the backdrop of Amalfi! Yet I retain from our encounter one of those impressions that leave their traces forever on our memory. With Merton a tension is created that never lets up but which never leaves you behind. He reveals his experience unreservedly and is respectful of silences and pauses. At the same time he is curious, insinuating, playful as any good investigator into the human spirit should be.

In the name of the Sociological Theories and Social Transformations Section of the Italian Sociology Association I wish to express my heartfelt thanks to the National Research Council for its contribution to the financing of the conference and the publication of this volume. My thanks also to the other organizations which made the conference possible, in particular, the Department of Sociology and Political Science of the University of Salerno, the Banca Nazionale del Lavoro, the Amalfi Tourist Office, and Sistem Form of Rome. I thank all my collaborators and in particular Simonetta Tabboni who has done an excellent job of editing this volume for publication.

Foreword to the American Edition

Some ten years since the Amalfi conference of 1987 it is with great pleasure that I send the American edition to the printer, to be made accessible to a much wider public. A rereading of its articles tells me that they have not lost the interest they had in the critical analysis of R.K. Merton's sociology those few years ago.

The memory of that first European meeting in Amalfi has also returned vividly to me from my rereading of these first pages. That Amalfi meeting has since been followed every year by another meeting dedicated to the great themes of modern culture. The conference papers have been collected in a series of volumes which I have edited for Edizioni Bulzoni of Rome. The fascination of these conferences has subsequently been added to by the Amalfi European Prize, awarded to scholars like Norbert Elias, Serge Muscovici, Zygmunt Bauman, Rainer M. Lepsius, Wolfgang J. Mommsen, Louis Dumont, and Charles Tilly. But the 1987 conference with Merton still holds a special significance even today. On that occasion European sociology bore witness to the debt it has to his work and his teaching and that witness is still alive in the pages of this book.

I wish to thank Irving Louis Horowitz for making this edition possible. I also want to thank Evie Robertson who translated most of the Italian texts, Yole Sills for helping to delete wholly ceremonial tributes from the translation, and Giorgio de Finis who was responsible for this new edition.

Carlo Mongardini
Rome, March 1996

Preface

Robert K. Merton

In retrospect, just as at the time, this Conference of the section on
Theoretical Sociology and Social Transformations of the Italian Sociological Association remains intellectually and organizationally impressive in its every aspect.

To begin with, there was an incomparable ambiance: the partly
retained and aptly reconstituted fourteenth-century convent, now known
as the Hotel Cappuccini Convento, on the rugged and beautiful Amalfi
coast. There could scarcely have been a more idyllic setting for the
lively interchanges among members of the *pro tem* thought collective—as Ludwik Fleck would have described it—gathered there to
examine selected sociological ideas and, in the process, to develop
those ideas further and to propose new ones.

Further, as students of organization were bound to note, the entire
Conference was organized with unobtrusive skill and gracious style.
Its composition was both transnational and theoretically variegated.
The participants were of course drawn in the main from Italy but not
alone from that host country. They came also from Austria, Canada,
Germany, Poland, the United States, and from as far off as antipodal
New Zealand. For such a polyglot assemblage, it mattered much that
the infrastructure of the Conference included provision for skilled and
considerate simultaneous translation. So, too, it mattered that the separate sessions provided for both designated and spontaneous discus-
sants of the theoretically connected papers which were prepared for
the occasion. This arrangement made for critical and spirited give-
and-take of a theoretically consequential kind. These sessions attended
by the participants as a whole were complemented, during planned

interludes of relaxation, by animated table talk among groups of participants, thus contributing further to the collegial atmosphere. This latter mode of discussion introduced an element of what Bronislaw Malinowski has described as "phatic communion": the use of conversation primarily to exchange expressions of social sentiments, thus serving rather more to establish an atmosphere of sociability than only to communicate cognitive ideas and social facts. (I believe that Malinowski would not have objected to this paraphrase of his anthropological idea.)

All this led to the Conference becoming a both a prime intellectual event and a gathering of the sociological clan. The three-day Amalfi meetings were, as we sociologists might put it in our tribal language, both intellectually instrumental and socially expressive.

Having commented at great length during the Conference upon the papers that make up this volume—to my mind, having commented at inordinate length—I make no effort in these very few introductory pages to comment on them further. Nor shall I identify and annotate the themes in my work that are examined in those papers and critical interventions. Instead, I shall set out in a separate paper the personal, social, and cognitive contexts of one of those themes: the unanticipated consequences of purposive social action and kindred social ideas.

Perhaps I may be allowed this further and concluding moment of phatic communion: for me, the 1987 Amalfi Conference was an illuminating, energizing, and much appreciated exchange of sociological ideas with colleagues who are ordinarily at too far a distance.

Part 1

Robert K. Merton's Place in Contemporary Sociological Thought

Introduction

Simonetta Tabboni

The international conference which took place in Amalfi on "Robert K. Merton and Contemporary Sociology" provided the premise for some timely reflection. It brought back into the limelight a classic who had been rather forgotten in Europe. It was an invitation to think again about an original theoretical approach which links a great range of analytical tools and empirical researches. It posed an interesting question for a period of great fragmentation in sociological models: what relationship is there between present-day sociologists and the thinking of the last great representative of the neo-functional model, of a theoretical approach which, (as indeed did the functionalist model), presented itself as the natural leader, the prime way forward for sociology to be practiced as a science?

The official responses to these questions, gathered together in this volume, came from all over the world. They are rich and various.

The connection between the characteristically nonsystematic nature, the openness and polyvalence in Merton's thought and the heterogeneity of these contributions is probably not fortuitous. The topics dealt with were numerous and widely different as were the geographical origins, the academic background and age of the many scholars present. It would not have been an easy undertaking to identify connecting threads, select lines of thought that could form a basis for a systematic account of the many responses the conference elicited to the question "what is the place of Merton in contemporary sociology?"

1

Perhaps it would not even have been a worthwhile undertaking. At any rate, all efforts at conferring such an order on the various contributions has been abandoned. The criterion which has been adopted is purely pragmatic: the material assembled has been organized according to the order which might seem most useful for teaching purposes. The four chapters by Paolo Ammassari, Volker Meja and Nico Stehr, Gianni Statera, and Filippo Barbano, whose subjects were all an evaluation of Merton's work, lent themselves to an introductory function. It is without doubt useful for someone approaching the study of Merton today to find articles that deal with the influence Merton had on the general direction of U.S. research as opposed to European research; his contribution, which was decisive, to the development of the sociology of science; his basic belief that the relationship between theory and empirical research is inseparable; and with the significance of the meeting of Merton's thinking and Italian sociology in the 1950s.

The second part contains the studies of the basic analytical categories of Mertonian analysis, the reflections on their relevance in general and in relation to the specific cognitive problems of contemporary social reality, while the third part has been given over to the short chapters, according to the criteria the writers themselves adopted to define their chapters.

The elaboration of concepts and their continual clarification have been Merton's passion; this is also the type of work for which he was best suited, bringing out both his creativity and his scholarliness.[1]

Merton has given prime importance to the construction of conceptual tools not least because of the central significance he gives to such construction in the course sociology has to take to throw off its state of scientific immaturity and reach conditions comparable to those in which the natural sciences operate. The most urgent task that sociologists have to face to close the gap that divides them from the way in which the other sciences operate is the elaboration of a precise scientific language, the abandonment of approximative terms adapted from everyday language, like a journalist's description of facts. Sociologists must refer to a set of unequivocal, universally accepted conceptualizations on which to base their researches. Field work does not give results if the person who performs it has not an adequate heritage of theoretical tools, just as those tools cannot take shape except in close connection with empirical research.[2]

Predictably enough, therefore, in view of the frontline role of Merton the theorist, most of these chapters take his elaboration of analytical categories as their subject. The chapters by Birgitta Nedelmann, Pierpaolo Donati, Peter Gerlich, Harriet Zuckerman, Alberto Izzo, Arnold Zingerle, to cite only these few, deal respectively with the concept of ambivalence, latent and manifest functions, the accumulation of advantage and disadvantage, scientific truth and unanticipated consequences.

These authors chose two approaches to the conceptual heritage elaborated by Merton, both of which were equally legitimate and equally suitable for developing their content. The first and most common approach was to embark on a mainly theoretical reflection. They examined the concept, went over its construction, then tested the concept for its general and current relevance. They paused over its lacunae or its particular inadequacy for the social reality of the conditions which are most often the focus of recent sociological reflection (complexity, the weakening of normative structures, the multiplication and impossibility of comparing cultural codes).

The second approach put the concept to the test of empirical research. A case-study created on the basis of the concept was discussed with reflections on the adequacy of the concept for explaining a certain reality and on its possible further theoretical developments.

This second application of his work was undoubtedly most appreciated by Merton. He spent a long time on these papers, clearly with pleasure and a desire to continue the research, giving further proof of his deep-rooted intellectual commitment to the guiding principle of necessary interaction between theory and empirical research.

Over and above the official responses, which are there to be read, the conference elicited implicit responses to the question of the links between contemporary sociology and Merton's thinking; it raised points of reflection that can be seen as very positive outcomes of the conference and are well worth taking time to consider more closely.

It emerged, for example, that the use the assembled sociologists tended to make of Merton's conceptual heritage generally followed particular inspirations on research, similar general directions: that it was certain Mertonian positions and concepts that had appeal and produced a desire for further exploration. This volume will try to focus on these implicit responses, look closely at the new interpretations and the powerful appeal of certain themes and put forward some suggestions about their general and current significance.

The choices made by the conference participants indicated without doubt that it was one particular part of Merton's work, not necessarily the best known or the type of analysis classically associated with it, that attracted most interest. It is enough to recall that only one chapter took as its subject the famous concept of anomie, for so many years at the heart of all research on deviance and, beyond deviance, not a single chapter on group theory and mass communications, and only two dealing with questions associated with the field of study Merton is most identified with, the history and sociology of science.

The Mertonian themes which proved most attractive were those linked with the criticism of classical functionalism, either as the abandonment of aspirations to global theory or as the progression beyond a prevalently structural, normativist position or, more especially, as the preparation of tools suited to registering the most fleeting and paradoxical aspects of social reality.

Briefly, there were three research areas where the assembled sociologists showed most interest in further exploration: (a) the proposal for a pluralistic theoretical approach; (b) the development of a series of concepts leading to a sociology that might be described as dealing with the subliminal in society. These concepts, apart from considerably extending the analytical field of classical functionalism and countering the most obvious instances of its shortcomings, define in various ways a single, fundamental intuition central to Merton's work which finds its most general expression in the essay on ambivalence; and (c) an innovative analysis of classic concepts such as anomie, made for the purpose of demonstrating its relevance within the general theory. No longer then as concepts that throw light on particular areas of sociological research but as theoretical tools that, taken over the whole range of their implications, show that Mertonian structuralism can provide satisfying answers to the central dilemmas of sociological theory. Many of Merton's concepts constitute lines of conjunction, for example, between theories of structure and theories of action, between theories of order and theories of change.

R.K. Merton is a great theorist who has never wished to link his name to any single theory of society, to any final, exhaustive answer to the big questions of sociological theory. His aversion to monumental works, grand theory, his preference for empirical research, elaborations of theories of the middle range, constructions which are never completed but are constantly being updated and further explored, for cognitive tools to use in the field, these are the most obvious and characteristic features of his style, as Filippo Barbano's chapter elucidates. His thinking gives an important place to the awareness of the many forms that rationality can assume, the profound irony, the ambivalence, the paradoxes contained in the norms and models of social behavior.

His theoretical position is first and foremost and avowedly open and "in progress."

This style of thinking in which the high level of theorization and the variety and heterogeneity of interests seem curiously intertwined, must have greatly fascinated students of Merton, his teachers and his pupils, who, in their descriptions of him, have had recourse to powerful and vivid metaphors. Pitirim Sorokin[3] has likened his writings to variations by Beethoven on themes by Mozart and Lewis A. Coser has painted him as the "fox of sociology" (Coser 1975: 88)—referring to Isaiah Berlin's famous division of thinkers into hedgehogs and foxes. Berlin's passage, which recalls a fragment of Archilochus, says that among animals and humans there are two opposite character tendencies, that of the hedgehog and that of the fox. While the hedgehog knows one basic thing and dedicates itself to cultivating that, the fox cultivates many things and, being curious, dedicates itself to the most diverse undertakings and accumulates a wide variety of knowledge. Among humans, too, there exists this basic difference: there are those, be they scientists, artists, or common mortals, who seek for a general interpretative criterion by the light of which they will read all their experience, putting all their effort and talent into building an all-embracing system. And there are those who follow the most varied research objectives without any interest in giving them a systematic, coherent place in one global view of life. These latter research on many levels, their experiences are most varied and least collective; they do not feel the necessity to fit them into a general theory, into one interpretation of the world. These two intellectual personalities are indeed as opposite as the characters of the hedgehog and the fox.

The coherence and substantial unity of Merton's thinking are not immediately obvious. They are revealed in rather different ways from those most frequently found in the great theorists both present and past; they are most fully present more as the unmistakably Mertonian method, a recognizable research approach, a "signature," "the art of approaching a variety of substantively different theoretical problems under a unified theoretical angle of vision"[4] rather than as elements contributing to one totalizing construction. As has been rightly emphasized by Lewis A. Coser (1975), Piotr Sztompka (1986: 1–3), and Arthur Stinchcombe (1975: 11–13), they must be traced through a skillful piece of excavation, by comparison or connection, or by proof of the service they have rendered to research.

The fact that his academic fathers were monumental, monolithic personalities like Talcott Parsons and Pitirim Sorokin, "hedgehogs" in Berlin's sense, and men of their time in their passion for conclusive syntheses, works of great theoretical breadth, was perhaps a contributing factor in making him the rebellious son and the first "classic" to commit himself to dealing with the changing, changeable world of advanced modernity using partial, provisional tools, ones that did not even claim to be exhaustive (Frisby 1985).

Merton has taken his place at the center of contemporary sociology by adopting an approach which is the direct opposite of that adopted by his masters, by denying the form of their scientific commitment— the grand theory, the magnum opus to which one gives one's name forever—in order to win back fully the substance and the level of theorization.

The image of the social actor as drawn by Merton is wholly contained in a context of doubts and ongoing conflicts.[5] However, these uncertainties are not necessarily experienced with anxiety or particular distress. The unpredictability, the risk, the contradictions are recognized as the realities of everyday experiences, are even appreciated for their dynamic qualities, the interest and flavor they give to social life. The world of human interactions as seen through the eyes of Merton is like a fascinating kaleidoscope whose often surprising shapes and combinations excite constant curiosity till the key to their interpretation is reached, a model to explain them achieved. Concepts and models are often provisional, they need to be put to the test, reviewed now and then, certainly not definitively set into a totalizing theory.

Merton has respected and revitalized a demanding heritage by setting against his masters' all-encompassing systems a way of making theory agile and circumspect, equipped to take on the challenges of a social world which is increasingly differentiated and difficult to decipher, in which the actor not only assumes diverse, often conflicting, roles but relates to heterogeneous cultural spheres that do not admit of comparison.[6]

The Mertonian "sociology of the subliminal," that set of concepts such as the unanticipated consequences of social action, latent and manifest functions, ambivalence, whose conceptual affinity I wish to emphasize, was the center of attention of the conference, its most exciting kernel, the point at which the majority of the lectures and the short papers met.

The major focus of the conference was on the themes connected with Herbert Simon's "bounded rationality,"[7] a complex representation of the social actor, the awareness of the necessity for the researcher to register "another" reality beyond appearances, one which contradicts the first, more likely, interpretation.

All these reflections converged to highlight the importance that contemporary sociologists (or at least those present) gave to the need for greater study of one theme in particular, ambivalence, which has so far not had its due attention in sociological reflection.

To adopt Sztompka's criterion for dividing Merton's work into themes (the classicist theme, the cognitivist theme, the structuralist theme, the ironic theme), (Sztompka 1986: 5) it was undoubtedly this last theme which exercised most fascination, which elicited the desire for further study. The theme of irony has for that matter occupied much attention in the American debate, and has been the subject of interesting monographs.

The centrality of this theme in Merton's work has been underlined by Louis Schneider in the 1975 *Festschrift* in Merton's honor. Schneider's analysis of the significance that the development of the ironic theme may have for sociology deserves careful consideration because it challenges a basic approach to looking at the social reality being investigated and assumes an enormous importance in the current difficulties of sociological analysis: "Where there is irony, there is a sense that things are not the way they are 'supposed to be.' Ironic outcomes of action involve an element of the unintended or unexpected. . . . But irony also suggests a 'knowing' or wry smile just because one witnesses the bafflement or mockery of the fitness of things, of their supposed-to-be character. This does not, however, preclude a certain affinity with the comic. There is certainly such a thing as tragic irony. Indeed, irony would appear to lend support to the contention of those students of laughter who claim that we laugh because, if we didn't, we would cry." On the other hand, and this he seems to emphasize: "Irony is emphatically not the same as cynicism or sarcasm or satire or a jaundiced view of the world. To allow a careless identifica-

tion or coalescence of it with these things is to render it—and properly
so—suspect for purposes of sociological analysis; and the present object is precisely to help rescue it for its uses for such analysis"
(Schneider 1975: 324).

Schneider has claimed that there are precise links between the functional approach and the theme of irony and that these links are particularly strong in the original version of functional analysis elaborated by
Merton. This claim deserves attention and it would be interesting were
Schneider himself or, now that he is gone, another student of Merton
to take it further.

Merton himself readily identifies with the ironic theme, and did so
explicitly in a letter to Schneider written on 14 September 1975. In
this letter Merton thanks Schneider for having chosen precisely this
theme for the *Festschrift* in his honor, adding that he had taken
Schneider's choice as further proof of the deep and lasting affinity
between them in their style of thinking.

Sztompka, too, has strongly emphasized the centrality of the theme
of irony in Mertonian analysis, claiming, unlike Schneider, that it
connects with a conflictualist view of the world: "In my interpretation
it entails a focus on distinct attributes of society: *complexity, contradiction, relativity, circularity, and paradox*" (Sztompka 1986: 253).

Reflections on how the ironic theme develops early, by acquisition
and progressive study, in Merton's academic career makes it possible
to form a hypothesis just as the astute and contrasting evaluations that
Merton has been subjected to open up many not insignificant questions on the relationship between Merton and contemporary sociology.

The hypothesis I should like to put forward is that the "ironic theme"
is in reality only one among Merton's basic inspirations, a total, unitary research tool, which appears as early as 1936, the year of the
"Unanticipated Consequences" (one of his first articles), and takes on
another form in 1949 with the famous essay on latent and manifest
functions, working its way through progressive stages to the final
formulation of the concept in 1963 (Merton and Barber 1963: 91–120
and Merton 1986) which potentially contains all the previous themes,
the concept of ambivalence.

Merton's intellectual progress often follows a path whose stages are
marked first by significant intuitions, then by the construction of "proto-
concepts," and finally by the formulation of a developed concept that
takes shape only after many years and much confrontation with em-

pirical research (Merton 1984; Tabboni 1985, partial Italian trans.: 163–187). In the case of the "ironic theme," though some differences can be seen in the line of development, it is substantially the same even if what we find are not proto-concepts but a succession of fully elaborated concepts, capable of application to research.

Unanticipated consequences and latent and manifest functions would seem to fit into the more comprehensive concept of ambivalence, and explain in different ways a rather ambivalent view of social life, human relations and the communication that sustains them (Watzlawick et al. 1967; Bateson 1972), and the normative structures that regulate them. Any conception of social reality, of course, that maintains the existence of conscious and unconscious levels of reality, manifest and latent or even structural and ideological, takes us straight back to the more general concept of ambivalence. What is the significance of the attention Merton gives to the theme of ambivalence, his elaboration of the concept of sociological ambivalence, if not the awareness shared by many of the founding fathers that the social actor very often chooses within a range of options about which he has conflicting feelings? Here too, Merton develops European themes, a theme dear to Georg Simmel in particular. Like Simmel, Merton is convinced that in social interaction the actor finds himself in situations of normal uncertainty between courses of action which seem to be equally desirable in that they would satisfy equally basic though opposed needs. Merton develops Simmel's thinking further by analyzing how ambivalence is actually written into the normative structures that frequently prescribe incompatible behavior and attitudes.

The essay on ambivalence is the culmination of long reflection, frequently concluded by the formulation of entirely new concepts stemming from observation of various aspects of reality. What, in fact, *is* the basis of intuition that lies behind the "ironic" concepts if not an awareness of the ambivalence underlying every human action, conditioning choice and revealing intention, an ambivalence that is only temporarily and not necessarily suspended in the decisional process and that is in any case never completely removed?

As for the discordant interpretations that Schneider and Sztompka have offered on the "ironic theme," these undoubtedly raise questions of significant interest. One might ask, for example: what is the significance of this theme for Merton's work as a whole, or his supposedly "conflictualist" worldview, the deliberately fragmentary nature of his theoretical approach, his early awareness of the various courses of rationality, the snares and "non-senses" that await anyone trying to come to grips with how a human society works?

Is Merton the first of the great American sociologists to expose himself to doubt, the realms of probability, the recognition of the constitutive limits of knowledge of the social world or is he rather the last and most astute exponent of an intellectual tradition which is fundamentally illuminist and scientistic in its basic convictions, a man whose intellectual finesse has permitted him to elaborate tools far ahead of his time which can tackle the cognitive difficulties that the present generation of sociologists has increasingly become aware of?

How far can one sustain the view that Merton is a conflictualist or a thinker who has been notably influenced by Simmel's approach to analysis of social reality?[8] What role, what priority in his intellectual make-up has Simmelian impressionistic inspiration, the dexterity of the juggler in noting ironies and contradictions and the illuminist's need to construct the basis of a science on traditional criteria, to get the better of disorder and the surprises of collective life by identifying their structural sources, cataloguing their forms and levels, reaffirming substantially the priority of structures in the explanation both con- formist and deviant behavior?

Another question, admittedly of minor importance, concerns the general system of values that underlie Merton's "ironic" tools. Does the ironic perspective assume a knowledge ethic that takes detachment as a necessary premise for competent intervention or is it rather a question of an ethic of indifference, a sort of resignation even if ex- pressed brilliantly? Is Mertonian irony to be interpreted as merely a stage in the process towards a possible committed sociological inter- vention or is it a tool of a disenchanted functional analysis tending to mere comprehension of what exists, contenting itself with smiling at its paradoxes? It would be interesting here to check the affinities and differences distinguishing the various ironic approaches, for example Merton's and that of Goffman and the Chicagoans.[9]

This is not the place to develop these themes, though each would justify closer study. It is important, however, to note their relevance in a general discussion of Merton's work for their link with one of the most crucial areas of reflection in contemporary sociology.

Many of the concepts Merton elaborated demonstrate his firm resolve to work by setting himself solidly "on the shoulders of giants," to connect up again with the European tradition of the founding fathers of sociological thinking. His idea of knowledge as selective accumulation, his willingness to reconnect with a tradition in order to make it fruitful again are well illustrated by the relationship Merton establishes early on with the most important of his "masters-at-a-distance," Émile Durkheim.

The famous essay "Social Structure and Anomie" is an obvious example of how, under what circumstances and with what attitude Merton draws on Durkheim's theoretical heritage and revitalizes it by developing it as a function of the new cognitive ideas emerging in the course of empirical research. The historical background of Merton's essay is the America of the Depression years, a period in which right-thinking people faced with the explosion of crime and deviance, lament the passing of individual moral values and look back with regret at the moral fiber of the honest American of the good old days. The help of Durkheim, the great analyst of structure, shows itself to be precious for the explanation Merton is seeking: his theory of anomie is re-examined and adapted to a different sociohistorical context and other empirical research situations. "The Durkheimian interplay between biological propensity and societal regulation was transformed in Merton's work into the discrepancy between culturally prescribed goals and socially available means of achieving these goals" (Coser 1975: 95). It is precisely by starting from the analysis of social structures and the pressure they exert on the individual that one can understand non-conformist behavior, that one can account for how on earth many individuals abandon lawful or previously customary ways of obtaining their ends when the field of opportunities narrows.

Piotr Sztompka, in his turn, develops the Mertonian concept of anomie in a decidedly original way: focusing on the four different concepts of anomie that Merton has recourse to, he shows its relevance in a theoretical context that goes well beyond the sociology of deviance where it had been mostly applied. The analysis of the different forms of anomie in its multiplicity of levels allows Sztompka to claim that Merton's sociology is not static and functionalist as is often held but clearly structural, dynamic and conflictual. Structure is a multidimensional construct for Merton, in fact, a network of models of social relations extending their influence on different levels: there exist not only normative structures, but also ideal and opportunity structures. Through the concept of anomie one can collect the contradictions that occur on the different levels and within each level.

Merton's chief concern, according to Sztompka, has always been not only to account for the specific contradictory configurations that work their way into the structures, but also to explain "the construction of the structures," the processes by which certain structures are produced and consolidated.

Since the dysfunctions, the conflicts, the tensions that the structures generate are the rule rather than the exception, the concept of anomie, like other Mertonian concepts, belongs contemporaneously to both the sociology of deviance and to general sociology.

The different concepts of anomie can be used to account for order and change, conformism and innovation; they constitute conceptual bridges linking traditionally opposed sociological approaches, such as theories of action and theories of structure. In fact, structures do not determine human behavior in a direct, unidirectional way; they open, facilitate, or obstruct certain fields of possibility for individual choice. The possible solutions for the individual faced with structural contradictions are so numerous on the different levels as to seem like free choice, albeit within certain constraints. Thus, the concept of anomie turns out to be much richer than was previously recognized because it identifies a characteristic structural condition that by favoring very different forms of deviance (criminal but also revolutionary and innovative behaviors) explains different forms and levels of social change, while it also connects the study of processes to that of social structures. It is a concept that bears a precious contribution for general theory.

Reading the report of the conference is not enough to explain a happy circumstance: the conference proceeded in an unusual and unpredictable way. This occurred because two things took on great significance; on the one hand, the "classic" stature of a scholar, on the other, his conception of collegial professionality to which we are not perhaps quite accustomed.

The conference could easily have taken on a chiefly celebrative appearance: the occasion for meeting one of the last great figures in sociological thinking could have led to highly dignified academic exercises with little to connect them to each other, to the recognition of an intellectual debt and to the fact, clearly acceptable but hardly stimulating, that "we cannot help but be Mertonians." Such homage to a sacred cow could have remained superficial, not been translated into a genuine exchange between participants and the personality around whom the conference was built.

The recognition of the topicality of Merton's thinking represented another small risk for the course of the conference. The discussion springing from the papers could have been confined to recording that many of the themes which have occupied sociologists in recent years (the unanticipated consequences of social action, the effort to overcome the dichotomy between theories of action and theories of structure, the revision of the conceptual schemata derived from utilitarianism, the limits of rationality and its diverse forms, social time) had been boldly anticipated in Merton's decisive contributions or owed their roots to his work.

The possibility of having a real dialogue between Merton and contemporary sociology would thus have been missed. Above all, a real contact would not have been established between the Mertonian method of tackling problems and the real interests of the participants, the load of real questions that every sociologist there presumably carried with them to the conference. Everyone could have agreed, paradoxically, that despite evidence to the contrary—the few sociological works and the few university courses dedicated to his thinking in Europe—Merton was really "very topical."

Fortunately, even the danger of a generic acceptance of Merton's contemporary relevance was avoided. What became obvious instead was the power of his thinking to generate discussion, to bring different points of view together and to raise untopical but valid questions. His thinking raised as many if not more problems than were declared solved and it was capable of application to quite disparate research interests. In other words, it became obvious that Merton is a "classic" if by classic is meant a powerful thinker, one whose ideas practitioners of a discipline cannot avoid tackling in the course of their studies or research.

But the decisive factor for the success of the conference was probably that the "classic" in question is also an unusual intellectual who joyfully squanders his time and his energies in discussion, and who nurtures a definite, indefatigable interest in other people's thinking. Along with his willingness to take part and become involved, however, there is a scrupulous attention to timing, absolute respect for punctuality and the rules that give everyone a chance to contribute equally to the debate, a diligent awareness of everyone's needs. This leads one to think that Merton's behavior does not stem from his having special gifts of expression nor from an exceptionally developed human generosity but rather from his precise and exacting understanding of collegial professionality.

In this respect Rocco Caporale's short chapter on Merton as a teacher deserves particular attention. It is the only written testimony we have that tries to give an idea of the atmosphere that Merton instantly created in the conference by his ability to transform it into a real event, into something far removed from a formal celebration. From Caporale's account one gets a clear idea of how the figures of the scientist, the teacher, and the intellectual mentor have never been separated in Merton; one gets a sense of his extraordinary propensity to take up every case with passion and of the central importance of the teaching role in his life.

The ability of a scholar to inspire and stimulate research interests in those around him, to be a good teacher day after day in dealing with those who have just come to the discipline and are learning how to use its concepts, the ability to offer tools for a scientific reading of the most ordinary realities, all these abilities are far too often undervalued. We do not often have word of how teachers teach: Merton offered us a remarkable example in the course of the conference. The figure described by Caporale was the same one that enlivened the scene at Amalfi: the discussion of every paper was conducted seriously, passionately, with a truly astonishing capacity to extend its confines and find exemplifications. Every subject dealt with was enriched by contact with this affectionate and life-giving interlocutor; even the papers dedicated to strictly defined, specialized perspectives became, on contact with Merton, topics that any sociologist could ill afford to neglect. In other words, subjects were immediately made meaningful by their connections with other aspects and other topics of more general interest. Merton's way of working and of tackling cognitive problems is at once demanding, relentlessly operative, and sustained by a strong urge to know and by the conviction that knowledge is possible. For diverse and serious reasons (among them the proliferation of approaches and the difficulty of communicating them, the difficulties of interpretation of "complex" societies) these qualities are not very common among sociologists today.

There were often strong differences of opinion during the discussions but these were also occasions of reciprocal enrichment between positions of doubt and more than legitimate mistrust on the one hand and the force, perhaps not always to be agreed with but certainly therapeutic, of a scholar whose thinking is at one with his desire to understand reality.

Perhaps this three-day encounter/confrontation with Merton, with his way of working and thinking which is indefatigably directed to research and empirical evidence, rigorously scientific yet full of sociological imagination, has restored some faith to practitioners of the "weak science": the faith that they can work as scientists and, though fully aware of the specific difficulties that acquisition of knowledge always implies and particularly in these times, they can nevertheless go forward in the conviction that this work is possible, that it makes sense and can even be a matter for passionate commitment.

A return to a study of Merton and discussion of his ideas frequently has this effect.

Interest in Merton's thinking is probably on the increase in Europe after a long period of relative indifference barely concealed behind a formal deference.

Studies of Merton in the United States, on the other hand, have never known a moment's pause. During the 1970s as also before, a significant number of studies by academics of a certain standing bear witness to the unceasing attention given to Mertonian themes and to the continuing flow of follow-up studies, reworkings and re-examinations associated with them. Nevertheless, from young American sociologists and from efforts to discuss Merton with them one forms a rather different impression from the general picture of attention or at least the regular examination of his ideas illustrated by the numerous studies mentioned above.

More than oblivion, the neo-functional model would seem to be suffering among these young sociologists from the consequences of a vaguely ideological line-up combined with questions of image. On the one hand, the accusation of conservatism directed at functionalism as a whole in the 1960s; on the other, the fact that many of the leading lights in the American debate taking place around Merton's thinking are his descendants, linked to him by close intellectual relationship and belonging to the highest academic echelons, all of this contributing to the creation of an aura of power and officialdom round the figure of Merton and the Mertonians. Naturally this has invited dissent.

Many sociologists of the new generation, identifying conservatism with functionalism and the latter with the thinking of Merton, (who of course has been one of its most active critics), largely discounted him, without reflecting too much on the losses that might be implied by such hasty action.

Merton's position was thus frequently disregarded, as if it were that of a venerable and a rather too-venerated sociological divinity, a symbol of academic power in its most conspicuous forms, whose great merits cannot be denied but from whom one must break away in order to follow new paths less tied to a particular academic establishment.

The situation in Europe and in Italy in particular was very different: here, Merton's eclipse was long and almost total, brought about, most probably, by the deliberately fragmentary nature of his thinking and the prevalently cognitive, objective emphasis with its opposition to all ideological involvement. In Europe and in Italy the sociological works which have always excited the most interest are those which offer a global synthesis of social reality with some exhaustive formula.

The aspiration towards all-encompassing explanations and totalizing theories of social reality is time-honored and lies deep in sociologists, particularly European sociologists, always less willing than Americans to undertake empirical research; besides, this aspiration is encouraged by their audience and rewarded by the media with not negligible gratification both to the pocket and to the ego.

If in a period when a discipline was being founded in a country—the Italian situation described by Barbano—Merton's works seemed precious and indispensable, it might have been difficult to remain faithful to Merton when that meant a rigid discipline of both theoretical and empirical work, without any concessions freely given to generalizations not validated by the research.

Furthermore, in a period when there was great pressure to line up ideologically (the 1960s and 1970s) Merton was not destined to have enormous success. As Robert Bierstedt has noted, Merton's sociology is far from being a "critical sociology," one which ties research to the realization of moral objectives and political ideals. Merton is much more interested in understanding than in changing the world. He is a sociologist, not a preacher (Bierstedt 1981). His purpose is to discover the patterns latent in social life that are invisible to the untrained eye. Merton has largely cultivated a cognitive vocation, he is a scholar whose interest in knowledge for itself does not seem mediated by other concerns except on rare occasions. Piotr Sztompka, too, has drawn attention to this aspect of Merton's intellectual character: "If I read Merton correctly, his ultimate goal is attaining a specific form of sociological knowledge that I would describe as *nomological under-standing of social patterns*. That is to say, his main preoccupation is to introduce a measure of intellectual order into human perceptions of social life. Such intellectual order is produced by generalised concepts, taxonomies, typologies, classifications, law-like formulas; in a word, by nomological postulates" (Sztompka 1986: 11).

The underlying message in Merton's thinking has always consisted of a firm and practical proposal to transform sociology into a "positive" science, albeit in the best and least naive sense of the term, into a rigorous, disciplined, methodical professionalization, a steady accumulation linked to empirical research through its heritage of working theoretical tools.

It must not be forgotten that Merton's ideal point of reference remains the natural sciences and that his lack of a systematic approach is linked to the recognition of the *temporary* state of inferiority of sociology as a science. His hope is that sociological research will reach the scientific validity of the "hard" sciences, that it will adopt the statutes of scientific method completely.

It is likely that the need for ideology in the 1960s taken along with the so-called crisis of the 1970s and the subsequent collapse of ideological commitment are all factors that have contributed to distancing European sociologists from Merton's type of largely cognitive commitment, deliberately limited in its objectives, but holding fast to the reality of empirical research and the illuminist faith that sustains it.

Now, probably, the times are ripe even in Europe for reapplying Merton's heritage (without necessarily taking it in its most markedly scientist perspective), preserving the greater awareness this period has given us of the limits inherent in any cognitive process (Mongardini 1983: 9–27), but building on the great wealth of his research subjects and tools.

The work is as promising as it is arduous. It is not comfortable to be "on the shoulders of Merton"—from this position there is no concession to generic dissertations on the way of the world, no digressions or speculations that are not to be supported by serious efforts at empirical research.

Notes

1. The importance Merton attributed to the formulation of concepts; their discovery, clear definition, and completed elaboration is evident straightaway in his words, the way in which he connects this precious kernel of scientific activity to recommendations stemming from empirical research. See Merton, in Powell and Robbins 1984.

2. Merton's theoretical talent has been widely recognized, of course. Studies of his work in the United States agree in underlining this aspect of his work and also the phenomenon closely connected to this, the very large number of quotations, references, and Mertonian concepts that all empirical research—not simply social science research—has contained in recent years.

   In this connection it is interesting to read the conclusion that Garfield (1980: 61) comes to on the basis of a study between 1970 and 1977 of more than 2,500 articles in which concepts elaborated by Merton were cited or used: "The strength of his influence derives firstly from his theoretical contributions. . . . In both the social and the natural sciences . . . two thirds at least of the citations concern concepts rather than research results. This confirms the impression that Merton's major contribution has been of a theoretical nature."

   The influence exercised by Merton on research, especially the regular recourse to his analytical categories on the part of authors of innumerable empirical researches, essays, and sociological undertakings of all kinds is an undisputable fact. As again Garfield says in the same essay: "The data are ample proof that his influence derives from the prolific production of unique sociological concepts that are widely accepted and used" (1980: 71).

3. According to Sorokin (1966: 455) " . . . like the Beethoven variations on themes by Mozart or the Brahms variations on themes by Paganini, the Merton variations are admirable in many senses."

4. According to Coser (1977: 567), "While rejecting the Parsonsian attempt to build an all-encompassing theory at this stage of sociology's development, Merton nevertheless taught his students the art of approaching a variety of substantively different theoretical problems under a unified theoretical angle of vision".

5. In comparing the images of the social actor as drawn by Parsons and by Merton, Coser (1975: 98), puts it this way: "While the latter [Parsons] thinks more or less in global categories, Merton's analytical strategies are characterised, *inter alia*, by an unrelenting attention to the ambivalences and conflicts to be found within the global structures, to the ambivalences in actors' motivations, to the ambiguities rampant in the field of perceptions on the basis of which these are created. As becomes a sociological fox, Merton is never satisfied to reach one vision of the whole and is always a little embarrassed to show that what is true for him is also true for the subject of the analysis. The Parsonsian actor *knows* the role possibilities that derive from the position he occupies, even if now and then he may find himself motivated to deviate from them. Merton's actor manages role-sets and status-sets that take him back to contradictory expectations and he navigates among them habitually. He takes great care to avoid the Scylla of excessive conformity and the Charybdis of deviance, frequently falling prey to both. This actor is not

simply a part of the society with a capital *S* of Durkheim and Parsons. He belongs to conflicting subgroups, reciprocally exclusive and appealing, which are at war with each other to win the loyalty and the collaboration of subgroups. Merton's world is a universe of warring gods and things are never easy to solve in this empyrean."

6. Merton has often drawn attention to the cultural complexity of his analyses. One of the clearest pieces of evidence of his awareness of this is in the essay on outsiders and insiders (Merton 1928: 881–893) in which the figure of the stranger and the outsider is for the first time placed against the background of a culturally complex society.

7. Compare Boudon 1977: 19.

8. Piotr Sztompka seems to incline to this hypothesis though it is put forward along with a substantially systematic interpretation of Merton's thinking. It is not easy to see, in fact, how the two interpretations can go together: the problem remains open and can be taken as one of the most interesting points in the development of Merton's thinking. Compare Sztompka 1986: 3, 27.

   Other scholars hold more or less divergent interpretations. According to Wallace and Wolf (1980), for example, Merton maintains a clearly functional position. "Contrary to most theorists of conflict, Merton is convinced that institutions and values can be functional (or dysfunctional) for society as a whole, not only for particular groups. Merton's accent on dysfunctions balances, to use a good functionalist term, Parsons's interest in social functions."

   L.A. Coser (1977: 567), too, having often emphasized the great significance conflict assumes in Mertonian theory, takes a subtler position than Sztompka, maintaining that Merton has only "tried to soften the previous rigidity of functionalist theory," without necessarily turning into a conflictualist for that: "Merton did yeoman's work in banishing the Panglossian optimism that all was always to the best in the best of all possible (functional) worlds. His analyses stressed instead the need to be aware of basically structural sources of disorder, of socio-cultural contradictions and of divergent values within given structures."

   It is interesting to follow how Merton's commentators have different estimates of his position stemming from a series of relevant questions. To turn again to Sztompka, functional analysis and structural analysis are complementary aspects in Merton's theory: "My emphasis on Merton's structuralist orientation may seem to contradict common appraisals in which his *functional analysis* is rather brought to the fore. As I have argued *in extenso*, this contradiction is apparent rather than real. Merton's functional analysis and structural analysis are not opposed but clearly *complementary* aspects of his overall orientation; they represent various phases in the development of the same approach to social reality" (Sztompka 1986: 251). In the opinion of Wallace and Wolf (1980: 80) on the other hand, Merton takes very small steps forward in specifying what the functional prerequisites are that can be satisfied in such various ways. Evidently he does not consider Parsons's schema a definitive framework for the question, but he does not offer one of his own.

9. See Giglioli 1971.

References

Bateson, Gregory. 1972. *Steps to an Ecology of Mind.* New York: Chandler Publishing Company.

Bierstedt, Robert. 1981. *American Sociological Theory: A Critical History.* New York: Academic Press.

Boudon, Raymond. 1977. *Effets pervers et ordre social.* Paris: Presses Universitaires de France.

Coser, Lewis A. 1977 *Masters of Sociological Thought.* New York: Harcourt Brace Jovanovich.

———.1975. "Merton's Uses of the European Sociological Tradition." In *The Idea of Social Structure,* edited by L.A. Coser. New York: Harcourt Brace Jovanovich.

Frisby, D. 1985. *Fragments of Modernity.* Cambridge and Oxford: Polity Press.

Garfield, E. 1980. "Citation Measures of the Influence of R.K. Merton" in *Science and Social Structure: Festschrift for R.K. Merton,* edited by T.F. Gieryn. New York: The New York Academy of Sciences.

Giglioli, P.P. 1971. "Introduction." In *Modelli di interazione,* by Erving Goffman. Bologna: Il Mulino.

Merton, Robert K. 1984. "Socially Expected Durations: A Case Study of Concept Formation in Sociology." In *Conflict and Consensus: A Festschrift for Lewis A.Coser,* edited by W.W. Powell and R. Robbins, 262–283. New York: Free Press. [Partial Italian translation in *Tempo e società,* edited by Simonetta Tabboni. Milan: Franco Angeli, 1985.]

———. 1976. *Sociological Ambivalence and Other Essays.* New York: Free Press.

———.1968. *Social Theory and Social Structure.* Enlarged, rev. ed. New York: Free Press.

———. 1972. "Insiders and Outsiders: A Chapter in the Sociology of Knowledge." *American Journal of Sociology* 77: 9–47.

Merton, Robert K. and Elinor Barber. 1963. "Sociological Ambivalence." In *Sociological Theory, Values, and Socio-cultural Change: Essays in Honor of Pitirim A. Sorokin,* edited by E.A.Tiryakian, 91–120. New York: Free Press.

Mongardini, Carlo. 1983. "Il dibattito nella sociologia e il significato di un ripensamento storico." In *Contributi di storie della sociologia,* edited by Alberto Izzo and Carlo Mongardini. Milan: Franco Angeli.

Schneider, Louis. 1975. "Ironic Perspective and Sociological Thought" in *The Idea of Social Structure,* edited by L. A. Coser. New York: Harcourt Brace Jovanovich.

Sorokin, Pitirim. 1966. *Sociological Theories of Today. New York:* Harper & Row.

Stinchcombe, Arthur. 1975. "Merton's Theory of Social Structure" in *The Idea of Social Structure,* edited by L. A. Coser. New York: Harcourt Brace Jovanovich.

Sztompka, Piotr. 1986. *R. K. Merton: An Intellectual Profile.* London: Macmillan.

Wallace, R.A. and A. Wolf. 1980. *Contemporary Sociological Theory.* Englewood Cliffs, NJ: Prentice-Hall.

Watzlawick, Paul, Janet H. Beavin, and Don D. Jackson. 1967. *Pragmatics of Human Communication: A Study of Interactional Patterns, Pathologies and Paradoxes.* New York: W.W. Norton & Company Inc.

1

Robert K. Merton's Structural Analysis: The Design of Modern Sociology

Volker Meja and Nico Stehr

Num schaut der Geist nicht vorwärts, nicht
zurück, die Gegenwart allein–ist unser Glück.
—J.W. Goethe, *Faust*

Introduction

History, utopia, ethics: issues of this genre are rarely investigated in contemporary sociology. The history of sociology may in fact be characterized in terms of the increasing exclusion of such topics from sociological analysis.[1] Norbert Elias (1987: 150) has described this development as a "retreat of sociologists into the present."[2] Sociology is now much more closely linked to the contemporary world, its focus has been intentionally narrowed,[3] and its orientation toward the present goes hand in hand with its increasing specialization and professionalization.[4]

These changes and therefore the growing intellectual differentiation of sociology begin historically with its institutionalization as a legitimate science, as a university discipline. In the United States, the professionalization of sociology began early and reached its peak during the 1950s and 1960s (compare Coser 1976; Hinkle and Hinkle 1960; McKee 1970: 106–107; Barber 1959; Friedrichs 1970; Lipset and Smelser 1961). The professionalization of sociology is accompanied by several other cognitive developments—for instance, by an increasing autonomy of sociological knowledge (Merton 1961: 23) and by the production of knowledge for use within the discipline. Despite the considerable intellectual diversity of sociology and its potential appeal to many audiences, fellow sociologists (and students of sociology) are today, especially in North America, often the primary audience of academic sociologists.[5]

A growing interest in detail, hand in hand with a generalizing ("scientized") terminology (which, however, has not led to a common language), increasing neglect of certain issues still central in classical sociology, and a loss of interest in sociohistorical problems (including theories of social change) are characteristic of the cognitive development of contemporary sociology. *Modern* sociology has essentially become a university-based discipline.[6]

Traditional European sociology, which was often self-consciously culture-specific, has always had a difficult time in American sociology.[7] The guiding values of American sociology were not, as in Europe, those of a "culturally aware" elite but rather those of the "average" citizen. This led to the North American emphasis upon the rational understanding of social conditions and their evolutionary transformation and improvement. The instrumental use of sociology even in the smallest contexts is a favored attribute of sociological knowledge in the United States (compare Mannheim 1932; Bendix 1951; Aron 1960; Bergsträsser 1961; Bramson 1961; Hofstadter 1959). American sociology has from its beginning in the nineteenth century been committed to a *gradual* improvement of American society. It has rarely questioned fundamental social structures. The orientation of American sociology toward the present, however, is in many respects congruent with the "modernness" of its society, inducing, despite the institutional differentiation of the discipline, an extraordinary symmetry between society and sociology. This symmetry is also revealed in the intellectual diversity of American sociology and in its tolerance and liberalism. Only in this restricted sense is American sociology oriented toward the future—that is, in the sense that for most American sociologists the present-day social organization of sociology exemplifies a desirable and rational form of social organization.

Modernity as a central term of our analysis requires critical reflection; this notion is frequently employed in a multifaceted and sometimes distinctly pejorative manner. If "modern" is merely seen as referring to that which is new or fashionable, varied usage is justified. The perpetual contest between preservation and change then becomes an anthropological constant. Modern is then not new, nor is the struggle to preserve it. But such usage of "modern" is also ahistorical. Yet, it is precisely its history-transcending aspect which we would regard as characteristic of the contemporary world. "Modern" signifies a historical period by denying it. It refuses historicity by considering universality a virtue. A modern consciousness has cut off its association with unique sociohistorical circumstances, as captured in the Mannheimian notion of socially "free-floating" intellectuals. It refers to ideas, which have transcended the multiplicity of their origins and have thereby fostered a new and distinctive identity—intellectual impartiality. We have moved from an age which was largely unconscious of the roots of its own ideas to an epoch in which such rootedness is linked to increasingly homogeneous social conditions. On the way to modernity in this sense, we have passed through a period of heightened sensitivity and concern with the existential connectedness of consciousness. Modernity, of course, neither comes about all at once nor simultaneously in all spheres of social activity. Discontinuities are everywhere evident. Yet in the scientific community, in Europe, North America, and elsewhere, efforts have been underway for centuries to create a style of modern thought increasingly freed from being bound to a specific time and a specific location. Success toward this goal had been—until recently in the social sciences as well—experienced as emancipation and as liberation from sacred and secular bonds. Modern consciousness is on the whole hardly unhappy with itself and represents an undeniable civilizational accomplishment, in science and elsewhere. However, it is increasingly evident that these aims and accomplishments are associated with multiple unanticipated consequences. Modern sociology sees itself as an expression of contemporary society and neither aims to bring about a "better" future nor, for that matter, warns against the danger of "utopia."

This brings us to the question whether the work of Robert K. Merton[8] is representative of "traditional"-classical or "modern" present-oriented sociology? This question can be decided only by looking at his sociological program more closely.

Norm and Interaction

One important feature of modern sociology is its development of a seemingly ahistorical language by adopting and operating with such terms as social system, function, integration, social order, social conflict, deviant behavior, values, social stratification, mobility, group, organization, behavior, role, and so on. This development is often interpreted, and sometimes even celebrated, as evidence of its increasingly scientific character (compare Simmons and Stehr 1982). There is a tendency for sociological terminology to become increasingly self-enclosed and to thereby forgo any directly observable linkage to specific social conditions.[9] The emergence of a specialized sociological language is accompanied by a definite *narrowing* of sociological research interests.[10] This development, which may appear to be contradictory, turns out to be quite consistent if one realizes that the delimitation of sociological research interests and the growing interest in detail may in the final analysis strengthen the universal appearance of concepts, since details are understood as individual examples of more general, even universal processes.

The characteristics of the socially neutral language of sociology are especially obvious in the terms *norm* and *interaction,* which are considered as indicative of universal empirical and theoretical problems of sociology.[11]

Alvin Gouldner (1956: 34–35), for example, refers to the *double polarity* of all sociological quests by arguing that "(a) a certain range of human behavior is influenced by *norms,* i.e., determined by value orientation, symbols, signs, etc.; (b) since we live in groups at almost every point of our life, our behavior is influenced by interaction with other individuals." Gouldner, following Merton, calls these fundamental themes of sociology "strategic empirical generalizations" and argues that one of the greatest difficulties in sociological theory concerns the integration of these two notions, and that existing theories can be imputed to one of these two poles. In this sense George C. Homans's exchange theory, for instance, emphasizes processes of social interaction, while Talcott Parsons emphasizes the significance of social norms.

Merton ([1949] 1968: 110), in contrast, defines the theoretical terms of interest to him as focused upon the comprehension of *structural* contexts and as viewing individuals as placed in networks of mutually interrelated social positions.

From Functional to Structural Analysis of Societies

Robert K. Merton, as a student of Talcott Parsons, was originally a proponent of functional analysis.[12] Yet he was never uncritical of Parsons. On the contrary, he[13] was one of the first critics of Parsons's theory, especially of its concept of science and its theory of the development of scientific knowledge.[14] The disagreements between Parsons and Merton will be discussed later on.[15] It should, however, be noted here that Merton soon saw himself increasingly less as a *functional analyst*; in a later important programmatic essay Merton (1975) refers to his theory as "structural analysis."[16] He (1975: 37–39) describes the difference between Parsons's classical structural-functional analysis and his own structural analysis as follows: "Substantively, the variant doctrine [of structural analysis] makes a large place for the structural sources and differential consequences of conflict, dysfunctions and contradictions in the social structure . . . [T]his orientation has been associated in its metatheoretical aspect with a particular image of the cognitive map of sociology. In that image, sociology has a plurality of theoretical orientations—distinct paradigms and theories of the middle range—rather than a single actual or soon-to-be-attained comprehensive theory."[17]

The differences between Merton and Parsons are by no means confined to theory-of-science issues alone but also include their reception of similar intellectual traditions and their attitudes toward analogies between organism and society (see Merton [1949] 1968: 102–103). A further significant divergence between Merton and Parsons is their different interpretation and use of the classical sociologists, in particular of Max Weber (Coser 1975; Horowitz 1983: 173–190).

Merton's identification with Parsons's functional analysis is in the last analysis minimal; his emphasis on theories of the middle range as a theoretical strategy indicates his much closer relation to empirical social research as well as a different evaluation of the role of empirical work for the development of sociological theories and sociological terminology (see Merton [1948a] 1968: 139–171).

In contrast to Parsons, who rarely discussed problems in the theory of science, Merton has never hesitated to self-reflectively incorporate theoretical and historical considerations into his analyses. A term by Franz Oppenheimer may also point to a preliminary explanation for this difference between Merton and Parsons: the "epistemological block-age" (*erkenntnistheoretische Bodensperre*), which Oppenheimer saw as a characteristic attribute of conservative thinking.[18] One could say that it is a characteristic feature of conservative thinking to relegate theory of science issues to the sphere of mere epistemology.

In the following section we will inquire how Merton's structural analysis can be evaluated politically and in terms of intellectual history.

Functional Analysis: Conservatism and Community

Ralf Dahrendorf (1963: 129) has diagnosed another characteristic of a conservative orientation in American sociology: "the occasionally almost romantic insistence on persistence, security, integration, that is, the scientific equivalent of *joining* and *neighboring*." And he adds: "American sociology is . . . conservative because American society it-self is conservative" (Dahrendorf 1963: 131). To be conservative, how-ever, also means to express apprehensions about the possible disinte-gration and the moving apart of social groups and institutions. A con-cern with the unity of society finds expression in the willingness of functionalists such as Parsons to apply natural scientific (in particular biological) conceptions to societal facts, in the goal to develop a *gen-eral* theory of social science, and in the emphasis upon a binding *normative superstructure* as well as the cohesion of social systems; in short, the mutualities of thinking and acting within social systems are emphasized.

As a result of the reference to methodological and substantive analo-gies to the natural sciences, moreover, social change can be conceived as relatively controlled change. In short, Parsons's functionalism is more than a *theorie pour la theorie,* more than an uncommitted theory by default supportive of the societal *status quo.* Functionalism rather involves an advocacy of social order and of *gradual* social change.[19]

Classical structural-functionalism in sociology and anthropology has been based on three interdependent postulates about social processes. Merton ([1949] 1968: 79–91) calls these premises: (1) the postulate of the *functional unity* of society; (2) the postulate of *universal function;*

and (3) the postulate of *the indispensability* of existing social structures and norms. Classical structural-functionalism therefore presupposes that all institutionalized forms of interaction and cultural patterns are necessary. From the existence of social formations, inferences are drawn about their function. For example, Davis and Moore (1945: 244), in an essay which has become a classic, describe the social function of religion as follows: "The reason why religion is necessary is apparently to be found in the fact that human society achieves its unity primarily through the possession by its members of certain ultimate values and ends in common. Although these values and ends are subjective, they influence behaviour, and their integration enables this society to operate as a system." The assumption of a universal functionality presupposes that all known forms of behavior ultimately have positive consequences. Merton refers to the claim of Bronislaw Malinowski (1926: 132) that "the functional view of culture insists therefore upon the principle that every type of civilization, every custom, material object, idea and belief fulfills some vital function." Such functional analysis, furthermore, adheres to the thesis of the indispensability of social structures and processes. The observations by Davis and Moore about the social function of religious beliefs point to the indispensability of religion for society as a whole. Religious beliefs have a dual function: they control social action and contribute to social integration. In other words, certain problems have to be solved in every society, and certain structural and cultural patterns are essential in order to do justice to these functions—to that of social integration, for example.

Merton's criticism of the functionalist program on all these counts led to a significant modification, even a transformation of the classical postulates (see Loomis and Loomis 1961; Barbano 1968). His critique of the methodological and substantive premises of functionalism involves a broadening of functional analysis by introducing a number of dichotomous terms.[20] Merton's analysis of the first postulate—that of the functional unity of society—results in the proposition to distinguish between the *functions* and *dysfunctions* of social processes, that is, it can no longer be assumed *a priori* that modes of behavior and norms necessarily always have positive consequences. Merton, in addition, modifies the postulate of indispensability by emphasizing *functional equivalents* or functional alternatives.[21]

As a further correction of functional analysis, Merton introduces the conceptual pair *manifest* and *latent* functions, which is meant to help avoid the confusion of motives with (objective) consequences of social action. The dichotomy of manifest and latent functions is also linked to the issue of the polarity of sociological analysis discussed later by Gouldner: the frame of reference for manifest functions are the contexts of social structures and constraints, whereas the frame of reference for latent functions refers to the importance of meaning in structural contexts. This distinction permits the raising of questions concerning the interaction, exchange, and the transformation of manifest into latent problem constellations (or vice versa).[22] It is in this context that other sociological notions of Merton, such as *unanticipated consequences* of social action (Merton 1936) and *self-fulfilling prophecy* (Merton [1948b] 1968: 475-490), reveal their significance (see also Honolka 1976).

As a result of Merton's modification of functional analysis, classical functionalism in sociology and anthropology began to lose many of its culture-specific features, including its clear preferences for a holistic-static perspective. It may be concluded that Merton has successfully modernized classical functionalism.

Structural Analysis: Liberality and Openness

Various authors pointed out early on, both critically and approvingly, that postwar American sociology is in many respects a product of some peculiar characteristics of American society. This may well be true also for Merton's structural analysis. One of the most significant features of Merton's sociology—both in regard to its concept of science[23] as well as in regard to its overall contents—is its "liberalism," especially in the sense of "openness,"[24] and its confidence in the moral authority of rationality.

Merton's attitude towards contemporary society is not characterized—as is Parsons's—by a consciousness of crisis that experiences the social order as endangered, but rather by an implicit acceptance of the existing social structure.[25] In contrast to Parsons, Merton emphasizes, both in principle as well as pragmatically, that structural analysis cannot account exhaustively for all social and cultural phenomena. This sort of metatheoretical openness corresponds to the assumption that social processes are neither uniform nor determined. Merton's thesis of the scientific plurality of sociological theories, as well as his claim that social processes are relatively open, reflect "modern" but nevertheless culture-bound assumptions. The metatheoretical plurality and the openness advocated by Merton are limited, however, since he wants to expose himself neither to the charge of *relativism* nor to that of political neutrality and abstinence. Merton's analysis of society, contrary to Parsons's, is characterized by a modern political liberalism—as opposed to partisan commitment.[26]

The essential components of Merton's structural analysis can be characterized by a number of substantive and methodological formulations.[27] Initially, it should be noted that Merton traces his own structural analysis back to Durkheim and Marx and not to the more recent French "structuralism." Merton argues that the theoretical orientations of Marx and Durkheim have proven to be complementary. Merton first attempted to show the convergence of certain assumptions of historical materialism and functional analysis in his essay "Manifest and Latent Functions" ([1949] 1968: 104–109). He points to the close affinity between such conceptions as "dysfunctions" and "contradictions," between "conditions of society" and "structural context" or "structural constraint," as well as to the emphasis of a sociology of knowledge perspective by both (see also Merton 1975: 32–33; Stinchcombe 1968, 1975; Gouldner 1970; Giddens 1971; Sztompka 1974; Alexander 1983). While Merton shows that the orientations of Marx and Durkheim are very different, he also demonstrates that their paradigms sometimes overlap. For example, Marx's thesis that social conditions determine human consciousness reminds him of Durkheim's collective representations (Merton [1948a] 1968: 160–161). According to Merton, it is the eventual aim to consolidate sociological terminology, approaches, and methods into a more comprehensive paradigm of theoretical analysis[28] which successfully links the investigation of micro- and macrophenomena.

The core social process, according to Merton (1975: 34) who adopts a formulation by Stinchcombe, is "the choice between socially structured alternatives." This process "differs from the choice process of economic theory, in which the alternatives are conceived to have inherent utilities. It differs from the choice process of learning theory, in which the alternatives are conceived to emit reinforcing or extinguishing stimuli. It differs from both of these in that . . . the utility or reinforcement of a particular alternative choice is thought of as socially established, as part of the institutional order" (Stinchcombe 1975: 12).

Merton conceptualizes the core processes on the macrolevel as the social distribution (i.e., the concentration and branching out) of authority, power, influence, and prestige which lead to the formation of structures of social control which, in turn, change historically, in part as a result of processes of the "accumulation of advantages and disadvantages."

The differentiation of social structures into interlocking networks of social statuses, strata, organizations, and political communities generates social *conflict,* but also common interests and values.[29] Consensus as well as conflict are not incidental, but rooted in social structure. At the same time it is important to differentiate between manifest and latent levels of social structures and functions.[30] One further essential assumption of Merton's structural analysis relates to the structurally generated *sociological ambivalence* of norms in the form of incompatible patterned expectations and "a 'dynamic alternation of norms and counternorms' in social roles" (Merton 1975: 35). These have been empirically identified and investigated by Merton, for example in the spheres of medicine, science, and bureaucracy (Merton 1976). Sociologically ambivalent normative complexes are part of normative structures—that is, differentiated social structures do not produce uniform expectations and interests.

Social structures, furthermore, generate differing rates of deviant behavior, which are interpreted differently by the members of society, depending on their social location. Merton's classical analysis of the interaction of social structure and anomie is based upon this assumption (Merton [1938] 1968: 185–214). Deviant behavior is to a significant extent the result of a socially structured discrepancy between culturally induced personal aspirations and unequal chances for the realization of these aspirations through legitimate institutional means.[31]

Merton further assumes that changes in social structure can be the result of external as well as internal factors and that these types of change "come about through cumulatively patterned choices in behaviour and the amplification of dysfunctional consequences resulting from certain kinds of strains, conflicts, and contradictions in the differentiated social structure" (Merton 1975: 36). Social change is seen both as involving intended, anticipated modifications of social structures as well as unintended and unanticipated consequences.

Merton's investigations of the most varied social phenomena all display the concrete features of his structural analysis. For more than half a century, one of his most important fields of inquiry has been his empirical and theoretical analysis of the social system of science. It is for precisely this reason that an example from this research program is especially suited to illustrate his structural analysis: the investigation of the Matthew effect in science ([1968] 1973). This essay is only one of his empirical studies which investigates the social organization of modern science and especially the effect of certain sociopsychological processes upon the distribution of rewards for scientific achievements. Merton assumes that this distribution in turn has important effects on the circulation of ideas and knowledge within the scientific communication system. He elucidates the causes of an asymmetrical accumulation of rewards in science and shows the consequences of the distribution system for this system itself.

Merton presupposes in his analysis the theoretical model of the reward system in science which he himself helped to develop; this model postulates that rewards in science are granted by scientific colleagues in the form of *reputation*. This reputation should ideally correspond to the order of the scientific merit in the judgment of the colleagues. "The recognition accorded scientific achievement by the scientist's peers is a reward in the strict sense identified by Parsons. As we shall see, such recognition can be converted into an instrumental asset as enlarged facilities are made available to the honored scientist for further work. Without deliberate intent on the part of any group, the reward system thus influences the 'class structure' of science by providing a stratified distribution of chances, among scientists, for enlarging their role as investigators. The process provides differential access to the means of scientific production. This becomes all the more important in the current historical shift from little science to big science, with its expensive and often centralized equipment needed for research. There is thus a continuing interplay between the status system, based on honor and esteem, and the class system, based on differential life-chances, which locates scientists in differing positions within the opportunity structure of science" (Merton [1968] 1973: 442–443).

Merton's observations point to his primary research interest: the so-called Matthew Effect. He cites the observation of a model laureate in physics: "The world is peculiar in this matter of how it gives credit. It tends to give the credit to [already] famous people" (Merton [1968] 1973: 443). In other words, the question arises if the reward system of science systematically favors established scientists. This complex pattern of "misallocation" of credit for scientific work, particularly in cases of collaboration and in cases of independent multiple discoveries made by scientists of different rank, is described by Merton as "the Matthew Effect." The experiences reported by eminent scientists, among other evidence, make it plain that the reward system of science "is leading to an unintended double injustice, in which unknown scientists are unjustifiably victimized and famous ones, unjustifiably benefited" (Merton [1968] 1973: 447). In short, the Matthew Effect leads to a serious inequity in the reward system which affects the individual careers of scientists.

Merton, looking at science as a system of communication, now inquires into the consequence of the Matthew Effect for the relative visibility of scientific work. He argues that a scientific contribution by a renowned scientist will have the greatest visibility in the scientific community, and he concludes that this development may in fact be functional for the development of scientific knowledge. The communication function of the Matthew Effect is increasing as a result of the exponential increase in the volume of scientific publications, which makes it increasingly difficult for scientists to keep up with work in their field. The reduction of complexity is accordingly accomplished on the basis of the reputation of the author(s). Merton emphasizes that for the development of science, "only work that is effectively perceived and utilized by other scientists, then and there, matters . . . Looking at the Matthew Effect from this perspective, we have noted the distinct possibility that contributions made by scientists of considerable standing are the most likely to enter promptly and widely into the communication networks of science, and so to accelerate its development" (Merton [1968] 1973: 450). He consequently claims that the dysfunctional aspect of the Matthew Effect on the individual level corresponds to a functionality of the same process on the collective level.

Merton also describes the role of leading scientists in recognizing important problems and hence their impact upon the advancement of scientific knowledge. He points to the interaction between specific individual dispositions of eminent scientists and the communication aspect of the Matthew Effect. For a number of reasons, the scientific contributions of an outstanding scientist have a greater chance to stimulate others than roughly equally outstanding work done by unknown scientists. This, Merton argues, is "a principle which provides a sociopsychological basis for the communication function of the Matthew effect. This principle represents a special application of the self-fulfilling prophecy, somewhat as follows: Fermi or Pauling or G.N. Lewis or Weisskopf sees fit to report this in print and so it is apt to be important (since, with some consistency, he has made important contributions in the past); since it is probably important, it should be read with special care; and the more attention one gives it, the more one is apt to get out of it. This becomes a self-confirming process, making for the greater evocative effect of publications by eminent scientists (until that time, of course, when their image among their fellows is one of leaders who have seen their best days—an image, incidentally, that corresponds with the self-image of certain laureates who find themselves outpaced by onrushing generations of new scientists)" (Merton [1968] 1973: 456).

However, this self-fulfilling prophecy may also become dysfunctional since this form of selective attention leads to a systematic neglect of other important work. The history of science is full of examples of important contributions by comparatively unknown scientists who were only recognized years or even decades later: "When the Matthew Effect is thus transformed into an idol of authority, it violates the norm of universalism embodied in the institution of science and curbs the advancement of knowledge" (Merton [1968] 1973: 457). Yet there are few studies of the system of social inequality in science which have systematically investigated the consequences of such practices for the advancement of scientific knowledge.

Finally Merton analyzes the impact of the Matthew Effect in regard to the accumulation of advantages and disadvantages in many systems of social inequality, and which consistently leads to the same result: "The rich get richer at a rate that makes the poor become relatively poorer" (Merton [1968] 1973: 457). These institutionalized social processes of social selection in science lead to an even greater concentration of top scientific work and of resources and thereby militate against all efforts to undo the institutional consequences of the Matthew Effect by, for example, establishing new centers of scientific excellence.

Summary

Merton is among the very few modern sociologists who have significantly shaped the institutional and intellectual development of the social sciences. His structural analysis has had a greater institutional and perhaps an even greater intellectual impact than Talcott Parsons's theory of society (compare Caplovitz 1972; Garfield 1980). Merton is certainly not a typical or even paradigmatic example of a "modern" American sociologist. Yet he is decidedly no "traditional" social theorist in the manner of Talcott Parsons. Merton's *structural analysis,* which emerged in a transitional phase of the cognitive development of North American sociology, has generally contributed to sociology's orientation toward the present.[32] His work may therefore be seen both as an expression and as a motivating force of modern sociology.

Probably the most important difference in the impact of the respective programs may be seen in the fact that Merton's influence has led to an enormous variety and breadth of empirical work in the North American social sciences.[33] This development is indeed closely linked to what Norbert Elias has called a "narrowing of the sociologists' focus of attention and interest to the immediate present" (Elias 1987: 150), which nevertheless "represents progress in the development of the discipline" (Elias 1987: 150), since sociologists are now better able "to study and in some cases solve short-term problems of their own society in a reasonably reliable manner" (Elias 1987: 150). Yet, in the face of this "almost explosive profusion of empirical sociological investigations" it is important to also pay attention to the structure and direction of long-term social processes which take account of "the intrinsic dynamics of human societies" (Elias 1987: 150, 152f.; see also Plessner 1924: 414). The analysis of long-term social processes is more urgent but also more difficult today than perhaps ever before. Merton's analysis of society could make yet another important contribution if it were to incorporate such issues, thereby initiating a return of sociological analysis to history.

Notes

1. This development did not occur without resistance. At different times and for different reasons, sociologists have warned against a restriction of sociological discourse (e.g., Mannheim 1940; Gerth and Laudan 1959) and have attempted to reintroduce the expelled issues.

2. Talcott Parsons referred to discourse which both attempts to be pure sociological discourse as well as present-oriented as "positive sociological discourse"—that is, as a genuinely sociological discourse liberated from the ballast of history and from explicit ethical-political considerations and goals (compare Parsons's 1936 programmatic critique of Karl Mannheim's sociology of knowledge). Parsons later (1968: 322) reiterated his convictions that sociology ought to restrict itself to a limited range of substantive social issues.

3. During the 1950s and 1960s, most sociologists were not only convinced that sociology was well on its way toward a genuinely modern science but they also believed that the theoretical diversity of the discipline had been significantly reduced. It is clear today that such hopes for cognitive homogeneity were premature. There is a renewed emphasis upon diverse theoretical perspectives which, however, does not imply that a trend toward a narrower scope of sociological theories and empirical research has altogether vanished. In fact, a narrowing of scope characterizes almost every perspective. This development supports our observation that the contemporary state of the discipline reflects both general societal factors as well as attributes of the modern system of science.

4. Smelser (1969: 6) describes this process as a positive one for sociology: "After all, sociology has already had a history of severing some of its connections with social philosophy, social policy, social problems, and social ideology—connections which are far from completely severed in the mid-twentieth century" (see also Lipset and Smelser 1961; Parsons 1961).

5. Instructive in this context is a principle advocated by Smelser (1969: 19) for use in any evaluation of sociological research: " . . . no investigative activity in sociology *is* scientifically *legitimate* unless it can be related directly to the core sociological enterprise: accounting for variations and interdependencies of data within a sociological framework" (emphasis added). In other words, Smelser stresses the intellectual autarchy of sociology and hence its autonomy within the division of labor of science. (See Scott and Shore's [1979] investigation of the consequences of this intellectual autonomy for efforts to produce practically relevant sociological knowledge.) Merton postulates a three-phase model of the development of sociology according to which sociology, having reached intellectual autonomy and institutional legitimization, in its final consolidating phase opens itself to other disciplines. However, one should not overestimate the possibilities of such intellectual openness of a "mature" sociology.

6. This professionalization of sociology has been evaluated very differently. Although the majority of sociologists have welcomed the "positivity" and the present-orientation of sociological discourse (e.g., Bierstedt [1957] 1974), others have viewed this development as not a progressive or rational one (Mills 1959; Sorokin 1956; Coser 1979). Parsons's 1959 essay may be considered as setting a signal for the politics of sociology: "Sociology the Profession—Its Scope and Style: Some Problems Confronting Sociology as a Profession." There Parsons describes the process of professionalizing and attempts to encourage its development.

7. Merton remarks about the "provincialism" of an American sociology focused on limited social problems: "Pitirim A. Sorokin helped me escape from the provincialism of thinking that effective studies of society were confined within American borders and from the slum-encouraged provincialism of thinking that the primary subject matter of sociology was centered in such peripheral problems of social life as divorce and juvenile delinquency" ([1949] 1968: xiii). See also Merton's investigation of "Patterns of Influence: Local and Cosmopolitan Influentials" ([1949] 1968: 441–490). Since European sociology, too, has fre-

quently been explicitly culture-specific—that is, tied to time and place—Merton's remarks about the "provincialism" of the American sociology he encountered can also be applied to European sociology.

8. For accounts of Robert K. Merton's intellectual biography see Hunt 1961; Sztompka 1986; and Crothers 1987.

9. Max Horkheimer (1934: 27) already deplored the elimination of a historically informed terminology: "The more a conscious connection with historical struggles is lost, the stronger philosophers tend to affirm that their thinking is rooted in it— an auxiliary conception which reveals by its very indefensibility that absent connection." Elsewhere Horkheimer (1935: 325–326) provides a more comprehensive interpretation of this intellectual development in the social sciences. "[T]his abstractness and merely pretended independence of the bourgeois scientific enterprise . . . [has] meanwhile . . . obtained a different meaning: instead of indicating courage and independence of thought, the abstention from general cultural and social involvement and the exclusion from analysis of actual historical interests and conflict indicates fear and an incapacity for rational action rather than a move in the direction of the real objectives of science."

10. This description of the development of sociology contradicts the optimistic account of the history of sociology typical during the expansion and consolidation phase in the 1950s and 1960s. See, for example, Edward Shils (1961: 1410).

11. This can be inferred from many programmatic statements; Parsons, for example (1968: 323–324), emphasizes that "the main substantive focus of sociological analysis . . . may be said to lie in the *institutional* aspect of the social. In the most general terms, this is the area in which the *normative expectations* operating in social systems, which are grounded in the culture and which define what people in various statuses and roles in *one* or more of various senses *ought* to do under various circumstances, are articulated."

12. Merton comments on this throughout his work. Despite interesting emphases— possibly as a reaction to specific occasions or as a result of a changed attitude— there remains throughout a certain distanced, diplomatic tone which is evidence for the ambiguity of his position: the pragmatic recognition of the dominance of structural functionalism which at the same time denied a claim to a monopoly. The position advocated is one of theoretical pluralism. In his "Acknowledgements" ([1949] 1968: xiv) in *Social Theory and Social Structure* Merton writes, for example, that he learned from Paul Lazarsfeld to articulate his reasons "for considering functional analysis the presently most promising, though not the only, theoretical orientation to a wide range of problems of human society." In his essay "Structural Analysis in Sociology" (1975: 36–7) he states in a similar manner that his variant of structural analysis "is deeply indebted to the classic mode of structural-functional analysis developed by my teacher, friend, and colleague-at-a-distance, Talcott Parsons. But the variant differs from the standard form in, for me, two major respects, substantive and metatheoretical."

13. Compare Merton's (1948: 164–68) observations. See also his remarks on the occasion of the commemorative session of the American Sociological Association for Talcott Parsons, "Remembering the Young Talcott Parsons," held in Boston in 1979 (Merton 1980).

14. Savage (1981: 19) observes that Merton's critique of Parsons is confined almost exclusively to Parsons's epistemological position and that Merton avoids a direct confrontation with the substantive aspect of Parsons's theory. Yet, such an observation is misleading since Merton's criticism of Parsons's theory is quite evident in Merton's work. A different approach to criticism requires very different social

or personal relations and attitudes. Compare, as a counterexample to Merton, the instructive biography of C.W. Mills by Irving L. Horowitz (1983), where Horowitz comments on the alienation between Mills and most of his colleagues, university-wide associates, and administrators at Columbia University as a result of Mills's repeated violation of collegial conventions—publishing strong criticisms of the scholarly position of some of his departmental colleagues, for example. Mills did not criticize Merton, however. On the contrary, after reading *Social Theory and Social Structure* he writes to Merton: "It was very depressing. I hadn't realized (in fact I had for some reason been refusing to examine the point) how very far I had wandered from really serious work in our discipline" (Horowitz 1983: 82).

15. We cannot, however, discuss here Merton's exposition and criticism of functionalism in *Social Theory and Social Structure*. Merton's treatment of functional analysis is regarded even by nonfunctionalists as one of the "most sophisticated general discussion[s] of functional analysis" (Giddens 1981: 42).

16. The concept of "structural analysis" is, it seems to us, programmatic in at least two respects: First, it signals, in a self-exemplifying manner, that Merton does not claim a monopoly for *structural* analysis. "Structure" and "structural" have multiple meanings and therefore cannot be restricted in a simple and convincing way. Second, the choice of the term itself points to a conscious distancing from functional analysis. The concept "structural" analysis, moreover, is gaining greater acceptance. Critics favorably inclined toward Merton's work describe his theory, at least up to the 1970s, as an example of a "*functional* structuralism" (Wallace 1969: 24) and they emphasize that Merton, in contrast to Parsons, prefers structures of social interactions as explanatory processes.

17. Merton (1948: 164–165) emphasized his metatheoretical differences with Parsons relatively early on: " . . . when [Parsons] suggests that our chief task is to deal with 'theory' rather than with 'theories.' I must take strong exception. The fact is that the term 'sociological theory,' just as would be the case with the terms 'physical theory' or 'medical theory,' is often misleading. It suggests a *tighter integration of diverse working theories than ordinarily obtains in any of these disciplines.* Let me try to make clear what is here implied. Of course, every discipline has a strain toward logical and empirical consistency. Of course, the temporary co-existence of logically incompatible theories sets up a tension, resolved only when one or another of the theories is abandoned or so revised as to eliminate the inconsistency. Of course, also, every discipline has basic concepts, postulates and theorems which are the common resources of all theorists, irrespective of the special range of problems with which they deal. . . . Of course, distinct theories often involve partly overlapping concepts and postulates. But the significant fact is that the progress of these disciplines consists in working out a large number of theories specific to certain types of phenomena and in exploring their mutual relations, and not in centering attention on "theory" as such. . . . To concentrate solely on the master conceptual scheme for deriving all sociological theory is to run the risk of producing twentieth-century equivalents of the large philosophical systems of the past, with all their suggestiveness, all their architectonic splendor and all their scientific sterility."

18. Compare Kurt Lenk's contribution to this discussion in Henning and Saage (1983: 26).

19. We want to stress, with Gouldner (1970: 335), that "in saying that functionalism's ideology is conservative, I mean to suggest, primarily, that its fundamental posture toward its surrounding society entails an acceptance of its master institutions, but not that it is *necessarily* procapitalist and antisocialist. Committed as it is to

the value of order, it can do no other than accept the kind of order in which it finds itself."

20. Compare the intriguing analysis of the method of functional sociology by Baldamus 1976.

21. Compare Niklas Luhmann's concept of *a functionalism* of equivalents: "The objective of verification is . . . no longer the identification of a regular relationship of certain causes generating certain effects, but the confirmation of the equivalence of several causal factors of equal value. The problem is not: does A always (or, with a probability attached) cause B, but: are A, C, D, E, in their ability to cause B functionally equivalent" (Luhmann [1962] 1970: 23). According to Luhmann, the functionalism of equivalents resolves a number of methodological problems of classical functionalism—that is, if one "conceives of the notion of function . . . as a regulating principle for the identification of equivalences within the frame of functional variables and thus replaces causal functionalism by a functionalism of equivalents . . . then the dispute about the question whether the functional method is essentially a static and conservative form of explanation of presupposed systems, or if it is able to incorporate problems of social change within the historical development is resolved. It analyses systemic relations with respect to other equivalent possibilities, i.e., also to possibilities of change, exchange and replacement and their feedback within the system" (Luhmann [1962] 1970: 17–18). These arguments by Luhmann were anticipated by Merton as early as 1949, but Merton's proposal to substitute the conception of functional equivalence for the postulate of functional necessity is not so much based—as in Luhmann—on the desire to counter traditional methodological objections against functionalism, but on the conviction that it is in principle impossible and not very useful to argue that certain social structures and social norms are indispensable (see Merton [1949] 1968: 86–90).

22. Merton's criticism and modification of functional analysis (Merton [1949] 1968: 104–109) has in turn been criticized (e.g., Nagel [1956] 1967; Rudner 1966; Ryan 1970; Mulkay 1971).

23. Compare Stehr (1985) for a discussion of the changes in Merton's conceptions of science and his conception of the *scientific community* during the nearly fifty years of his scholarly interest in the social and cognitive organization of science.

24. This "openness" is characteristic of Merton's sociology in a variety of ways; that is, it is evident in his indebtedness to different sociological traditions, in the variety of his research interests, as well as in his willingness to keep certain conclusions open or in suspension (see Coser 1975 and Sztompka 1986).

25. Robert Merton has indicated to us that he disagrees with our general interpretation of his "attitude toward contemporary society."

26. As Irving Louis Horowitz (1983: 175) states in his biography of C.W. Mills, contemporary American sociology is marked by its emphasis of "detachment over involvement."

27. This summary of attributes of Merton's structural analysis is based mainly on Merton (1975).

28. Despite his preference for sociological *theories of the middle range* Merton considers this strategy of constructing theories as a preliminary one only. His aim remains the construction of a general sociological theory of society (see Merton 1948).

29. Compare Dahrendorf (1967: 268–269); Gouldner (1973: x-xi).

30. Merton refers here to his discussed modification of functional analysis by introducing—with reference to Freud—the notion of "manifest and latent functions"

([1949] 1968: 73–138). The distinction between latent and manifest functions is to avoid a confusion between conscious *motivation* of social action and its *objective consequences* (Merton [1949] 1968: 114–138). Motivation and consequence (function) of social action can vary independently. (For a discussion of this distinction see, for example, Savage 1981: 138–142; Mennell 1974: 157; Giddens 1977: 106–108).

31. The literature on Merton's thesis about the relation between deviant behavior and socially structured conditions for a realization of socially sanctioned aspirations has in the meantime become quite extensive (compare Cole 1975). Among the most illuminating critical discussions of Merton's theses are those of the British criminologists Taylor, Walton, and Young (1973).

32. Lewis S. Coser (1975: 86) observes that "much of Merton's work, though by no means all of it, must be understood as a self-conscious effort to extract from the body of the work of his predecessors, and in particular from the diffuse, scintillating, but often confused and confusing heritage of European thought, the central core that needs to be transmitted to American students and practitioners alike if they are indeed to work within a living tradition." In the case of the sociology of knowledge, according to Coser (1975: 87), Merton attempts to "surgically remove those layers and tissues of a thinker's thought that show the mark of his time, his place, his milieu, so as to be able better to expose that vital core of his message which transcends the various existential limitations that might have entered into his perspective. By attempting to separate the 'objective consequences [from] the intent of an inquiry' he wishes to salvage the usable intellectual products of a past thinker."

33. Merton's *Social Theory and Social Structure,* as Bernstein (1976: 17–18) notes, has been especially influential: "A major reason for its success and influence is Merton's clear, moderate statement of the state of sociology as a young but growing science, and his optimism about its future development as a scientific enterprise slowly building and consolidating its theoretical functions." Thus another clear difference between Merton and Parsons becomes evident: their unmistakably different writing style. Parsons has often been accused of unnecessary complexity and of a Teutonic use of the language (which was parodied by C.W. Mills, and which has been repeated uncritically ever since), which makes access to his work difficult. Merton, in contrast, is not only an eloquent spokesman for a specialized sociological terminology, but also exemplary in his own cautious use of new sociological terms as well as in his self-exemplifying use of disciplinary language. Merton has managed to avoid an unnecessary specialization of sociological language while emphasizing at the same time the necessity of a differentiated language, without following Parsons's example in developing an extremely specific terminology. Merton has successfully introduced a number of sociological terms which have become an established part of sociological and even of educated everyday language. Parsons's intellectual influence in the United States has undoubtedly suffered because of his language while Merton's language has probably helped to increase his influence. The trivialization of Parsons's views and the refusal to engage in substantive debate with them has quite frequently been the result of prejudices against Parsons's language.

References

Alexander, Jeffrey C. 1983. *Theoretical Logic in Sociology. The Antinomies of Classical Thought: Marx and Durkheim.* Berkeley and Los Angeles: University of California Press.

Aron, Raymond. 1959. "La société américaine et sa sociologie." *Cahiers Internationaux de Sociologie* 26 (January-June): 55–80.

Baldamus, V. 1976. *The Structure of Sociological Inference.* London: Martin Robertson.

Barsano, Filippo. 1968. "Social Structures and Social Functions: The Emancipation of Structural Analysis in Sociology." *Inquiry* 11: 40–84.

Barser, Bernhard. 1959. "American Sociology in Its Social Context." In *Transactions of the Fourth World Congress of Sociology,* International Sociological Association.

Bendix, Reinhard. 1951. "The Image of Man in the Social Sciences: The Basic Assumptions of Present-day Research." *Commentary* 11: 187–192.

Bergsträsser, Arnold. 1961. "Amerikanische und deutsche Soziologie." In *Politik in Wissenschaft und Bildung.* Freiburg: Rombach.

Bernstein, Richard J. 1976. *The Restructuring of Social and Political Theory.* Philadelphia: University of Pennsylvania Press.

Bierstedt, Robert. [1957] 1974. "Wertfreiheit and American Sociology." In *Power and Progress: Essays on Sociological Theory,* by Robert Bierstedt. New York: McGraw-Hill.

Bramson, Leon. 1961. *The Political Context of Sociology.* Princeton: Princeton University Press.

Caplovitz, David. 1977. "Review of *The Idea of Social Structure: Papers in Honor of Robert K. Merton.*" *Contemporary Sociology* 6: 142–150.

Cole, Stephen. 1975. "The Growth of Scientific Knowledge: Theories of Deviance as a Case Study." In *The Idea of Social Structure: Papers in Honor of Robert K. Merton,* edited by Lewis A. Coser. New York: Harcourt Brace Jovanovich.

Coser, Lewis A. 1975. "Merton's Uses of the European Sociological Tradition." In *The Idea of Social Structure: Papers in Honor of Robert K. Merton,* edited by Lewis A. Coser. New York: Harcourt Brace Jovanovich.

———. 1976. "Sociological Theory from the Chicago Dominance to 1965." *Annual Review of Sociology* 2: 145–160.

———. 1979. "Two Methods in Search of a Substance." In *Contemporary Issues in Theory and Research: A Metasociological Perspective,* edited by William E. Snizek et al. Westport, CT: Greenwood.

Crothers, Charles. 1987. *Robert Merton.* London and New York: Tavistock.

Dahrendorf, Ralf. 1963. *Die angewandte Aufklärung: Soziologie und Gesellschaft in Amerika.* Munich: Piper.

———. 1967. *Pfade aus Utopia.* Munich: Piper.

Davis, Kingsley and Wilbert E. Moore. 1945. "Some Principles of Stratification." *American Sociological Review* 10: 242–249.

Elias, Norbert. [1983] 1987. "The Retreat of Sociologists into the Present." In *Modern German Sociology,* edited by Volker Meja, Dieter Misgeld, and Nico Stehr. New York: Columbia University Press.

Friedrichs, Robert W. 1970. *A Sociology of Sociology.* New York: Free Press.

Garfield, Eugene. 1980. "Citation Measures of the Influence of Robert K. Merton." In *Science and Social Structure: Festschrift for Robert K. Merton,* edited by Tom Gieryn. New York: New York Academy of Sciences.

Gerth, Hans H. and Saul Laudan. 1959. "The Relevance of History to the Sociological Ethos." *Studies on the Left* 1: 7–14.

Giddens, Anthony. 1971. *Capitalism and Modern Social Theory*. Cambridge: Cambridge University Press.

———. 1977. *Studies in Social and Political Theory*. New York: Basic Books.

———. 1981. *A Contemporary Critique of Historical Materialism*. London: Macmillan.

Gieryn, Thomas F., ed. 1980. *Science and Social Structure*. New York: The New York Academy of Sciences.

Gouldner, Alvin W. 1956. "Some Observations on Systematic Theory, 1945–55." In *Sociology in the United States of America*, edited by Hans L. Zeitterberg. Paris: Unesco.

———. [1959] 1967. "Reciprocity and Autonomy in Functional Theory." In *System, Change and Conflict*, edited by Nicholas J. Demerath, Jr. and Richard A. Peterson. New York: Free Press.

———. 1970. *The Coming Crisis of Western Sociology*. New York: Basic Books.

———. 1973. "Foreword." In *The New Criminology*, edited by Ian Taylor et al. London: Routledge & Kegan Paul.

Henning, Eike and Richard Saage, eds. 1983. *Konservatismus: Eine Gefahr für die Freiheit?* Munich: Piper.

Hinkle, Roscoe L. and Gisela N. Hinkle. 1960. *Die Entwicklung der amerikanischen Soziologie*. Vienna: Verlag für Geschichte und Politik.

Hofstadter, Richard. 1959. *Social Darwinism in American Thought*. New York: George Braziller.

Honolka, Harro. 1976. *Die Eigendynamik sozialwissenschaftlicher Aussagen*. Frankfurt am Main: Campus.

Horkheimer, Max. 1935. "Zum Rationalismusstreit in der gegenwärtigen Philosophie." *Zeitschrift für Sozialforschung* 2: 2–53.

Horowitz, Irving Louis 1983. *C. Wright Mills: An American Utopian*. New York: Free Press.

Hunt, Morton M. 1961. "How Does It Come to Be So? Profile of Robert K. Merton." *New Yorker* 36: 39–63.

Lipset, Seymour M. and Neil J. Smelser. 1961. "The Setting of Sociology in the 1950s". In *Sociology: The Progress of a Decade*, edited by Seymour M. Lipset and Neil J. Smelser. Englewood Cliffs, NJ: Prentice-Hall.

Loomis, Charles P. and Zona Loomis. 1961. *Modern Social Theories*. New York: D. Van Nostrand.

Luhmann, Niklas [1962] 1970. "Funktion und Kausalität." In *Sociologische Aufklärung*, edited by Niklas Luhmann. Opladen: Westdeutscher Verlag.

Malinowski, Bronislaw. 1926. "Anthropology." In *Encyclopedia Britannica*. 13th ed. London: The Encyclopedia Britannica Co. Ltd.

Mannheim, Karl. 1932. "Review of Stuart A. Rice: Methods in Social Science." *American Journal of Sociology* 38: 273–282.

———. 1940. *Man and Society in an Age of Reconstruction: Studies in Modern Social Structure*. London: Routledge and Kegan Paul.

McKee, James B. 1970. "Some Observations on the Self-consciousness of Sociologists." In *The Sociology of Sociology*, edited by Larry T. Reynolds and Janice M. Reynolds. New York: McKay.

Mennell, Stephen. 1974. *Sociological Theory: Uses and Utilities*. London: Nelson.

Merton, Robert K. 1936. "The Unanticipated Consequences of Purposive Social Action." *American Sociological Review* 1: 894–904.

————. 1948. "On the Position of Sociological Theory." *American Sociological Review* 13: 164–168.

————. 1961. "Social Conflict in Styles of Sociological Work." In *Transactions of the Fourth World Congress of Sociology*. Vol. 3. Louvain: International Sociological Association.

————. [1938] 1968. "Social Structure and Anomie." In *Social Theory and Social Structure*. New York: Free Press.

————. [1948a] 1968. "The Bearing of Empirical Research upon the Development of Sociological Theory." In *Social Theory and Social Structure*. New York. Free Press.

————. [1948b] 1968. "The Self-Fulfilling Prophecy." In *Social Theory and Social Structure*. New York: Free Press.

————. [1949] 1968. "Manifest and Latent Functions." In *Social Theory and Social Structure*. New York: Free Press.

————. 1968. *Social Theory and Social Structure*. Enlarged edition. New York: Free Press.

————. [1968] 1973. "The Matthew Effect in Science." In *The Sociology of Science: Theoretical and Empirical Investigations*. Chicago and London: The University of Chicago Press.

————. 1975. "Structural Analysis in Sociology." In *Approaches to the Study of Social Structure*, edited by Peter M. Blau. New York: Free Press.

————. 1976. *Sociological Ambivalence and Other Essays*. New York: Free Press.

————. 1980. "Remembering the Young Talcott Parsons." *The American Sociologist* 15: 68–71.

Mills, Wright C. 1959. *The Sociological Imagination*. New York: Oxford University Press.

Mulkay, Michael. 1971. *Functionalism, Exchange and Theoretical Strategy*. London: Routledge & Kegan Paul.

Nagel, Ernest. [1956] 1967. "A Formalization of Functionalism." In *System, Change and Conflict*, edited by N.J. Demerath III and Richard A. Peterson. New York: Free Press.

Parsons, Talcott. 1936. "Review of Alexander von Schelting's Max Webers Wissenschaftlehre." *American Sociological Review* 1: 675–681.

————. 1947. "Introduction to Max Weber." In *The Theory of Social and Economic Organization*, edited by Talcott Parsons. New York: Oxford University Press.

————. 1948. "The Position of Sociological Theory." *American Sociological Review* 13: 156–171.

————. 1959. "Sociology the Profession: Its Scope and Style." *American Sociological Review* 24: 547–559.

————. 1961. "Some Problems Confronting the Profession." In *Sociology: The Progress of a Decade*, edited by Seymour M. Lipset and Neil J. Smelser. Englewood Cliffs, NJ: Prentice-Hall.

————. 1968. "An Overview." In *American Sociology*, edited by Talcott Parsons. New York: Basic Books.

Plessner, Helmut. 1924. "Zur Soziologie der modernen Forschung und ihrer Organisation in der deutschen Universität." In *Versuche zu einer Soziologie des Wissens*, edited by Max Scheler. Munich and Leipzig: Duncker & Humblot.

Rudner, Richard S. 1966. *Philosophy of Social Science*. Englewood Cliffs, NJ: Prentice-Hall.

Ryan, Alan. 1970. *The Philosophy of the Social Sciences*. London: MacMillan.

Savage, Stephen P. 1981. *The Theories of Talcott Parsons: The Social Relations of Action.* New York: St. Martin's Press.

Scott, Robert A. and Arnold R. Shore. 1979. *Why Sociology Does Not Apply: A Study of the Use of Sociology in Public Policy.* New York: Elsevier.

Shils, Edward. 1961. "The Calling of Sociology." In *Theories of Society,* edited by Talcott Parsons et al. New York: Free Press.

Simmons, Anthony and Nico Stehr. 1982. "Language and the Growth of Knowledge in Sociology." *Social Science Information* 20: 703–741.

Smelser, Neil J. 1969. "The Optimum Scope of Sociology." In *A Design for Sociology: Scope, Objectives, and Methods* edited by Robert Bierstedt. Philadelphia: The American Academy of Political and Social Science.

Sorokin, Pitirim A. 1956. *Fads and Foibles in Modern Sociology and Related Sciences.* Chicago: Greenwood.

Stehr, Nico. 1982. "Robert K. Merton's *Wissenschaftssoziologie.*" In Robert K. Merton, *Entwicklung und Wandel von Forschungsinteressen: Aufsätze zur Wissenschaftssoziologie.* Frankfurt am Main: Suhrkamp.

Stinchcombe, Arthur. 1968. *Constructing Social Theories.* New York: Harcourt Brace Jovanovich.

———. 1975. "Merton's Theory of Social Structure." In *The Idea of Social Structure: Papers in Honor of Robert K. Merton,* edited by Lewis A. Coser. New York: Harcourt Brace Jovanovich.

Sztompka, Piotr. 1974. *System and Function: Toward a Theory of Society.* New York: Academic Press.

———. 1986. *Robert K Merton: An Intellectual Profile.* New York: St. Martin's Press.

Taylor, Ian, Paul Walton, and Jack Young. 1973. *The New Criminology.* London: Routledge and Kegan Paul.

Wallace, Walter L. 1969. *Sociological Theory.* New York: Aldine-Atherton.

2

Robert K. Merton: The Relation between Theory and Research

Paolo Ammassari

The Current Relevance of Two of Merton's Essays

Of the four fundamental Mertonian themes highlighted by Piotr Sztompka's *Robert K. Merton: An Intellectual Biography* (1986: ch.8)— the classicist, the cognitivist, the structuralist, and the ironicist—I have chosen the cognitivist to provide a thorough analysis of the methodological aspect based upon the relationship of reciprocal stimulation and conditioning between theory and research. I refer to the well-known Mertonian thesis: scientific and, in particular, sociological work is a "two-way traffic" between theoretical thought and empirical research.

The Mertonian argument is so well-known that, in a study of his body of work, as Sztompka's book is, this aspect ends up being almost marginal. Moreover, the very familiarity of the thesis weakens the author's ties of paternity, and inevitably precludes its evaluation within the context of a particular intellectual position and of a specific gnoseological perspective. Indeed, Merton's ideas are by now such a part of current textbooks that they appear to be common methodological notions. To a considerable extent, Merton's contribution in this area has, in fact, been subjected to that form of scientific reproduction which consists, as Merton himself has pointed out in other connections, in "banalizing" and "obliteration by incorporation." Therefore, if we wish to understand the current relevance of Merton's two essays on the relation between theory and research in its full actuality, we must reread them as part of the cognitivist theme and place them within Merton's more general conception of sociology and of science, that is to say, place them with reference to the epistemological assumptions implicit in this conception.

Sociological Theory and its Role in Empirical Research

In 1945, when Merton's first essay was published with the concise and allusively programmatic title, "Sociological Theory," sociological debate focused on the fragmentary nature, inconsistency, and theoretical insignificance of the findings of empirical social research, on the one hand, and on the other, the sterile, merely speculative, hastily generalizing, and abstractly systematic character of much sociological theory removed from linkage with empirical observation. At the end of the 1950s, these two themes were taken up again by C.W. Mills (1959) in his dual polemic against "grand theory" and "abstract empiricism." But in the mid-1940s they constituted the critical theses regarding the typical armchair sociologist ready to hold forth on the "real and significant" problems of society and history and the sociological field researcher, confident in his research instruments, and convinced and satisfied by the research findings that were thus attained.

In terms of controversy and, at times, even of polemics, these two positions were unyielding. The first would frequently deny the usefulness and significance of conclusions drawn from empirical research and the second would often consider the reasoning of theoretical analysis abstruse and obscure. Nevertheless, both were willing to acknowledge the possibility of a meeting ground on which rigorous observation could temper risky speculative generalizations and where theoretical implications could render empirical observations less obvious and fragmentary.

Assuming almost unanimous agreement on these considerations, Merton believed that both parties would undoubtedly be willing to bridge the gap between sociological theory and empirical social research.[1] Furthermore, he seemed certain that sooner or later empirical sociological research would meet the canons of scientific method and be more open to the influence of theory. Since, however, the term "theory" covers a wide range of cognitive activities, Merton thought it necessary to distinguish the different types and to clarify their diverse effects on empirical research.

Thus Merton distinguishes six different types of theoretical work, but attributes the status of "sociological theory" to only one of these. Summarizing the main arguments of his essay, Merton begins by distinguishing methodology from substantive theory. He observes how sociologists often laboriously elaborate the logical bases of their procedures, emphasizing how this praxis indicates the discipline's immaturity. He then excludes from theory-proper "general sociological orientations"—those theoretical orientations that are useful in providing a general framework for empirical inquiry, but that only provide a point of departure for theoretical work. He goes on to observe that the "analysis of sociological concepts" is an indispensable phase of theoretical work, but avoids the error of taking the part for the whole, by denying that one can justify the reduction of sociological theory to such analysis. He continues to discuss the scientific status of "*post factum* sociological interpretations*," pointing out that they can be useful in the development of theory provided that they are not treated as *ad hoc* hypotheses. Finally, he considers sociological generalizations, distinguishing "empirical generalizations" from "theoretical formulations." The latter are deducible from "a set of logically interrelated propositions" while the former are isolated propositions "summarizing observed uniformities of relationships between two or more variables" (95). Theory-proper and the orientation of empirical research toward theory emerge when statements of empirical uniformities can be drawn from the set of logically interrelated propositions.

At this point the numerous influences sociological theory exerts upon empirical social research become fully manifest. Indeed, theoretic pertinence (1) extends the cognitive *scope* of empirical findings; (2) contributes to the *cumulation* of both theory and research findings; (3) converts empirical statements into theoretical statements, thus increasing the *fruitfulness* of empirical research; and (4) provides empirical uniformities with a logical foundation and thus introduces *a basis for prediction*, which differs significantly from mere extrapolation.

In conclusion, Merton stresses the need for "codification" in the sense that a convention should be established that empirical research reports explicitly set forth the theoretical statements (in particular hypotheses) to which the research findings refer, a convention that, after all, has been fully acknowledged in sociological publications and has contributed to forming a model for the "research report" typical of American and, by now, of international sociological literature.[2] According to Merton, although the full theoretical orientation of empirical research is only achieved through the influence of theory-proper—defined as a set of logically interconnected theoretical statements—other aspects of theoretical work also have an inevitable impact on research. For example, general theoretical orientations limit the investigation and indicate the type of variables which are to be taken into account. On the other hand, by defining what is to be observed, conceptual analysis makes the character of empirical data explicit and frees us from the sometimes ambiguous or contradictory meanings buried in traditional concepts. Even this brief summary of Merton's essay should make evident the importance of his analysis and clarification of the diverse influences of sociological theory on empirical research. However, it is likely that Merton's reflections now seem scarcely controversial. If this is so, it is because they have been extensively included in handbooks of sociology. It is equally true, however, that at the time of publication, Merton's approach was definitely innovative and, as we shall see, in some aspects it remains so.

Two Ways of Understanding Sociological Theory

To demonstrate that Merton's perspective could not be taken for granted, it is sufficient to compare it to another essay published in the same year (1945) by Talcott Parsons. Parsons's essay—even its wordy title—is, in certain respects, the antithesis of Merton's. Parsons emphasizes the ambiguity of the term "theory" and laments the contraposition between theorists too steeped in the philosophy of history and empiricists too blind to the function of theory in scientific activity. Yet his approach is more a show of instrumental support in favor of the theoretical supremacy of structural-functionalism than it is a clarification of the relation between sociological theory and empirical research.[3] On the contrary, in bringing grist to the mill of a "generalized theoretical system" as the conceptual framework of the structural-functionalist perspective, he evokes the models of physical mechanics and biological physiology as models for sociological theory.

To me, his reasoning seems to be a flight into abstraction and wishful thinking. For his part, Merton warns instead that "every effort should be made to avoid dwelling upon illustrations drawn from the 'more mature' sciences—such as physics and biology—not because these do not exhibit the logical problems involved, but because their very maturity permits these disciplines to deal *fruitfully* with abstractions of a high order to a degree which, it is submitted, is not yet the case with sociology" (86).

The difference in Parsons's and Merton's conceptions of sociology as a science could not have been greater than in these two essays. In fact, these differences led to an open discussion with Parsons in 1947, and subsequently to an implicit polemic (Parsons 1948; Merton 1948; 1957). These debates mark the beginning of a new period in American sociology and not only because they coincide chronologically with the beginning of the postwar era. Whereas Parsons seemed certain that "we stand on the threshold of a definitely new era in sociology" thanks to the elaboration of a "well-articulated generalized theoretical system" (Parsons 1945: 212), Merton emphasized the current immaturity of sociology, whose differences with other sciences can be estimated in "centuries of cumulating scientific research" (Merton 1945: 87). He continues: "Pressures deriving from the respective theoretical gaps of the several social sciences may serve, in time, to bring about an increasing formulation of specific and systematic sociological theories appropriate to the problems implied by these gaps" (Merton 1945: 89). As opposed to Parsons's praise of the generalized theoretical system— logically closed and self-contained[4] as a theoretical panacea with which the future of sociology is assured—"Sociological Theory" sets forth the proposal of "*adequately tested, specific theories*" (ibid., emphasis added) as the only ones suited for the analytical and empirical work of the time. The idea and proposal of "theories of the middle range" are, therefore, already clearly present here with the same methodological and historical justifications that would be presented and developed in the subsequent dispute: the lack, in the present historical moment of sociology, of a sufficient accumulation of fundamental observations; the insufficient maturity of the discipline and the futility of comparisons with more mature sciences; the inadvisability of pursuing the usual pretense of a unified, omnicomprehensive, total theoretical system (Merton 1968: 46–48).

The counterposition present in the two essays is not confined to the

question of whether sociology is or is not ready for a coherent theoretical system at a high order of generalization. It also involves the
very concept of sociological theory and its requisite internal coherence. Whereas Merton urges us not to identify theory with the clarification of concepts (Merton 1945: 89), Parsons defines a theoretical
system precisely as a "body of logically interdependent generalized
concepts of empirical reference" (1945: 212). Whereas Parsons considers the system's logical coherence of the entire system an essential
requisite, Merton warns that "the pressure for logical consistency has
at times invited logomachy and sterile theorizing, inasmuch as the
assumptions contained in the system of analysis are so far removed
from empirical referents or involve such high abstractions as not to
permit of empirical inquiry" (Merton 1945:99).[5] Furthermore, while
Parsons sees the facilitation of describing empirical data and the selection as a fundamental function of theory from the indefinite number of
factual observations as a fundamental function of theory, Merton attributes the choice of variables to general theoretical orientations and
the construction of specific indicators through conceptual analysis—
two theoretical aspects that neither characterize nor exhaust theory-
proper. Finally, Parsons and Merton also differ in their understanding
of "empirical generalization," a concept utilized by both of them. Merton
(1945: 95, note 16) traces the concept back to Dewey who, in turn,
defines the concept by excluding from it any link to theory—a link
that Parsons, instead, asserts is indispensable (1945: 220). His use of
the term is not explicitly defined, but given the references to Comte,
Spencer, and Marx, it seems less connected with the uniformities found
in empirical research and more related to sociohistorical generalizations (Parsons 1945: 215–216). Thus, these divergent interpretations
are not confined to the bearing of theory on empirical research. On the
contrary, one can argue that these authors are interested in the impact
of theory only as a necessary implication of their conception of theory
as such and its role in scientific, and in particular sociological, work—
since, for both authors, sociology is a science, an empirical science.
Instead, the debate concerns the question of the status of sociological
theory in relation to development of the discipline. On the issue of
how the status and role of theory in sociology should be understood,
nothing was taken for granted, at the time of the publication of "Sociological Theory." On the contrary, sociology essentially had to face a
fundamental choice: to privilege theoretic work understood as specu-

lative construction, submitted once and for all to empirical work to be examined and (as was then believed, at the same time, hoped) "verified"; or to opt for an approach which by orienting empirical work theoretically would increase its fruitfulness, extend the scope of its empirical findings, and therefore promote its cumulativeness. Essentially, the choice was about the type of theory which sociology needed: one consisting of theoretical statements inferred from basic assumptions or one in which theoretical statements would be elaborated on the basis of empirical statements drawn from research findings. As mentioned, the choice involved two important aspects: (1) how "theory" was to be understood and (2) the evaluation of the then-present state of sociology as a scientific discipline. It is precisely in reference to these two aspects that Merton's perspective appeared totally innovative.

It was new, first of all, in terms of clarifying what constitutes a scientific "theory" in the strictest sense. In neither sociology nor in the philosophy of science did the term "theory" have an explicit and univocal definition.[6] Until the end of the 1950s, E. Nagel (1961: ch. 5) provided the most complete —and, I believe most balanced and convincing—analysis of the status of scientific theories in science. Yet even he could do no better than to rely on the unfinished classical work by N.R. Campbell (1920: 120–140) who defines scientific theory proper, as a set of theoretical statements intended as assumptions not directly confirmable. He distinguishes them from empirical statements, defined instead as observable and experimental "laws."[7] Tackling the subject again, Nagel elaborates and clarifies the distinction between "experimental laws" and "theoretical laws," and attributes the status of "theory" only to the latter. Several years before, on the other hand, Merton had already clearly distinguished empirical generalizations from theoretical ones. Furthermore, he warned against confusing either of these with general orientations or *post factum* interpretations, or even with the results of conceptual analysis.

But the originality of Merton's perspective is seen, above all, in his understanding of the procedures for elaborating theoretical statements. With respect to the danger of philosophical speculations uncontaminated by empirical data and deduced from basic assertions postulated in perfect and exhaustive conceptual systems, Merton proposes a less elating but more fruitful work of theoretical reflection. His proposal was aimed at "the conversion of empirical uniformities into theoretic statements" (1945: 98). The proposal, formalized two years later in the well-known terms of theories of the middle range, emerged from the aforementioned considerations regarding the role of theory in the current state of sociology as a scientific discipline. It should be noted that the fundamental aspects of his conception of science and sociology are juxtaposed in these reflections: a conception that, on the other hand, is firmly rooted in his studies of the sociology of science. These, in turn, are sustained, as we know, by his conscious sensibility about problems of the sociology of knowledge and those of sociology in particular. This "admirable conception of social science," as M. Brodbeck would say when she included Merton's two essays in her prestigious anthology of philosophy of the social sciences (1968: 458), is what gives Merton's proposal that originality and strength of conviction which still strikes us today. But before outlining this conception, it is necessary to examine his second essay, published in 1948.

Empirical Research and its Influence on Sociological Theory

When the essay, "The Bearing of Empirical Research upon the Development of Sociological Theory," came out, the dispute with Parsons was not completely over. On the contrary, by reaffirming the interdependence between theory and research, the essay tends to consolidate the Mertonian conception of sociological theory into a set of theoretical statements not deductively derived from a postulatory system of concepts but resulting instead from a reformulation of empirical uniformities.

In fact, the essay's thesis is that "empirical research goes far beyond the passive role of verifying and testing theory: it does more than confirm or refute hypotheses. Research plays an active role: it performs at least four major functions that help shape the development of theory. *It initiates, reformulates, deflects and clarifies theory*" (1968: 103).

The initial stimulus for formulating a new theory can come from an unanticipated, anomalous, or strategic datum. This is the well-known "serendipity" model: empirical research leads to a new hypothesis which, in turn, gives birth to a new theory. The reformulation of a theory can emerge from new data which cannot be accounted for by the original theoretical scheme: new empirical generalizations can give rise to the formulation of new theoretical statements. The deflection or reorientation of a theory can emerge following the use of new procedures and instruments of empirical research—in the sense that the theory which has promoted it is, in turn, influenced by the way empirical procedures and their specific results are employed. Finally, the clarification of a theory, or rather its concepts, is a frequent result of empirical research, since it is during the planning and implementation of research that concepts are analyzed and clarified in the attempt to make their definitions explicit and to indicate their empirical referents.

These four functions of empirical research are elucidated in counterpoint, as it were, to the arguments advanced in the preceding essay regarding the role of theory in empirical research. The serendipity model is contrasted with *post factum* and *ad hoc* interpretations and the two models are said to be governed by different logics: the former by the *logic of discovery*, and the latter by the *logic of justification*. A *posteriori* interpretations—occasioned by anomalous data that cannot be accounted for in the original interpretative scheme—can certainly not be considered proved by these. However, as a conjecture to be reformulated for further empirical research, it may prove to be a fortunate, new, and fruitful hypothesis. Thus, what is inadmissible within the context of verification becomes acceptable and, better still, particularly useful in the context of the invention of hypotheses.

By confronting new data, the reformulation of theory aims to take hitherto neglected aspects into account. From the viewpoint of empirical research, this re-emphasizes the important role of empirical generalizations as a "hinge" between theory and research. New empirical uniformities become pertinent to the object of analysis, and theory must take these into account by reformulating the empirical statements that express them into theoretical statements. On the other hand, it is only through such reformulation that empirical research findings can constitute a significant framework.

The clarification of concepts during the planning and implementation of all research "sensitive to its own needs" obviously represents the counterpart, on the level of empirical inquiry, to conceptual analysis carried out in theoretical inquiry. However, it does not necessarily represent a *trait d'union* between theory and research. This is obvious if one considers that although conceptual analysis is an indispensable phase in the process of conceptualization, the latter differs significantly in its logical characteristics and practical functions according to whether it is situated within the context of empirical or theoretical inquiry.

Finally, the refocusing of theoretical interests, stimulated by new methods of empirical research, highlights the positive *feedback* of research on general orientations and theory. It also highlights the impact that is exerted on theory by the availability of new research instruments, and, consequently, by new types of data, statistical types, in particular. In this case, the interdependence between theory and research in scientific work becomes, from Merton's perspective, a particular precursor of scientific development in both its theoretic growth and in the sophistication and pertinence of its technical and methodological equipment.

The second essay thus takes the themes advanced in the first essay regarding theoretical inquiry but, as it were, tips them towards empirical inquiry. The intention is to reaffirm a conception of sociological theory differing wholly from the one set forth by Parsons. This is evident if one considers that the capacity of empirical research to stimulate, reformulate, reorientate, and clarify theory is possible only if theory does not constitute a complete system, closed and logically self-sufficient, as Parsons would have it.[8] On the contrary, the presupposition—on which it is possible to configure these four functions of empirical research with respect to theory—is obviously that theory is not simply and solely deducible from the axioms constituting the fundamental theoretical nucleus; theory is open to the pressures derived from research findings and thus becomes able to convert empirical generalizations into theoretical statements.

The Sociological Conception of Science and Sociology as a Science

What makes Merton's reflections on science and sociology attractive and penetrating to a sociologist is, I believe, the fact that in them the conception of sociology as science is interwoven with the sociological conception of science. In fact, his being a sociologist was, above all, his being a sociologist of science. It is therefore not strange that in considering sociology as science, Merton defines science in sociological terms.

We are not dealing with the Chinese boxes generally evoked by the "sociology of sociological knowledge." On the contrary, it is by his very inauguration of "the sociology of science" as a discipline, by withdrawing it from the speculatively oriented sociology of knowledge, that Merton avoids falling into, as one puts it today, self-reference. He is able to grasp the very criteria of scientific adequacy as reconstructed logic. These criteria emerge as the result of the interaction between conscious activities of the scientific community and the social-structural conditions in which they take place. In a certain sense, which it is not possible to analyze in detail here, it is the study of the social conditions in which the type of scientific knowledge is produced that provides the criteria of scientific knowledge itself. In my opinion, Merton's methodological writings must be understood within the general context of his inductive reconstruction of the *social mode of practicing science*. Precisely because it is an eminently social activity, its fundamental characteristic is its being *public*.

The importance of the public nature of scientific procedures has not received the attention it deserves from the philosophers of science. And yet, I believe that all the other characteristics of scientific method follow from it. To begin with, the *reproducibility of procedures* would be completely problematic if it were not for their public nature. In its turn, reproducibility ensures, on the basis of shared theoretical premises, the *replicability of the results* and, therefore, the intersubjectivity that, at very least, constitutes the only possible guarantee of "objectivity."

Although Merton does not explain it in this way, the methodological aspect of the public nature of the procedures with which science is carried out becomes the epistemological foundation of scientific knowledge. Merton draws his conception of science, both of the "selective accumulation" of knowledge and of scientific objectivity itself, from the reconstruction of the social mode of producing knowledge: a manner that renders it public, replicable, and subject to the scrutiny and criticism of the scientific community. With reason, Sztompka speaks of "sociological epistemology" (1986: 75).

In this sociological conception of science there can be no place for definitive results—and both theoretic and empirical research are never-ending processes. In this, Merton's thought coincides with Popper's. Yet, according to a footnote to a well-known essay by Popper (1962: 221), only in 1956 was he convinced that the aim of scientific research should not be a "finished deductive system." It represents, if anything, an always surpassed means to richer and more controllable knowledge. In 1945, Merton proposed exactly this, even attracting Bierstedt's criticisms many years later (1981: 152–153), who, strangely enough, considers theory an end, meaning doubly *an end* and *the end* of inquiry.

Thus, in the Mertonian conception of science there is no room for the Comtean and Spencerian tradition (which, however, J. Agassi traced back to Newton and Popper connected to Plato and Euclid [ibid.]) to pursue finished and omnicomprehensive theoretical systems. In another quarter, Merton's concern that sociology would return to Spencerian speculative systems was acknowledged as valid by Parsons himself—even if, naturally, he held the critique to be unjustified with respect to himself, given that he did not propose a theoretical system, but a "systematic conceptual scheme" (1950: 352).

Regarding this role of conceptualization on the one hand, and of systematics, on the other, Merton's opinion differs even more radically. Nothing is further from his conception of science than a system of concepts finalized once and for all. In fact the bearing of empirical research on conceptual analysis implies a continuous clarification and redefinition of concepts in relation to the requirements of research, its problems, and its tools of data-gathering and analysis. It is the historical dimension of the conceptual apparatus of science and sociology as such that permeates an entire series of Mertonian reflections and methodological proposals (such as "Burke's theorem" or "sociological euphemism"). Nonetheless, the historicity of scientific concepts does not mean that there is no accumulation of knowledge or that history of theory is preferred to systematics. On the contrary, as is well known, Merton thoroughly criticizes the confusion between history of theory and theoretical systematics. He holds that the preference for the history of theory, in both academic curricula and publications is not scientifically justified. It must be emphasized that Merton's position is not at all contradictory. As a matter of fact, I believe that it is precisely the repeated claims by various authors of having acheived a "finished" conceptual system that calls for the study of history of sociological theory—not the clarification of concepts, which simply complicates matters in the course of both theoretic and empirical inquiry and only requires the revision of textbooks, without disquisitions of the various elaborations and conceptual clarifications introduced by every author.[9]

In the Mertonian conception of the evolution of scientific knowledge, these updatings and revisions are not supposed to constitute definitively consolidated and permanently acquired notions. The cumulativeness of scientific knowledge is, for Merton, a fact widely confirmed by technological applications; it should not be understood, in his thought, in a mechanically unilinear fashion. In this respect, one can say that Merton is Viconian, in the sense that "courses and re-courses" are always possible. Merton, however, does not consider the latest word, as such, to be closest to the truth. "The fallacy of the latest word" is a sophism that Merton resolutely combats, and not only to defend his earlier thesis (1984). In accord with his sociological conception of science, the achieving of scientific knowledge can be considered only part of the complex process of *selective* accumulation. With the typical disenchantment of the sociologist who includes this process among that of human and social matters, Merton does not believe in the assumption that he who comes afterwards must necessarily be right nor, obviously, that the last confutation must be just that.

Following Lakatos, Merton (1984: 1109) believes that this falsification theory is ingenuous and unacceptable. On the contrary, an informed falsification theory always proposes an alternative theory. In fact, if criticism—on which Merton, like Popper, bases the rationality of the growth of knowledge—were only *destruens*, there would have been no selective accumulation which undoubtedly characterizes scientific knowledge for Merton. Informed falsification theory (based on the emergence of alternative theories with greater explanatory scope) and the selective accumulation of scientific knowledge (with its corollary of the unacceptability of the idea of inevitable and unilinear scientific progress) imply a conception of science that differs from every kind of positivism. Although Merton probably considers himself a positivist, in view of his belief in the validity (N.B.: completely formal validity, not in terms of content) of natural science's methodological model for sociology, which is therefore a nomothetic and empirical science, I do not believe that he can be charged with being a veteropositivist, a logical neopositivist, or even a "critical positivist." His conception of science as a humanly conducted and socially conditioned undertaking places him in a sociological epistemological perspective in which the interdependence between theory and research constitutes the fulcrum of scientific activity. From this perspective and within the context of sociology, *serendipity* does not degenerate into pure inductionism. *Empirical generalizations* do not constitute the ultimate end of inquiry, but rather provide the empirical content of *theories of the middle range*. These represent only one moment—necessary, but transitory—in the construction of a proper sociological theory intended as a set of theoretical, logically interconnected statements. A set which is certainly subject to falsification, but which stems from an evolutionary view of science and, in particular, of sociology as a science, which I believe is the result of a mature critical rationalism. On this path toward a sociology that is consciously and rationally critical of its own theoretical aspirations and its own data gathering, Robert K. Merton has truly been a master-at-a-distance, just as Sztompka says. He has taught us not to be sociologists dedicated to pure speculation or solely preoccupied with counting heads, but rather to the merging of theory and empirical research in a meaningful enterprise.

Notes

1. Merton's optimism regarding the willingness of these two groups of sociologists to converge on common grounds (observation guided by theory and speculation tempered by observation), would abate as soon as he clarified that terrain as "theories of the middle range." In fact, the publication of his proposal brought about a polarization of sociologists' reactions as well as a dispute among scholars on the question of "present-day sociologists' most effective role." Later, Merton himself analyzed, in a disenchanted manner, this process of polarization from the viewpoint of a sociologist of science and from the viewpoint of sociology as a science (1957: 89 ff.).
2. Of course, Merton did not believe that standardization of the "research report" and, in general, of the "scientific paper" would assure that sociological work would be significant. On these aspects, see Merton 1957: 30 and Barbano 1975.
3. Parsons also dealt with the relation between theory and research in a speech delivered in 1937, at a meeting of the Society for Social Research (Parsons 1938).
4. The strictly coherent and perfectly self-enclosed nature of a theory is, for Parsons, a positive and particularly appreciated trait. In fact, according to Parsons, a scientific discipline needs, more than theories, a theoretical system with such a degree of logical integration that "every logical implication of any combination of propositions in the system is explicitly stated in some other proposition in the same system" (Parsons 1945: 212–213). But what constitutes the principal shortcoming of Parsons's proposal is precisely its perfect Cartesian, logically closed character: its almost complete impermeability both to theoretical considerations not present in the system or implied by it and to empirical observations not strictly deducible from it. For this reason, Parsons's proposal has been criticized from the outset for being "utopian" (Dahrendorf 1958) and the Achilles' heel of his entire body of work. In fact, in *The Structure of Social Action*, Parsons already affirmed that rational knowledge is a single organic whole (1937: 21). Merton, on the contrary, warns that to pursue integrated and all-encompassing systems from which all subsidiary theories are derived "is to risk producing twentieth-century sociological equivalents of the large philosophical systems of the past, with all their varied suggestiveness, their architectonic splendor, and their scientific sterility" (Merton 1968: 51). Should each sociologist pursue this type of theoretical work, the outcome would be, according to Merton, the theoretic balkanization of sociology.

5. On the problematic character of the concept of "unity" and theoretical "coherence," see Watkins 1984: 104–124.

6. Of course, no linguistic term has an unequivocal meaning, since, as is well known, all have cultural connotations, both at a social and at a personal level. Nevertheless, literary usage and in particular, philological thought has contributed to the general acceptance of the so-called denotative meanings of linguistic terms that we find codified in dictionaries. But naturally, beyond specific competence, the practical-ideological usage of the language remains. So even if a term appears fairly neutral, that is to say, has an extensively shared connotation and convergent denotation, it may be full of unwitting ambivalences and intentional ambiguities. This is what occurred to the term "theory"; during the nineteenth century it did not need an explicit definition in the domain of the natural sciences. Only with the emergence and the development of social sciences did the term "theory" become charged with, or suspected of, ideologically biased meanings extraneous to scientific work. Thus, the concept lost its denotative clarity and unequivocal usage.

7. It must be emphasized that Campbell's definition of theory as a set of theoretic statements not directly confirmable, that is, unprovable assumptions, has withstood the test of time; I believe it can also be found in the "theoretical ontology" with which Watkins defined the fundamental nucleus of a scientific theory—axioms that contain the theory's entire contents in themselves (1984: ch.3).

8. In an essay that ties the mircro-macro theme to the relation between sociological theory and empirical research, E. Besozzi (1986) sets forth the hypothesis that the object of study also orients the methodological attitude toward that relation. Thus Parsons, whose object of study is the "social system," can concentrate only on the general theoretical conceptual scheme, while the Chicago School or the Lynds, for example—who identify "social reality" as their object of inquiry—favor sociographic description instead. Only Merton's structuralism grasps the circularity between research and theory. The thesis is attractive, and I believe that it is generally valid even in relation to other methodological choices. For example, see Ammassari 1985 on the methodological consequences of choosing the "person" as an object of sociological inquiry.

9. But for this, according to Merton (1968: 27), it is necessary to free oneself from "adumbrationism." Nevertheless, this is a difficult suggestion to follow. To look for or, better still, grasp the links and anticipations in the writings of various authors is, in a certain sense, inherent in intellectual and scientific work. I also yield to the temptation: Popper had, in 1934, already outlined the circularity of the theory-research relation. He clearly emphasized that if the theorist is to guide the experimenter, the work of the latter is also mostly theoretical (Popper 1934: 103).

References

Ammassari, Paolo. 1985. "I fondamentali problemi di metodologia della ricerca sociale." *Studi di Sociologia* 23: 176–93.

Barbano, Filippo. 1975. "Sociologia e sviluppo della scienza nel pensiero di R.K. Merton." In R.K. Merton *Scienza, tecnologia e società nell'Inghilterra dei XVII secolo*. Milan: Franco Angeli.

Besozzi, Elena. 1986 "La circolarità teoria e ricerca empirica: il contributo di R.K. Merton." *Studi di Sociologia* 24: 442–64.

Bierstedt, Robert. 1981. *American Sociological Theory: A Critical History*. New York Academic Press.

60   Robert K. Merton and Contemporary Sociology

Brodbeck, May, ed. 1968. *Readings in the Philosophy of the Social Sciences*. New York: MacMillan.

Campbell, R. Norman. 1920. *Physics: The Elements*. Cambridge: Cambridge University Press.

Dahrendorf, Ralf. 1958. "Out of Utopia: Toward a Reorientation of Sociological Analysis." *American Journal of Sociology* 64: 115–127.

Merton, R.K. 1945. "Sociological Theory." *American Journal of Sociology* 50. Reprinted with the title "The Bearing of Sociological Theory on Empirical Research," in Merton [1957] 1968.

———. 1948. "The Bearing of Empirical Research upon the Development of Social Theory." *American Sociological Review* 13: 164–168. Reprinted in Merton [1957] 1968.

———. [1957] 1968. *Social Theory and Social Structure*. New York: Free Press.

———. 1984. "The Fallacy of the Latest Word: The Case of Pietism and Science." *American Journal of Sociology* 89: 1091–1121

Mills, C. Wright. 1959. *The Sociological Imagination*. New York: Oxford University Press.

Nagel, Ernest. 1961. *The Structure of Science: Problems in the Logic of Scientific Explanation*. New York: Harcourt.

Parsons, Talcott. 1937. *The Structure of Social Action*. New York: McGraw Hill.

———. 1938. "The Role of Theory in Social Research." *American Sociological Review* 3: 13–20.

———. 1945. "The Present Position and Prospects of Systematic Theory in Sociology." In *Twentieth-Century Sociology*, eds. G. Gurvitch and W.E. Moore. Reprinted in Parsons 1954. New York: Philosophical Library.

———. 1948 "The Position of Sociological Theory." *American Sociological Review* 13: 156–64.

———. [1950] 1954. "The Prospects of Sociological Theory." In *Essays in Sociological Theory* by Talcott Parsons, 348–69. New York: Free Press.

Popper, Karl R. [1934] 1959. *The Logic of Scientific Discovery*. London: Hutchinson.

———. 1962. *Conjectures and Refutations: Growth of Scientific Knowledge*. New York: Basil Books.

Sztompka, Piotr. 1986. *Robert K. Merton: An Intellectual Profile*. New York: St. Martin's Press.

Watkins, John. 1984. *Science and Skepticism*. Princeton: Princeton University Press.

3

Merton and the Sociology
of Science in Europe

Gianni Statera

The Origin of the Sociology of Science

The definition of the object and method of the sociology of science, its academic institutionalization, its spread and popularization, can be almost entirely attributed to Merton. Moreover, it is also in Merton's work that all the successes and failures of the discipline can be found *in nuce.* In broadest outline, Merton writes: "the subject matter of the sociology of science is *the dynamic interdependence* between science, as an ongoing activity giving rise to cultural and civilizational products, and the environing social structure. The *reciprocal* relations between science and society are the object of inquiry . . . But until recently, the reciprocity of these relations has received uneven attention, the impact of science upon society eliciting notice, and the impact of society upon science, little" (Merton 1968: 585).

Indeed, the latter often leads to a kind of determinism that Merton found logically and methodologically unacceptable. It was for this reason that, alongside the warning against the risk of overestimating the ideological-religious approach, he formulated his meticulous critique of the Marxist method proposed by the Soviets in London in 1931. In fact, the adoption of such a method in the search for the causes of the development of science leads to a feeling of accomplishment by succeeding in demonstrating *ex post facto* that the historical scientific discoveries (or at least most of them) served to meet certain technological requirements or, more generally, economic ones. And Merton found this method utterly inadequate for a sociology of science.

The Soviets had caused great turmoil in the ranks of the historians of science at the Congress on the History of Science in London in 1931 by insistently laying great emphasis both on the importance of the socioeconomic conditioning operative on scientific research in general, and, more particularly, on that part of research wherein tradition ascribed to free, individual creativity a primary, though not exclusive role: so-called pure science. Boris Hessen, in particular, had gone so far as to question the very idea of a separation between pure science and technology, analyzing a work customarily considered as a paradigmatic example of "pure scientific theory" uncontaminated by "practical" considerations—Isaac Newton's *Principia*, in terms of its being a response to precise socioeconomic needs.

Furthermore, the traditional idea according to which scientific progress was the result of a linear and ineluctable process, simply catalyzed by "intellectual giants of mysterious origin," had already been refuted at the beginning of the 1930s by the group of socialist-oriented British scientists (Hogben, Needham, Hyman, Levy), who had founded the so-called movement for the social relations of science. One member of this movement, which developed as a reaction to the scientistic utopia of the 1920s, was J.D. Bernal, who denounced the mystification inherent in the persistence of the idea of science as *otium* in his book *The Social Function of Science* (Bernal 1939).

Nevertheless, the "movement for the social relations of science" did not give birth to a real, genuine sociological approach to science; rather there arose a form of "scientific humanism" which later (in the 1950s) developed into a series of nonviolent protests. Moreover, the political repercussions of Hogben's and Bernal's politico-cultural ideas provoked an immediate antideterminist and liberal reaction, which culminated in the foundation by Michel Polanyi and John Baker of the "Society for the Freedom of Science" in 1940. Thus, the problem of the relation between science and society, at least with regard to the influence of the former on the latter, became the issue of politico-ideological polemic and not the object of sociological analysis. It is no accident that rediscovery by the British sociologists of science of

Bernal's theories was mediated largely through Russell's critical tradition and a rereading of Marx. But the fatherhood of the "new" sociology of science can be ascribed to the American historian of science, Thomas Kuhn.

Thus it was in America that the sociology of science, in the strict sense of the term, was born in its early Mertonian version, developed within an empirical perspective of limited breadth, and was finally endowed with new implications and suggestions until the prefigurement of an alternative approach. It is thus to America that we must turn to observe the development of the discipline, first casting our eye on Merton.

Adopting and perfecting the "sociological" method prefigured by the Belgian-American historian of science, George Sarton, and moving from an epistemological perspective influenced by Whitehead on the one hand and *Wissenssoziologie* on the other, in 1938 Merton published what would later come to be acknowledged as the first work to deal specifically with the sociology of science: his monograph *Science, Technology and Society in Seventeenth-Century England*—a paradigmatic example of systematic investigation of the social matrix of science in a historical period crucial for the development of science itself in the West. Subsequently, Merton continued to be interested in the relations between science and society, exerting an influence so strong that it can be said that, at least until the mid-1950s the history of the sociology of science can be identified with the elaboration of the analysis undertaken by Merton and his students concerning the normative structure of science; the social, political, and cultural conditions that pave the way for development in research; the complex relations that exist between the institutional imperative of science and the actual behavior of scientists; the nature of the scientific community; and so on.

The Merton Paradigm

> *Four sets of institutional imperatives—Universalism, Communism, Disinterestedness, Organized Skepticism—comprise the ethos of modern science* (Merton [1942] 1968: 607).

According to Merton these imperatives are both "technical and moral compulsives"; as a consequence they are "good and true" (Merton

[1942] 1968: 605). Indeed, they derive from fundamental methodological principles, but they are also considered morally good in the
sense that the "increase of certified knowledge" takes on a morally
positive connotation, at least to the degree that one deems morally
positive the commitment to the increase of certified knowledge. The
whole argument rests on the assumption implicit in the avowal that the
institutional goal of science is the "increase of certified knowledge,"
the assumption, that is, whereby science is seen as a cumulative process, an assumption which is anything but self-evident.

Moreover, it is immediately apparent that such "institutional imperatives" comprise the transposition of epistemological and/or methodological orientations onto the plane of cultural norm, with its ensu-
ing configuration as constitutionally ambiguous items arrayed in an
undefined interstitial area between the horizons of logical-method-
ological, moral, philosophical-ontological, psychological and properly
sociological discourse.

Thus Merton himself was forced to admit, in his important 1957
monograph on the debates about the priority of scientific discoveries,
that the institution of science, like other institutions, potentially includes incompatible values (Merton 1973). Among these, it is the
values of originality and of "humility" which induce scientists respectively to demand acknowledgement of their priority in a discovery and
to evince awareness of the limits of their results. Hence the typical
ambiguity of the scientist exemplified in Darwin's conduct towards
Wallace, who had anticipated him in publicizing in outline the theory
of evolution.

All this forebodes the risk of trapping the sociology of science
within the narrow boundaries of the scientific community, a risk that
did not escape Merton. At least at the procedural level, his definition
of the object and method of the discipline appears such as to enable a
sociological approach that shuns the risks of gross determinism and of
an idealization, or embalmment, of science. As we have seen, in fact,
it is in the *dialectical relationship between science and the social
system that the object of the sociology of science lies*; moreover, as
Merton clearly points out, although the institution of "science" is governed by norms and values endowed with their own specific peculiarity, these should in any case be analyzed in close relation to those
which obtain in the social system at large.

However, even a formulation of this kind leaves several problems unsolved: in what sense is the relation between social system and science dialectical? Should the latter element of the relation be conceived as a "social system" itself (as Storer does), as a "subsystem" in many ways heterogeneous, or simply, in a functionalist (or neofunctionalist) key as one of the many elements (institutions) which are variously functional, dysfunctional, and nonfunctional, in relation to the system? Merton's position in this regard is probably closer to the third alternative than to the other two. Nevertheless, it was precisely Merton's analysis of the ethos of science—characterized by institutional norms and imperatives apparently far removed from those of other institutions and from the dominant models of behavior in the broader social system—that gave rise to the rich stream of studies on the "scientific community," "the social system of science," and "scientists' values."

Therefore, it was precisely the more questionable part of Merton's work that inspired the so-called Mertonians, that legion of sociologists of science who elaborated the theoretical and empirical analysis of the normative structure of science. Norman Storer in particular analyzed in depth the prevailing ethos in what he defined as the "scientific community"—a sort of revived "republic of scientists" in which the irresistible psychological need for recognition and for the "competent response to one's work" predominate.

Storer holds back from exalted tones and from the mystique of the "purity" of science, clearly setting himself apart from theorists such as Polanyi, and elucidates that the most important reason for asserting that science can be seen as a social system depends on the importance of "norms for the continued and just allocation of the commodity, in this case competent response, whose circulation forms the basis of the social system" (Storer 1966: 84).

In other words, according to Storer, science can be perceived as a social system because the ethos that characterizes it accompanies a system of acknowledgements and rewards which sustain and endorse it, at the same time ensuring social control.

This formulation, developed more or less concurrently and along slightly different lines by Norman Storer and Warren Hagstrom, appears to facilitate the resolution of a problem identified by Merton deriving from the heteronomy between the system of acknowledgements operating in science and that which obtains in the wider social system. On the one hand, the internalization of the values of the "scientific" social system would lead to conformity with values such as "communality" or "humility." On the other hand, the quest for originality and vindication of priority in discoveries would seem to reflect the values predominant in the wider social context. Hence, in the framework outlined by Storer, these same tendencies in scientists are conditioned by the desire for recognition and rewards, which are not external norms but inherent in the social system of science. In other words, Storer reduces the import of an unmistakable source of tension and conflict between the social system and the "science" system by encompassing within the latter norms which, albeit deriving from the former, become constituents of the latter. That is, the conflict ends up becoming a *fact* inherent in science.

This clearly delineates the view of the so-called Mertonians (who, in fact, overstep Merton's original methodological formulation) and who develop a sociology of science entirely inherent within science itself. Thus, according to Hagstrom, in science there is a system of "exchange of gifts" whereby the contributions of science are the fruit of the desire to gratify the recipient of the gift rather than the outcome of a contractually defined utilitarian relation (Hagstrom 1965).

Consequently it becomes unnecessary either to specify the nature of the "gift" or the manner or moment of the "exchange of gifts" (discovery-recognition) which, in its comprehensiveness, may not actually occur at all. Hence the freedom subjectively perceived by scientists in the choice of problems, in their autonomy in evaluating the import of their results and deciding to make them public at one time rather than at another; hence, also, the objective need for the autonomy of science and the justification of the institutional norms that ensure its operation; hence, finally, the close connection between the development of scientific research and the liberal democratic social order underlined by Bernard Barber, who had explicitly identified the American society of the 1950s as the nearest to the ideal conditions of liberty, individualism, rationality, and the impetus to social progress with due respect for the needs of diverse socioprofessional groups and categories, which permit the full actualization of the norms of science (Barber 1952).

Merton's paradigm, in conclusion, was read and adopted in American sociology of science in a theoretically functionalist key, empirically focused on interinstitutional analysis—that is, on the analysis of the conduct of the scientific community.

The "New" Sociology of Science

The "new" sociology of science grows out of the attempt to develop a model of what the "old" sociology of science was unable to explain-the modification of scientific knowledge. Its standard-bearers include Stuart Blume, Richard Whitley, Peter Weingart, and Steven and Hilary Rose, all Europeans and all active since the mid-1970s. Primarily, what these scholars have in common is the need to define a paradigm which makes it possible to move beyond the prevalently interinstitutional dimension within which the sociology of science in North America, especially the branch concerned with the ethos of science, has established itself. In pursuit of this objective, they have rediscovered the "moment for social relations in science," returned to certain Marxist formulations, and often linked themselves to the analyses of Habermas regarding the ideological dimension of science and technology.

The "new" sociology of science takes as its starting point the approach laid out by Thomas Kuhn concerning not only the relationship between science and society, but also the acceptance, questioning, rejection, and replacement of scientific paradigms.

This permits an approach to science which favors a truly sociological (as opposed to the epistemological or predominantly normative) dimension of the analysis, and at the same time emphasizes not only what is referred to as "normal science"—the substantially unproblematical acceptance of a paradigm sanctioned by the scientific community—but the processes of transition from one paradigm to another as well. In both of these circumstances it is the consensus of the scientific community—clearly conditioned by complex factors more of a social than a cultural or psychological nature—which is in fact the criterion validating a paradigm. This opens up a fairly large area of research for the sociology of science, and one that by and large includes epistemology or at least conditions the epistemological analysis.

With Kuhn, and with the method of research based on his work, there is a modification in the position of the "pure" scientist, presumed to be at complete liberty to choose the relevant questions and theoretical models which will allow him to reach a solution. On the one hand, a central role is now given to the scientific community, and on the other, the characteristics of working scientists are described not only during "scientific revolutions" but in periods of "normal science" as well.

With regard to the first point, it is clear that the scientist Kuhn is talking about is not a "laboratory rat" but an individual who plays complex, differentiated and sometimes ambiguous social roles within both the scientific institution and the larger social system. Far from appearing as a figure who internalizes the values connected with "institutional norms" which are "right and good," the scientist experiences all the professional, economic, and political successes and frustrations connected with working for a public or private institution. He is influenced by prestigious colleagues. He sometimes affects the latest scientific "fashions" and is sometimes ignored because he does not. He is susceptible to all the influence and stimulus deriving from the concrete possibility of career advancement and/or acquiring professional, political, and economic prestige. Thus, in terms of methodological consistency and descriptive validity the "ideal type" of the pure scientist is demolished, and "science" as an institution loses its connotation of autonomous "social system" and instead takes its place in the ranks of socioprofessional subsystems.

The second and third points, closely connected to the first, lead, on the one hand, to a renewed questioning of the approach of North American sociology of science to the scientific community; and, on the other, to the risk of turning the sociology of science into nothing more than a subdiscipline of the *sociology of the professions*.

The fact is that, in Kuhnian terms, "classic" sociology of science, at least as it is most commonly formulated from a theoretical standpoint, may be accused of neglecting periods of "normal science" in favor of crisis periods in which "old paradigms" come under scrutiny and scientific revolutions occur. The emphasis on *systematic doubt* and *universalism* and the atmosphere of urgency pervading a scientific community composed of individuals bent on innovation, ever ready to question their own results and free themselves from their own "products" seem indeed to be features which define a situation of "permanent revolution." But this criticism is valid only if "normal science" and "scientific revolution" are formalized as "ideal types" set in opposition to one another. This is feasible in a diachronic analysis of the type so ably carried out by Kuhn, in which the history of science reveals the relative prevalence of one or the other of these "ideal types." From a synchronic, more purely sociological point of view, however, a research situation can never be defined in terms of "normal science," or in other words as fundamentally routine and unproblematical. Even a period which would be defined after the fact as "normal" might possibly (or even "normally") include characteristics such as sudden insights or elements of evidence which might put one "on alert," cause the suspicion that "something is wrong," or bring about a synchronically very real crisis, even though such a crisis may then become no more than apparent when viewed from a diachronic perspective. Later, this period which the sociologist has analyzed synchronically might be characterized diachronically as a period of "normal science." This in no way, however, implies that scientific research can be reduced to an ordinary professional activity in which the possibility of unforeseen and unpredictable circumstances is virtually nonexistent. This is true even when such research is done in industrial laboratories for purposes of experimentation along lines which are to a certain degree predetermined.

Clearly, Kuhn is too perceptive a historian of science not to be aware of all this. Nevertheless, as mentioned earlier, the "new" sociology of science clearly carries with it the risk that a slavish transposition of the diachronic Kuhnian model into synchronic terms will lead to the transformation of the sociology of science into a banal and insignificant branch of the *sociology of the professions or of corporations*, coinciding remarkably with the position of the North American empirical sociologists (Marvick, Kornhauser, Hirsch, Marcson, Glaser, etc.).

The importance of Kuhn for the sociology of science lies first of all in his basic premise: he rejects the cumulative conception of science and in so doing focuses attention on those moments which constitute "breaks," often conflictual, in science itself. Conversely, Kuhn is also significant for the emphasis he places on sociological moments of consensus as the only guarantee of the validity of scientific propositions.

In contrast to Merton, according to whom the institutional goal of science is the cumulative "increase in certified knowledge," Kuhn sees science as a field of permanent tension and conflict, which abates during periods of "normal science" (in which a paradigm is accepted peacefully), and flares up in periods of crisis during which opposing factions take the field and battle to establish a new paradigm which will then achieve a significant consensus in the scientific community. On the basis of this perspective it would seem possible to establish a sociology of science which does not set itself up as the appendage of an objectivist epistemology. The scope of the sociology of science is in fact incomparably wider if it does not pay homage to the myth of "objectivity," in the sense of reflection on reality through laws and/or theories, but instead emphasizes the utility of a variety of conceptual constructs in order not only to solve problems (theoretical or practical), but to propose scientifically pertinent new ones as well, leaving aside the "objective truth" which it is generally presumed such constructs must confront. Following Kuhn, the only plausible criterion for the validity of scientific propositions is sociological, and refers to the consensus of the scientific community. The determinants of a consensus (or the lack of one), the way in which a consensus is arrived at or dissolves, the characteristics of the process by which new problems and new paradigms arise—these in their turn are a function of social, economic, political, and cultural factors.

As mentioned above, Kuhn gives increased weight to the sociological dimension in scientific research and casts a new light on the image of the "pure scientist." Debating the question with Ben-David, he emphasizes *mediated social conditioning* to which even the academic researcher is subject not only in the *choice of problems* but also in the selection of the *conceptual categories* with which to tackle them. This conditioning, which Kuhn sees as dictated principally by technological needs today, would be mediated (although not necessarily diminished) by the scientist's community, which stands as a sort of reference group through which filters the social questions science is asked to deal with and administers the sanctions, from recognition to consensus, to marginalization and ostracism.

The scientific community, then, assumes a central role, even in the Kuhnian-type sociology of science; this suggests that we need to reconsider the idea of any "break" with the Mertonian tradition in this respect. It is true that, along with Kuhn, the scientific community described by Merton, Barber, and Hagstrom becomes a plural phenomenon (Kuhn refers to scientific communities) and above all it becomes secularized—the members of the scientific communities analyzed by Kuhn are no longer specialists, happily communicating amongst each other in complete autonomy, committed only to forwarding the cause, the triumph of truth. Nor do they now appear indivisibly constrained by ties of strict solidarity based on a common rejection of the instrumentalization of science, on the importance of tolerance, conjecture, antidogmatism, à la Michael Polanyi—the greatest representative of antiliberalism and founder of the Society for the

Freedom of Science. Yet they maintain a basic unity which is assured for Kuhn by the acceptance of a common paradigm: "A paradigm," writes Kuhn in the postscript to the latest edition of *The Structure of Scientific Revolutions*, "is something which is shared by the members of a scientific community, and, conversely, a scientific community is made up of individuals who share a paradigm" (Kuhn 1962).

This is clearly a vicious circle and Kuhn admits it: "Not all circles are vicious but this one is a source of real difficulty" also and especially because "the scientific communities can and should be distinguished before the paradigms by an analysis of the behavior of the members of a given community" (Kuhn 1962: 120). Added to this source of difficulty one has to note that throughout the book Kuhn uses the term "paradigm" with at least two different meanings: (a) as a constellation of beliefs, norms, and techniques shared by the members of a scientific community; and (b) as an example of a paradigm. To put it another way, it seems that methodologically the scientific community precedes the paradigm even if, from a logical point of view, one cannot establish any other priority than that stemming from the method of approach to the study of paradigms and scientific communities. But since it is the scientific communities and not some piece of ontological-gnosiological data that legitimate the paradigm, these very methodological problems concerning the validity of the scientific propositions have to be dealt with in sociological terms—that is, in terms of the Mertonian tradition.

The considerable degree of convergence between Kuhn's position on the one hand, accepted as a point of reference for a sociology of science differentiated from the North American version, and on the other the viewpoint of Merton—sanctioned by the postscript to the 1970 edition of *Science, Technology and Society in Seventeenth-Century England*—does not mean that the two coincide. In opposition to Mertonian rationalism, Kuhn points to the manifest irrationality which in most cases marks the process of transition from one paradigm to another. In opposition to the temptations of Mertonian objectivism, Kuhn proposes an epistemology grounded explicitly in a sociological matrix. In opposition to Merton's emphasis on the creative moment in science, Kuhn places his on the importance of technological conditioning in both the normal science stage and the crisis stage.

In the new sociology of science of the early 1970s it was Richard Whitley who clarified the distinctive character of the new school as opposed to the old. In his brief essay *Black Boxism and The Sociology of Science* (1972) he brought the real problem into focus for the first time. What Whitley argues is that a sociology of scientific knowledge which continues to regard science as a black box (which many of the exponents of the new sociology did) is utterly impracticable. He maintains that there is a close relation between organizational structure and cognitive structure such that it is not possible to move ahead with a modeling of the organizational and cognitive development of science independent of a specific awareness of the corresponding disciplinary matrices. In fact, it was not only the entire Mertonian school, faithful to the dictums of the organizational paradigm, that failed to take into consideration the type of cognitive matrix as an independent variable, but a good part of the new sociology of science as well. According to Whitley, "The sociologists of science are concerned more about the producers than the product" (Whitley 1972). The attack on the Mertonians is explicit. "The ideas," adds Whitley, "are considered as given and objectified in papers, each of them is held equivalent to any other." Which rests on an implicit assumption of the perfect rationality of the cognitive activity of the research and the purely cumulative conception of the development of science.

On the other hand, even a rigidly Kuhnian position is, like that of Merton, incapable of making sense of the global meaning of scientific change. In fact, according to Kuhn, paradigms are not comparable to one another. If this is the case, and if change originates in the appearance of anomalies whose roots are unknown, how is it possible even to recognize, much less evaluate, scientific change? But for Whitley not even this is the proper path for a sociology of scientific knowledge. The proper path, in his view, lies in the idea of making the sociology of science a translucent box, conceiving of scientific change as characterized by imperfect rationality. In this way, both the Scylla of perfect irrationality (absolute relativism) and the Charybdis of absolute rationality could be avoided.

And Now Back to Merton

Despite its real potential for innovation, Whitley's essay did not attract the attention it deserved and ended up among the large group of post-Kuhnian studies. Peter Weingart (1974) received the same treatment. Though he limits the field of application of the sociology of science to the study of scientific change (when, on the contrary, it is precisely the identification of the social mechanisms, which encourage the preservation of models and concepts, and so largely prevent change and innovation, that is of fundamental importance for the sociology of scientific knowledge), Weingart does pose a largely neglected problem: sociological analysis cannot make a generic study of change *tout court* but must take into consideration what is changing or has changed.

The research program of the new sociology of science, in which different methodologies come together in a general, essentially coherent model, is far from complete and perhaps, indeed, is still to be developed in all its empirical implications. Yet, this comprehensive program of the new sociology of science has already been challenged by new programs and new policies (especially in Europe)—by the English *relativists* of the Bath school, *ethnographers and ethnomethodologists* of scientific work (constructivists and "purists"), *the school of social interests* ("strong" and "weak" programs), and the *analysts of scientific discourse.* Thus the intellectual arena of the sociology of scientific knowledge has become overcrowded, with conflicting paradigms being proposed, and even more frequently, no real paradigm but more or less "alternative" models and methodologies. Furthermore, it is significant to note how the sociology of scientific knowledge reduces to some extent the scale of its research design and frame of reference (from the level of large establishments to increasingly smaller professional units, i.e., from complex organizations to single laboratories and research groups) and redirects its focus of attention away from the functional and structural regularities to the researchers' *performance* and from that to the types, channels, and mechanisms for communication and mediation of meaning.

Chubin and Restivo (1983) make a very simple distinction between "programmes and policies" defining "strong programme" in the sociology of scientific knowledge (characterized by the identification of sociological and scientific rationality) the analysis of scientific interests begun by Barnes and Bloor. The Edinburgh School (Barnes himself, MacKenzie, and Shapin), which limits itself to the analysis of scientific texts and the reconstruction of historical cases, can be placed alongside the Bath School (Collins and Pinch), which pays more attention to cases of "discovery" and the acceptance of that discovery.

The second great "family" of new trends can be seen to be laboratory studies, research carried out empirically on the activity of science in its natural context. The reference here is to Latour and Woolgar and their analysis of *discourse-in-action* which illustrates the social construction of knowledge. According to Chubin and Restivo, this constructivist "school" is closely connected to the ethnomethodology of science.

However, new programs and trends seem to have general thematic and methodological characteristics in common, according to the analysis made by Leonardo Cannavò (1984):

a. the inclusion of the day-to-day working of technical procedures within the field of analysis of the sociology of scientific knowledge;
b. the overall rejection of the distinction between social and scientific with the consequent possible confusion between the two areas (distinctions maintained by the new sociology of science precisely for the sake of operative clarity);
c. an essentially inward-looking approach to explaining scientific change, at least to the extent that factors external to the dynamics of the scientific system are largely overlooked;
d. the attribution of special heuristic importance to the practice of linguistic negotiation of scientific meaning with the resulting reproposal of a common-sense methodology on the one hand and of ethnomethodology-type research programs on the other;
e. the marked preference for qualitative methodology and hence the case study as *the* technique *par excellence*;
f. the reappearance of argumentation by example as opposed to by scientific inference;
g. the conviction—evidently taken from Kuhn but more so from Hanson, Toulmin, and Feyerabend—that scientific observation is inevitably theory-laden, and also that theory is underdetermined by data, as the conventionalist school among others had postulated; and,
h. the clear trend towards offering the specialist community theoretical points of discussion rather than research results.

The point is that, like any single scientific program, all of these programs and trends put together make up a very partial view. In various ways they propose the study of science (as process or product) through the collection and analysis of single cases (of spoken language, nonverbal and symbolic communication, and written discourse) by means of qualitative techniques whose aim is not explanation (which would imply agreed affirmation of the testing hypotheses) or exploration on the basis of selective criteria (typologies), but rather a sort of production of ostensible definitions of processes paradoxically "discovered" during the analysis without previously established, relevant hypotheses, or in the presence of hypotheses which are considered proved by the analysis of one or two cases.

A logical inconsistency becomes evident. Either the exponents of these trends consider their "schools" as networks for promulgating investigative procedures, without claiming that these procedures constitute theories or models, or they entertain some theoretical conception that justifies in general the recourse to certain methodologies. Indeed, every time case studies, which are *techniques* proposed as *method,* the underlying conception is that the cases are consistent, uniform, logical and self-evident, so only a few cases are required to demonstrate how things are.

Of the two the second hypothesis is the more plausible, though methodologically very shaky. But even then, the unresolved issues of the sociology of science, starting with the problem of methodology, reappear in the "new" as they did in the "old" sociology of science.

The latter, in what is basically a betrayal of the premises of the Mertonian paradigm, has developed in interinstitutional fashion, essentially as a sociology of the scientific professions; the former, aiming at doing better than Merton, leads to methodological inconsistency and often produces work of minimal relevance or value for generalization. Hence, a return to the definition itself of Robert K. Merton's program is perhaps worthwhile. Certainly, as Merton himself notes in quoting Whitehead, the scientific discipline which is reluctant to kill off its own founding fathers is lost. Yet, on closer inspection, this is exactly what has been missing in the sociology of science, whose most recent versions, while supposedly innovative, often get tangled up in the unresolved issues of the Mertonian paradigm (Statera 1978). To solve them it is worth returning to the original Merton program, which is a premise for revolutionizing the subsequent inadequate paradigm.

References

Barber, B. [1952] 1970. *Science and Social Order.* New York: Free Press.

Bernal, J.D. 1939. *The Social Function of Science.* (London: Routledge and 2d ed., Cambridge, MA: M.I.T. Press).

Cannavò, Leonardo. 1984. *Sociologia della conoscenza scientifica.* Rome: La Goliardica.

Chubin, D.E. and S. Restivo. 1983. "The 'Mooting' of Science Studies." In *Social Study Science,* edited by K.D. Knorr-Cetina and M.J. Mulkay. London: SAGE.

Hagstrom, W. 1965. *The Scientific Community*. New York: Basic Books.
Kuhn, Thomas. [1962] 1970. *The Structure of Scientific Revolutions*. Chicago: University Press.
Merton, Robert K. 1973. *The Sociology of Science: Theoretical and Empirical Investigations*. Chicago: University Press.
————. 1968. *Social Theory and Social Structure*. New York: Free Press.
————. 1938. *Science, Technology and Society in Seventeenth-Century England*. [Italian trans. *Scienza, tecnologia e società nell'Inghilterra del XVII secolo*. Milan: Franco Angeli].
Polanyi, Michel. 1958. *Personal Knowledge*. London: Routledge.
Statera, Gianni, ed. 1978. *La sociologia della scienza*. Naples: Liguori editore.
Storer, Norman. 1966. *The Social System of Science*. New York: Holt.
Weingart, Peter. 1974. "On a Sociological Theory of Scientific Change" in *Social Processes of Scientific Development*, edited by Richard Whitley. London: Routledge.
Whitley, Richard, ed. 1974. *Social Processes of Scientific Development*. London: Routledge.
————.1972. "Black Boxism and the Sociology of Science." *Sociological Review*.

4

The Informative-Formative Reception of Robert K. Merton's Work in Italy

Filippo Barbano

R.K. Merton in Italy in the 1950s: Two Types of Reception— "Informative" and "Formative"

The person now standing before you and about to speak on the work of Merton and its spread in Italy was a sociologist at the very beginning of his career towards the end of the 1940s. Like many of those who as university students were interested in the social sciences and for lack of other opportunities had tried to make contact via the Law Faculty, I received my degree a few years before, defending a thesis on the concept of "person" in the philosophy of law, a discipline whose presence in the Law Faculties had a *Bildung* tradition for juridical and political culture that went back to our Risorgimento.

At that time, sociology in Italy had neither mentors nor professors who could guide or transmit knowledge of it to the young, though I myself had had the good fortune to have as a supervisor of my thesis a teacher of philosophy of law who in his youth had actively collaborated in the *Rivista italiana di sociologia* (*Italian Review of Sociology*). However, being an avid frequenter of secondhand bookstalls from my schooldays, I had already become acquainted with the Italian edition of the great works of Herbert Spencer, and, above all, the

Trattato di sociologia of Vilfredo Pareto and the *Elementi di scienza politica* of Gaetano Mosca, as well as the *Sociologia del partito politico* of Roberto Michels. I asked myself why, despite the intellectual presence of scholars of such fame, sociology in Italy had had such a long period of obscurity for at least a quarter of a century, from the 1910s to the early 1940s.

The theoretical legacy of Pareto and Mosca fascinated me. But we scattered few neosociologists of those pioneering years could not see any immediate, practical implications in the work of those writers for the concrete social and political problems of a country such as Italy, at a time when it had just been freed from fascism and had to redo everything to become a modern democracy. In this state of necessity, more practical than theoretical, we were looking for links with a tradition of research, investigation, social inquiry that had been very much alive in our "first" sociology and whose traces had been lost but were in need of rediscovery: for example, research on the problems of the south, town and country, work, housing, poverty, the mix the of rural and the industrial that Italy was then, and so on.

We, the so-called pioneers of the rebirth of sociology in Italy, have often been accused of not having taken advantage in those years of the scientific and theoretical tradition of Mosca and Pareto as well as other lesser figures. There was talk of a sociology that was reborn, detached from its roots and forgetting of its fathers. If this is in a sense true with regard to the doctrinaire tradition to which Pareto and Mosca had reduced themselves, it is mistaken with regard to the subject of empirical research, which began again with renewed vigor in the years immediately after the Second World War, thus reestablishing a continuity between the "new" and the "first" Italian sociology which had been forcibly expelled from the culture of the country.

It was precisely this line of continuity that soon made one aware of a fact—that if it was indispensable to get to know the country by way of investigation and empirical research, this could not be done without a scientific design for the development of sociological knowledge (which Pareto and Mosca seemed to us far from offering) and, above all, without an appropriate research strategy. It seemed to me that the increased interest in empirical research, without an adequate advance in theory and criticism and a strong link to the empirical, had been one of the reasons for the rapid decline in sociology in Italy in the course of the nineteenth and twentieth centuries. In short, the practical necessity of doing research also posed the problem of constructing theory.

It seemed to me only too obvious that in a science which is in its own way experimental like sociology, empirical research should provide content for theory or validate theory. However, it was the obviousness of this relationship between theory and research that concerned me—that is, I wondered if continuing to take it for granted did not diminish the effectiveness, the purpose and indeed the very legitimation of the sociologist's work. Meanwhile, in the 1950s, from my theoretical interests in political sociology, and the processes and structure of public opinion in particular, I learned that avant garde research had been going on in the social sciences and sociology, especially in Anglo-Saxon countries, partly in Britain, but mostly in the United States. It was simply this curiosity in the new, a need to keep up to date, that led me to read the first, 1949, edition of *Social Theory and Social Structure*. It was for me a revelation, not so much because it proposed the integration of theory and research, but because it made their relationship explicit. It raised that integration as a problem in an important way and showed that it was a recognizable feature of the historical course of sociology which returns periodically, especially after crises or during periods of change.

I apologize for relating coincidences between my intellectual biography and the history of sociology in Italy in those years, but I must do so since this coincidence was in effect the beginning of the informative-formative reception of Merton's work in Italy. I said *recezione* thus correcting the word *ricezione* which somehow found its way into the program for this conference because—excuse the little grumble—poor telephonic reception (*ricezione*) led to an altered printed title of my talk. I shall be talking about the *formative* reception (*recezione*) and not the *informative* reception (*ricezione*) of Merton's work.

The notion of "*recezione*" I am using merits a brief digression. It came to me from the notion in historiography and juridical hermeneutics, especially in the History of Roman Law, in which the acceptance of that law and of modern juridical orders in Europe is the "formative reception" by antonomasia—that is, a considerable process of constitutive acceptance with an essentially formative effect for subsequent law.

In the history of sociology, the category of formative reception seems to me important for various reasons of increasing relevance. First of all, it substitutes for the often rhetorical or literary criterion, used in the history of ideas of the "good fortune" of a writer and his works. Secondly, on the question of formative reception as opposed to informative reception, what is perceived is not only what is transmitted, what is taken in is not only what is received. Messages and signals are received physically, forms are received mentally. Informative reception may start a process but it is not the complete reception. Secondly, formative reception may be irregular and consist of revivals of interest. Above all, when we refer to theoretical and conceptual contributions, the category of "formative reception" manages to render better than any other category the structure of the formations of thought in their historicity. The formative reception may even change its interpretative course, and reciprocally, the interpretative course of a theoretical formation may change the manner of its formative reception. For example, Friedrich Tenbruck's proposal for the interpretation of Weberian sociological formulation might cause a reevaluation of the formative reception of Weber, as did in fact happen in Italy. In the third place, the category of formative reception is heuristically richer than any other for getting into the processes of diffusion and circulation of scientific interests, cultural borrowings and exchanges, in short, all the interactivity, the "intertheoricity" that is highlighted nowadays by experiment, but which history, philosophy, and the sociology of science also reveal, now that the paleopositivist notion of unilinear cumulative "progress" has been abandoned.

I hope you will excuse this long parenthesis. I want to add only this, on the subject of Merton's diffusion in Italy, that if we adopt the category of formative reception, his theoretical formation is not reduced to an account of his fortunes and accidents en route, nor is it presented in an isolated manner. To return then straightaway to my point, I should say that Merton's work in the 1950s in Italy was part of what can be called a triple formative-informative reception from the cultural context of the United States, Merton being associated with Talcott Parsons and Paul Lazarsfeld. From the time of my personal reading of Merton in the 1950s, his work was put alongside that of Parsons; to this reception of these two figures for which I got the credit must be added, a few years later, the works of Lazarsfeld, this to be laid to the credit of the second generation of sociologists.

I am not interested now in remembering that the credit for introducing Merton and Parsons into Italy was honored only many years afterwards, or perhaps not until today. I feel it is more important to recall how the influence of Anglo-Saxon and particularly American sociologists, which was as widespread as it was controversial in Italy, was linked at that time to the charge of "Americanism" of which we were accused by some—a syndrome in Italy linked to the Cold War climate. It must be said, however, that the anti-Americanism in sociology in the 1950s had its roots not only in left-wing politics but also on the right; it reflected a widespread antipositivistic idiosyncracy, which at the same time was also transfiguring the formative reception in Italy of the philosophy of neopositivism.

So there we were, accused of "Americanism" when our interests, far from being private and circumscribed, had turned to other cultures precisely for their diversity. We were looking for elements of novelty and modernization but this was taken for a spirit of dependence. It goes without saying that we were looking at cultural contexts till then separate from our own, in the same spirit if not in the same conditions as, for example, Elio Vittorini and Cesare Pavese had looked at American literature years before, and at a time when apart from anything else Antonio Gramsci had already put the notion of Americanism in its right perspective in his well-known writings on Americanism and Fordism (which, of course, were read critically only decades later).

Implicit and Explicit Followers of Merton in the 1960s

Today, in the second half of the 1980s, the triple influence of Merton-Parsons-Lazarsfeld is commonly seen as an event of cultural *innovation* in the period that one might call the renaissance of sociology in Italy, the years between 1945 and 1950. One can, therefore, talk of a reception of Merton for those years as having the effect of innovation. Let us go on from there. Moving from the 1950s to the 1960s, interest was renewed in Max Weber, a sociologist long undervalued by our idealistic historicism. With the spread of the Weberian interpretative sociology, sociology in Italy regained the shores of European historicosocial culture, so much so that, in the common view on the history of sociology in Italy, the 1960s as the period of Weber's formative reception are considered by some to be the most authentic phase in the formation of the "new" sociology. This raises the question: what became of the cultural inputs which had just been received from the positive and pragmatic areas of sociology, and in particular from Merton?

Here we need to recall the date of publication of Italian editions of Merton's works. The first edition of *Teoria e struttura sociale* (*Social Theory and Social Structure*) was published by Il Mulino in 1959. The second edition, with its translation almost completely redone by Carlo Marletti and with a new introduction by myself was in 1966. There followed reprintings in 1971 and 1972 up to the fifth edition in 1974, with new contributions by Merton on the history and systematics of sociological theory, and my third introduction drawing attention to these new contributions. The first Italian edition of Parsons's *Struttura dell'azione sociale (Structure of Social Action)* was published in 1962 by Il Mulino, with an introduction by Gianfranco Poggi, and this was followed by Parsons's *Sistema sociale (Social System)* published by Comunità in 1965 with an introduction by Luciano Gallino. An extensive anthology of the work of Paul Lazarsfeld, edited and introduced by Vittorio Capecchi, was published in 1967. Thus, in less than ten years, the formative reception of the trio had all its essential texts available along with analyses of their work by other writers.

The 1960s can be called the *formative* years for Italian sociology. In those years the discussion of methodology was strongly affected by the influence of Weberism versus the abstract neopositivist methodologism. At the same time the inputs of Lazarsfeld and Merton in research methodology gave social research in Italy its orientation; it took off in those years, so much so that Lazarsfeld and Merton were from then on considered the typical representatives of *Survey Research* in the American fashion. The relationship between Merton and Lazarsfeld was quite clear: the methodology of research lay between social theory and field investigation. I should like to emphasize here that in the 1960s the formative reception of Merton had effects which were more *implicit* for their analytical and conceptual contributions to research than *explicitly* noted in the critical literature. Merton was more often referred to for practical research purposes in that period than quoted in theoretical works. This even when the starting point was one of Merton's own conceptualizations such as deviance or anomie, for example, which linked him with the European tradition, or cultural structure and social integration, groups, and socialization. These themes were often borrowed from Mertonian sources without being acknowledged, especially in researches on consumers, and on the disintegrative and integrative effects of emigration. The theme of unanticipated consequences was to be understood for its heuristic potential only much later.

In the 1960s we had the *explicit* followers of Merton's writings and his *implicit* exploiters; among the former some stayed with Merton's ideas, others did so to a varying extent, as, for example, Luciano Cavalli on the topic of anomie. Among the explicit followers there were myself and Alberto Izzo, as I urged during our long collaboration at the University of Trento, the first Faculty of Sociology to be established in Italy, this in 1962. Izzo read Merton's work but was opposed to him. (Others opposed Merton without having read him at all.) Izzo felt no attraction to Parsons and even less to Lazarsfeld; he was interested in a critical sociology with sources that were to be found in his interest in the sociology of knowledge. Izzo was particularly indignant at the Mertonian conception of the sources of the sociology of knowledge as in popular and mass culture. However, I venture to say that Merton became popular among the students of Trento. During the student uprisings of 1968 the "structural Merton" was among the few "bourgeois" sociologists still considered possible; also, of course, for his links with C. Wright Mills. My old students from Trento, Paolo Ceri, Darko Bratina, Antonio Schizzerotto, Bruno Tellia, and many others even today recognize the Mertonian foundation of their formation. I even spread the word about Merton in Genoa: Arnaldo Bagnasco, Giorgio Sola, Chito Guala, and others still consider the Mertonian contribution a very relevant preparation today. Angelo Pagani was my ally in Mertonism right from the beginning of his short life as a scholar and researcher.

Before finishing with the 1960s I must comment on the Parsons-Merton link as it was received in those years. If the link between Parsons and Merton was clearly understood, the difference between them was not equally clear but was conventionally explained away by functionalism. It is perhaps true that, I tended to insist on the polarity between Parsons and Merton in my first presentations. But so many divergences had emerged between them along the way that instead of polarity one may well say *diversity*. Diversity in their use of holistic functionalism, in their use of concepts such as latency, anomie, the formation of social groups and reference group behavior, and so on; but also a diversity in their way of constructing sociological theory and their presuppositions about it that is still decisive today. The integration of social theory and social research is precisely that interactivity between theory and research that is still much felt today in everyday works; it is that intertheoretical character of social analysis which is the enemy of hegemonic methods, and general, totalizing theoretical systems. Parsons was probably the last in the line of modern builders of grand theoretical cathedrals. Because Merton's middle-range theorizing implies economy, conventions and particular strategies of thought, the combining of neopositivist contributions with contributions of structural and situational analysis in his elaborations, he seems to me more open than Parsons to post-neopositivist and postmodern needs.

The Sociology of Science in the 1970s and Hermeneutic Needs in the 1980s and 1990s

We can now provide a balance sheet: From 1945 to 1950, the years of the rebirth of sociology in Italy, we have a formative reception of Merton that had an innovative effect on the modes of doing theory and research. In the sixties, the years of formation of the new sociology in Italy, the reception of Merton was implicit and related to questions of analysis in empirical research. Thus we come to the seventies. (Of course, these decades are not rigid.) Just as the passage from the fifties to the sixties was marked by strong formative innovations, so too with the passage from the sixties to the seventies when, all the while talking of crisis in sociology, the field actually took off so far as its institutionalization in the university was concerned—for example, in Trento social research became common practice and increasingly better organized. In my investigations into the history of sociology in Italy from 1945 to today, I call the seventies the years of "transformations" although they may seem to some to have been merely years of disorder, disorientation, disintegration, and search for identity. The contribution that the researches of the new sociology were meanwhile giving to knowledge of Italy as a society still does not have its history of successes and failures but one can say even now that the balance is positive, and that includes the Mertonian contributions in analytical conceptualization and research strategy.

Merton's presence in Italy in the 1970s can be illustrated more clearly in relation to these transformations and in their effects and though the picture is a complicated one, I'll try to make it as simple as possible. First of all, in the early 1970s, it began to be understood that the Gouldnerian crisis of Western sociology was a crisis of hegemony in the grand theoretical systems and the methodologies which they privileged, whether positivist or functionalist, interpretative or dialectical; it was, therefore, a crisis of theoretical and methodological strategies, rather than one of research and social analysis. In the successive decline of the grand theorizations, the status of theoretical work and its relationship with research once again became an important problem.

In the second place, in the 1970s, we witnessed the arrival of fields of study such as sociolinguistics, symbolic interactionism, ethnomethodology, and sociophenomenology. A brief note here on their reception: in the 1960s, Weber had been brought to Italy through Parsons; in the 1970s, Alfred Schutz appeared first of all through Thomas Luckmann's interpretation of his work as a sort of universal key to the social construction of reality, and also with a rough-and-ready reduction of Schutz to the sociology of knowledge. It was observed that even deviance results from a social construction of reality, and once again there was controversy over Merton's notion of deviance. Even his opponents, I am compelled to think, should be able to see that Merton may have become a classic precisely because one can never be sure to be free of him.

The fields of study recalled above, together with new heuristic procedures, gave new significance to the problem of sociology as a positive, naturalistic science. Phenomenology and sociophenomenology in particular created new heuristic and hermeneutic needs. Sociology seemed able to respond to these needs: sometimes in terms of criticism of the conventional sources—that is, of the data and concepts—and the ways of researching and preforming them, especially in *survey analysis*; sometimes in terms of historicity, sometimes in terms of the epistemological enrichment of traditional methods that had been impoverished by use (for example, the work of Franco Ferrarotti in Italy, using the method of studying biographies and life histories).

On the subject of the criticism of conventional sources, I cannot fail to mention that Merton had already proposed his own personal heuristic and hermeneutic transformation by bringing up for discussion in 1967 the relationships between history and the systematics of sociological theories; a proposal I took up in the introduction to the fifth Italian edition of *Social Theory and Social Structure* of 1974 without noticeable reactions in the sociological community, but which is now very much a part of the current research on nonconventional sources of social knowledge and their historicity: micro *versus* macro, quality *versus* quantity.

In the third place, in the 1970s, partly in response to the problem of the effects of complexity, which were reductive of social rationality and the sociologist's identity, Italy finally discovered conventionalism, i.e., the conventional status of the theoretical elements (concepts and theories) and of pluralism in possible research methods. In post-neopositivist fashion, the conviction spread even in Italy that the work of the sociologist, i.e, "doing theory" and "doing research" interactively and intertheoretically, is done, after all, in an epistemological triangle made up of rules, decisions, and consensus.

Questions were also raised about the legitimation of social knowledge. It was realized that, on the one hand, the consensual nature of scientific truths can be considered a response to this problem. On the other hand, if the context of the discovery is determined, these questions can also be answered by the contributions of the sociology, history, and philosophy of science. As far as contributions to the sociology of science are concerned, Merton's obviously could not be left out. In 1975, the Milan publisher, Franco Angeli brought out the Italian edition of *Science, Technology and Society in Seventeenth-Century England* to begin a new series on the sociology of sciences which I was editing. In 1978, Gianni Statera, my fellow Mertonian, produced an extensive anthology of Merton in his collection *Sociologia della scienza (The Sociology of Science)*. In 1980 the Italian edition of *La sociologia della scienza in Europe (The Sociology of Science in Europe)* edited by Merton and Jerry Gaston had already been published, and lastly, in 1981, there appears an Italian translation of the collection of Merton's work in the sociology of science, edited by Norman Storer and with my introduction.

The sociology of science took off in Italy and though it was obliged to be a low flyer, in the 1970s it represented another aspect of the "transformations" but not of course outside its own specific sphere. It was first necessary to discard the Mertonian conception of science as a value and an institution and then to rediscover the Mertonian contributions which explain how to see science as an activity, a practice, a mode of producing knowledge, a culture among other cultures and forms of knowledge, meanwhile playing down the hegemonic claims of sociology as a science and reconsidering the science of sociologists.

Despite the relative lack of interest in the sociological community, the Mertonian contributions in sociology of science are well known in Italy and often quoted by Italian historians and philosophers of science (for example, Paolo Rossi), who recognized in them a historicist, post-neopositivist trend.

And so we have come to the passage from the 1970s to the 1980s. In Italy, too, the faith in general theories and autonomous, hegemonic methodologies collapsed. Capecchi, the sociologist who in his day introduced Lazarsfeld into Italy, has an intellectual history that would be one of the more interesting to reconstruct (as I tried to do myself in a contribution to a collection of essays in honor of Franco Ferrarotti's thirty years of teaching) in order to trace his point of arrival, the abandoning of instrumental methodology and the affirmation of the pluralism of methods in "doing research."

We come again to Merton. Nowadays, when sociologists encounter the disadvantages of technocratic, strategic thinking and grand theory and recognizes that many strategies are possible in sociological thinking, then the problem of the validity of "doing theory" is raised once again. If such validity can no longer be seen as resulting from generalizations and accumulations of data, perhaps one can understand better today than ever before that theorizing of the middle range is not, naively, an automatic way of obtaining valid, general, and significant knowledge by merely summing up arrays of particular, insignificant contributions. In the past, the middle-range strategy for getting data has often been confused with middle-range theories which are, of course, common cognitive features of all the social sciences and are easily identified in their substantive historicity. Let us take even complex theoretical formations like those of Niklas Luhmann and Jürgen Habermas: apart from their self-referential presuppositions, systematic in Luhmann and critico-emancipatory in Habermas, they are constructed on the basis of a combination of contributions from research and theory acquired and reformulated in the interactivity and internalization of cognitive theories of the middle range or are taken as such on loan from various fields of the social sciences.

It is therefore easy to see how and why the relationship of theory and research is once again a problem today. On the one hand, the post-neopositivist epistemological experience has not in any way invalidated the terminology that Merton formulated years ago on types of work in theory and related research. On the other hand, the needs of the new resources and of the unconventional sources which require an enrichment of the list of contributions from empirical research to be connected to theory. But there is a more general aspect which makes the relationships between "doing research" and "doing theory" an everyday problem to be solved in the work of the sociologist and social researcher and it is the following: the extreme flexibility arrived at and permitted by the conventionalist spirit (the new scientific spirit as Gaston Bachelard called it in his day). In other words, the great freedom of conjecture granted to the sociologist within the epistemological triangle of rules-decision-consensus demonstrates every day that that triangle is historically and existentially inscribed as one says in a "hermeneutic circle." In that circle, social science and culture, scientific knowledge and definitions of the situation—in short, sociology as science and the science of practical sociologists—together open up the possibilities of re-examining the duration of internalized social time, the unanticipated consequences of behavior and social structures, the cognitive and symbolic processes present at the edges of systems, and any other experience or social process not susceptible to self-reference by the system.

The historical combination of all these new conditions of the relationship of theory to social research has already been otherwise identified. It can be discerned in the comparison between the epistemological formation of the social sciences and their hermeneutical experience, between positive, rationalizing social research and critical, historicizing social research. In Merton's works we can see a historicizing or hermeneutic turn in his thought after the essay on the history and systematics of sociological theory in 1967, and in his discussion of the Kuhnian conception of "normal science" and "paradigms," contained in the 1977 volume on the sociology of science in Europe.

And now, before drawing to a conclusion, I ask this: "How efficient are the Mertonian theory-research relations, which are so repeatedly strategic and fruitful for the heuristic needs of sociology, how effective are they for the hermeneutic needs of social research, which are now increasingly directed towards the *reading* (besides the observing) and even *textualizing* (besides the contextualizing) of social reality? In this connection, I am convinced that insofar as the new hermeneutic needs are restored to their linkage with theory and research, without being relaunched into the self-referencing of systems or, worse still, into the transcendentalism of an obscure and empathic social *eidos*, the hermeneutic experience changes from an improper method that is not a method at all. For the sociologist strongly supported by scientific interests that legitimate his knowledge and his role, it becomes a continual formative process of interpretative *Bildung*. In short, the epistemological triangle of the sociologist becomes inscribed in the theory-research circle which, in its turn, inscribes the hermeneutic circle. Not the other way around.

I have thus come to the end of the journey focused on the "informative-formative reception" of Merton's works in Italy from the 1950s to the present day. But there are circumstances in which the circulation of scientific interests shortens the time for "formative reception" so much that what is transmitted becomes immediately received, and this brings us back to the matter of "informative reception" which I only touched upon at the outset of this paper. One example of such a circumstance remains within easy memory. By coincidence, it has to do with the concept of "time" itself, a concept which interested Merton in his youthful days and one to which he returned in a work in honor of Lewis Coser published in 1984. In quite timely fashion the first issue of *Rassegna Italiana di Sociologia* (the *Italian Review of Sociology*) in 1985 contained an interview with Merton by Anna di Lellio on his concept of "socially expected durations" which I used formatively as the starting point for an article just a year later.

It goes without saying—and here I conclude—that while the formative reception of Merton continues, we expect and hope for much new informative and formative reception of Merton, a scholar I consider among my teachers and to whom we all owe much, and some of us very much, of our knowledge .

A Note on "Reception"

I refer to a letter from my friend Merton a few months back (December 1988) in which he writes among other things about the concept of *ricezione*: " I had been aware, of course, from your paper and interventions at Amalfi of your category of '*recezione*' as distinct from '*ricezione*.' But now that I find your analytical distinction put to repeated use in just about every part of your book—(*Sociologia, ermeneutica, storia: reciproche esposizioni* [1988])—I have come to understand its diverse value more fully, particularly as a heuristic concept to help clarify processes of diffusion of scientific and scholarly ideas. Although the final essay refers to the distinction in the subtitle, there would be value, I think, in your writing a paper focused on your conceptual contribution. As you indeed know, it may be a self-exemplifying observation in the historical sociology of science— new clarifying ideas do not automatically elicit attention, let alone agreement, when they are *ingredients* of published work rather than the *focus* of a paper or book devoted centrally to them. Do consider it."

While waiting to be able to dedicate myself to a more complete work on the subject, I take Merton's point. But not only because of the category of *recezione* that I used in Amalfi in connection with the diffusion of his work and thought in Italy. My Amalfi talk was intended to illustrate that Merton had an informative reception (*ricezione*) in Italy in the 1950s and 1960s rather than a formative reception (*recezione*), that is, his message was simply received rather than incorporated. Otherwise put, his reception was more implicit than explicit if a few contributions, including my own, are excluded. It was only from the end of the 1970s that Merton's reception became more explicit, accompanied by a crisis of interest in Parsons's theoretical system and Lazarsfeld's methodologism. This formative reception of Merton was like a return or a rediscovery of an author who, if not already renowned as a classic, is undoubtedly of strategic importance in the history of twentieth-century sociology. To find the support and guidance of an author of the past at the crossroads when those of today often seem far from certain where they are going makes that author either a classic or a crucial point of reference as the years pass.

Going beyond the scope of my Amalfi lecture, I should like now to gather together some statements that might be useful in clarifying the notion of *ricezione* (informative reception) and the innovative use that can be made of the concept of *recezione* (formative reception).

1. The examination of an interest in history and in particular the history of sociology in Italy has been crucial for providing examples and for better defining the notion of *recezione*. This has been the case when I have been faced with questions of method and historiographic judgement in three successive growth periods, the manner of their reception of ideas from other contexts, not to mention the effects and results of that reception. Let me recall them briefly: the years of the renaissance of sociology in Italy (1945–50) when Italy was forced to

get abreast of developments in social science and social scientific research outside Italy, chiefly in the U.S.A. This entailed the reception of Parsons's works (for their level of theoretical elaboration), of Lazarsfeld's works (for their level of methodological elaboration in empirical research), and of Merton's works for their theoretical criteria and the strategic mediation between empirical research and theoretical system in sociology. Then came the 1960s, years of formation and development, with the reception, on the one hand, of Weber and, on the other, of critical sociology/the Frankfurt School. And finally, the 1970s and 1980s when major undercurrents and transformations took place, due to a multiplicity, almost a surfeit, of new ideas (new *ricezione*): symbolic interactionism and ethnomethodology, social phenomenological philosophy, the Luhmannian thematic of complexity and self-referential systems, Habermas's communicative social action, and so on.

To sum up, in the course of the 1980s, observing, on the one hand, the varying "fortunes" (*fortuna*) of writers and their works, the increasingly frenzied circulation of concepts, the overlapping and entanglement of theories, viewpoints, explanatory criteria and research methods and, on the other hand, the sociologists' habitual practice of bundling together quotations and contributions of various and highly diverse authorship, from historicocultural contexts frequently very distant from each other, I realized the importance of the processes of *ricezione* with increasing clarity. In other words, I became convinced that cognitive and cultural features in sociology and social experience have their own *mobility.* The effects, definitely not positive, of dealing with that mobility as if writers and their works belonged neither to their time nor to their cultural context or, as if everything went with everything else, cannot be adequately understood and interpreted if we do not take into account the manner of reception of works and authors, concepts and theories, cognitive and cultural features. This type of mobility is not simply a question of the "fortune" of certain authors and certain works (a subject often believed important in the history of ideas). It is not "fortune," then, that explains, but the *interaction,* the public information and reception, in the context of the mobility of cognitive and cultural features.

What was characteristic of the tumultuous way of working with theory in Italian sociology of the 1980s was the acquisition of more and more undetermined things at the expense of anything determined.

This reached the point that sociologists came to be seen as studying anything and everything and mostly the obvious, an image that is part of the recent history of sociology in Italy. It is interesting to note how the effects of that tumult of proposals and especially of intellectual borrowings, taken from the most diverse and decontextualized sources, have in the end increased the need for a new evaluation of historical work in sociology. From this point of view, then, the notion of "reception" is confirmed above all as a historiographic category important for its related analyses and judgements.

2. The notion of reception is important not only for its historiographic criteria and judgments but also as a *heuristic* and *interpretative* category. First of all, a category in the framework of social interactivity (which is not only the psycho-collective interactivity of the 1910s-1920s nor only the symbolic interactionism inspired by Mead in the 1930s), but one seen from the angle of interactive social action. Interactive social action, especially communicative action, is not simply a question of conditions of functionality, linguistic competence, empathetic disposition, assumption of roles, and so on. The interactivity of social action, when it is not merely something determined, involves *the putting one's will into practice* that should be analyzed from the viewpoint of resources and then, the sources of those resources. When communicative interaction (or any other type) is not just determined in a functional *field*, the interactive situation identified in a *context* recalls a text, that is, *textuality*, in which the situation can be read and defined by either the actor or the observer. Situational social action is always translated into textuality. The textuality is established and is received. Where the textuality is understood, it is applied and a context is understood. The textuality is a social *form* of "reception," as in fact the history of research methods and the social analysis of sources (especially oral sources) illustrate rather well. Above all, textuality shifts attention from the field of the emitting of functional information to the context of reception and sources. This permits the collection of *qualitative* sources as resources of interactivity, to the enrichment of the oral resources. This, in turn, especially in a period of crisis of *quantitative* resources of empirical research data, makes the concept of "formative reception" interesting, even from the methodological point of view, and illustrates the dilemma (otherwise meaningless) that puts quantity and quality in opposition to each other in sociology.

The concept of formative reception, then, turns out to be important for correcting certain distortions in micro- and macro-sociological viewpoints. Since the context of reception is neither uniquely individual and private nor uniquely public and collective, it becomes the context of exposure to social visibility and public reflexivity for the textuality and/or the texts, the documentation, and the sources. Which is no light matter in a society like ours where the *exposure* of individual subjects as well as collective subjects, of cognitive as well as cultural features, to such visibility and reflexivity is on the increase generally from a myriad of viewpoints. Social visibility and public reflexivity are not the only conditions of such exposure, which is (analytically) also the textual way of presenting the cognitive and cultural features for the purpose of their transmission (Sormano 1988: my preface). From these brief notes it will be seen how a sociological theory of reception is corroborated by the aesthetic and juridical theory of reception which I deal with below.

A word of explanation needs to be given, then, on the presence of communication theory in sociology. In this theory, the notion of reception has long had its place, determined in functional *fields* of transmission or information transfer from their production (emission) to related channels and means. Functional analyses of communication, however, usually stop at the limits of the "receiver" and avoid the *context* of the "recipient," not dealing with the connections between the "receiving" of messages on the part of the social actor and the "incorporating" or understanding of them, the interpreting and applying of them by either the social actor or the observer. From what has been said, some of the distinctions between *ricezione* and *recezione* ought now to be clear: it is a difference not of process and its effects, but of the results of process.

The process of reception turns out to be, then, not simply a matter of transmission but, as I have said, of *putting into practice*, which in turn is not simply diffusion and circulation but interactivity as *formation*. The reference to the formative result of reception puts the self and the other into a context, just as it does audiences, specific groups, entire cultural areas, countries, nations, and continents. The contents of the process, in short, include announcements, written texts, oral contributions, borrowings, statistical data, and research reports. Finally, the manner of processing is not limited to transmitted information but also holds for different types of contact, transport, commerce, exchange, conquest, modernization, transfer of innovations, processes of internationalization, and so on.

3. An important contribution to a sociological theory of reception can be found in the historical events which, along with the influence of the philosophy and the associated history and sociology of science in the 1960s and 1970s, characterized the post-neopositivist criticism of the neopositivist way of considering the epistemological status of theory and cognitive contributions. This inspired equally strong interest and perspectives for a form of neohistoricism of science. These criticisms have profoundly shaken even the so-called conception of the "received view." In the neopositivist context, this conception of the epistemological status of theories, concepts, or research contributions was typically determined by verifying procedures and operations, accumulation, corroboration, falsification, and so on. That notion of the "received view" was completely ahistorical, without consideration for any other interactivity among the theoretical and cultural features than the methodological or logical one in terms of true or false.

When I spoke previously of the *neohistoricism* of science, I referred to that famous change in the epistemological status of concepts and theoretical factors in science in which we have gone from considering an interactivity limited to the *context of justification* and methodological and logical proof to an interactivity or dynamic of the theoretical factors extended to the *context of discovery*; I refer here to the best-known proposals of the so-called scientific revolutions and the widely historic notion of paradigm. This notion has drawn to it other historically meaningful notions, spreading the perspectives of a neohistoricism of science concerning research programs, research traditions, and images of science: all ways of redefining the theoretical factors in terms of epistemological historical status. With this widening of perspective there is increasing evidence of their interactivity and their mobility, together with the consideration of theories and concepts as cognitive and cultural factors, not to be reduced to the circumstances of the accumulation of notions or received views, or merely to their verificational and falsificational selection. This tendency, quite prevalent nowadays in the fields of the history, philosophy, and sociology of science is also naturally open to consideration of the contexts of the reception of theories and concepts as cognitive and cultural factors, thus also removing the cumbersome and never-achieved interdisciplinarity in favor of viewpoints on textuality and contextuality, intercontextuality, and intertheoricity.

However, the contextualizing and thus historicizing resource of the notion of reception also has other fairly convincing historicocultural sources.

A nonsociological source of the notion of reception (though it involves a sociological angle of vision on communication and the public) is to be found in the context of literary experience as communication: the *Rezeptionsästhetik*, the aesthetics of reception, a proposal of the so-called School of Costanza, which from 1966 onward was transformed into a theory of literary communication by writers like Hans Robert Jauss (1979). I consider it important to note that the literary experience of reception is interesting for sociology from the viewpoints considered above: textuality, sources, and exposure. I should like to stand straightaway against both the position that reduces the literary experience to sociology and the position that reduces the sociological experience to literature. I omit in these circumstances the historical intertwining of social knowledge and literary experience, especially when dealt with in a not entirely essential manner for sociology as by Wolf Lepenies (1987). The contribution of the aesthetics of reception to sociological theory is relevant not so much for the evidence of literary qualities as for the heuristic and hermeneutic meaning of the textuality into which the experience of the actor and the social observer is translated.

The introduction of the notion of *recezione* into my Amalfi talk on the spread of Merton in Italy caused awkwardness and difficulty, especially when it involved simultaneous translation. The problem develops for much the same reason as "The German denomination of *Rezeptionsästhetik* which carries with it a fatal misunderstanding: in French, as in English, the term *réception* is used only in the hotel trade! But since this term seems to have acquired common international usage in the history of aesthetics, I must first of all note that 'reception,' as a concept in aesthetics, has both a passive and an active meaning. The reception of art denotes a double act, comprising the effect which is produced by the work of art and the way in which the receiver takes in the work" (Jauss 1988: 135–6).

The active and passive meanings belong both to processes of informative reception which are determined in a functional field, and to processes of formative reception, given a written or oral context so far as results are concerned. However, the *active* meaning can be taken to characterize the result of processes of *formative* reception with respect to the passive effects of processes of *informative* reception, in the sense that the results of the informative reception are not differentiated from the contents of the transmission as they are in formative reception.

Consideration of the processes of reception is also important with regard to connections of the *present* with the historical transmission of the *past* and thus with regard to innovation in the criteria for judgment on *modernity* and *modernization*. Although it may seem remote to some, I must say that interest in certain historical processes of reception can reach far into the past, as, for example I found myself, reaching back to the historical facts of the reception of Roman Law in medieval Europe. The notion of "informative-formative reception" is institutionalized in the current Italian dictionary of legal terms: "termine con il quale si designa il fenomeno medievale e moderno della diffusione del diritto comune in Europa e piu' tardi in alcuni paesi extra europei (Brasile, Sudafrica, etc.)' [a term to designate the medieval and modern phenomenon of the diffusion of common law in Europe and later in some non-European countries (Brazil, South Africa, etc.)]" (*Enciclopedia del Diritto e dell'Economia* 1985: 956). Processes of modernization in this century, especially in their present consequences, can also be reconsidered from the point of view of a sociological theory of formative reception. For an introduction to these matters, I suggest my brief article (Barbano 1988: 221–30). A sociological theory of formative reception, worked out in a Weberian manner, can accumulate noteworthy examples from the case of the medieval reception of Roman Law in Europe, especially on the subject of the presuppositions and conditions for the reception.

This, through the written texts taken as a substratum: "Codes are incorporated, but laws are never incorporated as such" observes Paul Koschaker (1962). Without the *Corpus Iuris* there would not have been a formative reception of Roman Law, a system of juridical, rational, and cultural knowledge. In the same way, behind the processes of modernization in our century there lies a system of Western knowledge or knowledge that reflects the rationality and culture of the West. For the law, formative reception benefits from the absence in the countries it affects of a general, scientifically elaborated system of law. The presuppositions of twentieth-century modernizations remind us that the formative reception of a juridical system is not a question of quality. A foreign law is not incorporated because it is considered the best. "The 'incorporation' of a foreign law system is rather a matter of force, and is the consequence of a position of preeminence, at least in spiritual and cultural matters, of the incorporated law, a position which is, on the other hand, conditioned by the fact that this law is the law of a strong political power, either in present reality or within living memory of it and its civilization" (Koschaker [1958] 1962: 239).

It is not out of place to recall the role of juridical elaboration in the formation of both hermeneutic knowledge and modern social science. Apart from anything else, the concept of formative reception as distinct from informative reception is more than just heuristic; it is hermeneutic. Among the types of modernization whose spread was witnessed in the first decades of this century—economic-industrial, sociopolitical, and juridical modernization—all of these being modernizations that were received rather than incorporated, with the distorting effects this has caused, sociocultural modernization has always had a fairly modest, marginal and residual, theoretical and practical place, either as an effect or a consequence and even more so as a presupposition for the other types of modernizations. But let us not go into the results of that!

There is no need to add more to show the importance of the category of formative reception and its centrality in a theory of interaction and in the theoretical and practical area of sociocultural modernization. Modernization, after all, has always been part of the theory of economic development rather than the theory of cultural change. And so it is in the area of sociocultural modernization more than anywhere else that the meaning of informative versus formative reception becomes clear. There is almost everything still to be said on the subject of formative reception as *education* (or *Bildung*, if that is taken as a clearer term.)

All this is the underlying rather than general significance of this chapter. To read it is to learn that the formative reception of Merton's works and thought in Italy has been slow in taking hold despite implicit reception, borrowings (when they were not downright plagiarism); and that only several decades later has Merton's contribution been somehow recognized and legitimated as the result of an informative-formative reception. It seems to me that this is not only the fate of

Merton. On that score, my reflections on reception as interaction stem from the fact of the extreme facility with which Italian sociology receives ideas, often in accentuated and empathetic ways, more than simple cultural exchange implies. But none of these receptions seems to last long. It is drowned by other, greater, waves of reception, compromising every time any original sociological formation that is capable of preserving if not its own realization, at least its distinctive, autonomous point of view.

References

Barbano, Filippo.1988. "L'epoca postmoderna della modernizzazione: a proposito di 'ricezione-recezione.'" In *Sociologia, ermeneutica, storia: reciproche esposizioni* Turin: Tirrenia Stampatori.

Enciclopedia del Diritto e dell'Economia. 1985. Milan: Garzanti.

Jauss, Hans Robert. 1988. "Estetica della ricezione e comunicazione letteraria" in *Estetica della ricezione.* Naples: Guida.

Koschaker, Paul. [1958] 1962. *L'Europa e il diritto romano.* Florence: Sansoni.

Lepenies, Wolf. 1987. *Le tre culture: Sociologia tra letteratura e scienza.* Bologna: Il Mulino.

Sormano, A. 1988. *Sociologia e sociologi in Italia: Contesti e rappresentazione.* Milan: Franco Angeli.

Part 2

Concepts of Sociological Analysis

5

Sociological Ambivalence in the Thought of R.K. Merton

Pierpaolo Donati

Theme: The Construction of a Powerful but Problematical Concept

In Robert K. Merton's thought the construction of the concept of sociological ambivalence (hereafter referred to as SA)[1] has a special place as a specific notion for a discipline seen as autonomous. Undertakings such as this test the capacity of sociology to be considered a science and Merton has undoubtedly offered an original and far-reaching contribution.

If it is true that the theme of SA is associated with a series of basic papers written between 1936 and 1975 with an update in a more recent essay in 1983, then it is indeed one of the connecting threads of the whole of Merton's work. These papers have in many cases marked a milestone in contemporary sociological thought. For example, the famous essay of 1936 on "The Unanticipated Consequences of Purposive Social Action" has given rise to a vast body of literature, of which the work of Raymond Boudon (1977) on perverse effects is only one of the developments possible.

In reality, the Mertonian concept of SA is polyhedral, polymorphous. It lends itself, without doubt, to further examination and developments. In my opinion, the structuralist connotation that Merton gives to the concept of SA warrants particular investigation.

I propose to (a) examine the conceptual construction, the definition, and typology of SA in Merton's thought, (b) analyze the details of his sociological approach, and (c) lastly, give a critical assessment of the Mertonian theory on SA from a fully "relational" perspective.

The thesis that I have set myself to elucidate is that the Mertonian concept of SA is powerful but problematical in that (1) it has to be applied to societies which are highly structured and which therefore experience great normative conflicts and (2) its value emerges in the context of a functional vocabulary that institutionalizes conflict.

It becomes a reductive conception and so less useful as an interpretative and explanatory tool in those societies which encounter processes of de-normativization and at times when in social relations (specific or generalized) a symbolic dynamic prevails which is not retrievable by the functional framework.

The question is to understand if, in the latter type of society, that is in fact postmodern society, the Mertonian conception of SA can still fulfil the function, even in limited fashion, of explaining the structural connotations of the social dynamic (possibly as a theory of latent normativity), or if the theory has to be modified.

Problems of Conceptual and Typological Definition

Merton begins with the observation that the concept of ambivalence has a long history. It can be traced back to the dawn of human thought and there is no philosopher, thinker, or scientist who has not in some way taken it into consideration, at least (and usually) as *inner experience* (SA: 3).

The task Merton sets himself is that of bringing this concept out of cultural indeterminacy (to subject it then to scientific analysis) and out of the dominion of nonspecific conceptual frameworks of sociology, primarily those of a psychological type, which have not accounted for ambivalence as an intrinsic, structural characteristic of sociality.

In setting himself to develop an essentially sociological concept of ambivalence, he declares his intention of following what had already happened in psychology (above all in the psychoanalytic field with the work of Sigmund Freud). And thus the first definition he gives to SA is that of a notion *complementary* to the notion of psychological ambivalence (SA: ix, 5).

The starting point of the analysis is the observation that in all tales of experiences, myths, and narrations of ambivalence right from the Oedipus myth, "the structure of social relations is taken as a given in these accounts; it does not itself become the focus of systematic investigation" (SA: 4).

The first conceptual and defining axiom is therefore the following: the ambivalence of social processes has to be brought down to a specific and systematic analysis of the structure of the social relations in which a given process takes place.

Social relations (conceived of both as bonds and situational context) must no longer be left as peripheral and indirect objects of interest but must be made the central, explanatory focus of the analysis. Relations must no longer be considered "facts of historical circumstance" but as facts which determine the manner and the extent to which ambivalence comes to be socially constructed precisely *within the structure* of these very social relations.

Merton gives the example of the teacher-pupil relationship, which in past decades and centuries had been the subject of many *introspective* literary or psychological analyses (as a love-hate relationship) in either teacher or pupil, without any questions being raised about the different probabilities of the development of ambivalence depending on systematic differences in the structure of their relations and in the structure of the field of activity (SA: 5).

Merton's second step is to link the relations to the statuses and roles: the social relations are reduced to *status-role relations*. Here the influence of the common dialogue with Talcott Parsons is more than obvious.

And so here we have the essence of the defining orientation in sociology according to Merton: it refers not to personality (psychological) but to social structure.

"Unlike the psychological orientation, the sociological one focuses on the ways in which ambivalence comes to be built into the structure of social statuses and roles. It directs us to examine the processes in the social structure that affect the probability of ambivalence turning up in particular kinds of role-relations. And finally, it directs us to the social consequences of ambivalence for the workings of social structures" (SA: 5).

I shall come back to the question of the approach. For the moment let us simply note that the problem of definition of sociological concepts in Merton cannot be posed outside the general presuppositions defining a precise epistemology which forms the basis for an approach and the theories and models that may be derived from it and Merton chooses presuppositions that all fix on the social structure as the focus of interest, interpretation, and explanation.

This route leads our man to give two definitions of SA (SA: 6):

1. *"In its most extended sense* SA refers to incompatible normative expectations of attitudes, beliefs, and behavior assigned to a status (i.e., a social position) or to a set of statuses in a society."

2. *"In its most restricted sense* SA refers to incompatible normative expectations incorporated in a *single* role of a *single* social status . . . "

To give an example: the therapeutic role of the physician is ambivalent in the first sense (the widest) in that it is in conflict with other roles (researcher, administrator, colleague, member of a professional association, and so on) and it is ambivalent in the second sense (the narrowest) in that it is in conflict with itself (e.g., if, in order to heal, the physician has to hurt or cause damage).

From afar one feels the deep influence of Émile Durkheim in the anti-psychology debate. This influence can be better judged by bearing in mind Merton's precise affirmations closely modeled on passages from the French sociologist:

In both the most extended and the most restricted sense, the ambivalence is in the social definition of roles and statuses, not in the feeling-state of one or another type of personality. To be sure, as we would expect and as we shall find, sociological ambivalence is one major source of psychological ambivalence. Individuals in a status or status-set that has a large measure of incompatibility in its social definition will tend to develop personal tendencies toward contradictory feelings, beliefs, and behavior. Although the sociological and psychological kinds of ambivalence are empirically connected, they are theoretically distinct. They are on different planes of phenomenal reality, on different planes of conceptualization, on different planes of causation and consequences.

To be precise, *"The sociological theory deals with the processes through which social structures generate the circumstances in which ambivalence is embedded in particular statuses and status-sets together with their associated social roles"* (SA: 7, emphasis added).[2]

It is at this point that Merton faces the problem of the *types* of SA. The typology is made with reference to one criterion, the *sources* of SA and Merton distinguishes two types (SA: 7):

1. The source is in *the structural context of a particular status* (e.g., that of the intellectual in an organization in that he has to think for himself but at the same time share the values-objectives of the organization; or that of the bureaucrat who has to be impersonal in his dealings but also give personal attention to the client, etc.); or,

2. The source is in *multiple types of functions assigned to a status* (e.g., the expressive and instrumental functions of a family status, or those of professional care and human support in a physician, or the diverse teaching-research-administrative functions of the university professor, etc.).

From here Merton elaborates a typology using both definitions, extended and restricted. He distinguishes six types. The first is the simplest, the core-type, and the other five derive from it in that they follow by extension (SA: 7).

1. *Conflict within a single status and social role. The core-type of SA stems from contradictory demands made on those who occupy a single status with a particular social role.* For example, in the relationship between lawyer and client: here, as elsewhere, the ambivalence is created within the same person (or rather the same social role) in the sense that "acting in the interests of the other" and "acting in one's own interests" may not coincide (and often don't).

2. *Conflict within the set of statuses an individual occupies.* This type, Merton says, is the most analyzed on an empirical level. It is a question of SA coming from a conflict among the various statuses in an individual's set of statuses. For example, the contrast a lawyer may feel between his professional role and the family-friend role in his relationship with a client; more generally, the conflict between family and work roles in husband-fathers and wife-mothers; and so on for religious and secular, public and private roles. It is essentially a model of "conflict of interests or of values." A typical example would be electoral behavior under conflicting pressures: as a taxpayer I would like to vote for the party that promises tax reductions but as a believer or a professional I should vote for another party that defends certain religious values or interests of particular sections of the population, and so on.

3. *Conflict between the different roles in one single status.* This is

conflict among the several roles that may be associated with one particular status. For example, the status of the university professor, in that it includes different roles (teaching, research, administration, and more). The demands of these roles may be in conflict with each other either for questions of time, energy, and interest, or because the attitudes, values, norms, and activities requested are incompatible.

4. *Cultural conflict in shared basic values.* This refers to the contradictions that may exist among cultural values held by members of a society. These values are not ascribed to particular statuses but are expected of all the members of the collectivity, values like honesty, the family, patriotism, economic success, etc. The point is that the basic values of a society can be in conflict. Merton makes specific reference to North American society, quoting the famous research by Robert S. Lynd (e.g.: "Everyone should try to be successful" but "the kind of person you are is more important than how successful you are"; "the family is our basic institution" but "business is our most important institution and since national welfare depends on it, other institutions must conform to its needs," etc.) Merton observes that as long as these values are not organized into a set of norms for a specific role or roles, it is a simply a question of cultural conflict. But when they are, they produce the core type of SA.

Although this passage is not very clear, it seems that the institutionalization of values into norms is at the basis of SA as such. Merton never quotes the most patent case of modern societies torn between the institutionalization of values like freedom and equality, which are notoriously in conflict with each other on a normative level. In the light of the Mertonian theory, however, the welfare state is recognizable as a structural source of ambivalences which are never resolved or resolvable.

5. *Anomie inherent in the opportunity structure.* This is the SA resulting from the disjunction between culturally prescribed aspirations and socially structured paths for the realization of these aspirations. It is the *anomie* inherent in the opportunity structure of goals and means for which Merton has created a new, typically American typology compared with Durkheim's. Properly speaking, in the present analysis of SA, it is not a question of cultural conflict or social conflict but a "conflict between the cultural structure and the social structure" which emerges at times when cultural values are internalized by those whose place in the social structure does not give them access to oppor-

tunities for behaving according to these values and yet whose socialization has prepared them to see these values as fundamental.

6. *Conflict between different cultural groups.* This is the type of SA
that *develops among people who have lived in two or more different
societies and so have become oriented to different sets of cultural
values.* This is notoriously the situation of migrants, in those migration
processes that create the "marginal man" first spoken of by Robert E.
Park. More generally, there is the case of "reference groups" or those
who accept the values of a social group to which they do not belong.
This type combines elements of the fourth type (cultural conflict) and
the second type (conflict between statuses within a status set held by
an individual). This is typical of socially mobile individuals, who feel
contradictions between the values of the group to which they belong
and those of the group to which they refer (in their aspirations or
fantasies).

The typology is undoubtedly interesting but more than somewhat
problematical. As I shall explain later, it goes beyond the caveats and
limits of the Mertonian structural approach, which:

a. assumes values as not available to personal decision and not subject to
   reciprocal comparisons;
b. does not articulate the possibility of normative metacodes that can resolve the conflicts between the single norms; and,
c. is silent on the social actor as the subject of the structural web of
   relations.

As far as the typology just presented is concerned, the following
observations are necessary.

a. *The distinction between the core-type and the types deriving their
ambivalence from the multiplicity of their functions.* The structural
context of a status is not easy to distinguish from the multiplicity of
functions assigned to that status. On the one hand, the difficulties in
distinguishing are empirical: for example, the physician's status lies in
a context (concrete relations with the patient) which *necessarily* gives
him other functions (human, supportive, understanding, etc.), with respect to the function of professional competence of his role; Merton
himself places the physician-patient relation in both the core-type and
the other types. One must be careful then not to change "types" which
are essentially analytical into empirical types. On the other hand, there
is also a problem of analytical difficulties in that the same single

behavior may be used and interpreted in different ways—that is, it admits of diverse functional equivalents. For example, an act which is said to be done in the interests of the client, may (or may not) in certain circumstances be or become behavior in one's own interests.

b. *The SA conflicts that Merton defines as "normative" have multiple causes which are often not normative.* The same example of the physician-patient relationship along with many others reveals that the ambivalence in as far as it is normative conflict is not only inherent in and deriving from the social structure itself (the organization of the medical profession) but also from various imperatives, which may be ethical (practical) but also cognitive or expressive. These imperatives come not only from the multiple prescriptive functions of the status-role of the physician but also from the needs of the Other in a situation, if and to the extent that the Other (patient, client) knows how to express them and presents them to the Ego (the professional). If the Other, for example, had his own reliable human support network, he would probably not pose difficulties for the physician beyond the requirements of his profession.

c. *The complexity of relations that SA generates has a correlation in the complexity of the structure of social expectations, in which the subjective element is not secondary* as Merton assumes. One can well understand, as I have recalled above, Merton's desire to construct a sociological and not a psychological concept of SA but on the other hand social reality refuses to expunge the subject from the system of action as a whole as if all that is subjective were thus "psychological." In social action *"preconditions* (objective) and *prefigurations* (subjective) of action and its effects are consolidated into a 'rhythm' of interaction that, in taking for granted and anticipating future events in the present, allows the subject to adopt a line of conduct in which *tradition, time* and the *values* present in the social context, the displacement of self *interest* and the *effects* hoped for or feared take on a definite role, i.e., they are no longer simple or complex variables but are adopted as data on which to base the decision to behave in a particular way. The expectation presupposes the *development of a project* in which the single roles are already fixed" (Mongardini 1985: 99).

One has the impression, in short, that the Mertonian concept of SA (1) does not manage to define the corresponding typology in a sufficiently "relational" and therefore selective and flexible way, and (2) leaves out the most complex problems of how expectations are formed and how they work in social relations. Merton's great merit is obvious, however, in having pulled SA out of a nonsociological vagueness.

Approach: A Structural Variant of Functional Analysis

Merton defines his approach "that variant of functional analysis in sociology which has evolved over the years into a distinct mode of structural analysis" (SA: ix).

This structural variant of functional analysis was organized into "fourteen stipulations" (SA: ch.7) in 1975 by Merton. They merit a detailed examination and commentary, which is not possible here. It is, however, worth noting that Merton's manner of laying out his stipulations shows every sign of a functional approach amalgamating Marx and Durkheim. The notable absence is Weber and with him the sociology of action.

It seems to me that there are two basic criteria to emphasize in explaining the character of Merton's approach. This type of analysis is distinguished by:

a. the fact that it takes social effects back to *structural constraints* and *structural contexts which condition* the action and its outcomes;
b. the fact that "the social scientist normally finds *stochastic, not functional relations*" (SA: 149).

In other words, to come back to the theme of SA, according to Merton, the social dynamic as such is ambivalent (1) because it is *always conditioned* by factors (of bonds and of situational contexts) which are preceding, concomitant, and subsequent to the action subjectively considered that make intentionality irrelevant and lead structurally to opposing or conflictual requests (expectations, etc.), and (2) because the *functionality of the (relational) social dynamic has a probabilistic nature, in no way necessarily determined.*

The specificity of Merton's approach is brought out still more clearly in the differences between him and Pitirim Sorokin and Talcott Parsons. In Merton's view, the theories and classifications of these writers are certainly useful as conceptual tools for creating analytical and synthesizing typologies, but they do not take in the most fundamental characteristic of social reality, namely ambivalence.

Merton criticizes Sorokin for the fact that he defines the role (or rather the social relation) (SA: 15) as a "combination of designated properties" (direction, extensity, intensity, duration, type of influence) in analogy with chemistry. Social life, in Sorokin's view, would be made up of relations that were a combination of three types or pure forms (familistic, compulsory, and mixed).

Parsons, in his turn, follows the same logic in his definition of the social role, conceived as a combination of designated components (the famous pattern-variables). Thus, both these authors arrive at a description and interpretation of effective social relations as realizations of the *predominance* of one property or one component over another.

Such an approach is unacceptable to Merton since the focus on the domination of one attribute over another in roles or social relations is exactly what causes the ambivalence, or rather the functions and structures of the ambivalence, to be lost.

Thus the originality of the Mertonian conception is evident in relation to the *structure of the social role*. This last is not possible to define in terms of a combination of properties, attributes, or dominant dimensions, but as a *"dynamic organization of norms and counter-norms"* (SA: 17). Role behavior is not conformity to certain dominant expectations (e.g., affective neutrality or functional specificity) but it is the alternating of norms (of major importance) and counter-norms (of minor importance) that produces the ambivalence.

To sum up, ambivalence is structurally—because normatively— situated in the role; it is inbuilt.

In place of the theory and methodology that characterize roles on the basis of "dominant attributes," Merton proposes a theory centered on "normative complexity" (SA: 17). The social relationship thus becomes the expression of a role (its performance), but in such a way as to express the ambivalence inherent in the normative complexity of sociality.

In my view, Merton paves the way for the end of the rigidity of Parsonsian structural-functionalism which sees SA as a sort of subproduct of something (social order) which is intrinsically nonambivalent because it is integrated and stable. Nevertheless, he is still far from extracting from this all the implications that more recent sociological theories (such as those of Jürgen Habermas or Niklas Luhmann) have developed.

These theories, however, especially Luhmannian theory, owe much to Merton's approach, precisely because they start from certain general presuppositions advanced by Merton. Such presuppositions assume that the social relation must be seen as intrinsically dynamic because the connections between status and role come in the practical reality and cannot but be governed by an alternation of norms and counternorms. When a norm is defined and established, at least potentially, attitudes and behaviors in conflict with it are equally evoked.

Of course, Habermas, analyzed in this way, seems a good deal more "normativist" than Luhmann (for the emphasis the former places on communicative action, in so far as it is capable of "consensus"). And yet both share a *procedural* perspective on social norms where it is precisely SA conflict which plays a significant role. The difference between Habermas and Luhmann lies elsewhere: it lies in the fact that the former analyzes social relations from an institutional point of view (starting with language as the basic social institution) while the latter seems skeptical of such things, even cynical about them. Seen from this angle, then, the turning point marked by Merton's thought when he proposes his structural variant of functional analysis can be all the better appreciated. This turning point is in some sense presupposed in the current sociological debate too, in that it still marks a dividing of the ways in the comparison between Habermas and Luhmann, by favoring the shift to the latter's perspective.[3]

Merton's thought is to be placed at the beginning of this debate when he "discovers" that social roles (relations) cannot be defined in terms of dominant attributes because such a definition (approach) is not sufficiently flexible to take into account the contingencies of the social relations in their unceasing variations.

"Behavior oriented wholly to the dominant norms would defeat the functional objectives of the role. Instead, role-behavior is alternatively oriented to dominant norms and to subsidiary counter-norms in the role. This alternation of subroles *evolves* as a social device for helping men in designated statuses to cope with the contingencies they face in trying to fulfill their functions" (SA: 18).

The functionality (the functionalism) of the social dynamic is always critical, according to Merton. And so intrinsically, or at least potentially, it is a permanent source of conflicts, tensions, contradictions, differentiations.

If Merton can arrive at this conclusion, it is because he sees in social relations a dynamic of necessarily changing needs. All the same, he does not abandon the functional framework: "only through such structures of norms and counter-norms, we suggest, can the various functions of a role be effectively discharged" (SA: 19).

For Merton SA is basically an "oscillation between differing role-requirements" that remain *functional* requisites. The examples he gives with reference to the professions and a vast range of social problems remain within this framework according to which:

> The analysis of sociological ambivalence proceeds from the premise that the structure of social roles consists of arrangements of norms and counter norms which have evolved to provide the flexibility of normatively acceptable behavior required to deal with changing states of a social relation. (SA: 31)

In the case of professionals (such as physicians or lawyers), university professors, experts in voluntary organizations, organizational leaders in general, in all cases, SA is generated in specifiable conditions by actors who are trying to face up to the requisites of their roles and at the same time to the situations where they fail to meet these requisites.

In conclusion, Mertonian SA does not seem to escape an "institutional" logic. Can one then still speak of an "institutional" sociological approach? Personally I believe we can, and for the following reasons, which are also the underlying motives for a debate which is still going on today:

a. *Social phenomena are always analyzed by Merton as patterns of behavior.* Of course, they do not descend in linear fashion either from beliefs (doctrines or norms) or from individual attitudes, in that beliefs, attitudes and behavior form an *interactive* triad. And yet this triad in Merton's view always presents institutionalized rules, to the point where even to sidestep them (not use them or abuse them, etc.) is institutionalized (in virtue of what has been indicated above).

b. Merton assumes that *the norms are never totally realized*, and yet the distancing from the norms is never fortuitous but always structured according to patterned discrepancies (SA: xi).

c. The concept of SA is thus brought back to types of social conduct which recur *even if they are not normatively prescribed* in that they spring from structural-functional needs that are themselves hidden social norms (laws, rules, requisites) inherent in the social structure. It seems then that social normativity has to answer not to a logic *sui generis* but to supposed "functional requisites of the social structure" as their goal and ultimate logic. The "critical" elements of social action *have to* be resolved in a social function of a higher order.

These are the reasons why Merton's approach to SA can still be considered "institutional," though it is clear that it remains poised between a development into something more normative (like Habermas's) and the opening up to a more radical functionalism (like, as we have suggested, Luhmann's sociology).

An Overall Assessment

Merton's concept of SA is an important, perhaps the most important, *vaccination* for sociological analysis. Just as it is sensible to get the right injections before you go into an area where there is malaria, typhoid, or cholera, so to, if you want to get into sociological theory, you should prepare yourself beforehand with a good dose of that sociological vaccination that is called SA theory.

What is its use and what does it immunize you against?

1. In the first place, I think, it constitutes the basis for a critical use of functional analysis in sociology. Statuses, roles, and social relations are *never* totally functional (or totally dysfunctional either). Total functionality is not conceivable, because it would have to put together norms which are incompatible or potentially so. Normative expectations, even those that have been institutionalized, always have a margin of inconsistency. This margin is not merely chance (generated by contingency), but *patterned* in that it reflects the SA of the social *structures* themselves.

2. It serves as a "trail" in the identification of particular types of pathogenic relations (or rather systems of pathogenic relations). For example, the "double bind" "discovered" by Geoffrey Bateson (1976) is already all or potentially all contained in this theory, worked out independently and on a sociological, not psychological or merely communicational basis. In fact, I would say that the Mertonian theory goes beyond Bateson's since it says why the communication binds doubly *quite apart from* the characteristics either of the subjects or of the communication itself. For example, when a person presents schizophrenic traits, in that (s)he is in a double-bind-communication pattern, such a personality has to be understood in relation to the social situation (ties and frictions/connections and contestations) in which (s)he has been socialized in the course of life up to the moment under examination, and taking into account the structural and functional dynamic of the most comprehensive social system, normativity, and not only communication between two or three or *n* number of components.

3. On the basis of these two characteristics, the Mertonian concept of SA is particularly important for understanding and explaining numerous cases of *social innovation*, as in fact Merton has used it. And yet it

must be inferred that these cases remain linked to the structural dynamic of the social institutions. In other terms, as I shall explain later, *they do not attain to the alternative innovation which springs from within the social relations themselves in as far as they are intersubjective relations.*

I should like to draw attention to some doubts and weaknesses in the theory.

A Generic Concept?

From the conceptual point of view, the Mertonian notion of SA seems a bit too wide and generic. It includes concepts like: contradiction (contradictory demands and expectations), conflict, tension, incompatibility, inconsistency, and dilemma.

The "double valency" in which the social actor is caught may, that is, go from antagonism (positions that are in total contradiction to each other) all the way to mere difficulty in making a conciliation. Merton here seems to be taking rather lightly the epistemological aspects of the problem. He therefore runs into a series of possible confusions: for example, when the norms he speaks of are *only apparently* in contradiction/incompatible, or when they are *wrongly placed on the same level* whereas they are in fact on different levels that can be dealt with without contradiction or incompatibility. From this angle, in empirical phenomenology SA is often linked to the fact that adequate metanorms have not yet been elaborated by the actors; or to the fact that the symbolico-normative codes have to face new problems which require new rules (nonexistent) or necessitate new links between existing rules. In short, apparent incompatibility or incompatibility capable of solution is not distinguished from that which is substantial nor transitory incompatibility from that which is lasting.

Ultimately, *the Mertonian theory of SA requires a theory of normative production* (like *nomos* and *ethos* for the social world) *which cannot be only structural* but has to have recourse to a sociology of culture that in Merton—as among functionalists in general—does not exist or rather is presented in exceedingly reductive terms (Tenbruck 1985).

Merton gets by through saying that there is SA while the norms in question (contained in expectations or deriving from value orientations) *cannot be followed or expressed simultaneously in the practical behavior of the social actor*, who, as a result, is driven to oscillation between two poles (detachment and compassion, discipline and permissiveness, personal and impersonal treatment, and so forth).

It is clear that such a notion can lead to generic analyses. The only strong point in the Mertonian discourse is the fact that the lowest common denominator of the various meanings of SA is to be identified in the difficulties in following a norm that spring not from individual characteristics of the subject-actor but from structural incompatibilities. And yet one has to note that Merton himself makes exceptions to this rule at times, like when, in the 1936 essay on unanticipated consequences of social action, he puts the actor's ignorance, error and impulse towards immediate interests as sources of ambivalence.

A Nominalist Approach?

Merton does not escape a certain circular nominalism, which is of course common to many functionalists.

If it is the social structures (that is, the given status-role relations) that generate the circumstances and conditions in which SA is manifested and reincorporated into particular statuses and status-sets along with their associated roles, is there no risk that the social structure (the set of status-roles) is the origin and the end of the social processes in which the ambivalence is found? In short, the actor would be hyperdetermined by the circularity of the social structure in which (s)he acts.

If a person acts in an ambivalent way because (s)he is in a certain relational system that predicts, prescribes, and therefore generates SA, how can (s)he get out of it, even only on a level of finding a balance between the horns of ambivalence? And again: who and what will be able to change the social structures and the processes they produce in such a framework?

Merton's view that the social structures are characterized by an intrinsic, normatively conditioned ambivalence may be a good vaccine but it may also turn into a trap when we need to explain the prevalence or the emergence of a serious "value commitment" and when we need to understand behavior which is beyond "normal," the reasons for eruptions of novelty, charisma, breakdown and discontinuity, moments of great intentionality in social life.

The Problem of the Normative Character of Social Structure

Under the obvious influence of Durkheim and functionalism in general, SA is brought back to the normative character of social structure by Merton. What does this entail? Is it perhaps that SA has only one basis (determination and connotation) of a normative type? Are there no other sources of SA? In particular, what happens when the society (the generalized social relation) is denormativized?

These are problems that the Mertonian theory of SA inevitably leaves unanswered. In the theory's own conception of itself, its bearing has limitations that have to be overcome by other theories. Merton's appeal to theoretical and methodological pluralism is explicit in this connection (SA: ch. 7) and reveals the scholar's awareness of the insufficiency of his approach.

Conclusions: Towards a Fully Relational Theory of Sociological Ambivalence

In reality, I think that there is a deeper explanation of the caveats in Merton's theory, which after all he has in common with most sociologists. It centers on the fact that *an adequate conception of social relations is not reached*. By this I do not in any way mean to sustain the thesis that we must look for a monistic theory, but simply that theoretical exposition and methodological pluralism can find a deeper unity than a simple "rapprochement," juxtaposition, combination, or whatever of competing and conflicting points of view.

The difficulties we have encountered in the SA theory and especially those related to the adoption of a generic concept and the formulation of a typology which does not deal sufficiently with relations are in all probability related to the fact that (1) social relations are considered essentially from the "functional" angle, and in parallel, (2) they are strictly derived from the status-role. Hence the weight of a certain institutional normativity, linked to the given social structure.

The social relation, on the contrary, is essentially much more than functionality: it is *link* (structure) but also *signification* (symbolic reference). The lack of this second aspect explains why the Mertonian concept of SA is so generic (since its symbolic mediation is not investigated ad hoc) and why the typology is not relational enough (since it does not take into account or reflect the hermeneutic circle).

Finally, the Mertonian theory demonstrates its conditioning by a particular symbolic referent, that of the "highly structured" society. Obviously, the structuring is still to be understood in relative terms (or rather relational terms) both in the comparison between different societies and in the internal structuring of the single society referred to. But it is clear that the theory refers to that type of societal structuring that exists in some form up till the 1960s.

What happens when the social world becomes denormativized or, to use Mertonian language, the ties and the normative conditionality of status-roles are reduced, and with them the binding nature of generalized social relations?

Can one still speak of SA as Merton defined it and gave it its typology in a social world which is *no longer probabilistic but possibilistic*, where identities lose their limits, norms are separated from values, and social links weaken and fragment to the point that there is an infinite possibility of moves and countermoves? When, in short, the collective conscience represents society as a field of processes in which every move is possible and functionally equivalent? or, to put it yet another way, when the pragmatism that Durkheim rejected out of hand as a possibility for the collective conscience (Durkheim 1987) becomes instead the very form of the common conscience, as it does in today's society?

Obviously, there is no easy answer to such questions. In the first instance, however, I would say that, in a society which is minimally structured (relatively speaking, of course) like that of the 1980s, characterized by weak rationality, ethics without truth, neo-individualism and postmodernism, it is probable that:

- the Mertonian SA may lose importance in as far as it remains linked to the normatively structured side of society, while it should find new meaning in the symbolic codes which now predict and use it intentionally;
- other forms of SA will emerge, no longer related to the norms/rules of the prescriptive codes but belonging to the *semantic* dynamic—that is, with valency linked to the processes of signification.

In the fluid state of the social system, sociological syntax (as also Merton's) has thus to give way to a new sociological semantics of SA, which obviously changes the corresponding pragmatic forms too. These last tend now to be of the paradoxical type.

Of course, it is not for this reason that Mertonian theory is losing importance. It remains essential for catching the structural side of society. We must, however, realize that that side, from being manifest is tending to become *latent,* perhaps waiting to return to manifest again in different times and conditions. Since-and this is where the most profound truth of the Mertonian theory lies-ambivalence does not exist, as creativity does not exist, if there is not a normative code by whose rules it is possible to define double, confused, conflicting valencies, and therefore innovations requested. In fact, where any move is equally possible, SA is transferred from the social structure to the subject. But "private" (subjective) ambivalence is by this token deprived also of public significance and risks at any moment turning into mere confusion of imaginary symbols (Fornari 1976).

So it turns out that *a social world which is highly denormativized is a world which does not know how to deal with ambivalence.* It is afraid of it, it finds the consequent anxiety and frustration intolerable. This is the society that Luhmann describes.

The question many people are asking today about the present type of society (and by implication the Luhmannian theory that rationalizes it) is this: can the Luhmann-type social system, theorized as it is as a way of avoiding an excessive load of the ambivalence of social life-can it, will it be able to separate the symbolic code of the rules definitively from the symbolic semantics, thus giving institutional form to a social differentiation that would separate systematic SA (manageable by the system through codes of generalized interchange means) from properly symbolic SA (left to the imagination of signification and meaning, as "environment" of the system)?

It is for this new frontier that we are called on to develop a new theory. It becomes daily more urgent and dramatic especially in those fields which define human beings' relations with their interior and exterior nature.

Personally, I believe that Mertonian SA theory remains valid, but that it needs a more adequate conception of the social relation which is *both* structural link and symbolic reference, if we are not to remain within the insufficiencies of the structuralist approach, perhaps rounded out with the extrinsic juxtaposition of other approaches. It is no accident that in his most recent essay Merton concludes that it is sometimes difficult to distinguish the psychological, practical, and sociological forces that tend to put a brake on the search for help (from the professionals) and produce a deep ambivalence in those who seek help (SA: 40).

The royal way to greater clarification lies in seeking a sociological theory centered on a stronger theory of the social relation *as such*. A basic assumption of any such theory should be that the social relation is not (as Merton frequently assumes) an implementation or an extrinsication of the status-role, but *on the contrary* status-roles are defined by social relations, and these latter in their moment of creation are relations between subjects in a system.

Frequently, unanticipated or perverse effects, such as the existence of manifest and latent functions, or again the various ways adapting to means and goals (all Mertonian terms exemplifying the pervasive nature of SA) are the product of courses of action whose ambivalence is the reflection not of normatively structured conflict in which human beings act like mice in a maze but the result of subjective strategies or intersubjective needs whereby "one has to" assume and/or "one has to" say that one wants to do a particular thing or that one is aiming at a certain goal when in reality one is pursuing another course entirely.

Notes

1. See the collected essays of 1936 to 1976 in Merton 1976, hereafter referred to as SA. And the more recent essay written with Vanessa Merton and Elinor Barber 1983.
2. SA: 7 (emphasis added). Think, for example, of the position (function) and the role (professional profile) of the social worker as I have interpreted it in Donati 1981: 3–22.
3. For more details see Donati 1991.

References

Bateson, Geoffrey. 1972. *Steps to an Ecology of Mind.* New York: Chandler Publishing Company.

Boudon, Raymond. 1977. *Effets pervers et ordre social.* Paris: Presses Universitaires de France.

Donati, Pierpaolo. 1991. *Teoria relazionale della società.* Milan: Franco Angeli.

———. 1981."L'Operatore assistente sociale di fronte alla crisi del welfare state." *Studi di Sociologia* 19(1)

Durkheim, Émile. 1987. *Pragmatismo e sociologia.* [It. trans.] Florence: Ianua.

Fornari, Franco. 1976. *Simbolo e codice.* Milan: Feltrinelli.

Merton, Robert K. 1976. *Sociological Ambivalence and Other Essays.* New York: Free Press.

Merton, Robert K., Vanessa Merton, and Elinor Barber. 1983. "Client Ambivalence in Professional Relationships: The Problem of Seeking Help from Strangers." In *New Directions in Helping,* vol. 2, edited by B.P. DePaulo et al., 13–44. New York: Academic Press.

Mongardini, Carlo. 1985. *Epistemologia e sociologia.* Milan: Franco Angeli.

Tenbruck, Friedrich H. 1985. "I compiti della sociologia della cultura." *Annali di Sociologia* 1.

6

Robert K. Merton's Concept of Sociological Ambivalence: The Florentine Case of the "Man-Ape"

Birgitta Nedelmann

Introduction

There are several ways of approaching Robert K. Merton's important contribution to sociological ambivalence. One way would be to examine the analytical concept of sociological ambivalence with reference to its internal coherence, its relation to other related concepts, and its theoretical implications. Pierpaolo Donati has chosen to pursue this approach. Another way would be to compare Merton's approach to the analysis of sociological ambivalence with the approaches found in the classical works of sociology, particularly in Simmel. It seems particularly appropriate to adopt this approach as Merton developed the concept of ambivalence after reexamining the work of Georg Simmel (Levine 1978: 1278). But it might be assumed that neither Simmel nor Merton would approve of such a personalized way of discussing sociological concepts. Yet another way of approaching the concept of sociological ambivalence would be to investigate the countercultural impact of Merton's insistence on the social importance of dualism, contradictions, and paradoxes for American sociology. This question has already been dealt with by other scholars. Donald N.

121

Levine's *The Flight from Ambiguity* (1986) is one prominent example. However, that debate is best left to American sociologists.

These three approaches to Merton's concept of sociological ambivalence all carry some weight and are perfectly legitimate in themselves. In this chapter, however, I have chosen to pursue a fourth avenue to highlight what is considered to be Merton's main contribution to sociological theory. I shall present a case study and discuss the four main theoretical points arising from it.

When I was preparing this chapter (in May 1987), an intense public debate on genetic engineering was going on in Italy. The Florentine anthropologist Professor Bruno Chiarelli declared in public that the creation of a man-ape hybrid was technically possible. The purpose of this type of genetic engineering was to "produce a human sub-species which could do repetitive and unpleasant work" (*L'Espresso,* 17 May 1987: 173). When confronted with the question whether this type of scientific work could be justified from an ethical point of view, Professor Chiarelli declared: "I understand that the existence of human chromosomes in this hybrid upsets public morality. It would however be ethically acceptable to use [the hybrids] as donors of organs for transplantation" (ibid.).

These statements provoked a lively debate in the Italian press. The image of the man-ape captured the public imagination and developed into what was described as a scandal. Some of the most prominent Italian scientists became involved in the debate, among them the Nobel Prize winner Rita Levi-Montalcini.[1] I do not intend to focus on the broader issues, but will restrict my attention here to an examination of a local dimension of the wider issue. When the public debate reached its climax, the Academic Senate of the University of Florence (where Prof. Chiarelli held his chair) officially distanced itself from the scientific research conducted by Chiarelli. The Senate passed a motion declaring that Professor Chiarelli's statements were "unacceptable from an ethical-scientific point of view, that they offend the methodological seriousness of research and that the university is not at all involved in these results."[2] Only one member of the Senate voted against the motion. We will return to the reasons given by this member for his minority position later on. A journalist from the local Florentine newspaper *La Nazione* asked some members of the Senate why they voted on the motion. Their answers clearly demonstrate what Merton described as sociological ambivalence. This minor incident would probably have escaped my attention had I not recently read Merton's title essay on *Sociological Ambivalence*. Merton's article "The Ambivalence of Scientists" made me particularly aware of the merits of the Florentine case as a study of sociological ambivalence.

In this chapter I will discuss the following four points in detail:

1. Merton's concept of sociological ambivalence transcends the conventional dichotomy between "social" and "psychological" without excluding psychological reactions to social ambivalence from the analysis.
2. The case study will show that the concept of sociological ambivalence is eminently suited to empirical analysis. The clarity of the basic concepts in Merton's work, and the range of his theoretical approach makes it particularly suited to empirical investigation and confirmation.
3. Merton's concept of sociological ambivalence is based on a dynamic approach to role analysis. This approach enables him to examine systematically processes of oscillation of behavior.
4. Merton's concept of sociological ambivalence can be considered a major theoretical contribution to the analysis of intrinsic social processes or, to use a term widely used elsewhere (Mayntz and Nedelmann 1987), of social *eigendynamics*.

These points are discussed in detail below with reference to the Florentine man-ape case. In this chapter I shall restrict my analysis to a few selective illustrations. The empirical case as such deserves more detailed study in a further contribution.

Psychological versus Sociological Ambivalence

Sociologists often refuse to integrate the concept of ambivalence into their vocabulary because of its alleged psychological nature. They attempt to justify this rejection by quoting the terminology used in classic analyses of social ambivalence. Indeed, the terminology used by Max Weber, Émile Durkheim, and Georg Simmel can easily lead to a psychological misinterpretation of the notion of ambivalence. For example, when describing processes of oscillation between charisma and routinization, Max Weber talks of the individual "needs" for innovation on the one hand, and of order on the other. Émile Durkheim's notion of the dualistic nature of human beings is another classic example which lends itself to a one-sided psychological interpretation of ambivalence. It has given rise to the view that people's ambivalent action-orientation is built into their anthropological constitution.

Simmel's frequent references to dualistic desires, instincts, and needs have further strengthened this kind of psychological interpretation of ambivalence.

It is one of Merton's major contributions to have made a clear theoretical and conceptual distinction between psychological and sociological ambivalence. *Psychological* ambivalence refers to *personality*, *sociological* ambivalence refers to the *social structure*. Both types are of importance in the Florentine example. Psychological ambivalence proved an important factor in making this case an issue of general public interest. The image of the man-ape hybrid—in itself an ambivalent creature—gave rise to mixed feelings of fascination and horror, sexual attraction and revulsion. The broad appeal of films like *King Kong* and the recent success of *Max, amore mio* owe much to these mixed feelings. The press further exploited these psychological reactions in order to make a scandal of the man-ape case. Publicity for the film *Max, amore mio* frequently alluded to topical events: "The hot debates on the man-ape hybrid are going on. Charlotte Rampling could give her own version."[3]

Sociological ambivalence also played a role in the burgeoning of the man-ape scandal. According to Merton's conception, sociological ambivalence has its origin in incompatible normative expectations of attitudes, beliefs, and behavior assigned to a status or a set of statuses (Merton 1976: 6). Those occupying a particular status cannot withdraw from these expectations without violating the norms assigned to that status. Thus, for example, university professors are exposed to contradictory norms related to their roles as teacher, researcher, administrator, and representative of the scientific institution in which they work. Chiarelli's statements to the press enacted two contradictory norms which are built into the role of researcher: the *norm of freedom of research* (which is guaranteed by article 33 of the Italian Constitution) on the one hand and, on the other, the *norm of limitation of research,* which is brought into play because of the moral considerations of the researchers themselves. The Senate's decision can be interpreted as a vote in favor of the "limitation" pole of this built-in ambivalence. We shall deal with these two norms in more detail later. It is Merton's general distinction between psychological and sociological ambivalence that concerns us here.

We have already noted that Merton not only makes a clear distinction between sociological and psychological ambivalence, but also includes psychological reactions in this sociological analysis. Merton repeatedly makes it clear that "opposed feelings, beliefs and actions embraced in the concept of psychological ambivalence can in part be understood as response to conflict in patterned situations and social structure" (Merton 1976: 19). This comment is central to an understanding of the relationship between psychological and sociological ambivalence. Sociological ambivalence typically gives rise to oscillations in behavior. This variation can itself become the object of mixed feelings and insecurity. Both participants can become involved in what can be described as an emotional reaction to variations in behavior. In accord with Simmel's distinction between *primary* and *secondary* emotions (Nedelmann 1983), this type of psychological ambivalence could be called *secondary* (psychological) ambivalence. As this type has its origin in social structure, in sociological ambivalence, it belongs to the field of sociological analysis properly. The inclusion of secondary ambivalence in sociological analysis would have the advantage of allowing for a systematic investigation of the interplay between sociological and secondary ambivalence. Professor Chiarelli's highly emotional response to the Senate's decision might be explained at least partly in terms of secondary psychological ambivalence. Immediately after the decision he declared that he intended to "defend his dignity as teacher and researcher against attacks from all sides" (*La Nazione*, 16 May 1987: 13). Several months after the event the decision still aroused his strong feelings. He called the Senate's judgment a "heavy and hasty judgment of 'censorship' against me" (Chiarelli 1987: 119).

The Relevance of the Concept of Sociological Ambivalence

We have seen that the concept of sociological ambivalence refers to social structure. Merton isolates six structural sources which can give rise to ambivalence. He then goes on to construct six types of sociological ambivalence. This first type refers to ambivalence *within* a status. Merton is primarily concerned with this core type of ambivalence. The other types refer to contradictions *between* different statuses, roles, cultural values, culturally prescribed goals, and structural means as well as between different sets of cultural values. All six types are of significant heuristic value for the interpretation of the empirical case under examination here. In this chapter we shall examine only the first type, that is ambivalence within a status.

We must first of all clarify what Merton meant by this core type of ambivalence. According to Merton it "refers to incompatible normative expectations incorporated in a *single* role of a *single* social status" (1976: 6). Thus, for example, the role of the therapist is defined as a contradiction between norms that dictate that he should have "*both* a degree of affective detachment from the patient and a degree of compassionate concern about him" (Merton 1976: 8). In the Florentine example this core type is of crucial importance in explaining the Senate's decision. Firstly, it helps to identify which norms are in conflict and, secondly, the nature of the relations regulated by these norms.

As far as the first point is concerned, the members of the Senate were conscious that they were faced with two conflicting role expectations. As academics, university professors have to fulfill both the norm of "freedom" of research and the counternorm of "limitation" where ethical considerations are concerned. According to the first norm, academics are expected to pursue their own scientific interests without outside interference. However, the counternorm makes it clear that they are expected to limit their research and accept moral responsibility for the consequences of their activities. Some of the responses to press inquiries express this tension between dominant norm and counternorm.

As a professor of constitutional law put it:

We are not challenging the freedom of research. But when this affects the status of the individual or his body it must be subject to limits which take account of the morals of today's civilised society ... The creation of an inferior race has no parallels in history and is an affront to good sense.

Or another example:

Of course there has to be freedom of thought. But you cannot use the prestige of a university institution to cover investigations which have no scientific content whatsoever. There can be no beating about the bush. Deceiving public opinion like this is not exercising freedom but merely increasing one's reputation at the expense of others.

And as another member of the faculty put it:

The academic Senate has not come against freedom of research, but it is opposed to the sensationalist treatment of the issue in the press. The type of scare-mongering which aims at arousing emotions and interest is not a suitable medium for conveying objectively what the research involves. I personally disagree with the subject matter of this research, but I do not question the basic freedom to conduct research on any subject. In this case however there are ethical principles involved which simply cannot be ignored. (All quotations from *La Nazione*, 16 May 1987: 13)[4]

Merton's core-type of sociological ambivalence helps to identify which social relations are involved in them. In Merton's example, the therapist is related to his client by norms of engagement and detachment respectively. In our example, the norms of "freedom" and "limitation" of research regulate the relation between the university and the public, as represented by the local newspaper, various weeklies, television, and what is often described as "public opinion." The norm "freedom" of research is a social recognition of the autonomy of science as an institution. The public and the scientific community are thus considered to be fully independent of each other. The counternorm of "limitation" of research defines the relation between the public and the scientific community as being based on shared values and a common moral responsibility. The relation between the scientific community and the public is thus described as one of mutual dependence.

These distinctions give rise to two general questions. Under what social conditions is the dominant norm activated and the autonomy of science stressed? And under what social conditions is the counternorm activated and the shared moral responsibility of science stressed? Our case study can give a few answers to these questions. The counternorm of "self-limitation" became manifest when Professor Chiarelli publicly claimed his right to pursue his research without outside interference. He declared that he had "nothing against experimenting to discover what in fact is feasible" (*La Nazione*, 11 May 1987: 1). This statement prompted journalists to manifest their resentment against scientists and to make the research on the "man-ape" appear ridiculous. Humor, especially caricature, played a major role in highlighting this fundamental ambivalence. We will return to this point at a later stage. When the staff at the University of Florence realized that one of their colleagues was jeopardizing their reputation as scientists they brought the counternorm of "self-limitation" into play. A statement made by a member of the Senate, a professor of constitutional law, brings this out clearly: "I believe that reports in the press of negative reactions to Chiarelli's statements do not constitute criticisms of the research as such, however unusual and controversial this may be. They are reactions to abject and degrading scientific aims" (*La Nazione*, 16 May

1987: 13). The counternorm came to the fore even more when the professors realized that the publicity surrounding their colleague's statements threatened the prestige of their university. At this point it would be wise to recall one of these statements: "Of course there has to be freedom of research. But you cannot use the prestige of a university institution to cover investigations which have no scientific content whatsoever" (*La Nazione*, 16 May 1987: 13).

This raises one last general point. In this chapter I have limited my analysis to an examination of the contribution Merton's first core type makes to empirical study. If we brought the other five types of sociological ambivalence to bear on the present case, a more differentiated picture would emerge. It might be assumed that once one type of ambivalence has been brought into play the other types are present too. It is widely assumed that several types of ambivalence tend to occur together. As more people become involved in the process, the conflict between the institutional norms becomes more and more apparent. One of the reasons why the Florentine case escalated into a scandal is because ambivalences tend to accumulate and mutually reinforce each other in this way. This brings us to a consideration of the dynamic aspect of Merton's concept of ambivalence.

Merton's concept of sociological ambivalence is based on a dynamic approach to role analysis. Unlike Talcott Parsons and others, Merton does not confine role analysis to dominant role attributes only, but also takes into consideration minor counternorms. "*From the perspective of sociological ambivalence,*" Merton writes, "*we see a social role as a dynamic organization of norms and counter-norms,* not as a combination of dominant attributes." His analysis of sociological ambivalence proceeds from the assumption, "*that the major norms and the minor counter-norms alternatively govern role-behaviour to produce ambivalence*" (Merton 1976: 17). As Donald N. Levine has already pointed out, this apparently insignificant difference between the approaches of Parsons and Merton to role analysis has important consequences.

Merton systematically considers norms *and* counternorms, and focuses the analysis on the processes of variation in role behavior— "*since these norms cannot be simultaneously expressed in behaviour, they come to be expressed in an oscillation of behaviours: of detachment and compassion, of discipline and permissiveness, of personal and impersonal treatment*" (Merton 1976: 8). Seen from this analytical perspective, oscillation of behavior is not necessarily the expression of idiosyncratic inconsistency, but of conformity to the norms of the role. Variation in behavior is a "social device for helping people in designated statuses to cope with the contingencies they face in trying to fulfill their functions" (Merton 1976: 18). "As therapist and client, physician and patient interact," Merton continues, "different and abstractly contradictory norms are activated to meet dynamically changing needs of the relation" (Merton 1976: 18–19). This remark is of particular interest because it raises an important theoretical question: What are the consequences of oscillating behavior for the interaction process? We shall examine this aspect more closely in the following section.

Generally speaking, the oscillation of one person's behavior can provoke alterations in the other person's behavior. In this case, one can speak of the exchange of reciprocal ambivalences.[5] The alternation of one person's behavior triggers off a change in the other person's behavior and vice versa. If the therapist adopts a detached attitude this may prompt the client to expect a higher degree of engagement. If the therapist conforms to this expectation and shows more compassion, the client might become more withdrawn and thus lead the therapist to become even more detached. The two poles of the ambivalence have a reciprocal influence on each other in the interaction process.

The Florentine example is a clear instance of this. The shift towards the "limitation" pole of the majority of the Senate prompted other professors to take up the defense of the counternorm. The first to react in this way was of course the anthropologist under attack. As already mentioned above, Chiarelli declared immediately after the publication of the Senate's decision his intention to fight his case in court and to defend his dignity as a teacher and as a researcher (*La Nazione*, 16 May 1987: 13). There was just one other professor who reacted against the majority decision. He explained the way he voted in a special press declaration which deserves to be quoted at length:

Notwithstanding the gravity of the problems and the intensity of the emotions evoked by Professor Chiarelli's statements, it is nevertheless the responsibility of those holding public office to maintain a rigorous distinction between their right to criticise as individuals or as members of independent social, cultural and scientific associations and in their institutional function as members of public bodies, such as the *Senatus Accademicus*, the functions of which are defined by law within the framework of the Constitution.

From this point of view, each of the three elements of the proposal before the Senate appear totally outside the competence of such a body:

a. The Senate clearly cannot express any judgement of the scientific reliability of statements made by an academic because the majority of its members represent different faculties and thus do not have the necessary specialized knowledge when faced with this type of problem.

b. It is totally outside the competence of the senate, or any other administrative body, to make ethical judgments about the use to which actual or hypothetical scientific knowledge could be put. If these judgments are to be made at all by a public body, the competent one is Parliament acting in the exercise of its legislative functions and within the narrow limits laid down by articles 21 and 33 of the Constitution.

c. Finally, as far as judgments on the professional ethics of the researcher are concerned, and insofar as they bear on relations with the mass media; if they have legal consequences, they can be safely left to the relevant disciplinary bodies and their procedures.[6]

This declaration raises another question which is not discussed explicitly by Merton. Under what institutional conditions are alternations normatively acceptable or unacceptable? Merton seems to assume that alternations which arise from normative contradictions built into the social definition of roles are normatively acceptable (Merton 1976: 19).[7] However it would appear from the declaration made by the professor of administrative law quoted above that this is not always the case. Alternation in role behavior becomes normatively unacceptable if it comes into conflict with other normative expectations associated with another role. In the case under consideration here, it was considered that professors in their role as administrators did not have the right to use the institutional arena of the Senate to take a decision on a purely scientific issue. According to the professor quoted above, the appropriate institutional forum for dealing with such matters would have been Parliament, the courts, or voluntary academic associations. If the same academics had been asked for their opinion as researchers within, for example, the institutional context of an academic association, any movement towards the "limitation" pole would have been considered legitimate and normatively acceptable. Thus the professor of administrative law expresses a point of view which Merton has stressed in many different contexts, namely that the legitimate focus of social control in the established professions resides chiefly within the professional community itself (Merton and Gieryn 1982: 109–134).

If variations in behavior are considered illegitimate, this has consequences for the ongoing interaction process. It might generally be assumed that oscillations of behavior which are normatively unacceptable consequently lead to an accumulation of ambivalences. The interaction process is no longer only carried on by the exchange of reciprocal ambivalences, but also by the exchange of normative judgment concerning the legitimacy or illegitimacy of the shifting behavior. This type of metaconflict played a decisive role in blowing up the issue of the man-ape into a public scandal. Conflicts about the legitimacy of alternations in behavior might therefore be considered as a specific mechanism for driving on the interaction process based on sociological ambivalence. We will discuss this point further in the concluding section.

In his discussion of sociological ambivalence Merton emphasizes the structural preconditions and processes which give rise to ambivalence. *"The sociological theory deals with the processes through which social structures generate the circumstances in which ambivalence is embedded in particular statuses and status-sets together with their associated social roles"* (Merton 1976: 7). I would like to take Merton's ideas a little further in this chapter. I am not only interested in the structural preconditions of sociological ambivalence, but also in the type of social process which is generated by sociological ambivalence. Generally speaking, sociological ambivalence gives rise to interaction processes in which dominating norm and counternorm stimulate each other circularly. They function as cause and effect in the interaction process. Circular stimulation between two variables, in this case between two conflicting norms, is the main characteristic of autonomous (or *eigendynamic*) processes (Mayntz and Nedelmann 1987). Viewed from this perspective, Merton's concept of sociological ambivalence can be interpreted as a major contribution to the analysis of social eigendynamics.

In his title essay, Merton does not explicitly discuss oscillations of behavior as an endogenous process. However he demonstrates elsewhere that he is not against this type of analysis. One example is a work written with Paul F. Lazarsfeld—"Friendship as a Social Process" (1954). Here homophily—the observed tendency for friendships to form between persons with similar attributes—is interpreted as an immanent process (Lazarsfeld and Merton 1954: 18–66). A further example is his analysis of "The Matthew Effect in Science" which "consists in the accruing of greater increments of recognition for particular scientific contributions to scientists of considerable repute and the withholding of such recognition from scientists who have not yet made their mark" (Merton 1968: 58). The work of Harriet Zuckerman is another excellent example of this type of "self-reinforcing" process in science (1987: 149–150). It would be interesting to compare these various examples with particular reference to the structural preconditions which give rise to the intrinsic dynamics in each case.

One of the primary characteristics of social eigendynamics is that the reason for the continuation of the process is inherent (*eigen*) in the process itself. There may be additional situational and structural conditions which further stabilize and speed up the oscillatory process. In his analysis of the interaction process between professionals and clients, Merton identifies three such situational and structural conditions which cause the *accumulation* of ambivalence. Firstly, there is the client's anxious observation of what the therapist does.[8] Secondly, there is the norm to continue the relationship with the professional. The third factor is the professional's authority. In the man-ape case, all three factors contributed to the accumulation of ambivalence. The criterion of public scrutiny helps to explain why the genetic engineering issue was the focus of public attention for such a long time. Journalists are professionally trained to observe social events more keenly than laymen. The moment the speculations about the man-ape came into the public eye, all comments on the issue became particularly important and meaningful. What the scientists said, and especially what Professor Chiarelli said, *mattered* to the attentive audience (Merton 1976: 22). Given that they are exposed to intense public scrutiny, it is highly likely that statements take on an exaggerated importance. Like Merton's anxious client, the astute journalist develops an insatiable desire for information (Merton 1976: 23). In this situation, comments which would have gone unnoticed under "normal" conditions take on a new significance. Therapists are professionally trained to deal with a client's excessive attention to what is going on. Academics, however, are not prepared to deal with this, and often become the victims of astute journalists. They often become personally involved in public issues.

The norm of continuity also comes into play in the relationship between science and the public. Journalists have a professional obligation to follow up stories which have captured the public imagination. In our case study, humor played an important part in underpinning the norm of continuity. The image of a hypothetical man-ape made science appear ridiculous and was widely used to make ironic allusions to the ongoing crisis in Italian politics. In one caricature President Fanfani was portrayed as a man-ape. He was supported on his left side by the secretary of the Communist party, Natta, and on his right by the secretary of the Christian Democratic party, De Mita. Natta says: "We let him do the most unpleasant work." De Mita says: "Be quiet, then we'll come to a compromise" (*L'Espresso*, 24 May 1987: 12).[9] Humor in the form of political caricature was an important factor in speeding up the accumulation of ambivalence in the man-ape case. In coupling science with politics the caricature served a double function: it damaged the prestige of both scientists and politicians.

Merton argues that authority has the same function as continuity for the accumulation of ambivalence. The authority of the professional over his client gives rise to a mixture of anxiety and respect in the client. It is possible to argue that this social mechanism was also at work in the man-ape case. Professor Chiarelli's authority as a natural scientist gave rise to a mixture of anxiety and respect in the public. His frequent public affirmations that it was possible to create a man-ape hybrid activated deep-rooted ambivalent feelings of admiration and suspicion towards academics, and towards natural scientists in particular. Professor Chiarelli's behavior in public called forth an image of the essential duplicity of research scientists. Chiarelli became both Doctor Jekyll and Mr. Hyde. He showed an interest in scientific research regardless of the moral consequences, declaring to the press: "We witness a scientific discovery which in itself can neither be 'good' nor 'bad'" (*La Nazione*, 12 May 1987: 3). Yet he was also fully aware of the moral problems involved in the field of genetic engineering: "It is necessary to tackle the problem of the relationship between science and ethics now: the possibility of genetic manipulation makes this necessary" (Chiarelli 1987: 120). It was, however, only much later that Professor Chiarelli really espoused Mr. Hyde's cause, as we shall see when we look at how the affair came to an end.

Interaction processes which have their origin in sociological ambivalence have in principle no end. They oscillate between the two poles of ambivalence and can only be brought to an end if the structural conditions upon which they are based change, or if counterprocesses start up which are strong enough to end the process. Scandals do not go on forever. Often they stop simply because another scandal has been discovered. As Professor Chiarelli increasingly adopted the guise of Mr. Hyde in public, his colleagues felt less constrained to insist on the norm of "limitation" of research. Chiarelli's change in attitude was underpinned by reports coming in from research institutions outside Italy which declared that the creation of a man-ape hybrid was scientifically impossible. At the end of May, *La Stampa* published interviews with scientists from the York Regional Primate Center of Atlanta under the headline DRY COMMENT FROM THE "CENTER" IN ATLANTA: PROFESSOR CHIARELLI MADE A MISTAKE—THERE IS NO MAN-APE HYBRID (*La Stampa*, May 30, 1987: 2). When Chiarelli was asked by *La Repubblica*: "What is the problem?" He replied, "The problem is primarily an ethical one: this type of experiment does not cost more than about ten million lire [B.N] and could be done by anybody, as I said at the end of 1984.[10] I brought this issue up because I think it is necessary that the public becomes aware of the enormous possibilities of science. Today men are already able to influence their own future; regardless of the extrapolations of science fiction, the new biology is about to acquire capabilities which are similar to those offered by physics on the control of nuclear energy. Therefore it is necessary to go more deeply into the ethical problems which are related to these new developments" (*La Repubblica*, 30 May 1987: 19). This comment shows that Chiarelli himself had shifted more towards the "limitation" pole. He presents himself as somebody who has played the *enfant terrible* in order to initiate a discussion of ethical problems in contemporary science. In so doing he no longer gave his university colleagues any reason to act according to the "limitation" pole of their ambivalence. Thus they were once again free to oscillate towards the dominating norm of "freedom" of research.

Conclusion

We have chosen to explore the Florentine man-ape case not only in order to illustrate Merton's concept of sociological ambivalence. One of the primary motives for pursuing this case study was to show that Merton's sociological categories help us discover how social life functions. Merton's basic sociological concepts and insights illuminate many aspects of everyday life that would otherwise remain meaningless and trivial. His ideas help us *see* and *understand* social life from a specific sociological perspective. The sociological work of Robert K. Merton not only enriches sociological theory-building in general, it also enriches the lives of those who read him.

There are still some open questions related to the concept of sociological ambivalence. I will mention five of these briefly here.

1. In the present context it has only been possible to deal with the core type of sociological ambivalence. It would be worth examining the other five types mentioned by Merton and investigating the relationship between these different types. It would also be interesting further to examine Merton's own idea of the internal dynamics of the interrelationship between the six types of sociological ambivalence.

2. Another area of research which deserves further attention is the relationship between sociological and psychological ambivalence and what has been called here secondary psychological ambivalence. By focusing directly on this relationship it may be possible to overturn the old idea that ambivalence is a subject of psychological research only, but belongs properly to the field of sociology.

3. A third question of considerable interest is the social conditions under which the dominant norm is activated, and the social conditions under which the counternorm is mobilized. When do social actors orient their behavior towards the dominant norm, and when to the counternorm?

4. Merton's terminology of dominant norm and minor counternorm suggests that one norm is stronger than the other in structuring social behavior. What influence does this imbalance have on the *form of* process of oscillation? It might be assumed that social actors tend towards the dominant norm for longer periods than they are oriented towards the counternorm. The process of oscillation could be described in terms of unequal swings between the twin poles of ambivalence.

5. Finally, it might be worthwhile to examine more systematically the endogenous process which is initiated by sociological ambivalence. This would make a valuable contribution to theory on eigendynamics, and would lay important guidelines for empirical study. It would be particularly interesting to examine the countervailing processes which might stop the eigendynamic processes. Under what social conditions does the endogenous process itself initiate a counterprocess and what is the relation between the ongoing endogenous process and the exogenous process it starts up?

These are some of the questions Merton's concepts of sociological ambivalence leaves us with. I hope to pursue this area of research and demonstrate the merits of Merton's contribution by making further case studies.

Notes

I wish to thank Anna Bankowska for her help with translating Italian documents into English and for her thorough editing of style.

1. "This is beastly and repugnant," Rita Levi Montalcini commented (*La Repubblica*, 12 May 1987: 21); "These kinds of experiments are disgusting. Scientists must not even think of them," was another comment by the Nobel prize winner (*La Nazione*, 12 May 1987: 3). The famous Italian biophysician Alfonso Maria Liquori said, "This is obscene: I hope Chiarelli has been misunderstood" (*La Repubblica*, 13 May 1987: 17).
2. Dichiarazione resa alla stampa dal Prof. Brunetto Chiarelli, Estratto verbale del Senato Accademico, Università degli Studi di Firenze, 14 Maggio 1987.
3. "Infuriano le polemiche sull'ibrido uomo-scimmia. Charlotte Rampling potrebbe dire la sua . . . " (*La Repubblica*, 28 May 1987; *La Stampa*, 30 May 1987: 16).
4. It might be of interest to quote the biophysician Alfonso Maria Liquori of the "Centro Internazionale di Biologia Teoretica" again as a voice of the "self-limitation" pole: "The point is . . . that not everything that is scientifically feasible must be experimented. And it must not be protected by the secrecy of a patent. The patent is very serious and dangerous: it means to withdraw the possibility of control by means of research from the side of the scientific community . . . Not everything that at first sight might be 'useful' to human beings must be realized. Utilitarianism is the enemy of science" (*La Repubblica*, 13 May 1987: 13).
5. This terminology has been invented by Alessandro Cavalli.
6. Dichiarazione di voto del Prof. Orsi Battaglini, Senato Accademico del 14 May 1987. I am grateful to Professor Orsi Battaglini for letting me have his personal declaration.
7. "Action exclusively in terms of one component in the ambivalent pairs tends to be self-defeating, producing a lopsided development that undercuts the basic objectives of the complex activity" (Merton 1976: 63). From this observation of the dysfunction of one-sided norm-orientation it does not necessarily follow that oscillations are normatively accepted by the other actors.
8. This factor is also at work in creating the "Matthew effect in science." As Merton argues, the work of outstanding scientists is read with greater attention than the work of less well-known scientists. " . . . since it is probably important, it should be read with special care; and the more attention one gives it, the more one is apt to get out of it. This becomes a self-confirming process, making for the greater evocative effect of publications by eminent men of science. . ." (Merton 1968: 62).
9. "Buona, a mamma, ghe andiamo a fare il gombromesso" (*L'Espresso*, 24 May 1987: 12).
10. Chiarelli refers to his book: "*Taxonomy and Phylogeny of the Old World Primates*, published in 1986, which was by and large ignored" (*L'Espresso*, 24 May 1987: 45–46).

References

Chiarelli, Brunetto. 1987. "L'uomo-scimmia: perché ho sollevato lo scandalo." Intervista a cura di Giorgio de Finis. *MondOperaio* 7 (Luglio): 119–124.

Dichiarazioni rese alla stampa dal Prof. Brunetto Chiarelli, Estratto verbale del Senato Accademico, Università degli Studi di Firenze, 14 Maggio 1987.

Dichiarazione di voto del Prof. Orsi Battaglini, Senato Accademico del 14 Maggio 1987.

Lazarsfeld, Paul and Robert K. Merton. 1954. "Friendship as a Social Process: A Substantive and Methodological Analysis." In *Freedom and Control in Modern Society*, edited by Morroe Berger, Theodore Abel, and Charles Page, 18–66. Princeton: Van Nostrand.

Levine, Donald N. 1978. "Book Review of Robert K. Merton: Sociological Ambivalence and Other Essays." *American Journal of Sociology* 83 (5): 1277–1280.

———. 1986. *The Flight from Ambiguity*. Chicago: University of Chicago Press.

Mayntz, Renate and Birgitta Nedelmann. 1987. "Eigendynamische soziale Prozesse: Anmerkungen zu einem analytischen Paradigma." *Kölner Zeitschrift für Soziologie und Sozialpsychologie* 39: 648–668.

Merton, Robert K. 1968. "The Matthew Effect in Science." *Science* 159: 56–63.

———. 1976. *Sociological Ambivalence and Other Essays*. New York: Free Press, esp. 3–31.

Merton, Robert K. and Thomas F. Gieryn. 1982. "Institutionalised Altruism: The Case of the Professions." In *Social Research and the Practicing Professions*, by Robert K. Merton, 109–134. Cambridge: Abt Books.

Nedelmann, Birgitta. 1983. "Georg Simmel: Emotion und Wechselwirkung in intimen Gruppen." *Kölner Zeitschrift für Soziologie und Sozialpsychologie,* Sonderheft 25: 174–209.

Zuckerman, Harriet. 1987. *Persistence and Change in the Careers of Men and Women Scientists and Engineers: A Review of Current Research*. National Research Council, Office of Scientific and Engineering Personnel workshop "WOMEN: Their Underrepresentation and Career Differentials in Science and Engineering." Proceedings edited by Linda S. Dix, 123–156. Washington, DC: National Academy Press.

7

Accumulation of Advantage and Disadvantage: The Theory and Its Intellectual Biography

Harriet Zuckerman

The Theory of Accumulation of Advantage and Disadvantage

In science, as in other domains, the distributions of resources, achievements, and rewards are sharply skewed.[1] Numerous inquiries have shown that a small fraction of scientists receive more than their share of research resources, contribute disproportionately to scientific knowledge, and are accorded the lion's share of recognition. Moreover, disparities among scientists in access to resources, in contributions, and in rewards increase as they move through their careers, making for growing inequality between age-peers. The theory of accumulation of advantage and disadvantage attempts to account for such inequalities and has been a focus of empirical and theoretical research in the sociology of science since the late 1960s. In the process, it has shaped ideas about stratification in science and, in some measure, about stratification in other institutions as well.

As we shall see, the theory was intimated by Merton as early as 1942 ([1942] 1973) but a quarter-century would pass before he would put an explicit formulation in print (Merton [1968] 1973).[2] This chapter examines the theory systematically, traces its early intellectual his-

139

tory, and identifies a series of unresolved theoretical questions which pertain to the accumulation of advantage and disadvantage, especially in the careers of individual scientists.[3] It concludes by considering possible applications of the theory beyond the institution of science.

The theory of accumulative advantage and disadvantage[4] aims to account for the structures and processes making for social stratification in science. In particular, it explains why the distributions of role performance and rewards in science are sharply skewed and why disparities in scientists' resources, contributions, and rewards increase as they grow older; why already advantaged individuals become even more so while at the same time others become relatively disadvantaged. It treats the structure of stratification and certain aspects of individual, group, and organizational mobility.

In Mertonian language:

> When the role performance of an individual measures up to demanding standards, and especially when it greatly exceeds them, this initiates a process of cumulative advantage in which the individual acquires successively enlarged opportunities to advance his work (and the rewards that go with it). (Merton [1977] 1979: 89)

Put another way,

> certain individuals or groups repeatedly receive resources and rewards that enrich recipients at an accelerating rate and conversely impoverish (relatively) the non-recipients . . . the process [which operates primarily by affecting individuals' access to the opportunity structure] contributes to elite formation and ultimately produces sharply graded systems of stratification. (Zuckerman 1977: 59–60)

The processes posited in the theory are aptly illustrated by several examples from the careers of American Nobel laureates—the ultra-elite of science.

A sizeable fraction of future laureates took advanced degrees at the nation's most distinguished universities. Indeed, more than half (55 percent) of all future laureates were educated at just five universities—Harvard, Columbia, the University of California at Berkeley, Johns Hopkins, and Princeton (1977: 90). Moreover, much the same pattern holds for other members of the scientific elite: those in the National Academy of Sciences. These same five institutions graduated 47 percent of future members of the Academy but just 18 percent of all Ph.Ds in the sciences in the same period (Zuckerman 1977: 90).

Being educated at such institutions confers a variety of advantages.

Not least, scientific talent is concentrated in them. These young scientists had access to and were taught by senior investigators doing research of major significance. In fact, half (52 percent) of the future laureates were trained by Nobel laureates, most of the time before the seniors had gotten their prizes (1977: 99). The large proportion of future laureates having been apprenticed to older laureates is the outcome of the younger ones knowing which scientists were doing important research and electing to study with them (self-selection) and the somewhat older scientists identifying the young as highly promising and agreeing to take them on (social selection).[5] Future laureates therefore benefited from having early access to research at the scientific frontier and from socialization by scientists of the first class.

These young scientists, on average, became productive researchers early in their careers and remained so (1977: 146–149). Most met "demanding institutional standards" and "often greatly exceeded them," as the theory requires. For the most part, their talents were promptly recognized and many received their first appointments in elite universities (65 percent did so even though those same institutions employed just 9 percent of all faculty members at the time) and most of those who did not, found their way reasonably quickly to such institutions (Zuckerman 1977: 150–151).[6]

The evidence shows that these successful scientists did excellent scientific work early in their careers. It also shows how they benefited from processes of accumulative advantage. Working in elite institutions gave them more of the resources needed to get on with their work and provided interaction with scientists also working at the forefront of their fields. They learned from them and collaborated with them and were beneficiaries in this respect as well.

Moreover, their careers were not hindered by their being visible to and often the protégés of senior scientists who were gatekeepers in a variety of institutions—fellowship selection committees, research funding panels, and editorial boards of journals. As their careers progressed, future laureates continued to perform at a high level, often being rewarded copiously and thus gaining ever greater opportunities for enhancing their research performance.

The careers of these exceptionally effective scientists vividly exemplify the process of cumulative advantage. They call attention to the ways in which self-selection interacts with social selection in the allocation of resources and rewards to "provide a *stratified* distribution of chances among scientists for enlarging their role as investigators" (Merton 1979: 89). In turn, such scientists amass further resources and rewards which again enable them to enhance their role performance. Together, these processes produce and reproduce the accumulation of advantage in self-augmenting fashion. They also bring about the distinctive skewness in the distributions of performance and rewards in science as well as its elite structure.

Assumptions and Implications of the Theory

So much for a bare outline of the theory. Here, its principal assumptions and implications are examined.

The theory holds that *early* identification of promise will have both immediate and long-term effects on individual role performance and careers. Early identification brings early access to resources for research and the chance for scientists to establish a record of research performance. This, in turn, provides them with a head start over their age peers, this being particularly important in age-graded systems of evaluation like the one that prevails in science. Such systems benefit precocity and penalize late blooming; they put a premium on getting started early.[7] The longer-term consequences of early high-level performance are central to accumulative advantage.

However, the theory does not require that all those initially deemed promising will be permanently advantaged. It holds only that this occurs, on average, more often for these scientists than for others. Nor does it require that those who are initially disadvantaged will never come to be advantaged but only, on average, that this is less apt to occur for these scientists than for others. For advantage to accumulate, however, scientists must do some significant work at least some of the time; how much and how often is an empirical question not yet answered.

The theory also holds that scientists' past role performance shapes the opportunity structures they confront at successive stages of their future careers. Those who have done more in the past (who, as scientists say, have a "track record") are more apt than others to be given the opportunity to do more in the future, this in accord with the principle of meritocracy.[8]

But, of course, meritocracy does not always prevail. When functionally irrelevant criteria such as race, ethnicity, sex, religion, or other social origins govern the allocation of resources, the advantaged are no more competent on average than others and in particular cases may be less so. Here, disparities in role performance between the "haves" and "have nots" grow but only to the extent that role performance depends on access to resources. By contrast, when functionally relevant criteria govern resource allocation, disparities in performance grow especially rapidly because the advantaged have been selected solely on criteria relevant to high-level role performance. Not only are they more competent role performers than non-recipients but they may also use whatever resources they receive more effectively. In the former instance, then, advantage can be said to accumulate *additively* while in the latter, it accumulates *multiplicatively*. Thus, for all their similarities, these two models of cumulative advantage differ greatly in outcome.

> The resulting gap in attainment between the advantaged and the others [in the multiplicative model] is far greater than under the conditions of the additive model, in which the ability to use resources for further achievements is randomly distributed among recipients and nonrecipients. To the extent that resources are allocated to the same individuals on functionally relevant criteria [in accord with scientific merit] over the course of their careers, discrepancies in attainment tend to grow ever larger between the initially advantaged and everyone else. (Zuckerman 1977: 60)[9]

The combination of processes of accumulative advantage and a strong meritocratic emphasis in science also tends to reinforce marked inequality in scientists' contributions to knowledge. Indeed, such inequalities produced by cumulative advantage are often used by elites as self-serving justifications for inequalities in the distribution of resources and rewards and indeed for the sharply graded system of stratification in science. Inequalities in research performance and rewards are taken as evidence that the evaluation and reward systems operate efficiently and fairly, that those who are capable of doing the best work are most apt to receive resources and become most copiously rewarded. However, there is "no way of ascertaining whether other scientists would have done equally well had they been advantaged in the same ways as . . . members of the . . . elite" (Zuckerman 1977: 250).

So far, the objective benefits conferred by processes of cumulative advantage have been emphasized but these processes provide subjective benefits as well. These processes further encourage high-level role performance by providing recipients with psychic income, by reassuring them that what they are doing matters. The accumulation of advantage operates not only by providing stratified access to material rewards but also stratified access to psychic rewards.

Cumulative advantage and disadvantage should be particularly conspicuous when rewards do not merely provide personal gratification but can also be exchanged for additional resources. In some instances, of course, rewards and resources are not only interchangeable, but are one and the same. For example, the award of a major fellowship recognizes prior achievement and also facilitates further achievement. In the process, being rewarded contributes independently to scientists' capacity to improve the quality of subsequent role performance. Similarly, appointments to major departments of science in research universities serve as both reward and facilitation since such departments often enlarge scientists' research opportunities and the resources they can draw upon. This reinforces the upward spiraling of career achievement and rewards among elites.

In social-system terms, accumulative *dis*advantage is a correlate of accumulative advantage. Accumulative advantage for some leads to accumulative *dis*advantage for others. Accumulative disadvantage can refer either to relative or absolute deprivation of those not benefited by the reiterated allocation of resources, better role performance, and enlarged rewards. In fact, increasingly large disparities between the comparatively advantaged and disadvantaged can develop even when circumstances improve for both. Moreover, when resources are scarce and the run of scientists have difficulty in getting support for their work, disparities in performance can also increase between them and the few scientists who, under conditions of generally reduced resources for scientific work, remain relatively advantaged. The concept and the processes of accumulative disadvantage have received far less attention than those of accumulative advantage and provide opportunities for further inquiry.

Taken together, self-selection and social selection and the interconnections between the allocation of resources, role performance, and rewards contribute to accumulative advantage and disadvantage and these to the sharply graded stratification system of science. These processes are further amplified by the Matthew Effect and its contribution to the concentration of rewards received by the topmost stratum of scientists.

The Matthew Effect

The Matthew Effect consists in "the accruing of greater increments of recognition to scientists of considerable repute and the withholding of such recognition from scientists who have not yet made their mark" (Merton [1968] 1973: 446). It is the counterpart of the familiar observation that the rich become richer while the poor become poorer. The Matthew Effect is a special case of accumulative advantage and intensifies its self-augmenting tendencies. "This complex pattern of *misallocation* of credit for scientific work [is] . . . described as 'the Matthew Effect,' for as will be remembered, the Gospel According to St. Matthew puts it this way:

> For unto every one that hath shall be given, and he shall have abundance: but from him that hath not shall be taken away even that which he hath. (Merton [1968] 1973: 445)

The Matthew Effect can be most readily observed in cases of full collaboration and of multiple independent discovery, both being instances in which scientists' contributions are not just *comparable* but much the *same*. Senior as well as junior scientists repeatedly report that better-known collaborators tend to get credit for joint work at the expense of their lesser-known co-workers. They also say that credit for multiple independent discoveries tends to go to the better-known investigators ([1968] 1973: 443–445).[10]

In the case of collaboration, the Matthew Effect results from scientists assuming that the better-established collaborator has done the most work, even though no direct information is available on the relative contributions of the co-workers. In multiple independent discoveries, the more famous scientists get more credit mainly because their work is more visible and more easily remembered. In neither instance is the Matthew Effect the result of deliberate design. Rather, detailed information on the extent and kind of contributions by collaborators is scarce while in the case of multiple independent discoveries, the welter of scientific communications often makes it difficult to identify some pertinent research contributions. The Matthew Effect also comes about as scientists notice the work of already accomplished scientists, pay more attention to it and use it more often. Thus, on the psychological plane, the Matthew Effect involves processes of perception while on the social-system plane, it is reinforced by the enormous increase of communications in science.

The Matthew Effect amplifies processes of accumulation of advantage and disadvantage. It heightens the extent of inequality in scientists' standing and the influence of their work. In the case of accumulative advantage and disadvantage, inequalities derive, at least in part, from actual differences in the extent of contribution, differences which make the reward system appear to be effective and just. In the special case of the Matthew Effect, however, such differences derive mainly from judgments scientists make which are shaped by prior experience and features of the stratification and communication systems of science, both being unrelated to reliable information about the extent and quality of contributions of the various scientists involved in these conjoint events. These constitute consequential departures from the normative principle that rewards should accord with the extent of scientists' contributions.

An Intellectual Biography of the Field

The theory of accumulation of advantage and disadvantage did not appear full-blown. Instead, it emerged haltingly and piecemeal. In no sense did its development follow the familiar formal and often idealized model in which a set of propositions deduced from a general theory is subjected to empirical verification or falsification, with those propositions which hold their own being retained and those which do not, discarded. The theory of cumulative advantage initially developed as a provisional explanation of provocative and sporadically assembled observations and became increasingly elaborated as empirical inquiry focussed on theoretically pertinent phenomena.[11] As empirical research proceeded, investigators gave the theory new meanings, in part, to suit their own theoretical perspectives and, in part, to facilitate empirical inquiry.

Just when the theory of cumulative advantage and disadvantage was first formulated is one of those questions that intellectual historians relish but cannot decisively answer.

The idea-cum-phrase first appeared in exceedingly truncated form in 1942 in Merton's classic paper on the ethos of science ([1942] 1973). There, in his discussion of the norm of universalism, he writes:

Thus, insofar as laissez-faire democracy permits *the accumulation of differential advantages* for certain segments of the population, *differentials that are not bound up with demonstrated differences, in capacity,* the democratic process leads to increasing regulation by political authority. Under changing conditions, new technical forms of organization must be introduced to preserve and extend equality of opportunity. ([1942] 1973: 273, emphasis added)

Apart from underscoring the brevity and, some might say, off-hand character of this observation, I note two further implications. First, the passage suggests that there are two classes of differential advantage, one which is connected with "demonstrated differences in capacity" and another, which is not. It is the latter which violates the principle of universalism, is problematic, and calls for political intervention to maintain equality of opportunity. At this juncture, it would appear that the ways in which universalism, strictly applied, can also contribute to the accumulation of advantage were not being considered. Second, although the earliest intimations of the idea appeared in the special context of the institution of science, its connections with social stratification were clearly the focus of discussion. Later development of the theory mainly concerned science and scientists but need not have done so. As I indicated earlier, processes of accumulation of advantage and disadvantage are evidently widespread in modern society although they have been most intensively examined in the operations of science.

These early intimations were not followed up for a long time, either by their author or by others. They remained altogether fallow. Evidently, there were other ideas in that compressed paper on the ethos of science which did command attention so that the observation on the accumulation of differential advantages was not noticed, much less picked up and developed.

Indeed, the first forceful statement of the theory (rather than only the phrase) came some twenty years later in Merton's paper on the Matthew Effect, first presented in 1964 at the meetings of the American Association for the Advancement of Science, then as a National Institute of Health Lecture and finally put in print a comfortable four years later. The Matthew Effect, as I noted earlier, refers primarily to processes making for the *misallocation* of credit in science rather than to the general pattern of accumulation of advantage and disadvantage. However in examining the role of the Matthew Effect in concentrating resources and prestige in a few institutions, Merton clearly identifies the general pattern:

> the principle of cumulative advantage . . . operates in many systems of social strati-
> fication to produce the same result: the rich get richer at a rate that makes the poor
> become relatively poorer. (Merton [1968] 1973: 457)

It would not be until 1977, however, that Merton would publish a
more comprehensive statement of the theory in his *Episodic Memoir*
on the sociology of science. Here, drawing upon the illustrative case
of the career of Thomas Kuhn, Merton develops the theory of cumulative advantage as it applies to individual scientists, to scientific institutions, and the ways in which institutional and individual advantage
reinforce one another. He also examines the interplay between high-
level role performance and opportunities for further scholarly work,
precocity and its role in cumulating advantage, social linkages between eminent scientists (especially those in gatekeeping positions)
and younger ones, and the importance of access to resources, particularly to collaborators and colleagues of high quality—all of these reinforcing inequalities in performance and rewards. Moreover, he goes
on to make the central summarizing observation:

> The systems of reward, allocation of resources, and social selection thus operate to
> create and maintain a class structure in science by providing a stratified distribu-
> tion of chances among scientists for enlarging their role as investigators . . . *Mutatis
> mutandis,* cumulative advantages accrue for organizations and institutions as they
> do for individuals, subject to countervailing forces that dampen exponential cumu-
> lation. (Merton [1977] 1979: 89)

A case could be made then for the theory of cumulative advantage
and disadvantage having first been proposed in 1942, 1964, or in
1977—although the last option is plainly anachronistic since these
ideas had begun to have a social and intellectual identity by the late
1960s as others began to use and develop them further. Whatever date
one chooses, however, it is a central idea which has been around for
some time and one that has developed into an identifiable research
program.

So far, this account of the biography of the theory has focussed
entirely on Merton's central contribution. But as I have indicated, he
was not alone in thinking these ideas interesting. Soon after his paper
was delivered at the American Association for the Advancement of
Science (AAAS) and before its appearance in print, Derek Price (1965),
picked up the idea of the Matthew Effect. And not surprisingly, these
matters were vigorously discussed in our sociology of science group at
Columbia. Jonathan Cole, Stephen Cole, and I were, early and vari-

ously, taken by the notions of the Matthew Effect and of cumulative advantage (see S. Cole 1970; Cole and Cole 1973; Zuckerman 1970; Zuckerman and Merton 1972) as were Paul Allison and John Stewart (1974), Stephen Turner and Daryl Chubin (1974), and Simon Duncan (1974).

For Derek Price, who had been exploring the processes in science which lead "a very small core of good scientists, long-lived in their efforts, [to be] responsible for the vast majority of scientific work" (1965: 235), Merton's Matthew Effect was a thoroughly congenial idea. Price also noted that the tendency in science for excellence to be concentrated holds not just for individual scientists but that "this extreme inequality of science manifests itself in the distributions of . . . institutions and of fields."[12] Such concentrations in science are inevitable, Price asserts, and need to be taken into account by policymakers; " . . . science clusters round big people, big institutions, and big fields . . . science must continually play from strength and cluster round constellations of excellence" (1965: 235).

The Coles had a double interest in these ideas. In 1970, Stephen Cole undertook the first empirical investigation of the Matthew Effect, focussing on the impact of scientists' professional standing on the speed of reception of their work. Three years later, in their collaborative *Social Stratification in Science,* the Coles used the idea of cumulative advantage as a conceptual scheme for interpreting their findings on the careers of American university physicists, how "those who are initially successful have greater opportunities for future success" (1973: 119). They "conclude that doing good science brings rewards, and once those rewards are received they have an independent effect on the acquisition of further rewards" (1973: 120). Cumulative advantage is used here to account for departures from universalism in the reward system of science (1973: 119). The effects rather than the origins of cumulative advantage are of concern here. They also treat cumulative processes in their analysis of careers of men and women scientists (1973: 145–149) and take up the connections between cumulative advantage, labelling and the self-fulfilling prophecies that produce differential rewards (1973: 237–247).

A brief autobiographical comment may be pertinent here. I, too, found the complex of ideas of cumulative advantage and disadvantage illuminating while I was writing my dissertation on Nobel laureates in the early 1960s.

As that study proceeded, I had to confront two broad questions: first, to what extent had Nobel laureates done such excellent research because they were more talented and hard-working than others and to what extent was that research facilitated by social processes, which in conjunction with their unusual abilities and considerable efforts, enlarged their achievements and the gap between their contributions and others.' The interviews I had done with Nobel laureates suggested that many of them believed that ability alone did not tell the whole story.

The second question connected with the first: did the enormous prestige of these scientists simply reflect the extent of their scientific contributions or did they benefit also from social processes which enhanced their standing relative to others'? The merit principle would imply of course that prestige and performance would be in accord. But principle and practice do not always coincide. Here, as in the first instance, the problem was to identify the processes that intensified the already considerable prestige of these scientists. It was these interviews, as he begins the paper by noting, which led Merton to identify the Matthew Effect and the ways in which it heightens the standing of already distinguished scientists.

As the analysis of the laureates' careers proceeded, it seemed clear that they provided a prototype for processes of cumulative advantage. Moreover, their careers drew particular attention to the connections between their success in acquiring resources for their work and their capacity to use them. It was not simply that they were comparatively advantaged but that they were also especially effective in exploiting these advantages to enhance their scientific contributions—this producing the multiplicative as distinct from an additive version of the accumulation of advantage (Zuckerman 1977: 60). This distinction continues to seem important for analyzing both the process and the outcome.

For one thing, the different models of accumulation of advantage, additive and multiplicative, call attention to the fact that the extent of inequality between "haves" and "have nots" varies according to the criteria applied in allocating resources and rewards as does the rate at which it grows. The more often and assiduously the merit principle is actually applied in allocating resources and rewards, the greater the inequality and the more quickly it develops. Put another way, the more that functionally relevant criteria govern these processes and make for multiplicative rather than additive accumulation of advantage, the more inequality results. In short, meritocracy and marked inequality are inextricably connected in ways that are often not recognized by those who believe that it is possible to couple equality of opportunity and equality of outcome.

For another thing, the distinction between additive and multiplicative models of accumulation of advantage reminds us that applying functionally relevant (here, job-related) criteria, in allocating resources and rewards produces a sharply skewed distribution of role-performance with those performing at the highest levels comprising an elite of achievement. As I have noted, these processes have ideological functions also for they enable elites to claim, based on their superior role performance, that evaluation processes operate fairly and effectively, that the resulting system of stratification is legitimate, and that the advantages they have received are deserved.

Although the theory of accumulative advantage seemed especially apt in helping to account for the formation of the ultra-elite in science, it was clear much earlier that it had far broader applications. It made coherent a great variety of then scattered empirical observations about scientists' careers generally: the skewed distributions of research performance and of recognition and rewards.

Implications of cumulative advantage for stratification in science generally were explored in 1970, especially the unintended benefits which accrued to those identified as promising early in their careers, whose work was consistent with early expectations and who were "visible to those who make decisions on jobs, fellowships, research money, and awards" (Zuckerman 1970: 244; see also 236, 250). At much the same time, Jonathan Cole and Stephen Cole (1973) were using the ideas of cumulative advantage to make sense of the distribution of rewards to scientists over the course of their careers and among the various strata of the scientific community.

A further observation on the early intellectual history of cumulative advantage and disadvantage is in order. The decade between the mid-1960s and the mid-1970s were vintage years for sociological research on social stratification with the Blau and Duncan monograph, *The American Occupational Structure* (1967)[13] being a prime model for much of the research in that period. That study was not only impressive, it exerted a wide intellectual influence. There, Blau and Duncan were concerned with the extent to which ascribed rather than achieved characteristics contributed to social inequality. Their analysis of pro-

cesses of occupational attainment of American blacks and whites resonated for those of us who were interested in accumulation of advantage and disadvantage. For Blau and Duncan had demonstrated that
the relative standing of blacks and whites was not simply the outcome
of blacks having less access to education and holding poorer jobs. In
fact, something more was going on. Although educational attainments
strongly determined occupational standing overall, blacks and whites
with equivalent levels of education did not receive the same sorts of
jobs. In short, the returns blacks received on investments in education
were lower than those received by whites. It was clear to us that the
orientation of the Blau and Duncan study was quite consistent with the
one we had been using; comparing the rewards accorded to eminent
and lesser known scientists for similar contributions was much the
same as their examining the differential returns on the same investments for various subgroups in society. Moreover, that monograph
also reinforced our sense that the processes being examined in science
had counterparts elsewhere and could be conceptualized in similar
terms. It was also clear to us that students of social stratification in the
Blau-Duncan-Sewell-Hauser-Featherman tradition and those in the various Marxist traditions were unaware of work on cumulative advantage
and disadvantage or did not find it interesting.

This early history only hints at the existence of a body of inquiry
into cumulative advantage and disadvantage. These eminently research-
able ideas have given rise to further theoretical examination in the
sociology of science by Jonathan Cole, Stephen Cole, Jack A. Goldstone, Volker Meja, Michael Mulkay, and Nico Stehr. They have also
led to an increasingly coherent program of empirical and mathematical
investigations by Paul Allison, Judith Blau, Daryl Chubin, Jonathan
Cole, Stephen Cole, Mary Frank Fox, Jerry Gaston, Lowell Hargens,
Karin Knorr-Cetina, Tad Krauze, Scott Long, Robert McGinnis, Roland
Mittermeier, Nicholas Mullins, Angela O'Rand, Derek Price, Barbara
Reskin, Aaron Rosenblatt, Dean Keith Simonton, Robert Merton, and
myself.

Moreover, scholars interested in gender inequality (Shirley M. Clark,
Mary Corcoran, Vera Kistiakowsky, and Kathryn Moore), in studies
of careers of ministers (Broughton and Mill 1980), psychoanalysts
(Eleanor Schuker), Communist party members (Patricia Taylor), film
stars (Emanuel Levy), and corporate managers (Michael Useem and
Jerome Karabel) have come to apply the ideas of accumulation of

advantage and disadvantage. The Matthew Effect for its part has been examined not just in science but in education (Martin Trow, Herbert J. Walberg), aging (Dale Dannefer), information science, and library use (Stephen J. Bensman).[14] The theory of cumulative advantage and disadvantage is, it appears, diffusing into the larger domain of sociology—but slowly. The reasons for the slow diffusion are not altogether self-evident and while these have a certain intrinsic interest, this is not the time to explore them.

Nor is this the time to review the empirical findings of the now considerable body of research on cumulative advantage and disadvantage. To date, this research has focused on four patterns: (1) skewed distributions; (2) growing disparities with age in resources, achievements, and rewards; (3) reinforcement effects; and (4) the array of outcomes associated with the Matthew Effect. In brief, a variety of findings are consistent with the theory, but they are far from definitive at this juncture.[15]

The Theory of Accumulation of Advantage and Disadvantage: Some Unresolved Problems

The theory of cumulative advantage and disadvantage continues to evolve. Its constituent implications have yet to be fully identified, much less fully thought through. I mention just five of those implications here.

The first is most readily put as a question: if the processes of accumulation of advantage work as we have suggested, why is it that all resources and rewards do not come to be concentrated in the hands of a few individuals within each age cohort with the rest having none at all?

Robert Merton has long been interested in this puzzling question, especially as it pertains to scientific institutions—departments, laboratories, and universities—and has finally addressed it specifically in "The Matthew Effect in Science II" (1988). The same question must of course be raised with respect to individual scientists since we know that the concentration of resources and rewards is considerable but not total. The beginnings of an answer may be found in the careers of Nobel laureates. There we find that accumulation of advantage has its limits.

For one thing, there appears to be limits on scientific performance, these having both psychological and social structural sources. It is very difficult to continue to achieve at a high level, much less to improve year after year, as professional athletes are well aware. The same is true for scientists whose performance also varies from year to year. Moreover, success in science typically brings enlarged obligations as well as opportunities and these often interfere with continuing high-level performance in scientific work. It might be argued that the Nobel prize is unique in science in turning its recipients into celebrities, that the sequelae of the prize do not apply more generally to other successful scientists. To a degree, this is so. However, laureates are not the only successful scientists who find that new social responsibilities come with lofty recognition of achievement. Nor are they the only ones tempted into other positions which take them away from research. Success also sets in motion certain psychological processes which limit performance.

Some laureates find that they and others develop excessive expectations about the quality of their work and that these demands get in the way of continuing research.

There also appear to be limits on standing or prestige such that successive increments of recognition have less social and psychological significance than earlier ones. This holds for recipients and others. The awarding of the twentieth honorary degree or the dozenth award[16] does not elevate recipients in the stratification system as much as earlier ones nor are they apt to find them as gratifying.

There also appears to be a limit on the resources the system is willing to confer on individual scientists. The capacity of even the most energetic investigators to use resources eventually diminishes, making those in charge of resource allocation reluctant to concentrate them beyond a certain level. This reluctance is reinforced by a commitment to supporting the young and thus the need to reserve a fraction of available resources for them.

Thus there is reason to think that ceilings exist on scientific role performance, prestige, and resource allocation. Such ceilings prevent resources and rewards from being monopolized, interfere with cumulative advantage continuing without limit, and stand in the way of impermeable elites being established.

A second problem that needs attention can only be noted here: how does *dis*advantage accumulate? Is it only that nonrecipients become relatively poorer when recipients become relatively richer or is there more to the process? How do these processes operate under conditions of plenty and scarcity? Is cumulative disadvantage more common in certain fields than others and for what reasons? So far, too little attention has been paid to cumulative disadvantage in science and its possibly distinctive attributes. There is of course a substantial tradition of research on the culture of poverty which centers on such processes but the connections between this line of inquiry and the theory of cumulative advantage and disadvantage have not been identified.

Third, once individuals are beneficiaries of cumulative advantage, how long must they continue to demonstrate their merits by high-level performance? Put another way, what leads once-advantaged individuals to fail? To what extent are scientists with established records of performance given leeway if they enter an arid period in their research? Such questions have barely been formulated since far more theoretical and empirical research has concentrated rather more on success in science than on failure.

A related question is whether patterned differences exist among fields in the extent to which they allow for late blooming. Fields may well differ in the opportunities they provide for those who do not come into their own until comparatively late in the careers. Such individual patterns are apt to interact with social contexts to provide for comparatively high rates of early and late blooming in different sciences than would otherwise obtain. Yet little is known about such interactions and indeed, little is known altogether about the effects of social contexts more generally on cumulative advantage and disadvantage.

Fifth, last, and most important, is the extent to which the processes associated with cumulative advantage and disadvantage are generic, affecting stratification not just in science but also in other domains of social life. Indications that these processes may be widespread are found in studies of careers of individuals and institutions in politics (Taylor 1987), the professions (Broughton and Mills 1980; Schuker 1985), the arts (Levy 1987), education (Walberg and Tsai 1983; Trow 1984), and business (Useem and Karabel 1986), in both capitalist and socialist societies (Useem and Karabel 1986; Taylor 1987). They are found also in studies of the differential status attainments of academic men and women (J. Cole 1979; Clark and Corcoran 1986; Moore 1987; Zuckerman 1987) and of Blacks and whites (Farley 1984; 1987). Indeed, it might be claimed that processes of cumulative advantage and disadvantage affect structures and processes of stratification in meritocratic systems generally. Yet so little is known about extent to which cumulative—advantage and disadvantage actually obtain in different institutional domains, the conditions under which they operate and their connections with other processes of stratification, that this conclusion is clearly premature. It is equally clear however that these are the most consequential if unexamined implications of the theory; they require serious attention as the theory continues to evolve.

Notes

1. Such positively skewed distributions have been studied in other social institutions notably in the economy and in such diverse contexts as education, conformity to norms, language usage, and library use. Pareto's Law, for example, describes the positively skewed distribution of income and wealth ([1895] 1973) while Allport's J-curve (1934) originally described rates of departure from social norms and their extent. Zipf's Law (1949) describes an enormous variety of positively skewed distributions including city size, executive salaries, and insurance claims. Herbert Simon suggests that such distributions which are "J-shaped, or at least highly skewed, with very long upper tails . . . [probably arise from] a similarity in the structure of the underlying probability mechanisms" (1955: 425). See Walberg, Strykowski, Rovai, and Hung (1984) for an excellent review of the history of such positively skewed distributions in a number of fields and an analysis of their implications, especially for research and education.
2. The theory has since been developed by Merton (1968; [1977] 1979; and 1988), Zuckerman (1970; 1977), Cole and Cole (1973), Price (1976) and Gaston (1978) among others. See the bibliography for a listing of selected theoretical and empirical studies of accumulation of advantage and disadvantage.
3. See Merton (1988) for further analysis of the Matthew Effect and accumulative advantage as they affect the stratification of organizations in science.
4. The terms, accumulative advantage (and disadvantage) and cumulation of advantage (and disadvantage), are used in the literature and are interchangeable.
5. See Zuckerman (1977) for the ways in which apprenticeship to senior Nobel laureates may have enlarged apprentices' chances of receiving the Prize.
6. This is not to imply that the careers of Nobel laureates were entirely free of hardship. For example, Julius Axelrod, who later became a distinguished biochemist, was not admitted to medical school—probably because of restrictions on admitting Jews—and, in any event, would have had great difficulty paying for it had he been admitted. He worked as a chemist and research associate for fourteen years and did not get his Ph.D. until he was forty-three years of age, from the George Washington University, not one of the "distinguished" institutions that typically graduated his fellow laureates. Other laureates confronted similar obstacles.
7. For the connections between age stratification in science and cumulative advantage and disadvantage, see Zuckerman and Merton (1972, especially p. 53); Cole and Cole (1973, especially p. 113–116); Cole and Zuckerman (1984) and Merton (1988). Paul Samuelson once observed that head starts were no small matters in the scientific life, if one has somehow gotten a head start, all that is needed to stay out front is to progress at the same rate as others.

8. Two institutionalized rationales tend to maintain this pattern. One is normative—resources should be allocated in accord with the principle of universalism, that is, contributions to certified knowledge should be the main criterion used in deciding who is to receive resources for research. The other is utilitarian—since prior performance is apt to be the best predictor of future performance and since resources are scarce, efficiency is maximized when a scientist's track record is the principal criterion for allocating of resources.

9. See Zuckerman (1977: 59–63) on additive and multiplicative models of the accumulation of advantage.

10. An exemplary instance of the Matthew Effect in collaborative research involves the distinguished population geneticist, Richard Lewontin and his collaborator, J.L. Hubby. Here, one of two joint papers was cited far more often than the other—the one in fact in which Lewontin's name was listed first. They write:

    We seem to have a clear-cut case of Merton's Matthew Effect—that the already better-known investigator in a field gets the credit for joint work, irrespective of the order of authors on the paper, and so gets even better known by an autocatalytic process. In 1966, Lewontin had been a professional for a dozen years and was well known among population geneticists, to whom the paper was addressed, while Hubby's career had been much shorter and was known chiefly to biochemical geneticists. As a result, population geneticists have consistently regarded Lewontin as the senior member of the team and given him *undue credit* for what was a completely collaborative work that have been *impossible* for either one of us alone. (Lewontin and Hubby 1985: 16, emphasis added)

11. The ideas underlying the Matthew Effect, for example, may not have originated in the interviews with Nobel laureates but their development was surely stimulated by them.

12. For Price, these inequalities result from the characteristic pattern in science of "new knowledge being produced from old, rather than from any response to the wishes or characteristics of the society" (1965: 2235).

13. Andrea Tyree was of course a collaborator in the study.

14. In response to a preliminary version of this paper presented at the Russell Sage Foundation, Ronnie Steinberg observed that her own studies (1982) of the extension of legal rights to workers show that processes of accumulation of advantage operate in this domain as well but that she had been unaware of these ideas when she was engaged in her research.

15. Not definitive since empirical investigations of processes of accumulation of advantage and disadvantage must of course take into account the effects of differences in scientific talent or ability. These are notoriously difficult to measure, much less to measure retroactively as would be required by longitudinal studies including the past. For quite different reasons, needed data on the distribution of resources for research have also been difficult to come by. Thus investigations of cumulative advantage and disadvantage have not been as conclusive as one might like. Furthermore, some findings are not entirely consistent with the theory. In their investigations of the allocation of funds at the National Science Foundation, Cole, Rubin, and Cole (1977; 1978) report that scientists of greater repute are not significantly more apt to receive research support than others submitting proposals of the same assessed quality, nor are scientists associated with departments of high prestige. At the National Science Foundation, there is an explicit policy that evaluations of proposals take precedence over scientists' past performance in allocating funds, thus explicitly constraining the cumulative processes that have

been identified. Along different lines, Allison, Long, and Krauze (1982) find increasing disparities in published productivity in a cohort of biochemists, as the theory leads us to expect, but they do not find concomitant increasing disparities in citations. They go on to show, however, that a mathematical model of cumulative advantage need not imply increasing inequality in performance. It is only when the model takes "heterogeneity in the rate of cumulative advantage" into account, [that] inequality [must] increase" (1982: 615).

16. This is not hyperbole; Arthur Compton, the distinguished American physicist, for example, acquired twenty-four honorary degrees and ten other awards after receiving his Nobel prize.

References

Allison, Paul D. 1980. "Inequality and Scientific Productivity." *Social Studies of Science* 10: 163–179.

Allison, Paul D. and John A. Stewart. 1974. "Productivity Differences among Scientists: Evidence for Accumulative Advantage." *American Sociological Review* 39 (August): 596–606.

———. 1975. "Reply to Faia." *American Sociological Review* 40 (December): 829–831.

Allison, Paul D., J. Scott Long, and Tad K. Krauze. 1982. "Cumulative Advantage and Inequality in Science." *American Sociological Review* 47 (October): 615–625.

Bensman, Stephen J. 1982. "Bibliometric Laws and Library Usage as Social Phenomena." *Library Research* 4: 279–312.

———. 1985. "Journal Collection Management as a Cumulative Advantage Process." *College and Research Libraries* 46 (January): 13–29.

Blashfield, Robert K. 1982. "Feighner et al., Invisible Colleges and the Matthew Effect." *Schizophrenia Bulletin* 8 (1): 1–8 and commentaries 8–15.

Blau, Judith R. 1976. "Scientific Recognition: Academic Context and Professional Role." *Social Studies of Science* 6: 533–545.

Blau, Peter M., Otis Duncan, and Andrea Tyree. 1967. *The American Occupational Structure.* New York: John Wiley.

Broughton, Walter and Edgar W. Mills, Jr. 1980. "Resource Inequality and Accumulative Advantage: Stratification in the Ministry." *Social Forces* 58: 1289–1301.

Busse, Thomas V. and Richard S. Mansfield. 1981. "The Blooming of Creative Scientists: Early, Late and Otherwise." *Gifted Child Quarterly* 25 (Spring): 63–66.

Chubin, Daryl E., Alan L. Porter, and Margaret E. Boeckmann. 1981. "Career Patterns of Scientists: A Case for Complementary Data." *American Sociological Review* 46: 488–496.

Clark, Shirley M. and Mary Corcoran. 1986. "Perspectives on the Professional Socialization of Women Faculty: A Case of Accumulative Disadvantage." *Journal of Higher Education* 57 (January/February): 20–43.

Cole, Jonathan R. 1981. "Meritocracy or Marginality: Women in Science Today and Tomorrow." *American Scientist* 69 (July-August): 385–391.

———. 1979. *Fair Science.* New York: Free Press.

Cole, Jonathan R. and Stephen Cole. 1972. "The Ortega Hypothesis." *Science* 178 (27 October): 368–375.

———. 1973. *Social Stratification in Science.* Chicago: University of Chicago Press.

Cole, Stephen. 1970. "Professional Standing and the Reception of Scientific Discoveries." *American Journal of Sociology* 76 (September): 286–306.

Cole, Stephen and Jonathan R. Cole. 1987. "Testing the Ortega Hypothesis: Milestone or Millstone?" *Scientometrics* 12 (November): 345–354.

Cole, Stephen, Leonard Rubin, and Jonathan R. Cole. 1977. "Peer Review and the Support of Science." *Scientific American* 237 (October): 34–41.

———. 1978. *Peer Review in the National Science Foundation: Phase One of a Study*. Washington, D.C.: National Academy of Sciences.

Crothers, Charles. 1987. *Robert K. Merton*. Chichester: Ellis Horwood Ltd. and London: Tavistock.

Dannefer, Dale. 1987. "Aging as Intracohort Differentiation: Accentuation, the Matthew Effect, and the Life Course." *Sociological Forum* 2 (2): 211–236.

Duncan, Simon S. 1974. "The Isolation of Scientific Discovery: Indifference and Resistance to a New Idea." *Science Studies* 4: 109–134.

Faia, M.A. 1975. "Productivity among Scientists: A Replication and Elaboration— Comment on Allison and Stewart." *American Sociological Review* 40: 825–829.

Farley, Reynolds. 1984. *Blacks and Whites: Narrowing the Gap*. Cambridge, MA: Harvard University Press.

———. 1987. *The Color Line and the Quality of Life in America*. New York: Russel Sage Foundation.

Fox, Mary Frank. 1983. "Publication Productivity among Scientists: A Critical Review." *Social Studies of Science* 13: 285–305.

Gaston, Jerry. 1978. *The Reward System in British and American Science*. New York: Wiley-Interscience, chs. 7–8.

Goldstone, Jack A. 1979. "A Deductive Explanation of the Matthew Effect in Science." *Social Studies of Science* 9: 385–391.

Hargens, Lowell L., Nicholas C. Mullins, and Pamela K. Hecht. 1980. "Research Areas and Stratification Processes in Science." *Social Studies of Science* 10: 55–74.

Kantor, P.B. 1978. "A Note on Cumulative Advantage Distributions." *Journal of the American Society for Information Science* 229: 202–204.

Kirk, Stuart A. and Aaron Rosenblatt. 1980. "Women's Contributions to Social Work Journals." *Social Work* 25 (May): 204–209.

Kistiakowsky, Vera. 1980. "Women in Physics: Unnecessary, Injurious and Out of Place?" *Physics Today* 32 (February): 32–40.

Knorr, Karin D. and R. Mittermeir. 1980. "Publication Productivity and Professional Position: Cross National Evidence on the Role of Organization." *Scientometrics* 2 (2): 95–120.

Lawani, S.M. 1987. "The Ortega Hypothesis, Individual Differences, and Cumulative Advantage." *Scientometrics* 12 (November): 321–324.

Levy, Emanuel. 1987. *And the Winner Is—: The History and the Politics of the Oscar Awards*. New York: Ungar.

Lewontin, R.C. and J.L. Hubby. 1985. "Citation Classic." *Current Contents* 17 (28 October): 16.

Long, J. Scott. 1978. "Productivity and Academic Position in the Scientific Career." *American Sociological Review* 43 (December): 889–908.

Long, J. Scott and Robert McGinnis. 1981. "Organizational Context and Scientific Productivity." *American Sociological Review* 46 (August): 422–442.

Long, J. Scott, Paul D. Allison, and Robert McGinnis. 1979. "Entrance into the Academic Career." *American Sociological Review* 44 (October): 816–830.

Long J. Scott, Robert McGinnis, and Paul D. Allison. 1981. "Reply to Chubin, Porter and Boeckmann." *American Sociological Review* 46: 496–498.

Meja, Volker and Nico Stehr. 1989. "Robert K. Merton's Structural Analysis: The Design of Modern Sociology." In *L'Opera di Robert K. Merton e la Sociologia Contemporanea*, edited by C. Mongardini and S. Tabboni. Genoa: Ecig.

Merton, Robert K. [1977] 1979. *The Sociology of Science: An Episodic Memoir.* Carbondale, IL: University of Southern Illinois Press

———. [1968] 1973. "The Matthew Effect in Science." In *The Sociology of Science*, 439–459. Chicago: University of Chicago Press.

———. 1988. "The Matthew Effect in Science II: Cumulative Advantage and the Symbolism of Intellectual Property." *ISIS* 79 (December) 606–623.

———. [1942] 1973. "The Normative Structure of Science." In *The Sociology of Science*, 267–278. Chicago: University of Chicago Press.

Mittermeir, Roland and Karrin D. Knorr. 1979. "Scientific Productivity and Accumulative Advantage: A Thesis Reassessed in Light of International Data." *R&D Management* 9 (Special Issue): 235–239.

Moore, Kathryn M. 1987. "Women's Access and Opportunity in Higher Education: Toward the Twenty-first Century." *Comparative Education* 23 (1): 23–34.

Mulkay, Michael J. 1976. "The Mediating Role of the Scientific Elite." *Social Studies of Science* 6: 395–422.

O'Rand, Angela M. 1977. "Professional Standing and Peer Consultation Status among Biological Scientists at a Summer Research Laboratory." *Social Forces* 55 (June): 921–937.

Pareto, Vilfredo. [1895] 1973. *Manual of Political Economy.* New York: Augustus M. Kelly.

Price, Derek J. de S. 1976. "A General Theory of Bibliometric and Other Cumulative Advantage Processes." *Journal of the American Society for Information Science* 27 (September-October): 292–306.

———. 1965. "The Scientific Foundation of Science Policy." *Nature* 206 (April 17): 233–238.

Price, Derek J. de S. and S. Gursey. 1976. "Studies in Scientometrics, Part 1: Transcience and Continuance in Scientific Authorship." *International Forum on Information and Documentation, International Federation for Documentation* 1 (2): 17–24.

Reskin, Barbara F. 1976. "Sex Differences in Status Attainment in Science: The Case of the Postdoctoral Fellowship." *American Sociological Review* 41 (August): 597–612.

———. 1979. "Age and Scientific Productivity: A Critical Review." In *The Demand for New Faculty in Science and Engineering*, edited by Michael S. McPherson, 196–222. Washington, DC: Commission on Human Resources, National Research Council.

———. 1979. "Academic Sponsorship and Scientists' Careers." *Sociology of Education* 52 (July): 129–146.

———. 1977. "Scientific Productivity and the Reward Structure of Science." *American Sociological Review* 42 (June): 491–504.

———. 1978. "Scientific Productivity, Sex and Location in the Institution of Science." *American Journal of Sociology* 83 (5): 1235–1243.

Reskin, Barbara F. and Lowell L. Hargens. 1979. "Scientific Advancement of Male and Female Chemists." In *Discrimination in Organizations*, edited by R. Alvarez, K.G. Lutterman and Associates, 100–122. San Francisco: Jossey-Bass.

Schuker, Eleanor. 1985. "Creative Productivity in Women Analysts." *Journal of the American Academy of Psychoanalysis* 13 (1): 51–75.

Simon, H.A. 1955. "On a Class of Skew Distribution Functions." *Biometrika* 42: 425–440.

Simonton, Dean K. 1979. "Multiple Discovery and Invention: Zeitgeist, Genius, or Chance?" *Journal of Personality and Social Psychology* 37: 1603–1616.

Smith, David Lewis, Thomas Roche, and William Snizek. 1980. "Quality of Graduate Productivity in Sociology as Measured by the Citation Index: A Longitudinal Overview." *Research in Higher Education* 13: 343–352.

Steinberg, Ronnie. 1982. *Wages and Hours: Labor and Reform in Twentieth-Century America.* New Brunswick, NJ: Rutgers University Press.

Sztompka, Piotr. 1986. *Robert K. Merton: An Intellectual Profile.* London: MacMillan.

Taylor, Patricia A. 1987. "The Celebration of Heroes under Communism: On Honors and the Reproduction of Inequality." *American Sociological Review* 52 (April): 143–154.

Trow, Martin. 1984. "The Analysis of Status." In *Perspectives on Higher Education. Eight Disciplinary and Comparative Views*, edited by B. R. Clark, 132–164. Berkeley and Los Angeles: University of California Press.

Turner, Stephen P. and Daryl E. Chubin. 1974. "Another Appraisal of Ortega, the Coles and Scientific Policy." *Social Science Information* 15: 657–662.

———. 1979. "Chance and Eminence in Science: Ecclesiastes II." *Social Science Information* 18: 437–449.

Unger, Rhoda Kesler. 1982. "Advocacy versus Scholarship Revisited: Issues in the Psychology of Women." *Psychology of Women Quarterly* 7 (Fall): 5–17.

Useem, Michael and Jerome Karabel. 1986. "Pathways to Top Corporate Management." *American Sociological Review* 51 (April): 184–200.

Vijh, Ashok K. 1987. "Spectrum of Creative Output of Scientists: Some Psycho-Social Factors." *Physics in Canada* 43 (January): 9–13.

Walberg, Herbert J. and Shiow-ling Tsai. 1983. "Matthew Effects in Education." *American Educational Research Journal* 20 (Fall): 359–373.

Walberg, Herbert J., B.F. Strykowski, E. Rovai, and S.S. Hung. 1984. "Exceptional Performance." *Review of Educational Research* 54 (Spring): 87–112.

Zipf, G.K. 1949. *Human Behavior and the Principle of Least Effort.* Reading, MA: Addison-Wesley.

Zuckerman, Harriet. 1970. "Stratification in American Science." *Sociological Inquiry* 40: 235–257.

———.[1977] 1996. *Scientific Elite: Nobel Laureates in the United States.* New Brunswick, NJ: Transaction Publishers.

———. 1987. "Persistence and Change in the Careers of American Men and Women Scientists: A Review of Current Research." In *The Underrepresentation and Career Differentials of Women in Science and Engineering*, edited by Linda S. Dix, 123–156. Washington, DC: National Research Council, National Academy Press.

———. 1987. "Citation Analysis and the Complex Problem of Intellectual Influence." *Scientometrics* 12 (November): 329–338.

Zuckerman, Harriet and Jonathan R. Cole. 1976. "Women in American Science." *Minerva* 13 (Spring): 82–102.

Zuckerman, Harriet and Robert K. Merton. 1972. "Age, Aging and Age Structure in Science." In *A Sociology of Age Stratification*, edited by M.W. Riley, M. Johnson and A. Foner, 292–356. New York: Russell Sage Foundation.

8

Robert K. Merton's Four Concepts of Anomie

Piotr Sztompka

On the Significance of the Concept

Not many concepts among those used to grasp central aspects of the human condition are as influential as the concept of anomie. Perhaps the nearest contender is the notion of alienation. And not many articles in modern sociological literature have been as influential as that short piece of Robert K. Merton in 1938 entitled "Social Structure and Anomie." The only comparable case that comes to mind is K. Davis and W. Moore's paper on "Some Principles of Stratification." For almost forty years Merton's essay has been the subject of vigorous debate, and no more proof is needed of its continuing impact than our session today.

Most often the debate was focused in the sociology of deviance, and anomie was treated as an explanatory concept accounting for various forms of deviant conduct. Merton's clarification, elaboration, and application of E. Durkheim's notion was treated primarily as his contribution to the sociology of deviance. As S. Cole observed: "Until the late 1960s Social Structure and Anomie was probably the dominant theory in the area of deviance" (Cole 1975: 175). Even though labelling theory and conflict theory became more salient in the 1970s,

Cullen in evaluating deviance theories in 1984 writes: "Merton's perspective still occupies a central position in the field" (Cullen 1986). It still commands a considerable army of followers applying it in empirical research. On the other hand, the significance of the concept for a general sociological theory, as well as the centrality of its place in Merton's overall sociological system, has somehow been overlooked and neglected.

I propose to abandon for a moment an undoubtedly important but somewhat provincial horizon of a single sociological subdiscipline—the sociology of deviance—and to focus instead on the place of the notion of anomie in general sociological theory, and in the whole corpus of Merton's theoretical work.

Why is it so significant for sociological theory? Because it is a very powerful concept. First, it has a large, unexplored reserve of meaning; it is far from being exhausted in its heuristic fruitfulness for further, fine-grained conceptual developments. In a word: it has large *potentials of elaboration.*

Second, it indicates interesting empirical phenomena and important practical problems; it turns our attention to significant areas of research and application. In a word: it has large *potentials of relevance.*

And third, as a complex, multidimensional concept, it provides bridges between various one-sided perspectives on social processes and various separate fields of sociological study. In a word: it has large *potentials of integration.* For those three reasons, it has an important place in sociological theory.

But why is it also so central for Merton's own sociological system? Because it represents in a nutshell some of the most fundamental traits of his theorizing. First, it epitomizes his *structural and conflict orientation,* so often mistakenly identified as functionalist and static. As I argue at length elsewhere (Sztompka 1986), Merton's life-long preoccupation has been with the question of how a specific, contradictory, conflict-ridden configuration of a social structure constrains and/or facilitates specific patterns of human action, including deviance. And the concept of anomie is precisely about that.

Second, it illustrates Merton's interest not only in *structural determination,* but also in *structure-building.* He has always given some, though perhaps not preeminent attention, to the question of how certain structurally produced patterns of action feed back on the social structure, leading to its immanent transformations. The concept of anomie suggests at least two roads along which such structure-building processes proceed.

Third, it documents Merton's attitude toward sociological masters, rooted in his image of the development of science as *selective cumulation* of wisdom. In this case he places himself "on the shoulders" of Durkheim,[1] taking the concept from *Le Suicide* but extending its meaning and applications, and therefore seeing more, seeing further, and seeing better than the great predecessor. In his own terminology, he may be said to play a role of an "intellectual conduit" spanning two epochs—classical and modern sociology. This, if I am correct, is his crucial contribution to our science, and the concept of anomie is one of the best examples of such a role.

I will now try to give more substance to those claims. For this, we must take a closer look at Merton's fundamental notion of a social structure.

On Merton's Image of a Social Structure

It is not by accident that Merton titles his paper "Social Structure and Anomie." The idea of a social structure is clearly the core of his theoretical thinking.[2] What he means by that is, more or less, a patterned network of social relationships, making up a hidden, deep dimension of social reality and exerting constraining and/or facilitating influence on social life (e.g., on the actions and interactions, as well as the personalities of human individuals). Merton looks at human individuals as structurally located, anchored in the network of social relationships. The structural location of a person is described as his or her social status; an identifiable "position in a social system occupied by designated individuals" (Merton 1957: 368). A doctor, a student, a housewife, a father—are examples of statuses. Each social status, considered as the central building-block of a social structure, has three distinct aspects. Attached to it is a patterned set of social (shared) expectations concerning the proper behavior of any incumbent. This is the normative aspect of status, grasped by Merton's important concept of a "role-set" (Merton 1957: 369). Similarly, each social status has an attached set of "life-chances," options, resources, facilities available to incumbents. This is the opportunity-aspect of a status. Finally, each status has an attached set of patterned beliefs, ideas, creeds typically held by any incumbent. This is the ideal aspect of a status.

If one "brackets" the individual perspective and thinks of the social structure per se, as a sort of skeleton of the social world, it becomes obvious that for Merton social structure is not a unidimensional but *a multidimensional construct.* It does not consist exclusively of the *normative* "proscriptions, prescriptions, permissions, and preferences,"[3] as some critics claim in stubbornly labelling Merton as a "normative functionalist," but also of patterned, shared beliefs, creeds, ideas; that is, the *ideal* structure, as well as patterned vested interests, life-chances, access to resources, and so on, unequally distributed in human populations. In a word: what Merton designates as differential access to the *opportunity-structure.*[4] I believe that a valid representation of Merton's view treats the social structure as the combination of three dimensions (or levels, if you will), namely, the normative structure, the ideal structure, and the opportunity-structure.

Merton's pervasive concern is with the plurality, differentiation, and heterogeneity of the social structure: "The concepts remind us, in the unlikely event that we need to be reminded of this insistent and obstinate fact, that even the seemingly simple social structure is extremely complex" (Merton 1957: 370). And contrary to some simplistic and misleading accounts, he does not perceive social structure as harmonious, pervaded by consensus or kept in equilibrium. Just the reverse: malintegration, strains, tensions, contradictions, and conflicts within the social structure are the rule rather than the exception. To my mind, Merton is a conflict theorist *par excellence.*

Look at some of his central theoretical categories: dysfunction, role-conflict, sociological ambivalence; and—as our focus here—the concept of anomie. All of them refer to the "ugly face" of society, as Dahrendorf (1968) would put it. The concept of anomie stands out among them as it depicts particularly involved ugliness; it covers not only contradictions within *one level* of the social structure (mainly normative, as in the case of role-conflict and sociological ambivalence), but contradictions on all *three levels,* and even more importantly, contradictions *between* levels. To put it briefly, not only intralevel, but also interlevel contradictions. Thus, it is the only truly multidimensional concept of conflict in Merton's arsenal.

Owing to its multidimensionality it reflects better than other of the four concepts Merton's idea of *contingency and possibilism;* the assumption that structural arrangements do not determine human conduct in any simple, one-to-one fashion, but rather open up (or close down) a delimited field of possibilities for individual choice. The unique combinations of multilevel structural contradictions make a large variety of such "individual adaptations" variably feasible and likely. This is a message carried by the famous typology of deviant behavior included in Merton's classic article.

At Last: Four Concepts of Anomie

All this is only preparation of the field for the main claim of this chapter. We can now look more closely at those *structural contradictions* which are covered by the notion of anomie. Even though, in his 1938 article, Merton focuses mainly on one type of such contradictions, in later work he explicitly or implicitly distinguishes four of them. Those distinct types can be elaborated into four concepts of anomie.

At the most comprehensive level, dealing with the integration of normative components within the framework of a whole society, Merton claims that "full or substantial consensus in a complex, differentiated society exists for only a limited number of values, interests and derived standards for conduct" (Merton 1983: 53). He tends to assume the dominant reality of "cultural conflict," the far-ranging pluralism, ambivalences, and downright contradictions among normative components of the society. His general image of a society-wide normative structure clearly allows, under specified conditions, for prevailing deregulation of normative standards, a degree of "normlessness" or state of anomie. Indicating the significant origins of the concept in Durkheim's seminal work, Merton puts it this way: "The first thing to note about the sociological concept of anomie is that it is sociological. Anomie refers to a property of a social system, not to the state of mind of this or that individual within the system. It refers to a breakdown of social standards governing behavior and so also signifies little social cohesion. When a high degree of anomie has set in, the rules governing conduct have lost their savor and their force. Above all else, they are deprived of legitimacy. They do not comprise a social order in which men can confidently put their trust. For there is no longer a widely shared sense within the social system, large or small, of what goes and what does not go, of what is justly allowed by way of behavior and of what is justly prohibited, of what may be legitimately expected of people in the course of social interaction" (Merton 1964:

227). I propose to signify this first meaning of the concept by numerical subscript as *anomie*$_1$.

A special case of *anomie*$_1$ results from incompatibilities between various institutions within an institutional order. For example, in the educational order, the secondary school and the university may to some extent represent the same values and norms, may in this sense be mutually integrated; but they may also affirm quite different and even divergent norms and values (say: the value of conformity at school and the value of originality at the university; the norm of acquiring factual information at school and the norm of independent problem-solving at the university). Similarly, in the political order, the government may affirm autocratic values and the parliament, democratic values; while, in the economic order, the fiscal administration may emphasize norms of planning and the enterprises stress the principles of self-management and "free markets." Those examples may suffice to register the general theoretical idea.

Another analytically distinguishable kind of integration and dissensus refers to the link between norms and values regulating the same type of conduct. Again, the level of their integration is not taken as given but as contingent and problematic: "To say that these two elements, culture goals and institutional norms, operate jointly is not to say that the ranges of alternative behaviors and aims bear some constant relation to one another. The emphasis upon certain goals may vary independently of the degree of emphasis upon institutional means" (Merton 1938: 673). Norms may be congruent with values, in the sense that they prescribe behavior instrumental to the reaching of prescribed goals or incongruent with values, in the sense that the prescribed behavior does not serve to attain those goals, indeed may interfere with their attainment. In the latter situation, to conform to the norms means losing out in reaching the goal while if one retains the goal one must turn to the use of normatively proscribed (but technically more efficient) practices. Merton's example is taken from the domain of sport: "in competitive athletics, when the aim of victory is shorn of its institutional trappings and success becomes construed as 'winning the game' rather than 'winning under the rules of the game,' a premium is implicitly set upon the use of illegitimate but technically efficient means. The star of the opposing football team is surreptitiously slugged; the wrestler incapacitates his opponent through ingenious but illicit techniques" (Merton 1957: 135). More updated illustrations could include

drug-taking by competitors in sports or the financial undercover machi-
nations prejudging the score typical for some professional sports. It is
not by chance that a special prize instituted by UNESCO provides
rewards for outstanding cases of fair play; something which at least in
sports was once presumably taken for granted.

Merton addresses various modalities of incongruence between norms
and values in his theory of anomie, endowing the term with the second
meaning, as distinct from simple "normlessness," and referring rather
to the disjunction in the "norm-value" pairings. I shall signify this
concept as *anomie₂*. The polar forms of such disjunction include the
virtual atrophy of either values or norms within a pair. A less extreme
form occurs when "the original purposes are forgotten and ritualistic
adherence to institutionally prescribed conduct becomes virtually ob-
sessive" (Merton 1938: 673). The conduct of overzealous bureaucrats
or religious bigots provide fitting examples. And there is the opposite
form characterized by an overemphasis upon goals: "the range of alternative procedures is limited only by technical rather than institutional considerations. Any and all devices which promise attainment
of the all-important goal would be permitted in this hypothetical polar
case" (Merton 1938: 673). The domain of business, pervaded by the
overwhelming drive toward profits and economic success, provides
numerous illustrations.

The most extended and famous analysis examines one more type of
incongruence: the dissociation between normative structure and opportunity structure, described as a condition of anomie, in the third
meaning of that Durkheimian term. I shall refer to that concept of
anomie as *anomie₃*.

Merton believes that the full coordination of norms-values and opportunities is the exception rather than the rule. He refers somewhat
nostalgically to "those happy circumstances in which moral obligation
and self-interest coincide and fuse" (Merton 1973: 399) and elsewhere
maintains that "considerations of morality and expediency rarely coincide" (Merton 1973: 427). A more frequent condition is rather "the
disjunction between culturally prescribed aspirations and socially structured avenues for realizing these aspirations (what one of us has long
described as the 'opportunity structure'). It is neither cultural conflict
nor social conflict, but a contradiction between the cultural structure
and the social structure" (Merton 1976: 11). And it is this disjunction
that is precisely meant by *anomie₃*: "Anomie is then conceived as a

breakdown in the cultural structure,[6] occurring particularly when there is an acute disfunction between the cultural norms and goals and the socially structured capacities of members of the group to act in accord with them. . . . It is the conflict between cultural goals and the availability of using institutional means—whatever the character of the goals—which produces a strain toward anomie" (Merton 1968: 216 and 220). It will be noted that *anomie*$_3$ is, strictly speaking, a particular case of the dissociation or lack of fit between normative structure and opportunity structure. It occurs when access to opportunities somehow lags behind values and norms enjoining that action be directed toward indicated goals.[7] The opposite case, which Merton does not analyze, would occur when norms and values lag behind opportunities actually open to people, unjustifiably blocking their realization for all or some; in a word, by frustrating their vested interests. Example: anachronistic or obsolete laws, rules of etiquette, and so on.

The last type of interlevel dissociation, treated more casually and in large measure implicitly, obtains between the normative structure and the ideal structure, particularly that fragment of the latter which includes beliefs about norms and values, roles and institutions. In studying ethnic discrimination, Merton suggests: "Once we substitute these three variables of cultural ideal, belief, and actual practice for the customary distinction between the two variables of cultural ideals and actual practices, the entire formulation of the problem becomes changed" (Merton 1976: 192). He then mentions the types of immediate interest here: "so far as beliefs of individuals are concerned, we can identify two types: those who genuinely believe in the [official] creed and those who do not (although some of these may, on public or ceremonial occasions, profess adherence to its principles)" (Merton 1976: 192). Such beliefs, still treated here as if they were psychological, individual phenomena can be conceived of as patterned in a society and consequently as structural phenomena. Structural ideas about normative order are generally covered by the term "legitimacy" (in one of its meanings). Thus the shared, widespread, withdrawal of legitimacy from the normative structure must be treated as a state of ideal structure, not reducible to personal convictions held by this or that individual. At one place, Merton seems to introduce what I propose as a fourth concept of anomie, when he refers to the dissociation between normative consciousness (the fragment of the ideal structure) and the normative structure: "appreciable numbers of people become estranged from a society that promises them in principle what they are denied in reality. And this withdrawal of allegiance from one or another part of prevailing social standards is what we mean, in the end, by anomie" (Merton 1964: 218). This variety of the concept of anomie I wish to signify as *anomie$_4$*.

It can be seen now how the potentials of elaboration of the concept are put to work; how far Merton goes on from Durkheim's original idea, enriching, extending, and deepening it on the way.

Is the Typology of Any Use?

But isn't this a purely scholastic exercise in multiplying categories? Does it have any relevance for empirical research or social practice? Does it point to interesting problems and important issues? Here comes the second strength of the concept—its potentials of relevance. And the main point here is that only by moving from *anomie$_1$* to *anomie$_2$*, to *anomie$_3$*, to *anomie$_4$* can one conceptualize very significant forms and types of human action and explain their patterned occurrence. It is because various forms of structural contradictions covered by the four concepts of anomie delimit particular fields of possibilities for human action and make different choices *unequally* probable.

Thus, *anomie$_1$*, sheer normlessness, leaves the field for action wide open. In this fundamentally contradictory, inconsistent, incoherent world, "anything goes." Anarchic, chaotic, unpatterned behavior[8] is a likely result.

Anomie$_2$, antinomy between norms and values, produces a situation when deviance from at least *some* demands of the normative system (a partial deviance) is inevitable. It is not feasible to satisfy both kinds of expectation; the demands as to means and the demands as to goals. In effect, means become ends in themselves, or the ends justify all means. Evasion of some parts of the normative structure follows inescapably.

It is only when Merton leaves the exclusively normative domain, though, and adds the level of opportunity-structure to his analysis, that the picture of human action takes on more richness and color. *Anomie$_3$*, the dissociation between normative prescriptions and actual opportunities to follow them, produces the situation in which an individual is under pressure to search for *illegitimate* means or illegitimate ends or both. Various concrete configurations and interrelations of expectations and opportunity—discussed by Merton in detail—make one or another of the four famous "behavioral adaptations" more or less likely. To remind you, these adaptations are: innovation (following prescribed ends by illegitimate means), ritualism (following prescribed means with no consideration of ends), retreatism (abandoning both unrealistic ends and unrealistic means) and rebellion (actively pursuing illegitimate, novel goals by illegitimate, newly devised means) (Merton 1938).

Consider how much more vivid and exciting the picture of social life becomes. However one more conceptual step remains: the incorporation of the last dimension of a social structure, the ideal one. *Anomie*$_4$, the dissociation between normative prescriptions and shared beliefs, opinions, evaluations concerning them, is expressed in the *withdrawal of legitimacy* from the normative system. It produces the situation in which an individual faces a clear-cut dilemma; to act against one's own beliefs and follow norms and values considered as obsolete (or unjust or irrational or counterproductive, etc.) (opportunism), or to remain true to one's conscience, rejecting norms and values and acting without regard to what is expected (nonconformity), or even to act precisely against social expectations (negativism or counterconformity). Some will do this; some, that.

Taking the ideal structure into account also allows us to grasp another common type of action, what Merton calls "aberrant behavior" or "expedient deviance." In this case there is no withdrawal of legitimacy from existing normative structure, and deviance results only from the pressure of opportunities, which leads to the violation of norms and values, self-consciously adopted by a deviant. It is akin to innovation or rebellion in Merton's original typology, but, of course, it is a specific, distinct variety of those categories.

It is clearly to be seen that nonconformity, opportunism, negativism, counterconformity, aberrant behavior—are categories which are richer, more endowed with complex meanings, more pregnant with practical implications, than any of the earlier types. They are self-conscious, deliberate forms of conformity or deviance, whereas the previously identified categories are purely behavioral adaptations to objectively encountered field of possibilities. To put it metaphorically in order to bring the point home: there could well be innovators, ritualists, retreatists, and rebels among rats, but it is *only people* who can become opportunists or nonconformists or aberrants. A qualitatively new, and particularly telling, because exclusively human, dimension of deviance proves to be perceivable only in the context of the fourth concept of anomie.

All those seemingly scholastic distinctions provide an additional empirical bonus when applied to the crucial problem of structural transformations or *structure-building*. It is commonplace that deviance may lead to social change. But like all obvious truths it is highly misleading until one introduces more fine-grained categories. First of all, not every form of deviance generates structural change, some of them are clearly stabilizing, *reproducing* existing structures. This is certainly the case with ritualism, and to some extent retreatism (as long as not *all* people retreat). But also, though less clearly so, the same is true of aberrant behavior (expedient deviance). Thieves and assassins normally do not reform the normative system. Just the reverse, as Durkheim noted long ago, through the repulsion caused by their actions and through the mobilization of social sanctions, they unwittingly help to reaffirm and solidify current norms and values.

It is a different story with innovators, rebels, and particularly nonconformists. They may start far-reaching processes of structural reform, or even revolution. But—and this is a second implication of our distinctions—*the course* taken by the processes depends largely on the type of deviance initiating them. It seems that innovation, and to some extent ritualism, start structural changes via norm-erosion, patterned evasions, and finally institutionalized evasions which turn into new, emergent norms and values. On the other hand, rebellion, and especially nonconformity, initiate different, more direct and, in the latter case, fully self-conscious paths of normative innovations, the affirmation of new norms and values in behavior, their dissemination, legitimization, and finally, their incorporation into a modified normative structure.

Merton pays considerable attention to both kinds of structure-building processes, analyzing them in detail in many parts of his work[9]. Note that the concept of anomie allows us here to grasp a crucial, self-propelling or self-transforming capacity of a social structure. It describes a structurally produced condition, which, by facilitating various forms of deviance, originates significant structural transformation. It proves to be a central concept for the study of true social dynamics: immanent or endogenous social change.

The final strength of the concept, its potentials of integration, has been fully, though implicitly, documented throughout this discussion. To recapitulate: the idea of anomie seems to bridge the gap between the study of social structures and social processes, between the study of reproduction and the transformation of social structures, and also between the study of structural determination and structure-building or structural emergence. It provides the link between a sociology of deviance and general sociological theory, as well as a potential link, not yet fully explored, between a sociology of deviance and flourishing research on social movements and revolutions.

For one concept and one scholar who vindicated it for modern sociology, that is more than enough.

Notes

1. The allusion is of course to Merton's *On the Shoulders of Giants,* New York: Harcourt Brace Jovanovich, 1965, recently published in its vicennial edition (1985) [and now in its post-Italianate edition by the University of Chicago Press (1993)].
2. See especially chapters 5 and 6 in Sztompka 1986: ("On Sociological Orientation" and "On Social Structure").
3. I refer to this as Merton's "four P's" formula. See Sztompka 1986: ch. 6.
4. Two earlier levels are sometimes put together by Merton under the term: "cultural structure."
5. This was brilliantly interpreted by A. Stinchcombe 1975: 11–53.
6. Merton seems to suggest that $anomie_3$ regularly results in $anomie_2$ or $anomie_1$ at the level of normative structure.
7. Merton takes this case to be particularly consequential.
8. At least *socially structurally* unpatterned, as it may be patterned by biological necessities, physical environment, etc.
9. I deal with this aspect of Merton's theory extensively in chapter 7 of my book (cf. Sztompka 1986: 199–239).

References

Clinard, M., ed. 1964. *Anomie and Deviant Behavior.* New York: Free Press.
Cole, S. 1975. "The Growth of Scientific Knowledge: Theories of Deviance as a Case Study." In *The Idea of Social Structure: Papers in Honor of Robert K. Merton,* edited by L.A. Coser. New York: Harcourt Brace Jovanovich.
Coser, L.A., ed. 1975. *The Idea of Social Structure: Papers in Honor of Robert K. Merton.* New York: Harcourt Brace Jovanovich.
Cullen, F.T. 1986. *Rethinking Crime and Deviance Theory.* New York: St. Martin's Press.
Dahrendorf, R. 1968. *Essays in the Theory of Society.* Stanford: Stanford University Press.
Davis, K. and Moore W. 1945. "Some Principles of Stratification." *American Sociological Review* 10: 242–49.
Merton, R. K. 1938. "Social Structure and Anomie." *American Sociological Review* 3: 672–82.
———. 1957. *Social Theory and Social Structure.* Rev. ed. New York: Free Press

————. 1964. "Anomie, Anomia and Social Interaction: Contexts of Deviant Behavior." In *Anomie and Deviant Behavior*, edited by M. Clinard. New York: Free Press.

————. 1968. *Social Theory and Social Structure*. Enlarged rev. ed. New York: Free Press.

————. 1973. *The Sociology of Science*. Edited by N.W. Storer. Chicago: University of Chicago Press.

————. 1976. *Sociological Ambivalence*. New York: Free Press.

————. 1982. *Social Research and the Practicing Professions*. Edited by A. Rosenblatt and T.F. Gieryn. Cambridge: Abt Books.

Stinchcombe, A. 1975. "Merton's Theory of Social Structure." In *The Idea of Social Structure: Papers in Honor of Robert K. Merton*, edited by L.A.Coser, 11–53. New York: Harcourt Brace Jovanovich.

Sztompka, P. 1986. *Robert K. Merton: An Intellectual Profile*. New York: St. Martin's Press.

9

The Unanticipated Consequences of Action: Sociological and Ethical Aspects

Arnold Zingerle

Merton's Setting of the Problem and the Development of Different Analytical Frameworks

In the year 1936, Merton—then still a young scholar—published a short essay in which he decidedly proposed to study a hitherto underestimated matter: the unanticipated consequences of purposive social action (Merton 1936). At that time he was able to anticipate the importance which this matter would assume fifty years later. Everyone who studies the matter today recurs to Merton; and I doubt that this fact could be attributed in any relevant degree to the rituals of deference characteristic of scientific communities, though I admit that it would be very difficult to evade the influence of such a successful and highly estimated lifework as that of Merton. It is simply the acute sense of the problem conveyed by the author to the reader that makes this short essay indispensable even in today's discussions of the issue. It might be instructive here to reflect upon the historical, social, and cultural conditions of the scientific interest in studies on unanticipated consequences; we might try to examine some theorems of Merton's sociology of science on this occasion. Instead, I prefer to throw light on the topic as such, on the place assigned to it by Merton and on the background of other approaches to the topic; furthermore, on developments which took place especially in European sociological thought about the topic. In other words, I am concerned with a typology of reasoning and research on this subject in the context of more recent sociological ideas. My concern will thus not be with the further development of the topic within the intellectual biography of Merton; as is well known, the topic is present in many places in his work. It is sufficient to remember the study of Puritanism and science as a concrete historical field or the concepts of latent and manifest functions and the theorem of the Matthew Effect as related to theoretical fields. Starting from some peculiarities of Merton's essay, I shall point out different analytical frameworks for the study of unanticipated consequences. I shall then give an outline of three typical problem-generating contexts for the topic and I shall conclude with some remarks on the practical and ethical dimensions of the problem in connection with a comment on Max Weber.

The topic of unanticipated consequences of purposive action has, as is well known, an old tradition in social and political thought.[1] Merton's initial attempt to grasp the topic in sociological terms has a prefunctionalist action-theory design, and it is my conviction that the essay is indispensable precisely because of this quality. That is to say, it can hardly be replaced by an analysis mainly focused on structural conditions and consequences or functions of action; an analysis of that kind could only be a complement—even if in some cases a necessary complement—to an analysis in terms of action. It does not seem exaggerated to say that during the decades after Merton's essay the main stream of social scientists tended to lose sight of the phenomena of unanticipated consequences precisely because of the prevailing collectivistic orientation of theory. As an important part of this orientation, the well-known methodological principle of Durkheim to seek the determinative causes of social facts in preceding social phenomena, and not in the conditions of the individual mind, led to the elimination of the problems of unintended effects of action from the repertory of sociological thinking. Even the connection of individual actions with collective phenomena, which in some important cases constitutes problems of unanticipated consequences, must remain out of the analyst's view if he cannot recur to the action level with his conceptual tools.[2]

Instead of presenting an abridged version of Merton's very precise distinctions of the logical possibilities of unanticipated consequences and of their empirical referents, I prefer to sum up briefly what in my view are the main analytical advantages of Merton's procedure in the essay of 1936. They lie in the construction of types of cognitive failure in the assessment of the situation by actors with regard to possible unintended effects. The first two types may be read as corollaries to the Weberian type of instrumental rationality: the first refers to the lack of knowledge necessary for a correct anticipation of consequences, the second to the use of wrong information. The third type refers to actors who do not make use of the information they have at their disposal: either because they are pushed or blocked by the immediacy of needs and of interests or because they are dominated by values and by convictions to a degree that precludes a rational use of information (this second subcase can be identified easily as a corollary to the Weberian type of value-rational orientation).[3] In view of the universal importance of organizational life in modern society, I want to recall hitherto nearly unused chances of a transfer of these cognitive aspects to analysis of the behavior of corporate actors in the terms proposed, for instance, by Coleman.[4]

Merton has sought the genetic conditions of unanticipated consequences mainly in factors which limit or hamper a correct anticipation. He has never fostered the illusion that it could be possible to eliminate such fallacies in order to prevent unforeseen consequences. He took into account that even if cognitive fallacies were eliminated and actors anticipated correctly the consequences of their actions, the collective output of many individual actions could have reverse effects running counter to the original intention of each actor. Merton himself did not investigate this type of case further but, especially during the last decades, an increasing number of studies on this topic have been published. An outstanding example are the contributions by Boudon, who speaks about "compositional effects" which are to be analyzed through structures of interdependency (Boudon 1977; 1979). That leads me to give a very brief outline of three typical frameworks for the analysis of unanticipated consequences.

The main characteristic of the first is the unit of action. Analysis refers to this unit as the identical framework of all processes and intervening factors. Its particular strength lies in registering changes within the course of action, whether the effects occur outside or inside the actor. Merton, as well as Max Weber in some of his general statements on actions, can be placed here, but also for instance Wilhelm

Wundt with his theory of the heterogony of purposes, on which I shall comment later.

The second type of analytical frame refers to the unit of groups or, more precisely, the unit of group structures to which individual intentions and purposes are related. Many more recent studies of the effects of group membership diverging from individual orientations and values must be placed in this category. But also classical studies such as Michels's investigation of the oligarchic tendencies of political parties with democratic orientation must be placed here.[5]

The third type is characterized by the lack of a unit in the sense of the first two types. We have to distinguish between two subcategories. Within the framework of the first subcategory, individual actions are related to consequences which occur on a large scale without being attached to a definite unit. Here we must place all theories of the "invisible hand" type (Ullmann-Margalit 1978), which are concerned with the summative effects of individual actions, whether they are variations of the classic topic in economic theory from Adam Smith to Carl Menger (1983: t. 3, ch. 2, par. 4) or of more modern sociological conceptions like that of Boudon. The second subtype has no fixed conceptual framework except some underlying idea of unplanned long-range processes which lead to paradoxical effects. Max Weber's work on the Protestant ethic with its implications for long-range rationalization processes belongs here as well as Norbert Elias's conceptions of the concomitance of planned and unplanned processes (Elias 1977).

As some contributions on the topic have obfuscated the difference between the three types of analytical framework with the general label of "heterogony of purposes" (Stark 1967), I want to take this occasion to explicate the original meaning of this notion as given by Wilhelm Wundt in his writings on logic and ethics writings, in order to show that the term applies only to the first type of analysis which takes action as the unit, and that in this case the unanticipated consequences refer exclusively to changes within the course of action. "Heterogony of purposes" is understood by Wilhelm Wundt as follows: during the course of the action that is caused by will in order to arrive at a certain end, it is possible that because of the effects and secondary effects developing during the course of the action, the end varies and multiplies in such a way that the originally intended end is modified or not-intended ends develop. "Therefore," says Wundt, "the connection of a series of ends does not consist in the fact that the eventually achieved end has to be an imaginary part of the original motives of action, which finally led to the end . . . , but it is mainly mediated by the fact, that in general the effect of every single chosen action does not coincide with the idea of the end involved in the motive just because of the never-missing secondary effects. Especially those parts of the effect situated outside the original motive can develop into new motives or new elements of motives out of which new ends or changes of the original ends arise" (Wundt 1892: 266).

"Civilization" as Problem-Generating Context: Some Implications for Ethical Reasoning

In his essays of 1936, Merton makes a remark that can be taken as a point of departure for the construction of a typology of problem-generating contexts of unanticipated consequences; unfortunately, Merton himself has not elaborated this point nor has it been taken up in later discussions. Merton says that the unanticipated consequences are in general mediated through (1) "social structure," (2) "culture," and (3) "civilization." In a footnote Merton indicates the source of these distinctions: it is Alfred Weber's "*Kultursoziologie*" (Weber 1920–21),[5] the conceptual peculiarities of which may have caused the lack of reception of this aspect of Merton's essay, for they are rather unknown among sociologists even in Germany. A thorough explanation of those peculiarities would reach beyond the scope of this article. Suffice it to say that, following the theory of Alfred Weber, "social structure" encompasses the referents of the conceptual equipment of sociology as it is understood by the great majority of today's sociologists, that "culture" is to be understood as a comprehensive term for the creative forces by which each society is shaped in its characteristic form, by which the internal life of men is cultivated, and which find their expression in the highly valued achievements of the human mind such as religion, philosophy, and art; and that "civilization" is, in opposition to "culture," that part of human achievements in which human forces are bound and formed to master, at different and progressively evolving instrumental levels, the external necessities and challenges of life.

When we look at all the problems treated under the title of "unanticipated consequences," we can easily discern three problem-generating contexts related to the distinctions of Alfred Weber. First we have the large group of cases conditioned by social structure, as they are described in the various studies on the summative effects of individual actions or on the specific dynamics of organizational behavior. The second group refers to unintended effects mediated by culture. The complex of the "Protestant ethic" belongs without doubt to this group. With regard to analogous empirical cases we have to state great lacunae in the studies of historical sociology. The third group which refers to the civilizational complex deserves more attention in my opinion than sociology usually pays it. On the developmental level of modern society, civilization is dominated by the systemic connection between science and technical-industrial realization. Only today do we seem to be fully aware of the grave environmental problems and the fundamental problems of relation between men, culture, and nature which are involved in the technical-industrial civilization. With regard to our problem, an aspect which refers to the dimension of time is of central importance. The general acceleration of processes of life under the conditions of the technical-industrial civilization includes the attitude towards innovation and the norms regulating them. There is a fundamental break between the premodern past and our conditions of life, because rational economic behavior is formally oriented today towards permanent processes of innovation as such, without regard to material aspects, with the consequence that the acceleration of those processes makes it increasingly difficult to control undesired secondary effects by rational means. Compare, in order to reflect upon the entirely different conditions in the premodern era, the concept of time of Francis Bacon, who commented on the ubiquitous desires of men for innovations by pointing to time itself as the model of innovation which "indeed Innovateth greatly, but quietly, and by degrees, scarce to be perceived" (Bacon 1625: 101).

It is obvious that the civilizational situation of modern society contains particular challenges to ethical reasoning; yet this reasoning does not seem to pay enough attention to the implications of the analysis of unanticipated consequences of the problems in question. In his essay of 1936, Merton has also given an implicit indication of basic ethical problems contained in the topic of unanticipated consequences. In the final passages, he covers a great variety of empirical referents when he points to the dynamics of values which function to orient actions in a society with a certain degree of differentiation. Such an orientation may "release processes which so react as to change the very scale of values which precipitated them." This process, Merton says, "may in part be due to the fact that when a system of basic values enjoins certain *specific* actions, adherents are not concerned with objective consequences of these actions but only with the subjective satisfaction of duty well performed" (Merton 1936: 903). Or, action in accord with a dominant set of values tends to be focused upon that particular value area, while its consequences are not restricted to the specific area in which they were initially intended to center, but occur in interrelated fields ignored at the time of action.

Yet, Merton says, it is because these fields are in fact interrelated that the further consequences in adjacent areas tend to react upon the fundamental value-system. It is this usually unlooked-for reaction which constitutes a most important element in the process of regularized of the transformations or breakdowns of basic value systems, and Merton sees here the essential paradox of social action. The "realization" of values may lead to their renunciation. Merton paraphrases Mephistopheles of Goethe's *Faust*, speaking of the "Kraft, die stets das Gute will und stets das Böse schafft."

The most relevant empirical field for studies of this kind of unforeseen effects is the history of value-oriented social, religious, and political movements. Instead of reflecting upon this subject, I prefer to stress a theoretical aspect of the contradicting ethical principles connected with the problems which were expressed by Max Weber in the famous distinction of *Gesinnungsethik* and *Verantwortungsethik*: the "ethic of basic values" without regard to consequences on the one side, and the "ethic of responsibility," which in turn is based on the anticipation of consequences, on the other side (Weber 1926).

Weber, it is true, formulated this distinction within the context of political action. But it came up just during the last years of his life, during the same period when he was also writing down the sociological categories of the first chapters of *Economy and Society*. Thus, this distinction is a twin brother of the two basic rational forms of orientation in action, which he called *Zweckrationalität* and *Wertrationalität*, action-oriented "instrumental rationality" and action-oriented "value-rationality."[6] Several scholars have commented on this parallelism, but it is astonishing that most of them fail to point out clearly the relationship between the two distinctions that goes beyond mere parallelism.

Perhaps Weber's own terms help impede the understanding of the meaning behind them because from the beginning he opposes value

(*Wert*) on the one hand and end (*Zweck*) on the other. But a thorough reading of the definitions and explanations given by Weber himself will show that the core of the distinction lies in the opposition of values (or principles) and consequences. For Weber's definition reads as follows: "instrumental rationality, that is determined by expectations as to the behavior of objects in the environment and of other human beings; then expectations are used as 'conditions' or 'means' for the attainment of the actor's own rationally pursued and calculated ends" (Weber 1968: 24). In this sentence, the term "expectations as to the behavior" can be replaced, without the slightest violation of the substantive core of its meaning, by the word "consequences." This interpretation can be sustained further by the explanation given by Weber some sentences below the quoted definition. He says: "action is instrumentally rational, when the end, the means, and the secondary results are all rationally taken into account and weighed. This involves rational consideration of alternative means to the end, of the relations of the end to the secondary consequences, and finally of the relative importance of different possible ends" (Weber 1968: 26).

In other words, the link between the ethic of responsibility and "instrumentally rational action" is precisely the emphasis on an attitude oriented towards consequences as opposed to an attitude oriented towards basic, ultimate values or principles, and so I suggest that we designate the general distinction which covers the opposed twin concepts as the distinction between *axiological* and *consequential rationality*. In view of the basic relations between actions and consequences, this seems to have a clear normative significance for all problems concerning anticipation of the consequences of action. In a time of a permanently increasing need for regulative measures, the Weberian logic and ethic of consequential rationality offers a praxeology that especially takes those limits of action into account which derive from the awareness of consequences in the process of the realization of values and ends. As shown by many paradoxical processes within the science-technology complex of modern civilization, these limits are imposed by manifold limitations of knowledge, as Merton has repeatedly emphasized.

From this point of view, any work trying to cope with unanticipated consequences is certainly a troublesome undertaking. Still, it seems to me that it belongs to a set of specifically modern virtues that aim at the mastering of self-produced problems. To sum up, we have gone a long way from the despairing prophecy of the American essayist Henry Adams who, about a hundred years ago, after becoming aware of the tremendous acceleration of modern life, saw no other consequence than this: that we could not hope anymore to take lessons from history, all that we could teach would be how to *react* instead of how to *act* (Adams 1918: 497).

Notes

1. For a survey of the argument in the history of social thought compare Jokisch 1981. The selection made by the author includes Montesquieu, Smith, Ferguson, Comte, Tocqueville, Marx, Engels, Durkheim, and Max Weber. Wundt and Pareto are deliberately excluded. Merton (1936) also mentions Machiavelli, Vico, Graham Wallas, Cooley, Sorokin, Gini, Chapin, and von Schelting.
2. Compare Wippler (1981) and, for a criticism which (based on A. Schütz) elaborates the viewpoint of the actor as distinguished from that of the analyst: Merz (1982: 11–32).
3. See Coleman (1974) and the postscript to the German edition (*Macht und Gesellschaftsstruktur,* Tübingen, 1979) by V. Vanberg.
4. An unusual but inspiring view on this aspect of group-research is presented by D. Claessens (1977). For an interpretation of Michels's study on parties as a case of unintended effects see Wippler (1981: 255–258).
5. For the later development of this distinction, compare A. Weber 1951.
6. This is the translation by G. Roth and C. Wittich (see Weber 1968).

References

Adams, Henry. 1918. *The Education of Henry Adams: An Autobiography.* Boston and New York.

Bacon, F. 1625. *The Essays of Counsels, Civil and Moral.* Rev. ed.

Boudon, R. 1977. *Effets pervers et ordre social.* Paris.

———. 1979. *La logique du social: introduction à l'analyse sociologique.* Paris.

Claessens, D. 1977. *Gruppe und Gruppenverbände: Systematische Einführung in die Folgen von Vergesellschaftung.* Darmstadt.

Coleman, J.S. 1974. *Power and the Structure of Society.* New York

Elias, N. 1977. "Zur Grundlegung einer Theorie sozialer Prozesse." *Zeitschrift für Soziologie* 6: 127–149.

Jokisch, R. 1981. "Die nichtintentionalen Effekte menschlicher Handlungen." *Kölner Zeitschrift für Soziologie und Sozialpsychologie* 33: 547–575.

Menger, C. 1883. *Untersuchungen über die Methode der Socialwissenschaften, und der politischen Ökonomie insbesondere.* Leipzig.

Merton, R.K. 1936. "The Unanticipated Consequences of Purposive Social Action." *American Sociological Review* 1: 894–904.

Merz, P.U. 1982. *Zum Problem der korrekten Antizipation von Handlungsfolgen— einem Aspekt der sozialen Entstehungsbedingungen unbeabsichtigter Folgen aus absichtsgeleiteten Handlungen.* In *Unbeabsichtigte Folgen sozialen Handelns,* edited by H.J. Hoffman-Nowotny. Frankfurt am Main and New York.

Stark, W. 1967. "Max Weber and the Heterogony of Purposes." *Social Research* 34: 249–264.

Ullmann-Margalit, E. 1978. "Invisible-Hand Explanations." *Synthese* 39: 263–291.

Weber, A. 1920–21. "Prinzipielles zur Kultursoziologie" (Gesellschaftsproze, Zivilisationsproze und Kulturbewegung). *Archiv für Sozialwissenschaft und Sozialpolitik* 47: 1–49.

———. 1951. *Prinzipien der Geschichts-und Kultursoziologie*. Munich.

Weber, M. 1926. *Politik als Beruf.* 2d ed. Berlin.

———. 1968. *Economy and Society.* New York.

Wippler, Reinhard. 1981. "Erklärung unbeabsichtigter Handlungsfolgen: Ziel oder Meilenstein soziologischer Theoriebildung?" In *Lebenswelt und soziale Probleme. Verhandlungen des 20. Deutschen Soziologentages zu Bremen 1980*, edited by J. Matthes. Frankfurt am Main and New York.

Wundt, Wilhelm. *System der Philosophie.* Vol. 1.

———. 1892. *Ethik.* 2d rev. ed. Stuttgart.

10

Some Reflections on Latent Functions

Peter Gerlich

> *What we have not named or beheld as a symbol escapes our notice.*
> —W.H. Auden

Introduction

My remarks concentrate on five points. First, I sketch the background of my empirical research in Austria, particularly stressing the contrast between traditional legal and more modern social thinking there. Secondly, I refer to three examples from my work in which I tried, I hope with some success, to apply Merton's functional analysis or more specifically his concept of latent functions. Third, I add some reflections on Austrian political culture arising out of such theoretical interpretations. Fourth, I try to develop some considerations on further uses of functional analysis, and finally I conclude by presenting a few ideas on its political meanings and implications.

Legalistic versus Empirical Perspectives

In the country I come from, Austria, political science may have had a long tradition, but this practically disappeared during the nineteenth century while legal approaches took its place. The bureaucratic Habsburg Monarchy considered a legal perspective as an adequate method to describe and interpret public life. Modern empirical social science has had to fight an uphill battle against this attitude. This applies in particular to my discipline, political science, which was established on a permanent basis only a little more than ten years ago (Gerlich and Ucakar 1982).

Since then my few colleagues and I have considered it our task above all else to describe, analyze, and interpret our own political system. In doing so, we were and remain confronted with traditional legalistic understandings. These revel, so to say, in their emphasis on manifest structures and manifest functions and tend to ignore everything which does not fit these patterns. In the attempt to break out of these intellectual chains we have been helped a great deal by the methodology of modern social science, by doing empirical research, making use of it, and also by applying the conceptual instruments of functional analysis, especially as represented by the work of Robert K. Merton (1968).

I would like to describe how I personally benefited by this experience, giving a few—three—examples from my own research. Functional analysis and more specifically the concept of latent functions helped me at first to understand the implications of my rather myopic empirical research, it later guided the conceptualization of some of my analyses and presently may even provide the means by which we Austrians could come to grips with a crisis of our national self-understanding.

Three Cases of Latent Functions

My three examples are the following: first, a study of a parliamentary institution (Gerlich and Kramer 1969) which was undertaken in the mid-1960s under the guidance of Heinz Eulau,[1] who was one of the first to introduce modern political science into Austria; second, a study of the process of legislation which has occupied me during the last few years (Gerlich 1986); and, finally a brief study of the problem of the Austrian national identity that I prepared a short while before the Waldheim controversy arose and proved rather prophetic in this respect (Gerlich 1987). The study of the Vienna City Parliament—I may add parenthetically—was organized at the Institute for Advanced Studies, an institution founded by Paul F. Lazarsfeld, among others, who contributed so much to an empirically based, more sophisticated understanding of social reality. This study followed the pattern of so-called legislative behavior research (Eulau 1986: 179–204). We interviewed the members of this representative body and tried to reconstruct their role orientations from their own descriptions of what they were doing. To a large extent they described their official, so to say manifest duties: to represent their voters, to try to fulfill their campaign promises, to attend meetings, to speak in the plenary session, and so on. However, many of them also mentioned activities which were obviously very important to them, but which by no means constitute official tasks of the parliamentary deputy. On the contrary, these activities are even considered slightly illegitimate. The deputies described how they provided concrete services for voters who approached them. They accomplished what we call "interventions," bringing up individual cases to officials of the city and in many other ways trying to concretely support their supporters. As a matter of fact, we got the impression that these, so to say, unofficial activities constituted the main everyday concern of our respondents (Gerlich and Kramer 1969: 169–177).

I remember how I was not quite sure what to make of this. Our American mentor at that time suggested that we ignore these statements since they obviously did not concern the parliamentary institutions itself. But when I came across a copy of *Social Theory and Social Structure* (Merton 1968: footnote 2) and read the famous chapter "Manifest and Latent Functions" I started to realize what I was up against. Obviously our respondents partly described their participation in official or manifest functions of the representative institution and partly referred to something which could be interpreted as engaging in one of its latent functions (Gerlich and Kramer 1969: 191).[2] Parliament has manifest functions directed towards the whole electorate of political representation—that is the official case of representative democracy. But they also realize the latent function of servicing specific groups of especially party members or clienteles who in an extending welfare state obviously require such services. Since then I have found out that this kind of activity is going on in the framework of all parliaments, even nondemocratic ones, and the study of it has become accepted as an appropriate topic for research even by American scholars of legislative behavior (Loewenberg et al. 1985: 113–115).[3]

My second study concerns the process of legislation. In my conception this process not only includes parliamentary decision making but also what goes on before a bill reaches Parliament and—especially important—what happens after the bill becomes law and must supposedly be implemented (Gerlich 1986: 267–271). From the legal point of view, legislation is essential for government, since in Austria no state activity can be carried out that does not have a basis in a statute of Parliament. Lawyers also assume as self-evident that each statute actually becomes effective. It will because it has to. In order to find out what really happens I have conducted a number of case studies with the help of my students. We described the entire process and of course found that laws more often than not do not become effective, or at least do not become very effective. In describing the cases we look for certain cues. It is usually very important to find out which kind of group has in fact initiated the proposal and, so to say, is behind it. We distinguish politicians', civil servants', and interest groups' bills (Gerlich 1986: 357–368). The initiators usually pay lip service to the manifest function of legislation—namely to solve political problems in the interest of the public-at-large. And they insist at least outwardly that they have only this purpose in mind. But underneath you also find a more honest and realistic interpretation, although rarely admitted in the open. The legislative activity also serves specific group purposes. Politicians strive for reelection. Therefore their interest in a bill falters immediately as soon as the public has been told that the problem has now been solved by legislation. Politicians' laws are therefore hardly very effective. Civil servants try to justify and expand the activities of their respective bureaucratic units and (at least to that extent) they assure that legislation becomes effective. And finally interest groups: if the big groups agree—which is the rule in Austria—then laws are not only passed but also made very effective. In short, as soon as I know who has proposed a law and who has guided the proposal into Parliament and through it, I am fairly confident that I can predict how effective its implementation will be. To the manifest function of legislation, the solution of political problems for the benefit of the public-at-large, is added the latent function of serving needs of specific influential groups is added. In realistic terms, this latent function appears the more relevant. Lawyers of course rather dislike this kind of conclusion. But on the basis of more than fifty case studies, I feel confident about it. And these case studies have become rather meaningful through the application of functional analysis.

The third study enters more difficult territory. Partly because the problem of Austrian national identity is a complicated (Bluhm 1973) and rather emotional one and partly because it is (even or maybe particularly for a participant observer) difficult to conceptualize the problem and to understand what is going on in Austria at the moment. But my feeling is that functional analysis can provide guidance in this dilemma as well.

Already during the Habsburg period and especially after the dissolution of the Empire the German-speaking groups which today make up the population of the small Republic of Austria considered themselves part of a larger German nation. Because of this the Anschluss of 1938 uniting Austria with Nazi Germany was widely accepted even if there was dissatisfaction about the Nazi regime. During the Nazi period Austrians became much more aware of their specific identity and after 1945 greater efforts were undertaken to create an Austrian national identity. But these activities somehow remained on the surface and were conducted only manipulatively. Official Austria never really cleared up its past; it only ignored it and preferred not to talk about it. Politicians jumped proudly at survey results, which show that two-thirds of the population now agree with the statement that Austria is a nation. Closer scrutiny reveals that these sentiments are rather superficial and that the kind of strong identification which you find in more established nations is still lacking (Gerlich 1987). The Waldheim case brought much of this painfully out into the open. Both the president and the public were forced to remember their past, while trying to avoid it and resented the necessity of doing so. In functional terms, I believe that the official Austrian patterns of self-interpretation in their manipulative, harmonizing, and highly selective ways failed to fulfill their manifest function of creating a secure national identity within the population-at-large. I think that this has been on the one hand a rather dysfunctional process, because we do know that even ordinary people need a certain degree of national identification in order to be viable as personalities.[4] On the other hand, this lack of open self-interpretation has served certain latent functions. It has made internal social peace possible, it has protected those who were implicated in the Nazi period and in general it has helped to lay the groundwork for the reconstruction and prosperity of Austria after the Second World War; at a price however which has, for a long time, been underestimated.[5]

A Double-Edged Political Culture

In summarizing these empirical results a few more general remarks about Austrian political culture are in order. The very notions of manifest and latent functions alert us to the universal fact that in social and political life what is presented to the outside does not always correspond to hidden meanings and internal understandings. However I believe that this differentiation is carried to greater lengths in Austria than in many other countries. Official versions of things are full-heartedly presented to the public by politicians and other functionaries even if insiders know that in reality everything is different (Pelinka 1985: 9). This double-cdged or maybe ambivalent strategy also applies to political controversy. Let me try to give an example. Insiders describe how Austrian top politicians exchange friendly private information in the TV studio before the lights go on. When this happens, they switch from second to third person, start to shout at each other, and can hardly be restrained from physical attacks. After the lights go off again, they return to second person, congratulate each other and go off to the Heurigen together. The mass media go along with this kind of behavior, that is they don't expose it, mostly because they can be considered only formally and not really independent. Of course parts of the public resent this kind of double-dealing and, to my mind, that is one reason why the gap between voters and established parties widens and alternative movements receive increasing support (Gerlich 1985).[6]

I believe that there are *both* cultural and functional reasons for these patterns. The smallness of the country and the closeness of its elite, bureaucratic traditions of conflict avoidance and resistance to change on the one hand and the understanding that this kind of manipulative strategy serves the interests of entrenched power groups on the other, may play a role. However, some time-processes of change seem to be at work. The recent return to grand coalition government may be interpreted as an attempt to stop or even reverse these trends.

The Uses of Functional Analysis

But let us return, in perhaps a self-exemplifying way, to the functions of functional analysis. I think that my case studies and the general interpretations based on them demonstrate that it continues to play an important role in empirical social science. This certainly holds true if one applies the clear structure and detailed procedures which Robert K. Merton has proposed in his paradigm for functional analysis. I must say that I have always been rather critical of what has been described as classical functionalism. It seems rather naive and ideologically biased to me. In contrast, upon rereading it now I was again impressed by Merton's pragmatic concept of functional analysis (Merton 1968). His paradigm provides a framework for empirical research, particularly of a micro variety, makes it possible to put empirical findings into a larger context and even makes mere description of social and political phenomena more meaningful. More specifically, as I have tried to demonstrate, it may lead one to the discovery of latent functions, which I feel is a particularly suitable task for political science. It may also help to direct one's inquiry, to formulate hypotheses or to understand events or attitudes, which are at first difficult to explain.

It is interesting to note that the concepts of functional equivalents and functional requisites can also be meaningfully applied to the case studies I have presented. When Austria introduced an ombudsman institution a few years ago, the so-called *Volksanwaltschaft*, to which citizens can address any kind of complaint, it was quite clear to me that the function of this institution was to take some of the service load off the shoulders of parliamentary deputies and thus to serve the popular need for such kind of individual assistance. This assumption is supported to some extent by the fact that at once, and ever since, retired parliamentarians have been appointed to the three-person board of this body.

The Austrian institution of Social Partnership (Gerlich, Grande, and Müller 1986), the corporatist agreement which the big Austrian interest groups use to solve their problems by compromise and mutual adjustment demonstrates how the functional requirement of effective problem solving of specific interests is realized even outside formal legislative channels. Social Partnership has virtually become a second arena of decision making within the Austrian political system, in a sense even competing with Parliament and the executive.

Finally I might mention that the functional requirement of large-scale group identification is at least partly fulfilled by the development of a regional identity within the states or provinces of the Austrian federal system. In this development, I see a further example of the processes of political localism which Carlo Mongardini has analyzed in one of his recent papers.[7] A Tyrolean or Carinthian may even be a Tyrolean or Carinthian first and an Austrian only second (Bruckmüller 1984). It is also remarkable that a much more open and realistic attitude toward even the difficult parts of our history may be observed on the provincial level.

Political Implications of Latent Functions

As just mentioned I consider the description or discovery of latent functions a task that is particularly suited for political science. Political science is about power. It must describe and analyze how power is acquired, distributed, and made use of. These processes often take place in secret (Friedrick 1972: 175 ff.).[8] Ethnologists observe that it is easy to get information in everyday life situations, but gets more and more difficult as you get up higher within the social structure, because power, so to say, naturally tries to hide itself (Blok 1985: 30). Traditional systems in particular try to shroud government activity in secrecy. At least by intention, the process of democratization has also and always been a process of increasing publicity concerning all matters of government and politics (Friedrick 1972: 175 ff.). In this process, social and more particularly political science will contribute its part by collecting information and ultimately making it also available to the citizen-at-large. In Austria we certainly interpret our role in this way (Gerlich 1973: 1–18). And the analysis of latent functions will of course often be a very functional instrument in this respect. It does not come as a surprise, however, that such analytical activity is not always liked by those whose interests are at stake. Groups and individuals, who might be considered gatekeepers of inside understanding, protectors of latency if you will, frequently object to the findings and interpretations of our analysis. Politicians were quick to state that we had completely misunderstood the role of a deputy. High civil servants wrote articles pointing out that legislation was far too important an activity to be analyzed by so-called political scientists, who understand nothing of the law. Journalists resent our analysis of the role of the media and do not hesitate to tell this to their readers and viewers. Finally, whoever doubts the strength of Austria's national feeling, the sincerity of her understanding of the past is attacked from all sides.

I do not want to complain. Social science should not be immune from criticism. On the contrary. But it should also not become discouraged and give in to the temptation to analyze and describe only the obvious, only the manifest, official structures and processes. I think that the analysis of the more hidden and latent processes and functions is politically important not only in order to inform and enlighten the public within a democratic political system. It is also important because social science will never be able to provide relevant or even essential contributions to policy-making without the inclusion of latent aspects. I do not think that social scientists should as a rule become politicians themselves. But I do think it is their task to provide information for decision makers that can assist and evaluate policy-making. Without such information reform politics is often doomed to failure. Many politicians apparently do not yet realize that. My own research on legislative inefficiency for example provides many illustrations for Robert K. Merton's statement, with which I would like to close these reflections: "To seek social change without due recognition of the manifest and latent functions performed by the social organization undergoing change, is to indulge in social ritual rather than social engineering" (Merton 1968: 135).

Notes

1. See Eulau 1986. This collection of articles covering a life span of scholarly work also contains an abbreviated version of Eulau's *The Behavioral Persuasion in Politics,* which influenced us a great deal when first published (see pp. 19–75).
2. Later on I elaborated this analysis on the level of the national Parliament as well. See Gerlich 1973: 42.
3. The problems of representation in the contemporary world are also discussed by Mongardini (1985: 115–125).
4. This is especially stressed by Noelle-Neumann and Köcher 1987. Of course the Germans also have problems with respect to their national identity.
5. In this respect one might also refer to the high levels of indicators of individual troubles in Austria such as suicides, alcoholism, and psychosomatic illness, which contrast strongly with the obviously high levels of social peace. See Ringel 1984.
6. See also Mongardini (1985) for a more general-level discussion of the connected transformation of representative institutions.
7. The tendency towards political localism is also stressed by Mongardini 1985.
8. See Bok 1971. Both authors, and particularly the latter, do however stress that secrecy may in certain respects also be quite functional in government and politics (p. 171 ff.).
9. In this context I also explicitly proposed functional analysis as one of the appropriate methodological approaches of political science.

References

Blok, A. 1985. *Anthropologische Perspektiven.* Stuttgart: Klett.
Bluhm, W.T. 1973. *Building an Austrian Nation.* New Haven: Yale University Press.
Bok, S. 1982. *Secrets: On the Ethics of Concealment and Revelation.* New York: Pantheon.
Bruckmüller, E. 1984. *Nation Österreich: Sozialhistorische Aspekte ihrer Entwicklung.* Vienna: Böhlau.
Eulau, H. 1986. *Politics, Self and Society.* Cambridge, MA: Harvard University Press.

196   Robert K. Merton and Contemporary Sociology

Friedrich, C.J. 1972. *The Pathology of Politics*. New York: Harper & Row.

Gerlich, P. 1973. *Parlamentarische Kontrolle im politischen System*. Vienna: Springer.

———. 1985. "Ernstnehmen oder Augenzwinkern: Grün-Alternative Herausforderungen der traditionellen Politik." In *Demokratierituale*, edited by F. Plasser et al. Vienna: Böhlau.

———, ed. 1986. "Cause and Consequence in Legislation." *EJPR* 3, special issue.

———. 1987. "Nationalbewutsein und nationale Identität in Österreich." In *Das österreichische Parteiensystem*, edited by A. Pelinka and F. Plasser. Vienna: Böhlau.

Gerlich, P., E. Grande, and W.C. Müller, eds. 1986. *Sozialpartnerschaft in der Krise*. Vienna: Böhlau.

Gerlich, P. and H. Kramer. 1969. *Abgeordnete in der Parteiendemokratie*. Vienna: Geschichte und Politik.

Gerlich, P., E. Talos, and K. Ucakar. 1982. "Austria." In *International Handbook of Political Science*, edited by W.G. Andrews. Westport, CT: Greenwood Press.

Loewenberg, G. et al., eds. 1985. *Handbook of Legislative Research*. Cambridge, MA: Harvard University Press.

Merton, R.K. 1968. *Social Theory and Social Structure*. Enlarged edition. New York: Free Press.

Mongardini, C. [1985] 1987. "Crisis and Transformation in Political Representation in Western Europe." Paper presented at the International Symposium on The Crisis of Representative Democracy and Possible Alternatives, Geneva. Published in *The Crisis of Representative Democracy*, edited by H. Köchler. Frankfurt: P. Lang.

Noelle-Neumann, E. and R. Köcher. 1987. *Die verletzte Nation*. Stuttgart: DVA.

Pelinka, A. 1985. *Windstille: Klagen über Österreich*. Vienna: Medusa.

Ringel, E. 1984. *Die österreichische Seele*. Vienna: Böhlau.

11

Patterns of Manifest and Latent Influence: A Double Case Study of Influences on and from Robert K. Merton

Charles Crothers

Introduction

Mertonian formulations are unfortunately undervalued in contemporary debates in *general* social theory. This is largely due to the way in which Professor Merton works. Let me briefly sketch an analogy of the overall organization of Merton's very large stock of ideas. It is *unlike* the disorderly bedrooms of my children with their scattered heaps of untidy clothes. *No,* Merton is very careful in folding up his clothes neatly. But he does tend to leave them scattered about all around the room. What is needed is for the underlying semiconscious plan which I have, on occasion, had the temerity to attempt to scold Professor Merton for not being more systematic with the wider frameworks which undergird his more specific insights. I have as much success as I do in encouraging my children to tidy their rooms. Perhaps his style is similar to that of Goffman, who had a similar ability to fashion creative analytical insights, but is frustrating to systematize.

This chapter has five sections. In the first I attempt to develop a Mertonian approach in the sociology of knowledge. This, I see as centered around the investigation of manifest and latent influences on ideas that are employed in a particular social group.

But any attempt to trace influences on ideas must be based on very careful analysis of the set of ideas being studied. In my second section I provide my conceptualization of the basic units in Merton's theoretical apparatus, and the relationships amongst these.

The third and fourth sections provide two case studies: one, of the ideas influencing Merton; and the other, of the influence of his ideas on others. These case studies attempt to illustrate the model of patterns of influence sketched in the first section.

Rather than provide a concluding section, I intend instead to map out those areas in the overall framework of Merton's theoretical apparatus which I think are most in need of further theoretical work.

This chapter provides only an overview of the rather large topic it attempts to address, but it does attempt to establish a framework which can be built on.

Towards a Mertonian Sociology of Knowledge

Most commentators would see the "sociology of science" as Merton's "first love." Instead, I suggest that his constantly returning attention to issues in the sociology of knowledge betrays an even more abiding passionate interest in this area of study, which is a deeper and more general arena of analysis than the sociology of science. Although his work in these two areas of sociological inquiry is related, I do not think that it is correct to suggest that his sociology of science is formally derived from his sociology of knowledge in the way that some commentators imply. Merton's interest in the sociology of knowledge is a countertheme threaded through the more substantial research and writing programs (such as in the sociology of science) he has been concerned with during his career. The very depth of this interest to Merton is paradoxically measured in the irregular but recurrent attention to raising problems and indicating lines of solution in the sociology of knowledge, and to the glancing mode of attention to these.

But despite his recurring attention he has yet to develop an adequate statement of his sociology of knowledge. He continues to flirt, and not to attempt a systematic seduction.

Yet I think that a Mertonian model of the sociology of knowledge *can* be sketched out. This focuses on the set of ideas held by a social system. Or, more accurately, the set of ideas produced and constantly reproduced by a social system. A Mertonian analysis might begin with a description of these ideas. Merton's concern with systematically laying-out the central idea-units in any area of inquiry, and with depicting the relationship between these is made clear in his concept of a "paradigm."

But the main concern in a Mertonian approach would lie in providing a sociological explanation of how those ideas (rather than others) had been produced. In other words, what the *influences* leading to the holding of these ideas have been.

It must be recognized that the study of the influence of ideas is as difficult as the study of influence in political spheres. As in the study of power, influences in the knowledge sphere take several forms, and we must be alert to differences between the apparent or manifest wielding of influence, and the latent unrecognized and unarticulated shaping of influence. The surface forms of influence may be particularly important, but they also may represent socially required patterns of obeisance or the effects of political maneuverings. The shaping by unconscious sources may be powerful because it already prejudges the choices that appear to be under the control of the scholar. (Merton has pointed to the phenomenon of "Obliteration by Incorporation"—OBI— as a particularly powerful, and of course latent, mode of influence). It is necessary to trace through the patterns of influence at both manifest and latent levels.

In carrying out any explanation of influences on the adoption of ideas there would be a full deployment of the Mertonian theoretical apparatus (an adaptation of the schema to be laid out in the next section). The idea-producers would be shown to be located in particular status-and-role structures, to be limited by the various stocks of ideas available in their culture amongst which they select, and to be subject to different motivations and concerns as a result of the cultural values they share. These cultural and social frameworks would be shown to shape the *choice*-situations within which the idea-producers "work." Lastly, a Mertonian sociology of knowledge would show how the consequences of choices made in producing knowledge feedback to shape the knowledge-structures themselves.

If the area of knowledge concerned grows cumulatively, later decisions about knowledge will be affected by prior additions to the stock. Thus, the loop of the analysis is closed.

TABLE 11.1
Extended Model of Merton's System

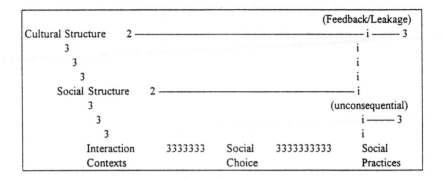

Before going on to apply this Mertonian perspective to the influences on and from Merton, I need to carry out a further preliminary task which is to lay out the architecture of Merton's theoretical framework. This involves attempting to identify the key unit-ideas in Merton's approach, and the relationships amongst these.

The Architecture of Merton's Theoretical System

In another study (Crothers 1987) I have been able to build on a remarkably acute essay by Arthur Stinchcombe (1975: 11–53) to provide an extended model of the operation of Merton's theoretical system. The key components in this model are depicted in table 11.1.

The first major component in Merton's analytical approach is the cultural structure, which is seen as a complex and often inconsistent set of ideas and meanings (knowledge, beliefs, values, conceptions and explanations, stocks of information) which shape and motivate human activity.

The second major component involves social structures (composed of people in statuses-and-roles, and more or less mobilized groupings based on these categories, and involving the differential distribution of resources and other properties to these positions). Social structure acts to amplify or dampen the influences set up by the cultural structure.

The third major component is the culturally and socially structured choice-situations with which people are presented, as portrayed in the anomie and other paradigms. In this component of his approach, Merton provides a logically organized framework of the dimensions of the choice-situation that people face, set at a rather more analytically abstract level than the somewhat wider array of particular forms of choice which may be empirically available. But this device usefully allows a focused description and then analysis of the influences which bear down on particular choices.

The last major component is the feedback and/or leakage effects of behavior (arising from choices) back onto cultural and social structures (feeding-back onto the structures which shaped the choice-situation in the first place, or leaking out, through the simultaneous occupancy of several statuses, to other structures. Usually, behavior is seen as having implications for the continuance or change of the cultural and social structures that channeled and affected the choice in the first place.

Thus, in the Mertonian approach the analysis proceeds through a sequence of macrosociological, microsociological, and then back to the macrosociological again. This is how Merton retains the insights, but bypasses the difficulties, of some forms of functional analysis.

Finally, the Mertonian analytical apparatus is fleshed out with other components (for instance, a loop involving the social forming of social character, interaction contexts, and socially expected durations).

A contemporary example might ensure that the application of this model is more clear. Since several countries have recently or are about to have an election (at the time of this writing, Britain, Australia, Italy, and New Zealand, for instance), the sociology of elections will provide an appropriate illustration. In an election, the voters are faced with an institutionalized choice between candidates of a few political parties. The way they make their voting choice is influenced by their position in the social structure. The net effect of the aggregate of votes is that in the short-term a party (or combination of parties) obtains governmental power, and in the long-term the viability of the various parties is each affected. Eventually, parties receiving little popular support are more likely to continue. Thus, the choice available to

TABLE 11.2
Page Reference Counts to Four Merton Collections

Sorokin, Pitirim	95
Marx, Karl	80
Parsons, Talcott	73
Weber, Max	69
Durkheim, Émile	58
Mannheim, Karl	52
Malinowski, Bronislaw	42
Freud, Sigmund	40
Engels, Friedrich	34
Bacon, Francis	33
Kuhn, Thomas	28
Scheler, Max	26
Simmel, Georg	26
Davis, Kingsley	26
Becker, Howard	23
Comte, Auguste	23
Whitehead, Alfred	21
Znaniecki, Florian	21
MacIver, Robert	20
Lazarsfeld, Paul*	74
Barber, Bernard*	68
Zuckerman, Harriet*	25

Key: * = Collaborators

voters in subsequent elections will be in part influenced by the way choices are cast in the previous election, as behavior can often have structural consequences.

The great volume of Merton's writings is full of a wealth of detailed suggestions about how various aspects of this analytical schema work, but it is not appropriate to provide further detail here.

Influences on Merton

As sketched in an earlier section, it does not do to simply assume the straightforward transmission of ideas from source to destination.

This is particularly true in the case of Merton as his stance towards "sources" has been an "innovative" rather than a strictly "scholarly" one. He has always sought to employ ideas from others in order to open up new insights, rather than be too concerned with tracing historical subtleties in the development of ideas. He has often used his scholarly skills in seeking a form of legitimation for ideas he has already developed, rather than merely been concerned with the extension or testing of ideas gleaned from predecessors. This makes the tracing of influences on Merton difficult.

There are several points at which Merton has himself noted influences on his work. In the acknowledgements to *Social Theory and Social Structure* he is grateful for the support of Sarton, Parsons, Lazarsfeld, and others. In a fugitive fragment of autobiography he particularly notes the influence of Durkheim on his approach to sociology.

These listings have been added to commentators. Sztompka lists the following in rank order of importance as influences (1986: 24–30):

1. Durkheim
2. Marx
3. Simmel
4. Weber
5. and among contemporaries or near-contemporaries Znaniecki, Malinowski, Sarton, Sorokin, Parsons, and (" . . . finally . . . ") Lazarsfeld.

This listing immediately shows some interesting divergences from more accepted rankings, especially in the "promotion" of Marx and Znaniecki and Malinowski, and in the "demotion" of Weber and perhaps Lazarsfeld. But this largely illustrates the difficulty of tracing influences without adequate theoretical guidance and a solid empirical research base.

Table 11.2 is offered as a research palliative in the meantime. It consists of a page count of the more frequent author citations in the indexes of Merton's most important four collections (*Social Theory and Social Structure, The Sociology of Science, Sociological Ambivalence,* and *Social Research and the Practicing Professions*). There are several difficulties in handling this set of data. (Indeed, Mertonian sociology of science has been active in both using citation data and in exploring their limitations, and can be drawn upon for advice in the handling of such data). Some names feature on the list as collaborators rather than sources, although undoubtedly they thereby constitute a major source of influence: they are listed separately at the end of the list. Other names feature strongly for special reasons: for example, Sorokin's sociology of science was the particular target of a review-essay, while references to Marx and Mannheim are particularly concentrated in Merton's review-essay on the sociology of knowledge. Nevertheless, the data provides some interesting pointers: the prominence of Weber is supported, but it also seems that Sztompka's intuition about Marx receives some support. There is an interesting grouping of middle-order sources.

But again, this set of data takes us only a small step further. To properly study influences on Merton it is surely necessary to subject each of the components in Merton's schema, and each of the relationships amongst them, to detailed investigation of sources, and to then assemble an aggregate picture. As a summary anticipation of such an exhaustive study, I now offer a brief interpretative overview.

The general set of components in Merton's analytical approach (as outlined above) are taken from the Harvard culture-society-personality "school" that developed in the mid- and late 1930s, and which included Parsons and Merton, as well as Sorokin. This shared approach was influenced particularly by both British social and American cultural anthropology, psychological theory, the three founding fathers, and Simmel. The Harvard work provides a meso- and micro-level underpinning and systematizing of the rather more macrosociological concerns, and idiosyncratic presentations, of the founding fathers. The Harvard school has been concerned to identify a significant array of deep sociological problems, and then to build a broad base of social theory that will address these problems and cumulate.

Merton's particular contribution is his particular *mix* of this set of components, and his particular way of assembling the components. His approach features more the primacy of the social structural level and the significance of choice-situations. It is pitched at a rather less abstract level, is more clearly linked to research studies, and includes a more obvious sensitivity to ambiguity, conflict, and change in social life. These emphases are in turn related to the particular sources Merton draws on more, including Simmel and Marx.

Influences from Merton

A variety of general citation studies of the structure of influence in sociology have shown the broad manifest influence Merton has wielded in sociology, and also other disciplines (see summary in Crothers 1987: ch. 2). However, such a broad scatteration of citation research has yet

TABLE 11.3
Research Programs Arising from, Strongly Influenced
by, or Unaffected by Robert K. Merton

Date	Research Paper	Research Program
1936	Unanticipated Consequences	"Perverse effects," etc. (Boudon, Elster), Technology Assessment, Social Impact Assessment
1937	Social Time	Diffuse
1938	Science, Technology, Society	"Merton thesis" debate
1938	Social Structure & Anomie	Anomie-and-Opportunity Structure
1939	Bureaucratic Structure	Columbia Org. Studies (Gouldner, Blau, Selznick, Sills, etc.) more generally (e.g., March and Simon)
1941/48	Intermarriage/Discrimination	?
1942	Science and Democracy	Democratic Theory (Hollinger)
1942	High School Graduates	None
1945	Sociology of Knowledge	Diffuse
1945/48	Theory & Social Research	Theory-Construction (Zetterberg, etc.)
1948	Self-Fulfilling Prophecy	Diffuse
1949	Local/Cosmopolitan Influentials	Diffuse (Gouldner: latent social roles)
1949	Manifest & Latent Functions	Functional Methodology Debate
1949	Applied Social Science	Diffuse (Methodology of Applied S.S.)
1950	Reference Group	Diffuse
1954	Friendship	Network Studies
1953/57	Professions	Professional Socialization Studies, Semiprofessions, Professionalization (Etzioni, Goode…)
1957	Role and Status Sets	Diffuse, Role-Theory
1967	History & Systematics Debates	Historiography of Sociology
1968	Matthew Effect	Cumulative Advantage in Science, Social Stratification in Science
1972	Insiders and Outsiders	Diffuse

to pin down the exact ways in which Merton's very considerable influence has worked. This gap in knowledge has been partly closed through a pair of detailed studies of particular areas of Merton's work (written by Jonathan Cole and Harriet Zuckerman, "The Emergence of a Scientific Specialty: The Self-Exemplifying Case of the Sociology of Science" and Stephen Cole, "The Growth of Scientific Knowledge: Theories of Deviance as a Case Study" and published in the Coser-edited *Festschrift*) which reveal the complexity and ambiguity of influences from Merton.

Another manifest influence has been through the subsequent intellectual careers of those sociologists who studied under Merton. After all, it must be remembered that Merton trained a large cadre of important social theorists over the course of several decades. But little has been published about such genealogical lineages apart from Mullins's preliminary listing (see *Theory and Theory-Groups in American Sociology*).

A useful way of summarizing Merton's impact is to trace the various special areas of sociology he has contributed to, or the various of his works which have spawned "research-programs" in the Lakatosian sense of a cumulative and advancing sequence of studies. Merton's role in setting up the sociology of science is well-known, but he has also assisted in the "birthing" or rejuvenation of several other specialties including the sociology of professions, the sociology of organizations, and so on. Table 11.3 attempts to provide a preliminary list of some of the research programs in which Merton played some part. In order to make the point that not all of Merton's work led to rapid breakthrough and development, I have included in the list several of his studies which seemed to fall on stony ground. An area of interesting investigation would be to try to identify the characteristics of those contributions which "took off" compared to those which did not. A preliminary review (based on comments in the two citation case-studies mentioned above) suggests that factors such as the availability of an audience (often attracted when a research area seems to be "speaking to" a social problem), the availability of a cadre of sociologists to work in the area, and the availability of technical aids to foster empirical research (for instance, citation data in the sociology of science) all assisted in leading to the development of research programs.

But, these research programs constitute only the more obviously shaped "manifest" influence of Merton's work, where particular direct traces are frequent and clear. In addition, there is a broad spectrum of largely latent influences of his writing across the whole range of postwar American sociology and other areas of scholarship. This broad penumbra of influence is indicated by the range of references to Merton's work, and needs further investigation.

I think that Merton had a considerable, partly latent, impact on a long period of postwar sociology. This arose in two ways:

1. through his methodological writings which put forward a robust and clear image of the necessity for a systematic and cumulative approach to the building of a scientific sociology; and,
2. from his implicitly developed analytical paradigm (I have presented a formalized version of this above) for studying social structures and its partly unconscious adoption throughout postwar American sociology.

The methodological writing, especially on the relation between theory and research, was sound, clearly written, and definitely articulated a methodological approach that had many supporters. However it was not especially original or sophisticated. Merton's methodological writings probably served more to legitimate preformed views than to be influential in creating a uniquely new approach in sociology.

His theoretical impact was widespread, but not as clearly perceived, largely because its impact was obfuscated by his methodological writings. His work was also overshadowed on a theoretical stage where there seemed to be room only for the work of Talcott Parsons. However, I suspect that the direct and deep influence of Parsons's work is often exaggerated. In fact, active contribution to his program came from only a few sociologists. For many others, he was more studied than used, and more often acclaimed than applied. Nevertheless, the availability of Parsons's theoretical work did support several themes of the American sociologists of the period. If the stage is rather less dominated in fact by Parsons, this leaves more room for other influences to be apparent. And clearly, of other influences, Robert Merton was particularly important.

Much of Merton's theoretical impact was subtle, and involved the consistent pointing up of a variety of specific frameworks (for instance, reference groups, role sets etc.) over a considerable period of time, without much of an apparent cumulative impact. But I think that, in addition, many sociologists dimly perceived something of the overall structure and thrust of the Mertonian approach (along the lines of the above section, and as articulated by such commentators as Barbano, Blau, Stinchcombe, and Sztompka). This approach and this checklist of explanatory strategies invoked resonances at a largely latent level. Thus, the latent effect of Merton's work has been considerable.

Several important characteristics of Merton's theoretical approach assisted in its adoption (the level at which it was couched, its relevance to key features of contemporary American social life, its linkage to social research methods, and not least the graciousness of its presentation).

Relevance to Contemporary Sociology

I will conclude by arguing the relevance of Merton's theoretical framework for contemporary sociology, although it might be more correct to sum up in terms of the extent to which the double case study revealed the appropriateness or lack of appropriateness of the Mertonian sociology of knowledge to the study of scholarly influences.

We demand several things from those theories we hope will be useful. A useful theoretical approach will generate interesting ideas about how a social system works and will guide the general approach of research on it. But theories are also subject to limitations imposed on them. It seems that all theories must make some attempt to cope with the awkward and contradictory demands of a set of philosophical antinomies (for instance, the structure versus agency, micro- versus macro-level, and subjective versus objective distinctions). Merton's analytical approach seems to work successfully between many of these. His sociology has a place for both determinism and free will, moves readily between micro- and macro-levels, and includes both objective and subjective aspects without seeming to be crippled by its simultaneous handling of these various oppositions. (The way in which these multiple features of Merton's theory are able to work needs urgent theoretical exegesis, to ensure that it cannot be exposed as a skillful and unsystematic eclecticism, but does rest on firm foundations.)

Merton's sociological approach formed a structure which mediated between many of the immediate postwar sociologies, and building further on it now may be a useful mediating strategy during the present "crisis" of sociology, as opposing sociologies take stances on opposite sides of the various antinomies and seem to resist amelioration of their isolating positions.

But for further work to be built on the foundations of Merton's sociology, it needs refurbishing from both Marxian and phenomenological directions. Although Merton has endeavored to overcome some of the relative lacks, in the Harvard school approach, of insufficient attention to conflict, change, and confusion, I am not sure that he has sufficiently succeeded. His handling of these points of difficulty seems to treat them as essentially departures from a general "social order" approach. It is possible that a wider set of basic assumptions about the foundation of social life is needed.

This is particularly so when we attempt to confront explanations of such "raw" aspects of social systems as violence, exploitation, and power. While Merton's schema can cope with explaining mild forms of these phenomena, it is, unfortunately, unable to apperceive their more exaggerated forms.

The refurbishing of the theoretical foundations may involve (to go through each of the components in his schema that I identified above):

- stressing the suppressive face of cultural structures (can this be extended to exposing the pathologies endemic in the scientific ethos?);
- examining the ways in which status-and-role structures are themselves underpinned by wider frameworks (an example of a study examining the structures which in turn generate role-structures is Harriet Zuckerman's recent work on role-models);
- analyzing the full strengths of limitations in choice-situations (by closer examination of the subjective experiences of choice-possibilities and also by evaluating the authenticity of these through objective analysis); and,
- more charting of the injurious effects of some cumulative cycles and feedback/leakage mechanisms.

It is only after such refurbishing has been carried out that Mertonian sociology can fully tackle the range of sociological problematics it ought to be able to face.

But even without such strengthening the Mertonian framework continues to furnish a particularly useful set of analytical tools for analyzing social structures. It has even been useful in a self-reflexive fashion, in providing a sociology of knowledge approach to examine the influences on and from Merton himself!

References

Cole, S. 1975. "The Growth of Scientific Knowledge: Theories of Deviance as a Case Study." In *The Idea of Social Structure: Papers in Honor of Robert K. Merton*, edited by L.A. Coser. New York: Harcourt Brace Jovanovich.

Crothers, C. 1987. *Robert K. Merton: Key Sociologist*. London: Ellis Horwood and Tavistock Publications.

Cullen, F.T. 1986. *Rethinking Crime and Deviance Theory.* New York: St. Martin's Press.

Dahrendorf, R. 1968. *Essays in the Theory of Society.* Stanford: The Stanford University Press.

Merton, R.K. 1957. *Social Theory and Social Structure.* Rev. ed. New York: Free Press.

———. 1964. "Anomie, Anomia and Social Interaction: Contexts of Deviant Behavior." In *Anomie and Deviant Behavior,* edited by M. Clinard. New York: Free Press.

———. [1965] 1985. *On the Shoulders of Giants.* New York: Harcourt Brace Jovanovich.

———. 1968. *Social Theory and Social Structure.* Enlarged and rev. ed. New York: Free Press.

———. 1973. *The Sociology of Science.* Edited by N.W. Storer. Chicago: University of Chicago Press.

———. 1976. *Sociological Ambivalence.* New York: Free Press.

———. 1982. *Social Research and the Practicing Professions.* Edited by A. Rosenblatt and T.F. Gieryn. Cambridge: Abt Books.

Stinchcombe, A. 1975. "Merton's Theory of Social Structure." In *The Idea of a Social Structure*, edited by L.A. Coser. New York: Harcourt Brace Jovanovich.

Sztompka, P. 1986. *Robert K. Merton: An Intellectual Profile.* New York: St. Martin's Press.

Part 3

Short Papers

12

Conditioning or Conditionings? Revisiting an Old Criticism of Mannheim by Merton

Alberto Izzo

Before getting into the main theme of this chapter, it is perhaps worth repeating what has long been pointed out, that Mannheim and Merton start out from very different epistemological premises and conceptions of science. This is easy to understand even from a look at their diverse social and cultural origins. Mannheim comes from the school of German historicism, from the phenomenology of Husserl and Scheler, and from Marxism. Despite his unquestioned openness to cultural trends different from his own, Merton remains linked to the Anglo-Saxon empirical tradition.

On this subject, the comparison of these two sociologists, a by now rather old, old student of Mannheim's has pointed to two different conceptions of truth, defining them as "scientific truth" and "existential truth." The first, which Kurt H. Wolff tells us is "sought in the solution of methodological problems may be called *stipulative* in the sense that the 'true' predicate is stipulated as suitable to the investigatory purpose in hand (or to the class of investigatory purposes of which the one in hand is an example). It may also be called *hypothetical* in the sense that it is contingent on the validation of a given hypothesis being examined in respect to its truth; or in the more compelling sense that, even if validated, the hypotheses remain hypotheses, namely propositions that can be validated only within the hypothetical, methodological, pragmatic, scientific attitude—that attitude

213

for which metaphysical propositions (concerning the nature of reality) are irrelevant. Finally, this truth may be called *propositional,* in the sense that it is predicated only (or predominantly) of propositions. It is clear that this stipulative, hypothetical, propositional truth, which is the truth sought in the solution of methodological problems, is also the truth sought in the solution of scientific problems. This is widely, if not generally, recognized by the philosophers of science and of value. It implies that science makes no claims about the nature of (ultimate) reality; it is not concerned with this reality" (Wolff 1974: 566).

These characteristics, Wolff's opinion again, are precisely those of "scientific truth." But in philosophy the term truth has meant and means something different: one refers to it as to the solution of problems which involve the very existence of man. He wants to be in truth, to live life according to criteria of truth. This kind of "truth" is that which is sought "in the solution of volitional and metaphysical problems" (Wolff 1974: 566). It may be defined by the expression "existential truth." The sense of truth and error which accompanies the existence of man is his criterion of truth, very different, then, from the scientific truth just mentioned. Even Paul Kecskemeti, on the subject of Mannheim, had distinguished two kinds of truth, in a distinction which is very near to what would later be elaborated by Wolff in his distinction between Merton and Mannheim. "There is . . . an unresolvable philosophical difference" writes Kecskemeti, "involved here: the difference between the existential concept of truth as 'being in truth' and the Aristotelian concept of truth as 'speaking the truth.'" Some philosophers adopt the first definition (as Mannheim did), and others the second" (Mannheim 1952: 31). To explain this difference in more concrete terms, one can recall that none of us has difficulty in considering *true* the syllogism "Man is mortal, Socrates is a man, therefore Socrates is mortal," but faced with the specific ways in which death can come in the world (think of death in war or famine), it is much more difficult for man's conscience to accept passively that this is its truth given as natural and untransformable. It follows that the first type of truth is linked to a neutral scientific vision while the second involves man's activity and is summed up in the question: "What must one do 'to be in truth' given that we find ourselves in a situation we consider false?"

This rather long preliminary on the two different epistemological orientations perhaps allows us to examine with greater clarity the meaning and the limitations of the criticisms that Merton, in times now long past (1945), directed at Mannheim on the question of the "connectives of knowledge and society" (Merton 1968: 552). Merton draws attention to a "fundamental indecision" (ibid.: 553) in the author he is criticizing on the relation between social structure and knowledge. In Merton's opinion "this lacuna leads to vagueness and obscurity at the very heart of his central thesis concerning the 'existential *determination* of knowledge'" (ibid. 1968: 552) Merton's point is formally unexceptionable. The vagueness and indecision he indicates in Mannheim's texts are undoubtedly there. But here I must raise the question which must be raised as to why there is this indecision and uncertainty. There are, in fact, two different and irreconcilable answers. The first possible answer is that Mannheim has not sufficiently clarified the *terms* of the problem, as he should have in keeping with the rules of scientific discourse, and this makes any empirical application of his hypothesis difficult. The other answer is that in concrete historico-social reality the infinite number of ways in which social relations take place does not permit of a single once-and-for-all identification in a watertight explanatory schema of the way in which the social conditioning of thought manifests itself, simply because not one way but many ways are given.

Merton anticipates this objection and forestalls his critics by saying that "although it may be agreed that it is unwise to prejudge the types of relations between knowledge and social structure, it is also true that a failure to specify these types virtually precludes the possibility of formulating problems for empirical investigation" (Merton 1968: 552). And here, perhaps, as well as in Mannheim, one might detect some uncertainty and indecision in Merton himself. One can, in fact, object that his "theories of the middle range" require formulation on the basis of the accumulated results of empirical research. But then the type of relation between social structure and thought has of necessity to take account of the results of analysis of the historico-social reality if it must not be preformulated. And since these results do not indicate a state of conditioning between the social structure and knowledge that is always of the same type, for reasons of methodological rigor such a type cannot be imposed on reality either, before the sociological analysis has begun. The very idea of the theories of the middle range would be compromised.

We can now come to Merton's more circumstantiated criticisms when he points out the various meanings for the expression "existential conditioning" of thought in a historico-social context as used by Mannheim. Merton says that "[O]n occasion—despite his explicit denial of any such intention—Mannheim assumes a direct *causation* of forms of thought by social forces" (Merton 1968: 553) And the examples he gives to support his criticism are all relevant. But it is still possible to ask if Merton by so doing does full justice to the interpretation of the explicit denial of causal connection between social structure and knowledge in the author he is criticizing. Mannheim's denial can be interpreted either in the sense that there is never a deterministic (cause-effect) relation between the conditioning factors and the factors that have been conditioned that he has selected for examination; that is, in the sense of a philosophico-anthropological position taken up once and for all, or in the very different sense that one cannot postulate a cause-effect relation in the problem under examination because even in the cases where the social conditioning of thought seems in specific circumstances deterministically given, it is historically transformable. Thus it seems one must explain Mannheim's idea so frequently repeated in his writings that the degree of critical awareness of social conditioning implies the possibility of at least a partial release from it. In an early essay Mannheim already had this to say: "If real men today are powerfully attracted by the modern study of mental and moral life, it is not because they have to convince themselves at any cost that all their behavior is objectively determined, so that they may excuse their deficiencies and let the anonymous social process decide about everything, instead of assuming the responsibility for a decision themselves. On the contrary, the deeper motive behind this study is the desire to descend into the laboratory where these hidden forces are at work, to gain an insight into the pattern of their interplay, and thus become able, at the bidding of an autonomous will, to master them and put them at the service of an educational work in personality formation which one can pursue consciously in full freedom and responsibility" (Mannheim 1952: 275). Merton does not seem to detect this dynamic, practical-political character of Mannheim's discourse on the "causal relation" that tends to be turned into its opposite through self-awareness. He interprets it simply in terms of a static interpretative schema, and on this level it is clearly lacking. But Mannheim's intentions were quite different.

The second way in which Mannheim interprets the link in question

Merton describes as "interest assumption." On the basis of this assumption the ideas and forms of thought are "in accord with" the
interests of the subjects and gratify them (Merton 1968: 553). Since
Merton himself relates this point of view to *Vulgärmarxismus* and
seems to suggest a deterministic reading of it, what one can observe in
this connection is not substantially different from what has been said
on the "causal relation."

In still other cases, in Merton's view Mannheim maintains simply
that "the subject limits his perspective in order to deal with a particular problem . . . Here thought is directed by the very formulation of the
problem, awareness of which may in turn be *attributed to* the social
position of the subject" (Merton 1968: 554, emphasis added). Since
Merton does not elaborate further on the meaning of "attributed to," it
is likely that there is not much to add about this meaning given to the
social structure-knowledge relation.

Much more important is what follows where it is stated that occasionally Mannheim considers certain structures "as simply prerequisite
to certain forms of thought." In these cases Mannheim's work "has to
do with the establishment of preconditions or even facilitating factors
rather than with necessary and sufficient conditions" (Merton 1968:
554).

At this point and almost parenthetically one should note in criticism
of Mannheim that he is left rather simplistically tied to the assumption
of German historicism whereby only the statements relating to human
reality and so the historico-social sciences, not the natural sciences,
are subject to social conditioning. If, indeed, the relation between
social structure and thought is conceived of in terms of "preconditions
or even facilitating factors rather than with necessary and sufficient
conditions," then it seems possible to maintain without risk of error
that social conditioning acts on the natural sciences too. Somewhat
strangely for one who was to become one of the best known sociologists of science in the world, and who had already done sociological
research on science even at the time of his criticisms of Mannheim,
there is no such observation in Merton's notes. This observation, however, seems useful precisely because it illustrates how different types
of thought conditioning can exist in the same historico-social reality.
Take the example of evolutionism. Many discoveries deriving from it
cannot be questioned today, yet from the point of view of the sociology of science it is not difficult to maintain that the politico-economic

structure of early liberalism may have "facilitated" its emergence and development. It is quite different to talk of so-called social Darwinism, an often improper extension of individualist-evolutionist principles, and in any case not sufficiently supported empirically to justify a determined and specific economic and political organization: protocapitalism or competitive capitalism. In the latter case, the social conditioning is expressed in the sense of ideological distortion, as happens, according to the youthful studies of Mannheim, in the incapacity of "conservative thought" (Wolff 1971: 131) to transcend the concreteness and immediacy of the facts and to grasp the intrinsic dynamism.

It is to be hoped that these examples serve to support the thesis that the relation between social structure and thought varies effectively according to the historico-social circumstances and also the kind of thought considered. Mannheim, therefore, could not point to one way in which social conditioning is activated without falling into a dogmatic categorization that is the opposite of his theoretical assumptions, and for that matter the opposite of Merton's too. Lastly, Merton refuses Mannheim's idea that one can identify "the presuppositions common to 'single expressions and records of thought'" (Merton 1968: 555) as if there were an intrinsic consistency to every conception of the world. Merton rightly observes that "abstractly inconsistent values are often rendered compatible by their distribution among various statuses in the social structure so that they do not result in conflicting demands upon the same persons at the same time" (Merton 1968: 556). Here Mannheim's thesis is certainly guilty of being simplistic. His thought was perhaps itself the result of "conflicting demands" to the point that he was unable even to grasp that for others the incongruence might not emerge consciously. Mannheim knew that conflicting and even irreconcilable tendencies were copresent in his thought and he was even ready to admit it (Wolff: 557–559). But he did not concern himself too much with this. What concerned him more than the internal consistency of his theory and the correctness of his methodology, was analysis of the unresolved problems that people of his time lived through. Typical of this attitude is the famous question that he asks himself in his best-known book: "How is it possible for man to continue to think and live in a time when the problems of ideology and utopia are being radically raised and thought through in all their implications?" (Mannheim 1936: 42).

Merton's orientation is very different. He is looking for a methodology capable of checking the hypotheses of the sociology of knowledge empirically. This in perfect consistency with the idea that sociological theories (like the theories of the middle range) cannot take on "all the urgent practical problems of the day" and have to confine themselves to "those problems that might now be clarified in light of available knowledge (Merton 1957: 68–69). Merton is inevitably ill at ease, therefore, faced with a writer like Mannheim, who clearly wants to identify the urgent practical problems of the day much more than reach a scientific solution for them which would be binding for everyone because supported by indisputable empirical proofs.

Most of the points Merton makes about Mannheim are valid, but only if one accepts the epistemological and methodological assumptions of Merton's sociology and if also one accepts to put Mannheim in an epistemological framework which is clearly not his. Merton is looking for a "scientific truth"; Mannheim, an "existential truth." The former criticizes the failed effort on the part of the latter to "set forth a systematic 'code of techniques'" (Merton 1957: 555) for the sociology of knowledge. Mannheim is facing the crisis of his times and the inherent problems for his contemporaries. The epistemological assumptions of the one and the other do not seem capable of conciliation. A methodologically correct solution to the problems in the Mertonian sense is not something that can be sought in Mannheim.

This discussion might seem to have only a historical and philological significance. And yet, one could claim otherwise for the simple reason that even today, diverse epistemological conceptions clash with each other to the point that rather than unity of vision, intent, and method identifying the nature of sociology, we are looking at conceptions so different from each other that we are forced to admit that even now there exists not sociology but sociologies. Convergence of the different schools, so long wished for and even announced by some, is not only far off but in light of the current plurality of indomitable epistemological premises (think only of sociobiology and phenomenology) it is to be presumed that it will never be attained.

References

Kecskemeti, Paul. 1952. "Introduction." In *Essays on the Sociology of Knowledge* by Karl Mannheim. London: Routledge & Kegan Paul.

Mannheim, Karl. 1952. *Essays on the Sociology of Knowledge*. London: Routledge & Kegan Paul.
———. 1936. *Ideology and Utopia*. New York: Harcourt, Brace and Company.
Merton, Robert K. 1957. *Social Theory and Social Structure*. New York: Free Press.
Wolff, Kurt H. 1974. *Trying Sociology*. New York: John Wiley & Sons.

13

Some Thoughts on Two Works by R.K. Merton

Paolo Almondo

I want to make a series of reflections centered on two particular works by Merton: the 1936 essay "The Unanticipated Consequences of Purposive Social Action" (UC) and the chapter on "Manifest and Latent Functions" (MLF) in *Social Theory and Social Structure* of 1949. The first of these has a significance in Merton's work that has only recently has begun to receive due recognition. The conceptual richness of UC is such that Arnold Zingerle's chapter leaves room for further observations. The second piece has been a classic since the beginning, a necessary stepping-stone for getting out of the method-ological aridity of functionalism. Its influence has, in my opinion, crossed the methodological domain so well defined in Merton's theo-rizing, that it can make itself felt even in contexts not particularly in line with theories of the middle range (another pillar of Mertonian thinking) such as in the work of Niklas Luhmann (1970).[1]

The fortunes, or rather as Barbano suggests, the informative-forma-tive reception of Merton in Italy has been marked by a destiny which is perhaps not anomalous but common to other national contexts as well. The paths he laid out have been made known and followed. Merton's lexicon is familiar, not to be acquainted with it is almost a sign of lack of education, or at least of poor sociological education. Then there are those people, and there are many, who make specific reference and use particular parts of his work but the critical debate on his work as a whole is relatively contained despite the fact that it was opened immediately at a high level by Filippo Barbano (1955 and 1959), further encouraged by Carlo Marletti (1970), and recently re-proposed from a different viewpoint by Italo Vaccarini (1982).

The fact of being very much quoted and having a more or less explicit following, and at the same time not being the object of a comprehensive critical survey of the type that Piotr Sztompka has recently provided (1986) may be partly explained by the relationship that Merton has established with sociology. Merton is absolutely out of sympathy with the need to refound the discipline that so often characterizes partisans of general theory. In his style of work, the foundations are considered already laid, and if they absolutely must be checked again, they are looked at in their individual parts and not as a whole. If there is a strong methodological guideline it is not directed at the epistemological assumptions but comes in the form of an invita-tion to sociological awareness of the conditions of the actual socio-logical work in daily scientific operation.

It is certainly much easier to write books on sociologists who have explicitly thematized the assumptions of sociological thought rather than on those who have been perfectly at ease with its deep structures and their elaboration. And it is certainly more difficult to circumscribe the multiplicity of Merton's contributions, constantly enriched by the double dialectic of theory-research and time, than the activities of sociologists who have pursued a general theory of society. Though Merton seems to exclude a theory of society, there is certainly an implicit theory of social life and this explains how it can happen that one finds his contributions accepted by some general theorists who are otherwise unmindful of his option for theories of the middle range. In my opinion, a compatibility or complementarity between Merton and Parsons, for example, is possible only as meta-interpretation quite out of context with the scientific validation of their respective approaches.

But let us come to the first of the two themes for this chapter. That Merton's contributions form a theoretical system in filigree is the hypothesis in part demonstrated by Sztompka in his fine book. Beyond an implicit system is it possible, though, to identify a programmatic, even if implicit, declaration? Can one trace an equivalent to the first three chapters and the last one of Parsons's *The Structure of Social Action* ?

The Unanticipated Consequences and a Theory of Social Action

I have no doubt that the essay on "The Unanticipated Consequences" has all the characteristics of such an equivalent and serves to reveal the *forma mentis* which is typically Mertonian; moreover, one that is perfectly analyzable in terms of the four themes proposed by Sztompka as characteristic of Merton's intellectual approach (Sztompka 1986: 4–5). Perhaps I suffer from a mistaken aesthetic need for unity, but reading that work brings to my mind the image of a fountain of waves producing harmonious effects, carrying many recurring themes in Merton's scientific work.

I shall leave to another occasion any systematic, documented exploration of the hypothesis and limit myself now to a few points in the course of an exposition intended to indicate a notable circumstance not only in the works of Merton. Indeed, in the essay in question, among other things, problems are outlined that can be considered as early indications of the debate on bounded rationality, but in a version, and herein lies its merit, which is already sociological.

From these pages of Merton's there emerges an image of the social actor for whom rational behavior is no guarantee of control of circumstances. The relative indeterminacy of social action does not weigh him down with a sense of the turbulence of his environment and of individual finiteness. Straightaway, the uncertain nature of prediction of human events is underlined, and, at the same time, it is made clear how that knowledge which serves for prediction is socially circumscribed and conditioned by its being intertwined with other equally important social needs. Rational scrutiny as an individual and social way of acting has to compete with a multiplicity of needs for the social allocation of resources and time.

I think we can agree that our author has no explicit theory of action and/or of the actor. It is more difficult to maintain that no assumptions are made in this respect, even if they can be understood differently according to personal interpretative inclinations. That human action is not merely human behavior is explicitly affirmed in UC, repeated in this conference along with the other general approach, shared with Parsons and most of sociology: we must consider human action as inscribed between cultural structure and social structure (between goals and conditions). It follows, among other things, that for Merton freedom is not a creative *a priori* for action, but that action takes place in the spaces created by the fortunately dynamic tensions between the constraints of cultural and social structure. Furthermore, one might suggest that precisely because of this differential between cultural and social structure, essential for a society which is not inert and without history, there arises the possibility and the necessity for scientific investigation. Again, all this is, for Merton, almost a question of sociological common sense that avoids theorizations but is practiced as analysis or as suggestion (remember, for example, that he will not speculate on the passage from latent to manifest but will turn it into a research interest).

To carry us forward it is useful here to take up a reference to the early Parsons in the brief period when their respective thematics did not diverge conspicuously. In *The Structure of Social Action* instrumental rationality (the intrinsic means-ends relationship), cardinal point of the utilitarian model along with the randomness of ends, is criticized if it is understood as the only element making up the relationship between actor and environment. Obviously, in Parsonsian use the criticism is directed at the exclusivist reductionism of positivism, and is designed to propose, with the inclusion of the nonrational, a wider ranging theory of rationality aimed ultimately at the evolutionist view of an adaptive upgrading of society. At any rate, it is clear that many of the constitutive parts of a sociological approach have on the one hand to reckon with, and are on the other hand necessarily hostile to, the theories that are based exclusively on individualism and the issues of rational choice.

I now come to a more precise point which enables me to go from Parsons to Merton. In *The Structure of Social Action* Parsons indicates two key points of logic that ensnare the utilitarian model: on the one hand, the appearance of the need to go beyond randomness or at least the givenness of individual goals and, on the other hand, the necessity to explain the departures from the rationality of action. In the second case, the problem is one of accounting for error and ignorance, taking them out of being mere practical circumstances. And ignorance and error are precisely the first two classes of factors accounting for unexpected consequences in Merton's UC.

Let us take a step back and recall a few of the affirmations that define the Mertonian analytical framework. First of all, social action does not always "involve[s] clear-cut, explicit purpose" (UC: 896) However, it seems evident that many human actions are directed to control of the consequences as can be seen from the rationalizations made in the face of the unexpected (UC: 895). Lastly, there runs an implicit distinction throughout the whole of Merton's analysis between the subjective rationality of the actor and the objective rationality that the observer presupposes, in an original reelaboration of the place of rationality in human action which anticipates the more general invitation to separate for analytical purposes subjective motives and intentions from objective consequences (manifest and latent functions) (Merton 1968: 78–79).

In this connection any summary would lose the stylistic economy of Merton's original text and I shall therefore quote him in full:

> Above all, it must not be inferred that purposive action implies "rationality" of human action (that persons always use the objectively most adequate means for the attainment of their ends). In fact, part of the present analysis is devoted to the determination of those elements which account for concrete deviations from rationality of action. Moreover, rationality and irrationality are not to be identified with the success or failure of action, respectively. For in a situation where the number of *possible* actions for attaining a given end is severely limited, one acts rationally by selecting the means which, on the basis of the available evidence, has the greatest probability of attaining this goal and yet the goal may actually *not* be attained. Contrariwise, an end may be attained by action which, on the basis of the knowledge available to the actor, is irrational (as in the case of "hunches"). (UC: 896)

The preliminary framework is completed in part by the observation that the "concrete consequences can be differentiated into (a) consequences to the actor, (b) consequences to other persons mediated through (1) the social structure, (2) culture, and (3) *civilization*" (UC: 895). On this last mediation we have heard the insightful lecture by Zingerle which confirms me in the idea that the conceptual richness of this essay by Merton is in proportion to its stylistic sobriety.

The first general limitation, the most obvious, to a correct anticipation of consequences is identified by Merton in the existing state of knowledge. It is interesting that Merton does not make it a question of ignorance in the individual actor but a general problem of the limits inherent and socially inscribed in human action. Indeed, the first element in ignorance that we might define as constitutive is identified as the preeminently "stochastic (conjectural) nature" of prediction in the sciences of human behavior themselves and so in the practical behavior of the actor (as Donati has pointed out in his lecture). This theme will turn up again in Merton's work on the "Role of the intellectual in public bureaucracy" (UC: 261–278, esp. 263–265) when he will show how the relative indeterminacy of the predictions of social experts explains the emergence of trusted chains of experts in the relationships with policymakers.

Moreover, regularities inferred by past events are no guarantee of the correctness of predictions for the future, given the impossibility of guaranteeing respect for the clause "other things being equal." Merton thus concludes with a brief summary: "Although no formula for the exact *amount* of knowledge necessary for foreknowledge is presented, one may say in general that consequences are fortuitous when an exact knowledge of many details and facts (as distinct from general principles) is needed for even a highly approximative prediction" (UC: 899).

A second element in nonguilty ignorance derives from the urgency for action imposed by practical life, which rarely gives enough time for an exhaustive examination of the situation and possible strategies. In this case, as also in the next one, Merton seems to propose a concept of objective time. Nevertheless, it would seem to me incompatible with the whole Mertonian perspective to reduce the importance of time to a mere quantitative factor, a *res externa*. Time has to be conceived as elaborated culturally and structured socially, as in part we shall see shortly. However, this sensitivity to time, far from the speculation and tautology of Parsons on time as constitutive of the finality of action, is found again exactly in the essay "Social Time: A Methodological and Functional Analysis," published together with P.A. Sorokin in 1937. On the subject of the concept of "socially expected duration" Merton himself refers back to this first study (Di Lellio 1985: 3–26, esp. 7–8).

A third element in ignorance derives from the lack of time and energy and therefore from the problem of their allocation among various needs. The prediction of consequences is one of many needs and time kept for cognitive activities is a function of the particular aspect of any specific social structure. Merton affirms in a vivid image: "An economy of social engineers is no more conceivable or practicable than an economy of laundrymen" (UC: 900). And, as can be observed, there is more: the impossibility of proposing an exclusive primacy for cognitive activities directed to the rational control of action.

From what we have seen so far, there emerges a figure of the social actor (individual or group) who may resort to rational strategies to control the future consequences of his actions but whose chances of being able to gain total control of the required information are circumscribed not so much by individual finiteness combined with environmental turbulence as by the social structures of time and resources in relation to the framework of social needs (functions?). A certain amount of cognitive deficit is unavoidable and, besides, the success of actions may discover other routes than rational and/or conscious domination. To say it with winged words: there is no need to bring the Mertonian actor down to earth, his Olympian quality comes to him precisely from the fact of being born in situations of bounded rationality and uncertainty for him is not a source of anxiety but the very stuff of life.

A second general factor that generates unanticipated consequences is identified by Merton in the errors that can occur at various moments during the course of an action: in evaluating the situation, in extrapolating the future from the present, in choosing the strategies and in the execution of the action itself. Merton lays particular emphasis on the snare of habit: habit usually springs from the success of a way of behaving in certain circumstances that is turned into a time-and-energy-saving routine guaranteeing automatic success. The force of habit with the consequent *ritualism* becomes a powerful brake both on the perception of new needs and on the satisfaction of old needs in a changing environment. Do we have here a foretaste of the Mertonian attention to phenomena of displacement of goals?

Having come this far, I hope (a) to have provided enough evidence to justify the hypothesis that in UC there is a sociological anticipation of the theory of bounded rationality, and (b) to have indicated some passages which can legitimately be considered as the first entries of themes that will run through Merton's work. Before going on to the second subject of this chapter, functional analysis, I should just like to add one or two further observations.

In the course of the conference there have been hints of possible connections between the sociological approach outlined in UC and the methodological individualism and proposals of Raymond Boudon on the topic of perverse effects. Perhaps some connection is traceable in the assertion that the relationship between actor and consequences is mediated by the social structure.

The social structure could also be considered as, in part, a product of the aggregate of effects of individual actions, but, as we have seen, Merton does not seem inclined to lay down laws or hypothesize on processes and mechanisms on the basis of reasoning about the aggregate of individual rational actions. I should say that in the specific case he does the opposite. What social margins are conceded to a concrete act on criteria of an instrumental rationality that is not even necessarily destined to be successful? Nevertheless, the thematic of perverse effects is undoubtedly in perfect harmony with the continued and not guileless interest shown by Merton in the often paradoxical character of human action.

This aspect of Merton's work, highlighted by Sztompka, is already fully in evidence in UC, both in the recurring methodological reflections and in, for example, the paradox of "the boomerang effect" of certain basic values (as in the Protestant ethic). In fact, the essay concludes, and not in any way pessimistically, on the greatest of paradoxes in the field of the social sciences, a perfect anticipation of the concept of self-fulfilling prophecy. I refer to the disturbing observation that a correct prediction of undesirable effects may be taken into serious consideration so that adequate steps are taken to prevent their happening, and thus the direct evidence of the correctness of the prediction is wiped out. The intervention has altered the balance of equality of conditions. This paradox, Merton adds, would make it necessary to do a very careful analysis of the implications for "social prediction, control and planning" (UC: 904).

In this last reference there emerges another recurring Mertonian reflection: the use of the social sciences or even the theme of social engineering. I shall deal with this subject in the observations on functional analysis that make up the second part of this chapter. To link the two parts let me say this that, even if it is difficult to maintain that there is a foretaste of functional analysis in UC, it is certain that many of the concepts that will go into its composition are already present from the point where intentions and consequences are separated, the basis on which the distinction between manifest and latent functions is laid. Moreover, Merton will expressly recall the 1936 essay on the question of this distinction he had made (1968: 105, n.8).

The Paradigm of Manifest and Latent Functions

The title of Merton's contribution—"Manifest and Latent Functions"—and the fortune of the distinction to which it alludes have ended by reducing the meaning of a well expressed series of indications to only one and that the one which is most open to criticism. I refer here to the perplexities expressed by Colin Campbell (Campbell 1982: 29–44).[2]

Let me reformulate the criticism in the following way, focusing especially on the definition of manifest function. The definition is expressed like this: "*Manifest functions* are those objective consequences contributing to the adjustment or adaptation of the system, and which are intended and recognised by the participants in the system" (MLF: 105).

First of all, there is a basic ambiguity: it is not clear if the awareness refers only to the connection that links the actions and the consequences, or if it also extends to the functionality of the consequences. This second hypothesis seems to me too strong, retraceable only in experiments of social planning and those crowned with success at that.

And so, if I read Merton correctly, it is wise to limit the definition to the first hypothesis, but one must also see the necessary consequences:

1. the true kingdom of functional performance turns out to be the latent function (and I think that many of the examples Merton cites back this up);
2. the distinction takes on a double valency, one which is pedagogical—an invitation to go beyond the appearances of things—and the other which is preliminary to the analytical excavation;
3. the interesting question is raised of the function of any inertia in the latent function (due perhaps to the copresence of groups with different, but balanced, power and different, but balanced, interests?): I shall return to this later in my discussion of "The Position of Sociological Theory"; and,
4. the need to reconstruct the dynamic relationship that is set up between intentionality and functionality is, however, salvaged.

In my experience of teaching and scientific communication I have the impression that the attractiveness of the distinction between manifest and latent ends up by obscuring other aspects of perhaps greater significance, but fortunately not the trichotomy function-dysfunction-nonfunction which is, in practice, often reduced to a dichotomy. Certainly, very little attention has been given to (a) the descriptive protocol for functional analysis and (b) the concepts of structural context or structural constraint, of functional balance. The concept of functional alternative is salvaged but without real appreciation of its value as an analytical tool and as a possible cardinal point in the criticism of classical functionalism.

Pierpaolo Donati's chapter has put forward a very clear case for the prospects of analysis inherent in the concept of sociological ambivalence. In my view, similar attention would be worth giving to the concept of functional alternatives.

The Concept of Functional Alternatives

As MLF is laid out, the criticism of the notion of functional indispensability and the emergence of the concept of functional alternatives appear at the end of the section critical of classical *functionalism* and proposing the renewed *functional analysis*. I wonder if in reality the idea of functional alternatives does not sum up well the Mertonian purposes and express the precise way Merton theorizes about social life, so much so as to allow us to consider it the point of departure and not of arrival in the renewal of functional analysis.

Let me recall that the criticism of the third postulate splits into two: the indispensability of the function and the indispensability of the element that performs a given function. As far as the first is concerned, Merton's diplomacy in criticism—a serious and well-based comparative analysis between societies would be needed (Merton and Parsons 1948: 156–164, 164–168)[3]—perhaps covers a much more deep-rooted conviction of the impossibility of proposing, at least in the present state of things, a general theory of society(ies). Merton's interest is wholly concentrated on the questioned hypothesis of the indispensability of the element that performs a given function.

The breakdown of a necessary relationship between a function and the element that performs that function is the first step towards wedging the prospect of multiplicity and change into the image of an extremely compact and so relatively unchangeable society. In my view, the Mertonian protocols owe something to certain value premises as well as to the prudence that comes from an awareness of the logic of development in the sciences. These value premises translate into a "possibilist" image of society—an off-center image we would say nowadays—never given over to a paralyzing synchrony between cultural and social structure[4] that frees us from the obligation to dominate the whole (i.e., to abandon a theory of society) and focuses our attention on circumscribed and realistic areas of analysis.

And there are practical as well as scientific consequences: the logical possibility of actions for reform is opened up, given that working on the part is certainly less foolishly ambitious than intervening on the totality, all the more so if we conceive of this part as released from a dependence on the whole and so is able to sidestep the system. Briefly, the concept of a functional alternative is a good explanation of the need to break the plan of society as a totalizing social system by introducing dynamic elements, further qualified by the perspective of middle-range theories.

In general, this may be more or less acceptable: less so the force of the functional alternative as a theoretical and practical analytical tool. Here one has a veritable sociological scalpel allowing exposure of the deep anatomy of the systems under investigation. The mental experiment—and why not? the practical experiment too—in which the concept is seen in operation, "What would happen if one introduced one element in place of another?" forces us to define and retrace a given system to test the compatibility of an alternative element with a given structural context to check the degree of structural tension.

The underlying purpose is to measure the degree of room for coercion and so also of propensity or willingness for change in a circumscribed system. Various degrees of "permeableness" in a system are thus represented: from indifference to the substitution of an element, to the possibility for improving the functional balance thanks to the contribution that the substitution of an element brings to the adaptation of the system, to the impossibility of partial modifications that simply expose the necessity for more radical transformations of the system as a whole.

The potential of such an analytical tool can be explained only by a theoretical and practical redimensioning of the image of a sociality coincident with society, conceived as well as an organic whole, unitary and static. These are roughly the reasons why, in my opinion, the concept of functional alternative is not just a tool derived from criticism of holistic functionalism but on the contrary can be considered a constitutive part of the criticism.

Now I want to go on to some problems relating to functional analysis and I shall then conclude with the topic of social engineering. I don't want to link up directly with the methodological developments contributed by various scholars—in particular by Francesca M. Cancian (1968) and Johan Galtung—to the revision of functional analysis proposed by Merton. Instead, I want to stay within Merton's own proposals.

The Method of Functional Analysis

One of the first problems is how to identify a system subject to functional analysis. In this connection I would formulate the hypothesis that the codification of the paradigm is not enough: it must be integrated with a later suggestion of Merton's, the logic of the examples presented and indications provided from outside.

This precious suggestion is contained in his closer examination of the first point of the paradigm—*items subject to functional analysis* (MLF: 109–114). The section concludes with a summary, defined as descriptive protocol (MLF: 114), in five points from which one deduces that the point of departure is not the function but an element (or more than one, which occurs simultaneously or is subsequently acquired in the course of the analysis). The function, or rather the functional balance, is a point of arrival, not an original assumption. Through the "location of the participants in the pattern within the social structure-differential participation" the connections in the system are reconstructed. But what are the boundaries of the system? When should one stop in order to prevent infinite regression down the dangerous slope towards society as a whole?

Obviously there is no mechanical rule that can be applied. Even Merton's intuitive sense of balance offers little help. Help comes, however, from the methodological codification Merton offers towards this balance: the theories of the middle range. A functional analysis can be usefully linked to the available theories of the middle range and their contribution can provide indications on where to establish the limits of the system. Or again, the various practical goals may be compared in order to arrive at elements that serve to narrow down the analysis on the basis of the feasibility principle. In all cases the ruling principle is to include all that can be theoretically and empirically kept under control and to avoid the level at which the implicit assumptions, the data which are interesting but difficult to coordinate and the attractions of *post factum* interpretations multiply uncontrollably.

Should we interpret this as an invitation to micro analysis on the assumption of greater controllability? Certainly not. In the first place, of course, micro is not at all the kingdom of simplicity; and secondly, Merton himself has dealt with topics that concern society as a whole. In one of these cases, in fact, he has given us an example of positive self-limitation in analysis. I refer to the studies on "Social Structure and Anomie" (Merton 1968: 185–248) where the goal of success in American society is assumed as a given whose functional consequences can be studied without getting involved in an explanation of its functional role.

This last reference to examples of functional analysis allows us to introduce the second point in the paradigm. I believe that if the examples Merton gives offer exemplary and educational illustrations of the method, they also introduce some methodological variations. In the case we are considering, there emerges quite clearly as a structuring element of the analysis the "solidarity" that gets established between social groups through the objective convergence of their interests, directed both to the satisfaction of socially approved needs and of those which are socially disapproved.

The key words are groups and interests. And here a third point in the paradigm is particularly useful, the one that confirms the hypothesis that these two terms are not specific to a given subject for study but extend to a more general indication. An early, brief criticism of functionalism can be found in Merton's discussion in 1947 of Parsons's paper "The Position of Sociological Theory." In the last part Merton admits to serious reserves about the way in which Parsons represents deviant behavior in relation to institutional models (168) Against the Parsonsian image of conditions of quietly dominant institutional values that would attribute distancing from the norm to prevalently individual deviancy, Merton puts forward the idea of groups with varying degrees of interest in the institutional models. He maintains that if a theory of institutions does not systematically take account of the groups that sustain particular institutions, one ends up by neglecting "the important role that sheer power plays in society."

If, finally, one bears in mind the attention Merton pays to the problems associated with reference groups, one can legitimately ask: is the functionally strategic action—and therefore action which need not be wholly conscious—of groups simply an example among many of functional analysis or is it a substantive indication which completes the most disembodied method? In the second prospect one can see some solution to another problem which I have not mentioned, that relating to the identification of the function(s); furthermore, more central and precise definition is given to the concept of functional balance. Even the concept of system adaptation lends itself to the possibility of patching up the relationship between the manifest and the latent. Nevertheless, one has to conclude on this point by observing that in fact not all Merton's functional analyses are so oriented even though, clearly, some are. Merton is never a boring reproducer of examples or a pedantic practitioner of his paradigm of functional analysis.

The last affirmation introduces the following question: to what extent does Merton really explain the functional method in studies which he himself declares are inspired by such an approach? He certainly does not lead the reader by the hand and point out his adherence to the method at each stage of the way. It is left to the reader to perform the intellectual exercise of checking such adherence. The studies quoted on "Social Structure and Anomie" lend themselves well to this purpose. The functional machinery of the two chapters in question is reconstructible only through the analysis as a whole and reveals an interesting qualification as well.

I'll begin with the qualification. One can think of a definition that links subjective and objective aspects of anomie in these terms: a *very high potential for breakdown in a state of social equilibrium* is produced by a split between cultural goals and social structure in the pursuit of goals in any given social system. The model case of split is one where there is a strong emphasis on a cultural goal (for example, monetary success in American society) "imposed" on the mass of the members of a social system, without adequate normative support when the legitimate means for its pursuit are not available for all or at least for a substantial majority.

The analysis is against a background of a state on the brink of total disorder announcing transformations. The split between means and goals produces, however, a series of role behaviors that Merton defines in his famous typology of adaptations. (Let us not get confused here: this is not yet adaptation in the functional sense, but in the sense of different ways of reacting to the split.) A first reduction of the destructive potential comes through the substitution of the goal of monetary success by other kinds of measured success; for example, artistic or professional prestige. But this is only a partial solution in that it obviously cannot be applied to everyone. It is a limited resource; if it were applied generally, the system would be transformed into something else with totally different cultural characteristics.

The real answer that reduces the destructive potential to within tolerable limits or that eliminates it altogether is to be found in the qualitative and quantitative form adopted by the distribution of the various behaviors, deviant and otherwise, in the particular system of social stratification that characterizes the social system under investigation. Merton provides precise indications in this direction, goes some of the way but does not complete a procedure that would lead inevitably (?) to linking aspects of class structure, cultural system, and political regime in a given society.

Social Engineering and Applied Sociology

I want to conclude now with some observations on the theme of social engineering in Merton. They will inevitably be superficial in that they touch on the vast theme of the relationships between cognitive valency and operational valency in social research and have to take into account the encyclopedic attention Merton gave to the sociology of science.[5]

In MLF and in particular in the pages relating to the formulation of the paradigm for functional analysis, Merton frequently refers to social engineering or aspects of it. Let this one citation suffice: "The points at which a functional analysis presupposes an implicit political outlook and the points at which it has bearing on 'social engineering' are concerns which find an integral place in the paradigm" (MLF: 109).

It is clear that Merton's use of the term "social engineering" does not imply the totalizing ideology of social planning but the more circumscribed applied sociology of the public social services.

Mertonian ideas on the organizational and ethical characteristics that guarantee the necessary autonomy of science are well known. Nevertheless, considering his work as a whole, one has the impression that he is far from having an aristocratic conception of scientific work; i.e., he is not indifferent in the making of its programs as to their translation into action or use for practical ends. I believe that the passage I have quoted, taken from a purely methodological reflection, is a clear example.

Generally, one can formulate the hypothesis that the imperative of objectivity and detachment has a double valency for Merton: one totally within the scientific ethos, the other projected onto the plane of practical action to characterize competent social interventions, far removed from moralizing or foolish dreams of utopia. This second valency may be translated into the recommendation: "The objectivity of the analysis is an excellent ingredient for reducing false starts in social interventions and perhaps also for their efficacy."

Laying no claim to exhaustive or systematic coverage, I should like now to quote, beginning from the most recent, some parts of Mertonian production that show his continued and not at all academic interest in the social utilization of scientific knowledge in the direction outlined briefly above.

A first indirect proof may be the historical period and the social context chosen as the subject of his first monograph in the sociology of science (Merton 1938). Going further and involving the social sciences, in UC there is, as we have seen, a specific affirmation on the problems of control and social planning. And as we have seen, in the extreme economy of exposition in that essay, every affirmation has its own specific relevance. I should like also to quote a circumstance which I like to think is not fortuitous. The contribution in question was published in the course of the first year—1936—of the *American Sociological Review*, which carried three articles at the beginning of the first issue: the first by F.S. Chapin, "Social Theory and Social Action"; the second by P.A. Sorokin, "Is Accurate Social Planning Possible?"; the third by E.A. Ross, "Some Contributions of Sociology to the Guidance of Society." In short, the climate was such even if Merton will be less rhetorical and more circumspect, almost as if he thought that the reciprocal respect between society (the State in particular) and social science typical of a democratic regime is what in the long run produces the most benefit for both.

There are occasions other than in his writing when Merton expresses his support for social commitment but at the same time warns against the risk of reducing the researcher committed to public action to the role of technical bureaucrat.

There is an exemplary illustration of this in an affirmation in the 1951 essay "Social Scientists and Research Policy"[6] written with Daniel Lerner: "If the social scientist is to contribute significantly to human welfare, he must be ready, willing, and able to ask and seek answers for such questions as: can we get human welfare without the 'welfare state'? If so, how? If not, how can we get the welfare state without the total state" (306–307)? The words speak for themselves, I think.

Finally, as further proof of what I am arguing, let me refer again to the essay "Role of the Intellectual in Public Bureaucracy" in which Merton reflects on the fate of a generation of American social scientists who placed their hopes as reformers in work for the federal government. By way of a circumstantiated analysis of the mechanisms and processes that cancel out the good intentions of the social researchers recruited by the policymakers, Merton arrives at the conclusion that the independent intellectual maintains, thanks to his freedom of thought, a significantly greater ability to influence the definition and resolution of problems.

Moreover, it would seem that so far as the conception of applied sociology is concerned, Merton is much nearer to what has been defined as the enlightenment model rather than models like the clinical-engineering or strategic-cooperation-with-the-client type.[7] And yet he has much to say even to those who, like myself, incline more to the these last two models, without in any way forcing them to embrace the first model. Indirectly, it is a lesson in vigilant toleration: another reason why we cannot but be Mertonians.

Notes

1. In Italy the Luhmann-Merton relationship has been dealt with by Italo Vaccarini 1982.
2. It is clear here that the distinction between subjective and objective consequences is absolutely not in discussion.
3. The overall meaning of pages 86–89 in MLF which contains the elaboration of the criticism of the indispensability of functions is well summed up in Merton's discussion of Talcott Parsons's "The Position of Sociological Theory," both of these in *American Sociological Review* 13 (April 1948) 156–164 and 164–168. The summary is on page 168(e) of this brief text which may be considered an integral part of MLF.
4. See, for example, how Merton hypothesizes on the "dysfunctionality" of an absolute conformism in his introduction to part 2 of *Social Theory,* and at 301–302.
5. Sztompka (*An Intellectual Profile*) insists on the central role of the sociological analysis of scientific institutions in Merton's theoretical system.
6. In attributing parts of the paper, Merton has ascribed to himself the second part from which this quotation is taken.
7. I refer especially to J. Ben David 1973 and Kathleen A. Archibald 1970.

Robert K. Merton and Contemporary Sociology

References

Archibald, Kathleen A. 1970. "Alternative Orientations to Social Science Utilization," *Social Science Information* 9 (2): 7–34.

Barbano, Filippo. [1959] 1971. "Introduction." In *Teoria e struttura sociale*, by Robert K. Merton. Bologna: Il Mulino.

———. 1955. *Teoria e ricerca nella sociologia contemporanea.* Milan: Giuffré. Esp. 100–108, 129–134.

Ben-David, Joseph. 1973. "How to Organise Research in the Social Sciences," *Daedalus* 103 (2): 39–51.

Campbell, Colin. 1982. "A Dubious Distinction? An Inquiry into the Value and the Use of Merton's Concepts of Manifest and Latent Functions." *American Sociological Review* 47 (February 1982): 29–44.

Cancian, Francesca. 1968. "Varieties of Functional Analysis" under the heading "Functional Analysis." In *International Encyclopedia of the Social Sciences*, vol. 6, 29–43. New York: Macmillan.

Di Lellio, Anna. 1985. "Le aspettative sociali di durata: Intervista a Robert K. Merton." *Rassegna Italiana di Sociologia* 26 (1): 3–26, esp. 7–8.

Luhmann, Niklas. 1970. *Soziologische Aufklärung.* Köln Opladen: Westdeutscher Verlag. [Italian translation. 1983. *Illuminismo sociologico.* Milan: Il Saggiatore, 31–35].

Marletti, Carlo. 1970. "Alcune riflessioni sull'efficacia della pratica di ricerca empirica in sociologia." In *Sviluppo e struttura*, by Carlo Marletti. Rome: Bulzoni, 9–66, esp. 18–26.

Merton, Robert K. 1968. "Manifest and Latent Functions." In *Social Theory and Social Structure*. New York: Free Press.

———. 1938. "Science, Technology and Society in Seventeenth Century England." In *Osiris: Studies on the History and Philosophy of Science, and on the History of Learning and Culture*, edited by George Sarton. Bruges: St. Catherine Press. [Italian translation. 1975. *Scienza, tecnologia e società nell' Inghilterra del XVII secolo.* Milan: Franco Angeli].

———. 1936. "The Unanticipated Consequences of Purposive Social Action." *American Sociological Review* 1 (6): 894–902.

———. and Daniel Lerner. 1951. "Social Scientists and Research Policy." In *The Policy Sciences,* edited by David Lerner and H.D. Lasswell. Stanford: Stanford University Press, 282–307.

Parsons, Talcott. 1947. "The Position of Sociological Theory." Paper given at the annual reunion of the American Sociological Society, 28–30 December 1947. Published in *Social Theory and Social Structure*, by Robert K. Merton, 168. New York: Free Press.

Sztompka, Piotr. 1986. *Robert K. Merton: An Intellectual Profile.* London: Macmillan and New York: St. Martin's Press.

Vaccarini, Italo. 1982. "Per una rivalutazione delle teorie sociologiche di Robert K. Merton." *Studi di Sociologia* 20 (2).

Zingerle, Arnold. 1997. "The Unanticipated Consequences of Action: Sociological and Ethical Aspects." In *Robert K. Merton and Contemporary Sociology*, edited by Carlo Mongardini and Simonetta Tabboni. New Brunswick, NJ: Transaction Publishers.

14

Robert K. Merton, the Teacher: Episodic Recollections by an Enthusiastic Apprentice

Rocco Caporale

The subtitle of this chapter is wilfully plagiaristic, but well suited to the occasion. A few months ago in New York, I invited a group of distinguished social scientists to a reception held in honor of Professor Tullio Tentori of the University of Rome, and, of course, I made sure that my mentor Robert Merton was invited. He promised to come, but at the last minute excused himself. A few days later I received a note of apology in which Merton explained his absence: he had to meet a deadline for an essay on the great historian of science George Sarton, his own mentor at Harvard several decades ago.

The article he enclosed was entitled "George Sarton: Episodic Recollections by an Unruly Apprentice." As I read the essay, I had a profound feeling of *déjà vu*, of affinity, of an intellectual, almost genetic linkage with Professor Sarton, my sociological grandfather as it were, whose deep sense of professional commitment I had experienced through Robert Merton, my mentor and sociological model.

Because of the privileged relationship I had with Professor Merton, this chapter will differ considerably from the others in this volume. I shall not deal with critical aspects of Merton's theorizing; rather I shall present some anecdotal bits and pieces from my personal experience as a graduate student at Columbia University under his mentorship, to highlight the significance of this scholar as master-teacher and guide in the intellectual pursuit.

This chapter, however, has significant theoretical implications with regard to the notion of *exemplification* frequently alluded to in this meeting.

Exemplification is a widely used pedagogical strategy to drive home a particular point and show the applicability of a conceptually engineered interpretation of reality. In sociology, however, exemplification acquires a deeper meaning that borders on typification and on the critical case, and yet never leaves the level of concreteness and reality.

Essential to the process of theorizing is the requirement that every theory worth its salt must be susceptible to exemplification, or run the risk of remaining abstract and largely irrelevant to real life. One of the most biting criticisms that could be made of Parsonsian-style theorizing is precisely that it is often so refractory to exemplification that it almost becomes the conceptual construct for an imaginary society.

Merton's theorizing, on the other hand, never leaves the realm of the daily and the ordinary, but emerges with a fresh insight into social processes and phenomena that many sociologists take for granted to the point of not being problematic at all. The Matthew Effect reflects the daily observation of maldistribution of rewards, reference group theory makes sense of discrepancies in motivated behavior, the differential patterns of deviance from norms and compliance to them answer the question that moralists and legislators should pose about the ultimate responsibility of human responses to ambivalent situations (the issue of predictable "rates" of behavior and individual guilt), and so on.

It can be said that Merton's seminal concepts and theoretical statements generally display this deep-rooted and intimate connection to concrete social experience and daily life. Unfortunately the same cannot be said of some other theoreticians, concerned more with devising a beautifully architectured conceptual structure than using theory to make sense of life.

I was privileged to be one of the few Italian sociologists who had Robert K. Merton as their master-teacher and as such, I have a sense of duty to share with my Italian friends, on this unusual occasion, one of the most valuable experiences of my life. Because I see in Professor Merton a cogent illustration of the feasibility of wedding the highest capability for theoretical thinking to pedagogical excellence and professional enthusiasm, thus making the sociological enterprise meaningful in real life terms, rather than just an academic exercise to justify one's occupational position.

It can be said that in the early 1960s the sociological enterprise in the United States reached its zenith at Columbia University. Graduate students were arriving from many countries to study under such world-renowned teachers as Paul Lazarsfeld, pioneer of so much in sociological methodology and a founder of mass communications research; Herbert Hyman, originator of the concept of reference groups and master of secondary analysis; William J. Goode, leading theorist and researcher in the comparative sociology of the family; and Sigmund Diamond, the distinguished figure in historical sociology. Other, younger teachers, of later fame, included the mathematical statistician Theodore Anderson, and the sociologists Allen Barton, Amitai Etzioni, Samuel Klausner, Eugene Lavine, Juan Linz, Thomas O'Dea, Ivan Vallier, and Hans Zetterberg. As the then chairman of the Department of Sociology, Robert K. Merton presided over this constellation of luminaries.

It was the end of January 1960 and I had been shopping for a congenial doctoral program at Columbia. I had been admitted provisionally to the program in social psychology and signed up for classes with Professors Otto Klineberg, Richard Christie, and Goodwin Watson.

I liked some of the classes I attended, but after two weeks of experimenting I felt extremely uncomfortable, utterly unmotivated, and academically restless. Something prompted me to seek an alternative and that afternoon I ventured into the anthropology department where I met a spunky, short lady and, as I later learned, that epitome of anthropology, Professor Margaret Mead. I ventured to tell her that I wanted to change departments, but was not sure as to which program was suitable for me. Professor Mead glanced through my transcripts and then looked at me in utter disbelief at my academic window-shopping: how could anyone with my background doubt for a minute my suitability for anthropology? As I continued to hesitate, she grumbled disappointedly and suggested that I look into the sociology program.

On to the second floor of the sociology building, where Mrs. Esther Davis, the departmental secretary, promptly directed me to the chairman. The shelves of his enormous office were crowded with books and reviews, and on his desk a variety of pipes blended naturally with a variety of manuscripts and the latest arrivals from the publishing houses.

Professor Merton was intrigued, asked me lots of questions and fascinated me with his aristocratic demeanor, his genuine interest in my problem, and, above all, his patience. At the end of our conversation I had no more doubts: I wanted to become a sociologist.

Pretty soon I was informed that Columbia University was granting me fifteen credits of advanced standing for my previous studies, a President's Fellowship for four years, and, best of all, that Professor Merton was to be my advisor and mentor of my dissertation. I felt accepted, chosen, wanted, sustained, and at home—and I knew to whom I owed it all.

I enrolled in his course "Analysis of Social Structure," and saw my life change dramatically. It was hard to get up very early in the morning and drive all the way from Westchester to Columbia to be on time for the 9:30 A.M. class. The long drive turned out to be a joyful anticipation of a profound and rich intellectual experience.

Merton would lay his pipe on the desk and begin lecturing from extremely well-prepared notes, with the clearest diction, and the most crystalline logical flow. One topic was the emergence of social norms and the bases of social order. From Hobbes to Montesquieu, to Durkheim and Sumner, to the interaction process analysis of Bales and Parsons, the experiments of Pepitone, Asch and Sherif, he would compellingly unravel a complex and fundamental problem, effortlessly designing an astonishing synthesis of human struggle and showing the far-reaching capability of the sociological imagination.

Accustomed, as I was, to a very different lecturing style by the Italian professors of that time, I was surprised and elated, to say the least. What Merton was saying not only made sense of the world around me but (in a George Mead sense) helped explain *me* to *myself*, to the point of giving some validity (so I thought at that time) to the Comtean notion of sociology, as the discipline that could do what other "sciences" had failed to do: give empirically validated meaning to the human experience. I enrolled in every course and seminar he offered for the next four years!

As a student in search of meanings I found two compelling qualities of Merton's teaching that made my quest for meaning much easier:

unlike most other professors in the department, his theorizing had the beauty, elegance, and solidity of a Renaissance building, but it could be applied without strain to concrete, everyday, real-life situations.

I could not say that I disliked the other professors; it was only a matter of quality I felt absent in most other lecturers. Not infrequently, for instance, good old Paul Lazarsfeld had us totally lost as he moved through armies of two-by-two tables; William J. Goode lectured on the family, a real-life topic if any, but at the end of two hours of intense lecturing we were not sure we had grasped the implications of his extensive familiarity with the subject and their theoretical valence; Professor Anderson would fill all the blackboards on the four walls of the classroom with equations, switching skillfully from right hand to left hand (he was ambidextrous), but more often than not left us totally overwhelmed; Juan Linz would go over ten articles and five books in a single lecture and assign a fifty-page reading list on the history of sociology, successfully engendering in us a sense of utter hopelessness. How do you catch up with minds of this order? How do you reconcile the pressure to absorb a frightening amount of required material when you struggle to see its relevance to a daily life filled with all kinds of insurmountable problems?

There was no ennui, tedium, or academic overkill in Merton's class. The fully packed classroom became, as it were, one body, one mind, fully alert, charged by the calm but energetic thinking of this man who painstakingly was driving us away from half-truths and confused thinking to a mountaintop of clarity, order, and even intellectual harmony.

In the years that followed I took down classroom notes by the bookfull: even today I cherish them and find them rich in inspiration and the best preparation for my course in theory and for a variety of lectures on related topics.

The richness and relevance of the material presented in Merton's class acquired greater value because of the clarity and crispness of his prose, classically enhanced by the use of a choice vocabulary, yet simple and coherent to the point of sounding like a genuine piece of English literature. When we sought relief from the perverse obscurity of Parsons, or from the jargon of *AJS*'s writers, Merton's crystalline essays took on an aura of redemption: the highest level of sociological theorizing could make sense, even to the man in the street, to the novice graduate student, as well as to the journalist and the politician.

It comes as no surprise that of the sociological concepts that have found their way into the popular usage of educated people, a good many are the product of Merton's thinking and literary sophistication.

When the time came for me to select a topic for my dissertation, Professor Merton suggested that I study the attitude of the Catholic community on the issue of birth control. Already then (in 1962) he had accurately anticipated that this issue would become a battleground of the decade (as in fact it did, especially after *Humanae Vitae*). But I had my mind set on spending some time in Italy to study the Roman Catholic religious system in the throes of change brought about by the Vatican Council.

Accommodatingly, Merton went along with my choice, like a father who scales down his stride to the diminutive steps of a child. That year at Columbia an entire cohort of graduate students was writing dissertations on leadership in various spheres of activity. Harriet Zuckerman was interviewing Nobel prize winners, Adolpho Critto was studying political elites, and a Chinese-American student (whose name I forgot) was studying business elites.

My desire to study religious elites well suited Merton's keen interest in the relationship between science and religion. He arranged for me to receive a research grant and I was off to Rome.

I still preserve the draft of my dissertation, in large part rewritten in red ink by Merton. Painstakingly, he went over it line by line, to make sense of my thinking while at the same time editing my faulty English style. Years later I realized the value of his dedication to students and pedagogy, when I experienced personally how much a graduate student's demand can erode a scholar's research time, and when I heard widespread complaints from Italian and American students about their mentor's lack of interest in their dissertation research.

I never found Merton grudging the time that my limited preparation was costing him.

Finally it was defense time. While Professor O'Dea and Professor Vallier were genuinely enthusiastic about my manuscript, Professor Goode and Professor Etzioni had strong reservations and attacked me violently. In the long discussion that followed, I watched with amusement five outstanding sociologists debate my dissertation and passionately argue with each other, until at one point Professor Etzioni, obviously appalled at the turn of events, suddenly stopped and asked: "who is defending this dissertation, anyway?" To my great surprise

Robert Merton replied with aplomb: "I am!" Amidst the general laughter that followed, I felt the intensity of affection and the mysterious bond that this man of science could evoke in his students; and, I realized that all the toil and struggle of the previous four-and-a-half years were worth every bit of the energy I had invested in them.

As I reflect on the deep empathy that links me to this extraordinary man I realize that, in comparison with several other students in my cohort, I did not spend as much time with Merton as I would have liked to. Yet our relatively few meetings were so intense and so imbued with psychic osmosis that I felt, and still feel, an almost filial bond to this man whose writings and whose life I could take at one and the same time as a model of deep human richness, dedication to duty, brilliant thinking, and intellectual achievement.

I need not apologize for the personal flavor of these recollections: I am sure that every one of the hundreds of students who studied with Professor Merton would stand by what I said, and could add a host of more tasty bits and pieces that would enhance even further, if possible, the figure of this man as a teacher.

I like to hope that these biographical reminiscences, this sort of sociological gossip, if you will, may represent an invitation to all, but especially the teachers amongst us, to give due consideration to the other side of the sociological enterprise: the transmission of knowledge through the pedagogical encounter of two generations of searchers.

As we discuss and debate Merton's theories and the achievements of this man of science, I believe it is imperative to call our attention to the coherence between the intellectual productivity and the human side of this scholar, who has drawn upon a sociological imagination, and the master teacher who validates the profession through his exemplary performance.

This is what *exemplification* is all about. I am sure that somewhere on the shelves of Merton's study there is a manuscript he has been working at for several years and which one day we may see in print with the title: "An essay on the sociological function of exemplification." In the sociological profession no one is better qualified to write this essay than Robert K. Merton, exemplary teacher of an epoch that may not return.

15

Notes towards an Analysis of the Relationship between Ambivalence and Rationality

Alessandro Cavalli

The generation of Italian sociologists who started their sociological studies between the late 1950s and the early 1960s has been marked by a singular experience: among the first books that we read and studied was without fail *Social Theory and Social Structure* by Robert K. Merton. Since I believe in the decisive influence of early experiences, that is, in the possibility of generalizing on the ethological theory of imprinting, I think one can say that ours is a generation of sociologists which grew up under the influence of Merton, even if we are no longer always aware that we have received this inheritance and that we carry it with us. Thus, every now and then, I realize almost with astonishment that much of what I have cultivated in my sociological garden in all these years turns on Mertonian themes: social time and ambivalence.

In this chapter I want to make a series of observations on the latter theme, which has already been dealt with very authoritatively during the conference by Pierpaolo Donati and Birgitta Nedelmann. Forgive me though, if, before I say anything on the theme of ambivalence, I make a brief premise of an almost autobiographical nature.

Personally, I have always felt uneasy about lining up in support of any one side in the dichotomies that have seemed to divide the sociological community in the last thirty years—the sociology of consensus versus the sociology of conflict in society, explanatory versus interpretative sociology, structural sociology versus the sociology of action. I have always felt myself to be on both sides at once, without entirely sharing the theoretical, epistemological, and methodological credo of the opposing trends. For this reason, I dare to define myself an eclectic sociologist, in the hope that this adjective does not simply conjure up negative associations. So if my observations on ambivalence are delivered in the language of action theory, that does not in any way signify a rejection of an approach in structural analytical terms.

Any action theory has to start with the assumption that intentional action is possible, that human beings are not only moved by needs and forces which are beyond their control, which operate through them and of which they are largely unaware. An action theory, then, starts with the assumption that basically people are consciously able to set themselves objectives and make choices between alternative courses of action. Of course, the possible options, either in terms of resources or in terms of values and norms, are structurally given and it is true that people are not always aware of the social nature of the processes producing the alternative options for action from which they make their choices.

The theory of rational choice has long been put forward as the basic nucleus of action theory. It says, to make a crude synthesis, that the actor will choose the course of action that seems most advantageous in terms of cost-benefit correlation. There is no room in rational choice theory for ambivalence. It assumes, in fact, two conditions: (1) that the costs and benefits of the various alternative courses of action are measurable by the actor; and, (2) that among the various alternative courses one and only one leads the actor to expect an appreciable advantage over all the others. Now, the definitive case of these conditions is clearly a special case, a case which does not occur often in the experience of social actors. On the contrary, paradoxically, when we are able to make rational choices, we do not have the subjective sensation of making real, genuine choices. When we see very clearly where the benefits lie, we do not feel we are making choices. If you ask me whether it is better to organize a seminar on Merton and contemporary sociology in Amalfi or in Sesto S. Giovanni, I do not feel I am a champion of rationality if I say I prefer Amalfi. I don't even need to explain the reasons for my choice because I feel they are generally acceptable. Situations of this type do not pose problems. The real problems of choice for the actor come when (a) it is not possible to establish with certainty the costs and benefits to expect from alternative courses of action; (b) the relative advantages are equal, or in the language of neoclassical economic theory, the alternatives all have the same utility, that is, they are situated in Pareto's terms on an equal distribution curve; and (c) the actor has to justify, to himself and others, the criteria on which he bases his choices. These situations are very frequent in reality, the actor's "rationality" is tested before ambivalent choices, choices, that is, where the assumptions of rational choice are not realized. This is the paradox of rational choice.

Faced with situations of this type, the actor has a further choice before him, and this is very often an ambivalent one too: he can abstain from action, that is, he can choose not to choose, or he can *intentionally* modify his own expectations, if at the same time he is prepared to accept a higher level of risk and uncertainty.

This last point is very delicate. In a situation of ambivalent choice, the actor has to start a decision process aimed at reducing the level of ambivalence in the choice (and therefore aimed at making the choice possible), unless, of course, he chooses not to choose and so he escapes from the ambivalence of the situation by postponing the decision or shelving it completely. If he chooses to choose, that is, if he takes a voluntaristic option, the actor has to modify his preferences (their utility curves in economic theory) almost intentionally during the process. He has to give an answer to the following question, first of all for himself: what do I really want, what are my real objectives? This inevitably implies some degree of manipulation of the actor's identity by the actor himself. In fact, the actor's identity gets a chance to define itself not in situations where the rational choice model can be generalized, but where the actor has to manage situations of ambivalent choice and is therefore obliged to make clear to others, but first of all to himself, the scale of priorities he is going to adopt either to get out of the ambivalence, or to choose to stay within the ambivalence. In fact, we owe to the ambivalent nature of the choices that we have to make in the course of our lives, the fact that we can define our individuality/identity in a world of human beings capable of being rational.

Merton has demonstrated in masterly fashion how society produces conditions of structural ambivalence; he has thus reintroduced into contemporary sociology a category, ambivalence, which was central to classical sociology starting with Weber and Simmel. Many sociologists have forgotten Merton's lesson. For myself, I can only declare my intention to cultivate this theme in my sociological garden, while trying to combine the themes of ambivalence and identity in an action theory perspective. I hope, therefore, that this brief chapter is merely a small foretaste, as well as being witness to the great debt of gratitude we all owe to Robert K. Merton.

16

Robert K. Merton for an "Open Society"? Or, a Concept of Society Beyond Functionalism

Giuliano Giorio

This extremely brief chapter should be viewed as notes on some points in the chapter by Volker Meja and Nico Stehr. Among sociologists the ups-and-downs in the fortunes of Merton's nevertheless fundamental work are well-known: from the years in which any sociologist of note could not but make reference to his works,[1] to a sort of partial abandonment which was largely linked to superficially held, political prejudices that drew fashionable consensus,[2] and finally to a more recent widespread recovery even in Italy.[3]

Alongside the various problem areas touched on in these chapters, there is another I feel one should not neglect—a possible Mertonian meaning of the concept of "society" itself that, as far as one is permitted to know had led Coser in the early 1970s to consider from a general viewpoint whether Merton's thought should be declared as extending well beyond a static dominant vision of functional analysis (Coser 1971: 566–567). I should like to draw attention to this question again, quite specifically, going beyond a simplistic and perhaps now generally accepted insertion of Merton's thought into a holistic or systematic all-encompassing category, which has been given the more extensive discussion due to it elsewhere (Giorio 1985).

On this subject, obviously, it seems possible to refer in the first instance to certain points in the work that is best known and most quoted, Merton's *Social Theory and Social Structure* (1949), which became available in Italy immediately after the second edition (1957), along with a fine introduction by Professor Barbano.

But one should be warned that in this book the concept of society does not seem so much to be dealt with explicitly as an "autonomous paradigm" in the context of the work, as much as it gradually becomes obvious "functionally," (not by chance one might say), through the subsequent evolution of closely argued thoughts proposed for common reflection over the decades.

It is well known, in fact, that among the "prevailing postulates in functional analysis" (Merton 1957: 25) Merton puts "the postulate of the functional unity of society" in first place before the "sociological functions" of the social and cultural elements and their indispensability.

For Merton the first declaration of the postulate is to be found in Radcliffe-Brown in the sense of "a social system (the total social structure of a society together with the totality of social usages . . .) has a certain kind of unity, which we may speak of as a functional unity" (Merton 1957: 25–26). To this is added the opinion of Malinowski who "continues to speak of standardized practices and beliefs as functional 'for culture as a whole' and goes on to assume that they are also functional for every member of the society" (Merton 1957: 26). And still in Merton's view, Kluckhohn would complete the discussion with his affirmation that "cultural forms [would turn out to be] adjustive or adaptive . . . for the members of the society *or* for the society considered as a perduring unit" (Merton 1957: 26).

Consequently, for Merton "the degree of integration [of a society] is an empirical variable [precisely!] changing for the same society from time to time and differing among various societies" (Merton 1957: 27). Furthermore, Merton takes for granted that "all human societies must have some degree of integration" but—he hastens to add—"not all societies have that *high* degree of integration in which *every* culturally standardized activity or belief is functional for the society as a whole and uniformly functional for the people living in it" (Merton 1957: 27).

Naturally, Merton is also ready to recognize that "the assumption of the complete functional unity of human society is repeatedly contrary to fact," in the sense that "social usages or sentiments may be functional for some groups and dysfunctional for others in the same society" (Merton 1957: 27). Moreover, he also feels he must challenge the positions of certain social anthropologists in that he does not believe it is possible to transfer without qualification the assumption of the "highly integrated nature" of "aboriginal civilizations," in other words, a transfer "from the realm of small nonliterate societies to the realm of large, complex and highly differentiated, literate societies" (Merton 1957: 28). He gives "a functional interpretation of religion" as an example (Merton 1957: 28). In reality, says Merton, "integration is provided by any consensus on any set of values" (Merton 1957: 30) and for this reason too, he maintains it is best not to adopt "the unqualified postulate of functional unity. This unity of the total society cannot be usefully posited in advance of observation" (Merton 1957: 30).

Merton seems to use another indirect reference, too, to the more general problem of defining the concept of society when he tackles new developments in the history of reference groups in connection with the field of social psychology. These deal mainly with the responses of individuals to the stimuli which they receive in the realm of personal relations and in the wider social realm. Merton develops this last concept, the idea of "collectivity," borrowing from von Wiese, Becker, Znaniecki, and Parsons; "collectivity" understood, however, as social structures composed of "people who have a sense of solidarity by virtue of sharing common values and who have acquired an attendant sense of moral obligation to fulfill role-expectations" (Merton 1957: 299). And he considers it necessary, almost in anticipation of more recent identifications of this concept with that of "community" (Giorio 1983: 18–54) to specify straightaway that "all groups are, of course, collectivities, but those collectivities which lack the criterion of interaction among members are not groups" (Merton 1957: 299).

At this point, then, it would not seem altogether without interest, a word from the man himself with reference to his later reflections on the relations between the two concepts of "society" and "collectivity," and on any further elements contributing to greater comprehension of the meaning he intends to attribute to them. [At the conference Professor Merton took up the invitation.] However, it must also be added that the same scholar formulates another series of observations which, interesting in themselves, bear on "theories of the middle range"; this, in a comment on the so-called Thomas theorem: "If men define situations as real, they are real in their consequences" (Merton 1957: 421).

In Merton's view, indeed, "Were the Thomas theorem and its implications more widely known, more men would understand more of the workings of our society" (Merton 1957: 421). Merton goes on to explain that "the first part of the theorem provides an uneasy reminder that men respond not only to the objective features of a situation, but also, and at times primarily, to the meaning this situation has for them" (Merton 1957: 421–422). Following this, Merton justifies the assertion on the basis of the results of specific investigations on "the self-fulfilling prophesy and the vicious circle" (Merton 1957: 435) in order to identify in "these patterns of behavior" "a product of the modifiable structure of society" (Merton 1957: 435) till he discovers that precisely because of legitimate doubts about "man's capacity to control man and his society" (Merton 1957: 435) this same capacity must effectively be also established institutionally if it is to be effective.

It would seem, therefore, that Merton's argument develops within anything but a static perspective; on the contrary, it takes on an explicitly dynamic configuration. Not for nothing did Barbano astutely observe, more than twenty years ago, how the scholar from Pennsylvania [Merton] seemed to take up a position in one of his discussions "on social structure," about "the viewpoint of the process through which the individual constructs for himself his practical image of society." That is, he reconstructs its "objectivity not only by means of the analysis of the interactions, the reciprocal relations and the implied related subjective dispositions" (Barbano 1966: 126–27). And along with our teacher and friend from Turin [Barbano] we can thus rightly emphasize that "the reconstruction of the analytical properties of social structure . . . [represents] a decided step forward compared with any positivist and naturalist way of describing and classifying based on taxonomic criteria" (Barbano 1966: 126–27)—a method by which, then as today, not a few limit the very object of sociological knowledge.

In this wider perspective, lastly, one must mention other possible indicators which might well be considered above those of mundane everyday social experience. In fact, among those who appear to have accepted the Mertonian idea of "social restructuring," some have felt they must also attach to it what they see as relevant implications "in relation to the more far-reaching conceptions of 'man.'" To this, they add the search for every possible guarantee of "that modest margin of autonomy which global society still concedes to utopian thinking," in the sense of a continual and active claim to "individual autonomy, as far as it is possible and of some use in the context of a sociality which has become more and more restrictive and determining" (Demarchi 1976). One might ask, then, if a hypothesis such as this can still fit in with Merton's more recent reflections. Consider, for one example, Luhmann who, again with a clear reference to Merton in an interpretation coming a good fifteen years after Merton's fundamental work, seemed to demand "a restructuring of the social system that [should substitute] a prevalently segmentary differentiation with a prevalently functional differentiation" (Luhmann 1970 [It.trans. 1983: 176]).[4] Or consider Donati, who again brought up again the problem already tackled by Mongardini on the role of the subject-actor in social mobility, who is commonly thought to develop increasing tensions at least on the level of an adequate rationality. Thus, Donati's work is presented in more sophisticated terms than the preceding Luhmann hypothesis.[5]

Notes

1. See, for example, the references in the works of Wagner 1963, Martindale 1960, Jonas 1968, etc.
2. This is perhaps the explanation for the silence of not a few Italian writers in the 1970s.
3. See, as an example of this, Italo Vaccarini 1982: 135–155.
4. For interesting reflections in this connection see in particular Carlo Mongardini 1983: 197ff.
5. A concept of "rationality" can also be traced in Toynbee's general (and thus debatable) historical perspective. See Toynbee 1934.

References

Barbano, Filippo. 1966. "Significato e analisi delle strutture nella antropologia e nella sociologia." *Studi di Sociologia* 2: 126–127 passim.

Coser, Lewis A. 1971. *Masters of Sociological Thought*. New York: Harcourt Brace Jovanovich.

Demarchi, Franco 1976. "Struttura." In *Dizionario di Sociologia*, edited by Franco Demarchi and Aldo Ellena, 1279. Rome: Edizioni Paoline.

Giorio, Giuliano. 1985. *Società e sistemi sociali*. pp. 96–98, 129–132, 237–241. Milan: Franco Angeli.

———. 1983. "L'Organizzazione di comunità in ambiente montano." In *Territorio e comunità: Il mutamento sociale nell'area montana*, 18–54 passim. Milan: Franco Angeli.

Jonas, Friedrich. 1968. *Geschichte der Soziologie*. Hamburg: Rowohlt Verlag.
Luhmann, Niklas. 1970. *Sociologische Aufklärung-I*. Köln Opladen: Westdeutscher Verlag. [Italian trans. 1983. "Introduction" by D. Zolo. In *Illuminismo sociologico*, edited by R. Schmidt, 176 passim. Milan: Il Saggiatore.]
Martindale, Don. 1960. *The Nature and Types of Sociological Theory*. Cambridge: The Riverside Press.
Merton, Robert K. 1957. *Social Theory and Social Structure*. New York: Free Press. [Italian trans. [1959] 1966. "Introduction." In *Teoria e struttura sociale*, 2d ed., by Filippo Barbano. Translated by C. Marletti and A. Oppo. Bologna: Il Mulino.
Mongardini, Carlo. 1983. "In margine all'ultimo libro di Luhmann." *Sociologia 2*.
Toynbee, Arnold J. 1934. *A Study of History*. London: Oxford University Press.
Vaccarini, Italo. 1982. "Per una rivalutazione della teoria sociologica di Robert K. Merton." *Studi di Sociologia 2*.
Wagner, Helmut R. 1963. "Types of Sociological Theory." *American Sociological Review 5*.

17

Robert K. Merton's Contribution to Sociological Studies of Time

Simonetta Tabboni

The study of time has not been an issue that has absorbed Merton to any great extent, although he has returned to it from time to time over the years. It is enough to say that there are almost fifty years between his first and his most recent essay on the subject. Nevertheless, Merton's contribution to this field has made a considerable impact and pointed the way for future studies in this area. Merton is significantly well equipped to give a detailed account of the American approach to the analysis of temporality, as it was he and Pitirim Sorokin who laid the basis for a theoretical study of time in 1937. This paper, "Social Time: A Methodological and Functional Analysis" (Sorokin and Merton 1937a), broke new ground in the United States, marking the beginning of a completely new line of research. In 1982 he developed these ideas further in a lecture (Merton 1982b), and then went on to write an essay on the social aspects of duration, which was published in 1984 (Merton 1984a).

Merton's work was in the great European tradition, building on the pioneering studies of Émile Durkheim, Henri Hubert, and Marcel Mauss, whose studies on the theme of time provided many profound insights. However, the intellectual climate of the late-1930s did not seem particularly favorable to a renewal of interest in the study of time, and American sociologists showed no particular interest in

Merton's attempts to develop it further.[1] The themes put forward in Sorokin's and Merton's essay were not taken up by anyone else, although Sorokin, who had been the moving force behind these studies, remained interested in these issues and went on to develop them in *Social and Cultural Dynamics* ([1937] 1941) and *Sociocultural Causality, Space, Time* (1943).

In retrospect these initial studies can be seen as premature and isolated attempts to transplant European and Durkheimian ideas into a somewhat unfertile and nonreceptive American soil. They met with little success. Still, when American social scientists become interested in the subject of time again, they will no doubt take up from where Sorokin and Merton left off, continuing the Durkheimian emphasis on the normative and collective aspects of time and the way in which time is seen as a unifying force.

The works of Moore (1963), Coser and Coser (1963), and especially Zerubavel (1981) are direct developments of the themes of the 1937 essay, firmly rooted in the Durkheimian tradition.

In this sense Merton's second essay on time of 1984, which focuses on the concept of socially expected durations (SEDs), marks the logical conclusion of a particular line of research which had been started in the United States by Merton and Sorokin, following on directly from Durkheim. Perhaps this explains Merton's comment on the relation between his essay on SEDs and the large body of work produced on the subject of time from the 1960s: "However, these and kindred materials, both early and contemporary, provide part of the substantive basis for a methodical analysis of the concept of socially expected durations in connection with the sociological problems and understanding it helps to generate" (Merton 1982b).

This amounts to saying that the diverse approaches to the theme of time adopted by American sociologists need to be supported by an adequate theoretical framework if they are to stand up to close scrutiny. Merton put considerable emphasis on the fact that social time and SEDs formed part of the same continuum, both in the paper he presented at San Francisco in 1982 (1982b) and in the interview with Anna di Lellio in 1985, in which he said:

> In highly industrialized societies, certain types of social expectations of time are highly complex and have a considerable impact. This can be more clearly understood if we bear in mind the concept of social time which Sorokin and I developed in an article we wrote in 1937. Even although at that time we had no idea of what

social expectations of time were, in that article we maintained, in the best Durkheimian tradition, that the more there is a generally perceived social need to coordinate and link aspects of time, the greater the development of models of social time which are distinct from calendar time and time as measured against the movements of the stars. (Merton 1985b: 8)

After having made clear the basic premises of Merton's approach, a number of questions remain to be answered. The first concerns the exact nature of Merton's project and the theoretical directions he is following within the American tradition of studies on the "sociology of time." We must attempt to identify the strengths and weaknesses of his contribution to the study of social time and to ascertain what are likely to prove the most promising developments of his line of thought.

In his essay on SEDs, as on many other occasions, Merton goes back to Burke's theorem to explain his intellectual development, the reasons for his particular approach, why it proved to be particularly fruitful and why he left other directions relatively unexplored. Burke's theorem must have fascinated Merton and provided the answer to a question which, although apparently banal, often arises when assessing the evolution of a theory, namely why certain issues are explored in great depth while other related fields of inquiry are left unexplained, neglected, or judged as irrelevant. According to Burke: "A way of seeing is also a way of not seeing. If we focus on object A, object B gets left in the shadows" (Burke 1935: 70).

I would like to apply Burke's theorem to Merton's work. Thus I will not only elucidate fully those aspects of his work which he himself has highlighted and which lend themselves, as in fact happened, to being taken up and developed further; I will also attempt to give an account of those elements which have hitherto been neglected. It is particularly interesting that the aspects which Merton failed to develop in depth take on a particular importance if they are viewed in the context of his exhaustive treatment of other aspects of temporality and the fascination which certain themes and theoretical orientations exercised on him throughout his intellectually productive years.

I would like to show how Merton's focus on the normative and integrative aspect of time, his emphasis on collective representation and the supreme importance of the social, prevented him from recognizing that the study of time was of greater sociological interest than he had first realized. Another consequence of Merton's approach was that the world of the social and the world of the individual were seen

as potentially opposed rather than interwoven. This opposition between the social and the individual provides the basis for his relatively
static vision of the social aspects of temporality and his neglect of
historical tools of analysis.

The Opposition between Social and Individual Time

In his essay of 1937 with Sorokin, Merton made it quite clear that
he accepted and wished to develop his own version of the Durkheimian
tendency to regard collective representations as sacred, to ascribe a
positive value to the social and to see it as an extremely powerful,
almost omnipotent force. Merton makes no mention at all of the issue
of individual time and the way it is closely connected with changes in
social time, actually helping to bring them about. The very fact that
Merton is able to describe in such detail the essential harmoniousness
of temporal norms, the basic patterns which carry a determined set of
collective meanings, seems to indicate that social time is implicitly set
against individual time, although this is never stated directly. Like all
other norms, collective temporal norms are imposed on the individual
consciousness with an almost divine authority. In short, individual
time is not considered as a problem.

However, this means that we have no way of understanding how
and why individual time contributes to forming the structures of social
time, which are the main focus of Merton's attention. As he puts it
apropos of SEDs, they "constitute a fundamental class of patterned
expectations linking social structures and individual action" (Merton
1982b). Individual time tends to be seen as existing between certain
patterns of opposition or adaptation. It is never perceived as a creative
force. In fact Durkheim was even less convinced than Merton that
these two aspects of time could have a reciprocal influence upon each
other. He expressed grave doubts about the possibility of bringing
these two levels of human experience together and breaking down the
barriers between them. For Durkheim, the gulf between social time
and individual time could not be bridged.

The individual and society could only be brought together if society
were very much the dominant force. When, in the concluding pages of
The Elementary Forms of the Religious Life, Durkheim asks how it
comes about that " . . . the individual is capable of raising himself
above his own peculiar point of view and of living an impersonal life"

(Durkheim 1964: 445), when, in other words, he raises the issue of the relationship between individual and society, he expresses the solution in the following way:

> Perhaps some will be surprised to see us connect the most elevated forms of thought with society: the cause appears quite humble, in consideration of the value which we attribute to the effect. Between the world of the senses and appetites on the one hand, and that of reason and morals on the other, the distance is so considerable that the second would seem to have been able to add itself to the first only by a creative act. But attributing to society this preponderating rôle in the genesis of our nature is not denying this creation; for society has a creative power which no other observable being can equal. (Durkheim 1964: 446)

Merton's analysis of social time bears some traces of the Durkheimian emphasis on a sociological definition of time, which stresses time's social and integrative quality. For Merton, time extends beyond the domain of measured time, beyond the abstract chronology of the days and hours measured on the clock face to which modern societies turn because they need a common language and which allows them to understand each other and to coordinate their common activities. Time for Merton is the sum of change experienced and observed: the essence of social time lies in the experience of the collectivity. Thus Merton not only paid scant attention to the notion of individual time, he also largely ignored the aspects of time which were linked to the theory of action (see Sztompka 1986: 27).

Merton's theories about the social origin of time, its qualitative nature, and the ways in which it differs from measured and quantitative definitions of time do not bring out the uniqueness of individual time and the choices it involves, neither do they clarify how social and individual time are connected. There is a considerable imbalance between the subtlety of Merton's analysis of the social aspects of temporality and the fact that he largely ignores the individual's experience of time and how individual time contributes to modifying the rules we call social time.

If we return to Burke's theorem, it appears that the fact that Merton lays particular emphasis on the normative aspect of time makes it difficult for him to become aware that it is the very adoption of a temporal perspective that makes it possible to approach a solution to one of the most difficult dilemmas of sociological theory, namely the search for ways of connecting theories of action and theories of structure. In fact Merton continued to devote his attention to this difficult issue, but he tried to find a solution to it by pursuing other avenues of inquiry than the one on time.

If we consider that people really use the notion of time to describe experiences of change[2]—and a norm which connects directly the social and the natural at the level of the individual—then this makes it easier to establish a link between these different planes of human experience. As Norbert Elias has maintained, to understand what time is we have to abandon the dichotomies which have traditionally been used in the West to separate the individual from the social and the natural. Elias's definition of time can help forge a link between the different zones of human experience: in its present state of development time is a symbolic synthesis on a very high plane, a synthesis which enables us to relate natural, social, and individual processes of change (compare Elias 1984).

Elias's analysis of time complements the Durkheimian approach to the question. His approach progresses along the same lines, but enriches it with new insights. Elias is not content merely to demonstrate the social nature of time: he also offers an explanation of why time has become what it is today. Elias attributes the development of a series of changes wrought over the centuries of human society, which he refers to as "the civilizing process." Time is no longer merely the collective rhythm of different activities, but a social construction which varies in the course of the process of civilization, becoming today one of the most constraining social habitus, an extremely abstract symbol, a cognitive instrument borrowed from the natural sciences.[3]

This work of historical reconstruction is not accomplished by reference only to the normative definition of time. In addition to the social norm, Elias takes into account the active intervention of individuals and their different experiences of time in explaining the historical change that this concept has undergone throughout the centuries and its concomitant changing social practices and representations.[4] These reflections on the theme of time enable us to reach some understanding of how the social, the individual, and the natural levels of human existence are linked. Elias's work gives us an insight into how normative bonds and subjective intentions, constraints and choices contribute to the solution of what constitutes individual time. Individuals construct a wide range of different time schemes, they each have their own particular way of going about things and coming into contact with the collective temporal norm. People are continually adjusting and readjusting the facts to suit their own particular needs and skills and continually reassessing the relationships constituted by different social times.

The study of time helps us understand the interplay of structural constraints and individual intention in social action. It is likely that one of the reasons why the various elements of time have exerted such a fascination for sociologists is that the study of time offers a good opportunity to explore the nature of individual choice. Time implies order, constraint, but also meaning and a degree of free choice. The study of individual and collective temporality seems to offer sociologists a way out of a deadlock and opens up an interesting perspective on an extremely complex theoretical issue: how and to what extent do social structures determine individual behavior, and how in turn do individuals modify social structures to suit their own purposes?

The Concept of Socially Expected Durations

In Merton's second essay on time from 1984 (Merton 1984a) the focus alters slightly; he refines and improves his method of approach, leaving aside previous lines of inquiry. The concept of SEDs evolved over a long period. It gradually took shape during various collaborative empirical research projects that he undertook. The idea began to take shape on the basis of the findings of a study of the behavior patterns of the inhabitants of Craftown—a new community of about 750 working-class families which had been established in 1941 in an industrial area near New York. Merton found that the inhabitants' relationships with others and their readiness to make friends and to participate in leisure activities were directly dependent on how long they expected to stay in Craftown. As he put it: " . . . it was found that the *expected* duration of residence worked independently of the actual duration to affect these behaviors" (1984a: 275). When Merton temporarily gave up empirical research at the end of the 1950s to return to more theoretical study, his intention was "to identify the major properties of social structure" (1984a: 278). He now felt ready to attempt a definition of the broad concept of the socially expected durations (SEDs).

Merton distinguishes three types of SEDs. The first are socially prescribed durations supported by institutions. Second, there are what he describes as collectively expected durations (these include, for example, predictions about how long an economic crisis or a government coalition will last). This type of socially expected duration is difficult to define precisely. Finally, there are the temporal expectations which are to be found in interpersonal relations of various types, ranging from formal contractual relations to more intimate and community-oriented relations. Although these types of relations are generally more stable, they too are expected to last for a particular length of time.

Merton's notion of socially expected durations introduced the theme of time into social theory. It must be said, however, that although Merton was fully aware that time was part of the social structure, the impact of his approach was blunted by his failure to take account of the origin and evolution of the concept. Merton has always been primarily interested in social structures, in the elements of collective life which exert a powerful constraining influence on human behavior. By focusing on the social expectations of duration, which is how Merton sees human behavior in relation to time, he largely ignores the sphere of individual experience and the fact that an individual's experience of time is historically conditioned.

In addition, although the concept of socially expected durations enabled Merton to develop a structural analysis of the social world, he often failed to take the historical dimension into consideration. Although the historian Reinhart Koselleck uses the concept of time in a completely different way from Merton, it is nevertheless instructive to compare his approach with Merton's, as it provides an interesting counter to an approach which focuses too narrowly on normative expectations. The starting point for Koselleck's study of temporal structures (Koselleck 1979) is an analysis of the reasons why certain linguistic usages occur, take root, and spread and the circumstances in which this comes about. The basis of Koselleck's approach is a detailed analysis of the links between social history and the history of concepts. Koselleck's exploration of the development of meaning is certainly far removed from the empirical social scientific approach adopted by Merton from which the concept of socially expected duration gradually arose.

Koselleck also highlights the importance assumed by what he defines as "the horizons of expectations" in collective life and in the way people choose to behave. However, unlike Merton, Koselleck considers that if this concept is to be used to explain the past and possibly to predict the future, then it must be seen in relation to what he describes as "the regions of experience." Koselleck discusses expectations and experiences in general, and his perspective remains a historical one. Nevertheless, it is still possible to compare his approach with Merton's, given that both are primarily concerned with the temporal factors which influence collective behavior and that expectations and experiences of time form part of the wider sphere of expectations and experience. All this brings home the fact that Koselleck and Merton use the term "expectations" to suit their own particular purposes; neither makes any reference to general definitions of the concept.[5]

For Koselleck, then, "horizons of expectations" are inextricably linked with "regions of experience." Experience and expectations are antithetical temporal concepts which can only be understood if they are seen as interrelated. All human action springs from the reciprocal tension that is generated between these two related concepts. If expectations are a structural element of every society and if society exists in a diachronic dimension, what defines history is the ever-present and necessary difference between expectations and experiences. This process works in both directions: expectations never confirm experiences, something new is always happening, which in turn modifies previous expectations, thus altering the overall picture. Experiences do not confirm expectations, but are modified retrospectively by the appearance of new experiences, so that the past is never a closed book, it keeps evolving and changing and is continually being modified by successive events. The past is continually being brought to life and remodelled as events progress.

The difference between expectations and experiences, which according to Koselleck is a basic anthropological fact, is all the more significant—and its effects more widely felt—in the modern era, in which time takes on a new meaning, the future is seen as unpredictable and unsettled, and people are generally convinced that things will happen in the future that would have been inconceivable in the past. It is indeed the case that Merton developed the concept of SEDs on the basis of empirical research findings which showed that there was a precise correlation between SEDs and the ways in which the working-class inhabitants of Craftown behaved.

However, this does not necessarily imply that these findings would have been borne out by other research conducted in different sociohistorical contexts. Indeed it is possible to envisage cases in which such a correlation could be explained by other factors. It could be linked, for example, to certain foreseeable aspects of economic and collective life, to a general sense of stability and security which gives people confidence in the norms or conventions on which their social expectations of duration are based. Alternatively, if similar research were carried out against a background of socioeconomic crisis and fluctuating rates of employment, for example at the end of a war or in a climate of general uncertainty where the overwhelming experience was of a general lack of stability, it is unlikely that this correlation would be found to exist. If the sociohistorical circumstances of the workers studied by Merton had been different, if, for example, they had experienced periods of unemployment or underemployment or participated in political or union struggles, their experience would have had to be considered a significant variable forming an interactive nexus with expectations of various types. Experience and expectations have a reciprocal effect on each other, just as the expectations which influence human behavior, like any other structural variable, develop on the basis of past experience as well as on the basis of a more or less binding normative system.

Individual experience is also part of what we call SEDs, and SEDs themselves are the result of the interaction which takes place between experiences and expectations. In fact, expectations arise out of existing norms, convictions, and customs. How does it come about that SEDs play such an important role in social life? How is it that individuals behave predictably as regards the expectations which they hold on the basis of certain rules—some of which have a formal-legal character and some of which are rooted in custom or derive from generally held beliefs?

Rules alone cannot explain certain forms of behavior unless they are viewed within the historical framework in which they occur, develop, and are used. If we do not take into consideration the experiences which constitute the background and support of a normative system, either ensuring that the rules are enforced and guaranteeing their legitimacy or alternatively providing evidence of fragility and precariousness, then we cannot be fully aware of the true nature of socially expected durations. SEDs evolve out of a historical process; they are the product of the interaction between expectations and experiences which develops over a period of time.

The concept of SEDs is an extremely useful research tool if it is conceived as the product of a historical process in the course of which individuals compare their expectations and experiences. It is a useful concept for describing how the various social actors view the reliability of the norms and customs in force on the basis of their own experiences.

The Sociology of Time Today

Reviewing sociological studies of time today, we can single out two approaches which have been extremely influential in determining the course of research. First, there is the French tradition, dominated by Durkheim and developed by Sorokin and Merton, which provided the real inspiration for American research on the issue. Second, there is the German tradition, largely based on historical tools of analysis, including scholars such as Elias and Koselleck, Luhmann and Rammstaedt. These two traditions have tended to develop along separate lines and have had little or nothing to do with each other. It seems likely that the proponents of these different approaches would emerge with more interesting findings if they were prepared to learn from one another and adopt elements of each other's approaches. Fresh impetus has recently come from the Franco-American tradition, led by Merton, with the formulation of the concept of socially expected durations. This has had the effect of focusing attention on the social origins of time and on its innate capacity to order human life.

Current developments have meant that the focus of research has become increasingly sociological in the strict sense of the word. There has been a tendency to focus on the integrating function of temporal norms and to uncover the vast range of conventions and temporal norms upon which social life rests (the work of Eviater Zerubavel is a case in point). Present research aims to make increased use of theoretical concepts—such as Mertonian SEDs—in an attempt to impose some order on the mass of empirical observations and findings and to make them part of a coherent system. It is primarily the normative aspects of time which are being studied at the moment; the study of temporality is being brought back to the study of social structures.

In the German tradition, on the contrary, the concept of time is first and foremost defined from a wider historical point of view.[6] Experience is also a subject of investigation,[7] and attention is focused not only on the temporal norm, but also on the historical development of the notion of time and the factors which appear to have influenced it most in the course of its history.[8] In this tradition the main interest lies in the changing form that time has assumed while common experiences and prevailing values were also changing, and how time has fulfilled a variety of different functions throughout history. Attempts have been made to identify the variables which may have influenced the change, and the emphasis has been on a historical approach rather than a sociological one (if it can be assumed that this distinction is meaningful).[9] Both these traditions, the Franco-American and the German, are rich in relevant concepts and characterized by acute insight, although both have their own particular "blind spots" à la Burke. For this reason it would be useful to bring the two approaches together, starting with the work of scholars such as Merton.

To return to the question asked at the beginning of this chapter, it now appears that Merton's contribution to the sociology of time could be developed further in two directions. First, it could follow the lead of other studies which have demonstrated an increasing awareness of the fact that temporal norms are closely interwoven with the fabric of social life. Second, advances can only be made if the range of analysis is broadened to include new approaches. Merton has already shown that he is aware of this and is continually extending his interpretative scheme.

In his paper of 1982 Merton outlined some possible future developments of the concept of SED:

> The further analytical and interpretative questions are legion: what are the attributes and parameters of SEDs? How do SEDs vary in structure, operation, and consequence? What, in particular, are the anticipatory behavioral adaptations of individuals, groups, organizations, and collectivities to social expected duration of the several kinds? In short, how do SEDs come to take certain forms rather than others; what are the parameters of the various forms; and finally how do they operate as temporal components of social structure to affect patterns of organizational and individual behavior?

However, it is not possible for Merton to pursue his interest in the normative aspects of time much further as long as they continue to be analyzed independently of changing social experiences. Although he has to some extent investigated how the concept of time has evolved throughout history (Sorokin and Merton 1937), he does not seem interested in studying why and how the concept changes or in identifying which kind of long-term processes influence it. Above all he does not tackle the problem of how the mutual interaction between social

and individual time develops, how individual initiative modifies existing temporal constraints while partially accepting them. Interactions
can only be analyzed historically. In short, what is missing in Merton's
entire approach is an attempt to find points of contact between the two
poles of the "paradox of human action" (Abrams 1982): freedom and
constraint.

Notes

1. This is confirmed by Merton in his ASA paper of 1982 in which he describes his
   own work and the intellectual climate in American sociological circles during that
   time. He also mentions the intellectual isolation of his mentor, Pitirim Sorokin.
   See Merton 1982b.
2. There are many classical psychological studies on time which link thinking on
   time to broader perceptions of change (see, for example, James 1909; Fraisse
   1967; Piaget 1971). This issue is dealt with convincingly by a number of sociological studies (see, for example, Rammstaedt 1975; an unpublished paper by
   Cavalli 1986; and some passages in Norbert Elias's *Über die Zeit* 1984).
3. Norbert Elias deals with these themes at some length in his *Über die Zeit*.
4. This does not mean that the concept of time should be "historicized," nor indeed
   was this what Elias was saying. On the contrary, although its historical evolution
   should also be taken into account, it remains the main task of the sociologist to
   arrive at a definition of the concept per se. If the notion of time as it stands takes
   into account the relation between the subject and a particular experience, the
   analysis of its genesis enables us to arrive at a better understanding of the context
   and the social circumstances in which the concept takes on meaning.
5. An exploration of the concept of expectation would have been useful before
   formulating the concept of SEDs. As Carlo Mongardini has pointed out:
       Role-expectations, or, more generally, structural expectations in the broader
   sense as used by Merton, are only the same facade covering microprocesses
   which go against the current of the production or reproduction of collective life.
   These microprocesses help the social actor adjust to his environment. This adjustment process in turn produces expectations and consequently action. These
   microprocesses comprise the following elements: (a) the gathering of information
   on and perceptions of the environment which are the preconditions of action; (b)
   the awareness of the fact that the social actor is able to alter the situation to his
   advantage, and indeed is likely to do so. This has some effect on the way he sees
   what he is going to do; and (c) the setting up of a plan for interaction which is
   composed of partial expectations and expectations of expectations (which are
   attributed to the other). (Mongardini 1985: 104–5)
6. As far as I am aware, Norbert Elias is the only sociologist to tackle the problem of
   the sociological definition of time. His lucid definition forms an invaluable base
   for future developments in the study of time head-on: "The concept of time is
   dependent upon...man's capacity to link two or more sequences of continuous
   changes. One of these sequences acts as a yardstick for the other or for others"
   (Elias 1984). Elias expresses this idea more clearly still: "the word 'time' is a
   symbol of a link which a group of people, that is a group of living beings with the
   biological capacity to remember and to make sense of their experiences, estab-

lishes between two or more series of events. One of these is then used as a frame of reference or yardstick for the other or others." Compare Elias 1984.
7. I am referring to the previously quoted studies by Rammstaedt 1975 and Koselleck 1979.
8. Both Elias (1982; 1984) and Koselleck (1979) have made important contributions to this particular area of study.
9. On this point see Philip Abrams's brilliant polemic, *Historical Sociology* (1982). I am in broad agreement with the views expressed in Abrams's book.

References

Abrams, P. 1982. *Historical Sociology*. Shepton Mallet: Somerset, Open Books.
Burke, K. 1935. *Permanence and Change*. New York: New Republic Inc.
Cavalli, A. 1986. "L'esperienza del tempo." Paper presented at conference, Time and the Sacred, 22–23 May in Florence.
Coser, L.A. and R. Coser. 1963. "Time Perspective and Social Structure." In *Modern Sociology*, edited by A. Gouldner and H. Gouldner. New York: Harcourt Brace Jovanovich.
Durkheim, E. 1964. *The Elementary Forms of the Religious Life*. London: George Allen and Unwin.
Elias, N. 1982. *The Civilizing Process*. Vol. 2 of *State Formation and Civilization*. Oxford: Basil Blackwell.
———. 1984. *Über die Zeit: Arbeiten zur Wissenssoziologie*. Vol 2. Frankfurt am Main: Suhrkamp.
Fraisse, P. 1967. *Psychologie du temps*. Paris: PUF.
James, W. 1909. *Psychology*. New York: Henry Holt and Co.
Koselleck, R. 1979. *Vergangene Zukunft: Zur Semantik geschichtlicher Zeiten*. Frankfurt am Main: Suhrkamp.
Merton, R.K. 1982. "Socially Expected Durations: A Temporal Component of Social Structure." Paper presented at the annual meeting of the American Sociological Association, September.
———. 1984. "Socially Expected Durations: A Case Study of Concept Formation in Sociology." In *Conflict and Consensus: In Honor of Lewis A. Coser*, edited by W. Powell and R. Robbins, 262–283. New York: Free Press.
———. 1985. "The Social Aspects of Duration." Interview by Anna di Lellio. *Rassegna Italiana di Sociologia* 26 (1): 3–26.
Mongardini, C. 1985. "L'aspettativa come categoria sociologica." In *Epistemologia e Sociologia*. Milano: Franco Angeli.
Moore, W. 1963. *Man, Time and Society*. New York and London: Wiley.
Piaget, J. 1971. *Biology and Knowledge*. Edinburgh: Edinburgh University Press and Chicago: University of Chicago Press.
Rammstaedt, O. 1975. "Alltagsbewusstsein von Zeit." *Kölner Zeitschrift für Soziologie und Sozial-Psychologie* 27: 582–592.
Sorokin, P.A [1937] 1941. *Social and Cultural Dynamics*. New York: American Book Company.
———. 1943. *Sociocultural Causality, Space, Time*. Durham, NC: Duke University Press.
Sorokin, P.A. and R.K. Merton 1937. "Social Time: A Methodological and Functional Analysis." *American Journal of Sociology* 42: 615–629.

Sztompka, P. 1986. *Robert K. Merton: An Intellectual Profile*. London: MacMillan and New York: St. Martin's Press.
Zerubavel, E. 1981. *Hidden Rhythms: Schedules of Calendars in Social Life*. Chicago: University of Chicago Press.

18

Serendipity in the Work of Robert K. Merton

Maria Luisa Maniscalco

It is well known that Robert K. Merton's thought has played a fundamental role in contemporary sociology—from his criticism of abstract functionalism as founded on general schemata not grounded in history, through an approach that not only does not take for granted the stability and functional integration of the various parts of a system but, on the contrary, considers the possibility that the system may be badly integrated and contradictory.[1]

Mertonian production ranges over a wide field of interests from systems theory to an interest in social problems, from the history of sociological theory to field research, from the sociology of science and knowledge (with particular reference to the mass media) to social structure analysis.[2] Despite the plurality and diversity of his interests, however, Merton's work constitutes a coherent system of thought in which certain recurring and unifying leitmotifs can be distinguished.[3]

One of the first unifying motifs can be traced to the attention he gives to "social problems," that is, the most critical aspects of the life and organization of contemporary society, aspects he considers by examining the relationships between mechanisms for order, for creating stability, organization, social reproduction, and consensus on the one hand and the phenomena of conflict, disorganization, deviance, and anomie on the other. A second motif lies in the constant striving to find a basis for explanatory sociological theories in structural elements (both facilitative and obstructive), in individual situations, his-

273

torical configurations, and social contexts. Yet another can be found in his interest in problems of cognition, which he examines from the starting point of a belief that cognitive objectives are best reached through the restrictive criteria of evidence, more or less common to the various sciences, requiring empirical proof, detachment, and objectivity. This epistemological basis is the source of his obvious concern with questions about the interrelationships between theory and research in sociology.

Merton has dedicated a good deal of his scientific effort to the problem of integrating theory and research, and this not only the chapters in his basic work, *Social Theory and Social Structure*.[4] In fact, both his references to the classics, and his conception of functional analysis and (middle-range) sociological theory are delineated as methodological and conceptual instruments for facilitating this integration. Merton's long and productive scientific association with Lazarsfeld, for example, is well known.

In this context I would like to make one or two brief observations to draw attention to the concept of "serendipity," important for its role in the process of scientific discovery and for the methodological value, often implicit, hidden, and uncodified, that it gives to all Merton's production, and for the significance it acquires in his widest vision of what constitutes scientific knowledge. Merton actually dedicates only a few pages and a few references to the "serendipity pattern,"[5] where perhaps a greater emphasis and more explicit definition might have been called for.

Pursuing his practice of seeking greater precision for propositions or important concepts in sociological analysis by creating specific terms, often neologisms,[6] Merton designates as "serendipity" the emergence during the process of empirical research of an anomalous datum that is unexpected but important insofar as it reorientates the theory or suggests ways of developing a new theory.

The introduction of the word serendipity into Western culture—from *Serendip*, one of the names for the island of Sri Lanka in ancient times, and in its turn a name which can be traced back to an even more ancient Sanskrit root—has always been attributed to Horace Walpole, an English aristocrat and man of letters who wrote in a letter to his friend, Horace Mann, that he had read the fable of "The Three Princes of Serendip" and had been struck by how the main characters "were always making discoveries by accidents and sagacity, of things they were not in quest of" (Walpole [1754]1903). Walpole used the neologism *serendipity* to stand for the lucky discovery of things that you are not looking for.

If it was an English gentleman who coined the term in 1754, recent research by an Italian scholar, Pietro Dri, in the Trivulziana Library in Milan has shown that the legend of the three young princes—and so the idea of serendipity—had already been known in Europe for some two centuries. In fact, Dri's research has brought to light the original edition published in Venice in 1577 of a little book entitled *Pellegrinaggio dei tre giovani figlioli del re di Serendippo* (*The Wanderings of the Three Young Sons of the King of Serendippo*), the work of a certain Cristoforo Armeno who explains the origin of the text on the cover of the book that "it had been brought from the Persian language into Italian" (Dri 1994).[7] In a period when Venice was the commercial and cultural gateway to the Indies, it was this foreigner, a guest in the city of lagoons, who introduced the story of the three young princes of Serendip to the West and along with it the idea of serendipity as the art of finding things that you are not looking for.

This recourse to the etymology and semantics of the word is not intended so much for its literary curiosity value, but rather to signify that the term is rich in appeal to the imagination and certainly not without its aura of magic. In this manner, as we shall see later, it forms a sort of bridge between art and science.

Although Merton paid some attention to the diffusion of the term serendipity, even outside limited academic circles, and to the shifts in its meaning, as well as its ideological uses in the course of diffusion (Merton and Barber [1958] 1997), he never went beyond that, as has been said, to codify the concept more precisely, even though he supported a creative role for empirical research vis-à-vis theory (Merton 1957: 96, note 18). One can fully agree with his vision of creative attitudes toward research since the serendipity model is rich in conceptual and methodological stimuli; it is now a question of developing its great implicit potential along with its cognitive implications.

I want to spend the rest of my time making some observations on related concepts, examining some in depth and starting with the basic Mertonian definition.

Merton considers serendipity as inherent in the research process itself; it consists of the possibility of discovering important elements more or less by chance which are unexpected in the sense that they are "lateral" to the research project. "Serendipity," he writes, "refers to the fairly common experience of observing an unanticipated, anomalous and strategic datum which becomes the occasion for developing a new theory or for extending an existing theory" (Merton 1957: 104).

In a larger theoretical framework the principle of serendipity represents a particular aspect of the more general Mertonian theme of unanticipated consequences of action applied to the field of scientific knowledge. As we see from the definition of serendipity, Merton sees serendipitous scientific discovery as composed of three basic elements, the first of which brings us back to its involuntary, unpredictable nature. Let us look at these three elements.

Unpredictability (an unanticipated datum) means that a datum emerges in the course of research which does not fit in with the hypothesis and the analytical scheme the researcher has adopted. Here, plainly, Merton is thinking of the considerable role that chance elements play in scientific research. Of course, a scholar as aware as he is of the mechanisms—not only social mechanisms—that underlie scientific discovery and science in general could not fail to be sensitive to this substantive moment in the path towards knowledge: it is well-known that many scientific discoveries in all fields have emerged by accident in the course of cognitive investigations with quite different objectives.

If Merton seems to emphasize in this first element the free play of chance, so to speak, the second brings the subjectivity and leading role of the knower back into the limelight.

Anomaly (anomalous datum) emphasizes that the observed datum seems to contrast with the paradigms of "normal science" or with well-established certainties. This arouses the curiosity of the scholar and encourages him to follow the new line of research and continue his observations. Merton thus emphasizes that it is precisely the apparent lack of coherence that elicits curiosity and generates the creativity of the effort to make sense of the datum through suitable theoretical explorations (Merton 1957: 241, note 13).

Unexpected, paradoxical, and strategic results exert a creative "pressure" towards extension of the theory or elaboration of a new one. This observation is of particular interest since it emphasizes that both subjective and objective elements are closely related in the concept of serendipity. A first superficial observation might have it seem that the emerging datum has clarifying value and theoretical relevance in itself. This has the Mertonian model rejecting those outdated conceptions of science which would have it that objectivity lies in the external datum in itself and thereby leads to its being noted in its specificity. On the contrary, Merton emphasizes in Weberian fashion that despite its literal etymological meaning, "data" are not at all "given"; that is, they do not automatically provide meaning and relevance until the inevitable aid of concepts gives them shape.

A further significant modification of the model of scientific discovery through serendipity appears in the third element.

Relevance (strategic datum): the unanticipated and anomalous fact must be relevant, that is, it must play a strategic role in the research, allowing for elaborations that make way for new theories or extensions of existing theories. Even here, however, it must be pointed out that the datum assumes theoretical importance and thus becomes relevant only at the moment when the researcher intervenes creatively and constructively by considering it significant and then selecting it. In effect, serendipity also involves, and perhaps especially, the creative and intelligent use of elements which have emerged by chance. Such practice becomes easier as a result of a specific mind-set produced by long familiarity with empirical research. In fact, Merton's introduction of the notion of serendipity into sociology is first made with reference to the discovery by chance of valid but unsought elements by a mind that is theoretically prepared and, above all, is not remote from a disciplined empirical observation.

Having traced the outline of the principle of serendipity briefly, we can go on to its epistemological presuppositions and its cognitive implications.

With regard to epistemological presuppositions, attention to serendipity in the context of discovery obviously rests on a general conception of scientific research as a journey towards the unknown through tracts that are somewhat unpredictable and unprogrammable. Whereas research results are usually presented as having followed a strictly logical course, eliminating anything that does not fit in by a kind of *a posteriori* rationalization, recourse to the element of serendipity as inherent in cognitive process amounts to returning to scientific knowledge the wholeness and depth of a thoroughly human enterprise in which the rational and the irrational,[8] the purposeful and chance, the psychological and social, the interior and exterior worlds, are all inextricably mixed up together. Merton recalls attention more than once to this aspect of the process of attaining scientific knowledge in his criticism of the common practice which tends to undervalue and fail to communicate the information concerning the course the research actually followed, which then has no way of being recorded in the standard pattern of scientific literature which is usually expressed in a logically persuasive rather than historically descriptive form.

Besides, as in all other forms of knowledge, in sociology, too, it is fundamental to identify the problem areas: the main difficulty, however, lies right here in their identification; according to Merton, it is more difficult to find out what the real problems are than to solve them.[9] To this it must be added that it is their solution that sometimes causes ideas and observations on new problem areas to come to light; such a process can be seen as a particular type of the "serendipity pattern." In reality the isolation and solution of new research problems is based on a "puzzle" made up of the sum of intellectual and social influences, both present and past, planned and accidental meetings, data, ideas, intuitions, errors, oversights, departures from the original path of the original research, and so on.

Serendipity, both in the objective and the subjective sense, performs the heuristic function of exerting pressure for the elaboration of new theories. If it is seen as a capacity for redirecting cognitive interest and to manage in this way to collect anomalous and unanticipated data which were not anticipated within the established theoretical framework, serendipity fits into a general conception of science as a process which works on different levels and where one of the crucial things is knowing the right questions to ask.[10]

From the subjective point of view, serendipity represents the art of finding what was not being sought. This necessitates, as has been said, a particular mindset on the part of the researcher: reasoning for serendipity means lateral thinking, changing the direction of one's reflections and one's thought, finding connections between the most diverse elements and contradictions among those that have most in common in keeping with that capacity that Pareto described as the "residue of instinct for combinations." It is necessary also to be ready and open to receiving what is new, free from academic attitudes, not tied to the interpretative framework that has been adopted or to the hypotheses which have been instituted and must be confirmed at all costs. Serendipity is not only the result of chance but is correlated with the scientific imagination of the researcher; it calls up interior worlds and the aura of things sacred that emanates from them. Thus, it represents a subjective category since it expresses and gives added importance to the individual characteristics of the scientist, who betrays his own nature if he shuts himself into the repetitive confirmation of a particular model.

However, as Merton has emphasized, serendipity cannot be applied by just anyone. Only the person with a scientifically prepared mind can note the novelty, the originality, and the significance of the unexpected, discordant event. Serendipitous discoveries are, therefore, the fruit of a happy combination of intellectual creativity and methodological rigor.

To get a better picture of serendipity as a cognitive category one must show that it rests, in a modification of the term from classical functional analysis, on two fundamental prerequisites that Merton does not explain but which are connected to the whole of his wider conception of scientific knowledge. I wish to show that the element of lucky chance, in order to become scientifically important, must not only meet with a creative, able mind but also with an environment that is suitable from both a technical-cultural and a sociopolitical point of view.

So far as the first goes, the times must be ripe, in the sense that the theoretical and cultural development and the surrounding technical resources must be such that the anomalous character of the data can be fully appreciated, its rupture and discord with the paradigm and therefore, that the potentiality of the theory can be realized in an extension of knowledge. In this connection Merton loves to recall Newton's well-known aphorism : "If I have seen farther, it is by standing on the shoulders of giants,"[11] in order to indicate the dependence of discovery and innovation on the existing cultural base. However, the situation of the physical and natural sciences differs from that of the social sciences and sociology in particular; the former operate in a more typically accumulative context, the latter, oscillating between the two orientations of empirical science and humanistic knowledge, does not reach a standard of rigorous accumulativeness. It must be remembered, however, that so far as the development of science in general is concerned, Merton rejects both the idea of uniform accumulation of knowledge and the notion of radical scientific revolutions; science does not cumulate in unilinear but in selective fashion and every "revolution" still shows links with the past. One might suggest an analogy here between Merton's theory of the extension of knowledge through serendipity and the theory of evolution through natural selection, not so much in the original and partly outdated Darwinian conceptions, but bearing in mind the more advanced positions such as "punctuated equilibria" (Gould and Eldridge 1977; Gould 1980; Stanley 1981); in both cases, elements which surface sporadically and by chance are then selected and preserved on the basis of their strategic importance in the given context.

As was mentioned earlier, a further element proves necessary before serendipity can unfold its full potential. Along with the technical-scientific conditions, a sociopolitical system that favors the birth and reception of new ideas must also be there. In fact, it can happen that the development of certain areas of knowledge is such as to allow the emergence of serendipity but this cannot occur because of resistance to it from social, political, religious, economic, or other sources. That is the typical condition of periods of decadence in knowledge when different questions are no longer asked and new answers to the old questions are no longer sought.

It is possible then to formulate two hypotheses. The first sees the scientist and researcher betray his vocation, abandoning investigation of the grey areas presented by a cognitive paradigm, and pretending he does not notice that the paradigm has lost its coherence if it is not actually on the point of collapse. The scientist thus becomes the tutor and guardian of institutionalized knowledge, the "mandarin" of the dominant cognitive ideology, the priest of the power that emanates from it. The second hypothesis witnesses the recovery and theoretical and/or practical reappropriation of what has been perceived through serendipity but through "alternative" channels with respect to established cognitive schemes and existing reality. Knowledge then shuts itself up in the secret society of the sects[12] within which "other" realities and "other" experiences can appear in the most unexpected manner and the scientist can turn into a magician.[13]

Associated with serendipity are cognitive implications whose significance, as I have indicated at the outset, permeates the whole of Merton's work. To recall only a few of them, they are present in the role the American scholar accords the rereading and reexamining of the "classics," in which anticipations, foreshadowings can be detected—in short, elements of "serendipity lost" in light of the changes brought about in the structure of knowledge with the passing of time. Often it is only after a long period of time that it is possible to intuit fertile directions which would lead to success in developing an original idea.

Of significance, also, is the path followed in the formation of certain sociological concepts through a slow and irregular evolution from proto-concepts (that is, initial, rudimentary, often indefinite ideas occasionally used in empirical research and frequently derived from it) to full-fledged concepts.[14]

Both preceding examples can be summed up in the so-called Burke's theorem (which Merton recalled quite recently) according to which "a way of seeing is also a way of not seeing: a focus upon object A involves a neglect of object B" (Merton, in Powell and Robbins 1984). In fact, the very logic of the knowledge process implies that it is necessary to introduce such theoretical constraints, choices of perspective, limits on the subject for research, that always and inevitably operate as reductive elements in societal multidimensionality. Hence the importance of assigning greater emphasis and constant attention to serendipity—meaning the ability of thought to change direction when faced with the challenge of the contradictory nature of reality and to avoid freezing reality into a rigid theoretical system. In this sense the "serendipity pattern" becomes an integral part of a mental attitude derived from the realization that any theoretical model whatsoever includes and accounts for only a part of the phenomenon under examination.

Another fundamental implication is represented by the need to establish the correct reciprocal relation between theory and empirical research. While empirical research frequently has the exclusive or at least primary function of confirming or refuting hypotheses, Merton uses the concept of serendipity to maintain that "it also initiates, reformulates, refocuses, and clarifies" theories and sociological conceptions.[15]

The fundamental role that serendipity plays in the process of discovering new scientific knowledge underlines the significance of a theoretical reevaluation of observation and empirical research, which becomes seen also as a brake on the tendency, all too frequent in sociology, to construct one's own "object" for investigation by conceptual selection of reality and objectifying the respective concepts; thus elaborating theoretical constructions in terms that prevent understanding of the connections between events.

Although I have referred essentially to the social sciences in this chapter, it is obvious that the concept of serendipity can be more widely applied in other fields;[16] it is, in fact, closely connected to any process of research that is scientific only insofar as it is open to data, hypotheses, and events which the accepted interpretative framework neither predicts nor includes.

Notes

1. Coser (1975: 98) observes in this connection that Merton's analytical strategies are characterized by careful attention to the contradictions and conflicts present in social structures as well as actors' ambivalence of motivation and ambiguity of attitude; this leads him to claim that "the Mertonian world is a universe of warring gods."
2. Merton's cognitive course is clearly brought out in a recent excellent intellectual biography by Piotr Sztompka 1986. The essential steps in his thinking have also been revisited by Charles Crothers 1987.
3. For Sztompka the key to the interpretation of Merton's intellectual identity lies in four central ideas that he designates as: (a) the *classicist theme*, i.e., the tendency towards "aurea mediocritas," meaning the propensity to reconcile and mediate between extreme positions in order to formulate interim solutions for theoretical and metatheoretical problems; (b) the *cognitivist theme*, i.e., the methodological approach centered on the conviction that cognitive goals in science are reached largely by the same criteria in the various sciences, while practical utility is not necessarily connected with those goals; (c) the *structuralist theme*, the pervasive idea of using configurations, models, and structures in all fields of his endeavor; and (d) the *ironic theme*, traced to the awareness of the complexity, contradictions, and paradoxical nature of the human condition, with its unexpected effects and the circularity of social processes that make everything in social reality relative and intricate (Sztompka 1986: 5).
4. This work, as is well-known, was first published in the United States in 1949. Other significantly extended editions followed; the text notes refer to the second edition of 1957.
5. Given the prolific nature of Merton's production, this information may be incomplete, despite a careful search for other works in which he might have developed the concept of serendipity further.
6. In Merton's opinion, the not-always-to-be-recommended practice of introducing new terms into the technical dictionary of sociology is sometimes indispensable in order to give the language of sociology a sufficient standard of scientific precision. Apart from the introduction of the terms "serendipity" and "eponymy" and the associated concepts into the language of sociology, we owe many neologisms and definitions to Merton such as "self-fulfilling prophecy," "specified ignorance," "the Matthew effect," the "Eureka syndrome," "the Phoenix phenomenon," and so on.
7. Compare Pietro Dri (1994: 17). In the original version of this paper (1989), reference to the etymology of the term was limited to Walpole's letter. Pietro Dri's recent rediscovery of the sixteenth-century Venetian volume has made an update necessary in the revision for this English language edition. As proof of the Venetian precedence in matters of serendipity, Dri reproduces a long passage in

archaic Italian which Cristoforo Armeno declares he translated from the Persian and subjects it to a close in terms of a scholarly comparative literature analysis.

8. The term *irrational* refers here to the subjective sense not as operating in terms of the logical schemes on the basis of which the researcher usually operates.

9. In this connection see, for example, "Notes on Problem-Finding in Sociology" in *Sociology Today,* ix-xxiv.

10. Merton's position on this is made very clear in the concluding essay "Social Problems and Sociological Theory" in Merton and Nisbet 1961: 697–737.

11. Newton's famous observation is taken up by Merton as the title of an erudite sociological "novel" in which he makes a synthesis not without its ironical moments of the principle of historicosocial accumulation (Merton [1965] 1985).

12. On the role of the social formation "sect" (not only in its religious sense) as a place for experimenting and preserving alternative forms of knowledge, see Maniscalco 1992.

13. On the relationships between science and magic Carlo Mongardini (1983: 37) writes: "In periods of decline in knowledge it is as if magic has collected to itself all the most avant-garde, most antitraditional positions and has preserved them to open the road to new cognitive paradigms."

14. Emblematic here is the case of socially expected durations (Merton, in Powell and Robbins 1984: 262–283).

15. Various examples of serendipity in the course of research are attributed to Merton; among the many, we can recall the concept of "relative deprivation" elaborated during one of the pieces of research contained in *The American Soldier* (Merton 1957: 241, note 13).

16. It is in the physical and natural sciences, in fact, that Merton's conceptualization finds its widest and most complete application as the historical proof suggests. One need only recall the vigorous action of serendipity as accidental invention or discovery in the well-known episode of Archimedes, the famous Greek mathematician, whose problem was to determine whether a crown was made of gold or base metal, a task given him by Hiero, King of Syracuse; likewise for Newton and many cases, recent and not so recent, as for example in the blessed intuition of seeing the healing powers of certain molds. For the relationships between science and serendipity, compare Halacy 1967 and Roberts 1989.

References

Coser, Lewis A. 1975. "Merton's Uses of European Sociological Tradition." In *The Idea of Social Structure: Papers in Honor of Robert K. Merton,* edited by L.A. Coser, 98. New York: Harcourt Brace Jovanovich.

Crothers, Charles 1987. *Robert Merton.* London and New York: Harwood & Tavistock.

Dri, Pietro. 1994. *Serendippo.* Rome: Editori Riuniti.

Halacy, D.S., Jr. 1967. *Science and Serendipity: Great Discoveries by Accident.* Philadelphia: Macrae Smith.

Maniscalco, Maria Luisa. 1992. *Spirito di setta e società: Significato e dimensioni sociologiche delle forme settarie.* Milan: Franco Angeli.

Merton, Robert K. 1984. "Socially Expected Durations: A Case Study of Concept Formation in Sociology." In *Conflict and Consensus: A Festschrift for Lewis A. Coser,* edited by W.W. Powell and R. Robbins, 262–283. New York: Free Press.

———. [1965] 1993. *On the Shoulders of Giants: A Shandean Postscript.* Chicago: University of Chicago Press.

————. 1961. "Social Problems and Sociological Theory." In *Contemporary Social Problems*, edited by R.K. Merton and R.A. Nisbet, 697–737. New York: Harcourt, Brace and World.

————.1957. *Social Theory and Social Structure*. 2d. ed. New York: Free Press.

Merton, Robert K. and Elinor G. Barber. 1958. *The Travels and Adventures of Serendipity: A Study in Historical Semantics*, ms. (This book is now in press: *I viaggi e l'avventura della "Serendipity."* Bologna: Il Mulino.)

Mongardini, Carlo. 1983. "Sul significato sociologico del pensiero magico." In *Il magico e il moderno,* edited by Carlo Mongardini. Milan: Franco Angeli.

Roberts, R.M. 1989. *Serendipity: Accidental Discoveries in Science*. New York: Wiley Science Edition.

Sztompka, Piotr. 1986. *Robert K. Merton: An Intellectual Profile*. London: Macmillan.

Walpole, Horace. 1903. Letter to Mann, 28 January 1754. In *The Letters of Horace Walpole*. Vol 3, edited by Philip Toynbee. Oxford: Clarendon Press.

19

R.K. Merton: The Model of Theory-Empirical Research Circularity as a Way Out of the Micro-Macro Dichotomy

Elena Besozzi

In the course of a recent collegial reexamination of the debate on macro and micro approaches in sociology at the Department of Sociology of the Catholic University of Milan, I put forward the contribution of R.K. Merton on the circular relationship between theory and empirical research, with regard to Martindale's hypothesis (Martindale 1968) that Merton's cannot be considered a macro approach in any strict sense. Much nearer to Merton's work seems to me what Barbano has to say in his introduction to the second edition of *Teoria e struttura sociale* (Barbano 1986): Merton's work is more a commitment to building a bridge between positive sociology—based on criteria of observation and scientific explanation—and interpretative sociology which, beginning with Weberian interpretative sociology, seeks to understand the experienced or existential significances of social action.

This effort on the part of Merton to link two, often contrasting, sociological positions is almost equivalent, in my view, to the construction of an innovative sociological approach that moves some distance toward resolving the micro-macro dichotomy.

This comes about through two of Merton's choices:

1. The first concerns the subject for study, which for Merton is not the social system from which social structure can be deduced by analytical procedure, but rather the social structure itself with its empirical implications (such as dysfunctions or latent structure). The social structure is characterized as a structural situation and therefore implies a definition of the situation, or, as W.I. Thomas held, an analysis of the representations which individuals use as a basis for evaluating a certain situation and which are thus predisposers to action.

2. Merton's second choice concerns the methodological framework, which assumes as a basic option that the relations between theory and empirical research must be considered reciprocal. In my view, it is precisely through the construction of this relationship—and the resulting elimination of the dichotomy between theory and research—that the foundations are laid for eliminating the dichotomy between micro- and macrosociology in Mertonian functionalism.

A basic characteristic of contemporary sociology concerns its inability to reconcile the micro and the macro level (Bovone 1986:306) in relation to two assumptions of deeply divergent origin: the assumption about action for the micro approach and the assumption about system for the macro approach. As Smelser (1981) points out, the macrolevel is concerned with structure; the micro, with the process by which the structure is constructed and preserved. Macro theories, roughly, deal with the problem of the integration and influence of the social structures on individuals, while the micro theories concentrate on the problem of the meaning and applications of social structures.

Examination of the Mertonian model of the circularity between theory and empirical research—supported by relevant examples such as the advance in behavior theory in light of important concepts emerging from research, for example "relative deprivation," "reference group," etc.—permits us to draw attention to the following implications:

1. Subject and method in Merton are profoundly connected, so much so that the model of theory-research circularity cannot be seen on its own only as a problem of methodology. This circularity makes it possible to note the same circularity between the structure and subject of the action, between the system and the actor in the situation.

2. The Mertonian methodological approach implies, therefore, a dialectic between micro and macro (where micro refers to macro and vice versa) and where the problem of the meaning of action is reformulated in terms of a direction which is not generically functional. Even if, as Bovone (1986) emphasizes, it is possible to escape from the micro-macro debate by positing a micro foundation for macrosociology and

by considering micro and macro as part of a continuum, in my opinion, this Mertonian methodological approach nevertheless contains an important program that may lead us to a solution of the epistemological and methodological crisis in which sociology finds itself.

3. The Mertonian position, finally, is proved to be firmly anchored to the classics such as Durkheim and Weber (in whom there is not so much evidence of counterposition as of co-presence of micro and macro). It seems to have also influenced more recent positions such as that of Boudon in his commitment to retrieving the founding features of a theory of action in the light of methodological individualism. In fact, Boudon (1980: 55–56) emphasizes that though Merton's effort is constantly towards analyzing the reactions of individual actors to the restraints imposed by the system, it also focuses on transformations of the social structure and its various types of equilibrium resulting from the dysfunctions caused by the behavior of its actors and, above all, by the fact that roles are not absolutes given to subjects for their interpretation but are open, compound, often ambiguous and contradictory and that they come equipped with a variability that ensures a measure of autonomy to the social actor (Boudon 1980: 76–77).

The reciprocal relations between theory and empirical research and, above all, the equal status given to them both therefore allow Merton to remain within a functional approach, while challenging the legitimacy and generalized indispensability of existing social structures. That orientation allows him to ask questions such as "functional for whom?" when it comes to regular empirical audits, thus laying the basis for a functional analysis whose starting point is also the individual or group of individuals.

References

Barbano, Filippo. 1986. "Introduction." In *Teoria e struttura sociale*, 2d ed., by Robert K. Merton. Bologna: Il Mulino.

Boudon, Raymond.1980. *La logica del sociale*. Milan: Mondadori.

Bovone, Laura. 1986. "Micro-macro: una dialettica congenita della sociologia" *Studi di Sociologia* 24, (3–4):306.

Martindale, Don.1986. *The Nature and Types of Sociological Theory*. Cambridge: The Riverside Press.

Smelser, Neil J. 1981. *Sociology*. Englewood Cliffs, NJ: Prentice-Hall.

20

Sztompka's Analysis of Merton's Writings: A Description and Some Criticisms

Charles Crothers

Introduction

It is important in discussing the general themes in Merton's writings that we examine the frameworks put forward in Piotr Sztompka's book-length study entitled *Robert K. Merton: An Intellectual Portrait* (1986). This is a very comprehensive study and any further analyses of Merton's work must be aware of it and build on it. But it is not an easy book to grasp and summarize, as it involves several complex, multilayer and interwoven typologies. However, my purpose in providing a description of the book is, in part, that I can *then* raise some criticisms of it and suggest an alternative line of interpretation.

Description

In his book, Sztompka tackles the task of summarizing Merton's voluminous output in several major substantive chapters that follow introductory summaries and biographical materials. These substantive chapters begin with Merton's views on science, and then elicit Merton's approach to sociological method, his general sociological orientation, his views on social structure and his analyses of social process.

The early emphasis which Sztompka accords Merton's science of science as something of a common matrix from which more specific strands of his thinking emerge makes a very insightful point. This is because Merton's work might well be seen as "triangulated" around the study of the development of science. He has not only studied this sociologically, but has also reflexively incorporated various lessons from this study into his own approaches to scientific work in sociology. I think a major drawback of Sztompka's chapter-structure is that it postpones until rather too late in the book an adequate treatment of Merton's structural analysis of social phenomena that is—to my mind— by far the most important contribution he has made to the advancement of sociology.

But the chapter-structure is only the outer form of the presentation of Sztompka's argument and it is to its inner structure that we must turn. Sztompka's portrayal of Merton's writings is set within a broad portrait of what Sztompka sees as an overall system of Mertonian thought. This overall system is considered to be anchored in the classic nineteenth-century heritage of the systems-building founding fathers of sociology, and Merton is portrayed as the last of this lineage. However, Sztompka does point out that this "system-building" has not been the way Merton has proclaimed his tasks, but is constructed in Sztompka's own analysis.

Sztompka sees Merton's system as spanning both "meta-scientific" (i.e., methodological) and "scientific" levels. In both his conclusion and opening chapters Sztompka has provided an analytical conceptualization of the extent to which Merton's thought forms a system on both these levels. The properties of this systemness are identified as:

- coherence;
- generality and abstractness (based in a common core of theory);
- continuity over time; and,
- thematic unity (itself composed of four themes: a general classicist approach, a cognitivist stress, a structuralist focus and an ironic stamp).

Of these four themes it is suggested that the classicist approach is a master-theme in Merton's work. This, Sztompka suggests, is located in Merton's concern to order scientific issues, to strike an intermediate stance in relation to issues (the Aristotelian "golden mean") and to express his positions in well-disciplined prose. Sztompka assumes in his more detailed handling of Merton's work that it is permeated by these themes.

Within this general framework of Merton's writings, Sztompka's analysis of Merton's *sociology* (at the "scientific" level) involves a two-level framework in which *social life*, as enacted in raw concrete reality, is explained by a complex abstract theoretical model of *social structure*. Sztompka indicates that in the Mertonian view the anatomy of social structure in turn comprises three dimensions:

1. normative structure (norms and values, roles and institutions, and role-sets);
2. opportunity-structure (access to resources, means, etc.); and,
3. ideal structure (*beliefs* about norms, values, opportunities, etc.).

These three dimensions are then each cross-classified by a further dimension relating to "scale" and comprising first-order, second-order, and third-order components which correspond in a way to the sequence of elementary particles, atoms, and molecules (as in the sequence—within the normative dimension—of values, roles, and role-sets).

Having established these three dimensions, Sztompka criticizes the overindulgence in only the normative aspect in Merton's own work and even more so in the appreciations of critics and commentators. He then adroitly goes on to show the relevance of these three aspects in Merton's analyses of anomie, social change, and the general operation of social systems. It is in this attempted tidying-up over several areas of Merton's work that Sztompka's schema shows particular signs of creative development.

The creative potential of Sztompka's scheme is demonstrated in his chapter on "anomie." Sztompka argues that Merton's use of anomie is a central conceptual device in which multiple strands of his thought cross over, and also reminds us, that in Merton's approach, anomie is often a social condition leading to structural change.

Sztompka focuses particularly on a typology of four types of anomie, which he is able to identify separately in terms of his more general approach to Merton's sociology. This application, therefore, forms a crucial test of the usefulness of his general approach in analyzing Merton's writings.

Sztompka labels the general form of anomie—that is, when there is "a breakdown of social standards governing behavior" (and little social cohesion)—as *anomie*$_1$. A more specific form, *anomie*$_2$, arises from incompatible multiple sets of norms. Another, *anomie*$_3$, arises in the classic Mertonian sense out of a mismatch between goals and the means available to achieve these. Sztompka points out an interesting variation of this type of anomie, in which the mismatch involves the available means having a surplus capacity which is stifled by "low expectations," as well as the type covered by the more usual assumption that it is "high expectations" that are frustrated by undersupply of available means. Lastly, he identifies *anomie*$_4$ as a mismatch between ideal structure and normative structure in which there is a withdrawal of allegiance from prevailing standards. In identifying these different forms of anomie Sztompka is applying his prior conceptualization of the three key dimensions (normative, opportunity, and ideal) of social structure.

There are, of course, several points of useful detail in Sztompka's chapter on anomie which I have not attempted to cover: especially how different sequences of change may arise out of different types of anomie. And of course his book very considerably amplifies the basic typologies which I have tried to summarize here.

Criticisms

But to take Sztompka's work seriously we must carefully analyze it further. This criticism must take place at several levels:

- in terms of the overall characterization of Merton's writings;
- in terms of the overall characterization of Merton's sociological schema; and,
- in terms of the details of the description and commentary.

My criticisms in this short chapter are confined completely to the first of these levels.

While I agree with much of what Professor Sztompka has to say about the extent of systematic-ness he has uncovered in the writings of Merton, I would like to indicate that a subtle and yet profound change in the basic image he presents may provide a more useful understanding of Merton's writings, and also provoke examination of more general theoretical and historical issues. I offer a brief sketch of a critical commentary in the hope that others more knowledgeable may take points further.

Sztompka portrays Merton's work as that of the last of the nineteenth-century system-builders in sociology. While wishing to retain much of the force of this imagery because it nicely points up much of the implicit consistency in Merton's writings, I would prefer to alter it to suggest, rather, that Merton is the first of the twentieth-century science-builders in sociology. I think that Sztompka has seriously misjudged the way in which the consistency across Merton's writings is manifest. In order to rebuild the image of system-ness I must establish a particular link back to some widespread characteristics of thought of the seventeenth rather than the nineteenth century.

In many ways, Merton is a creature of the seventeenth century rather than the nineteenth century, as Sztompka portrays him. For several years—and while at the impressionable age of carrying out postgraduate work!—much of Merton's work was on the late-seventeenth century. In later writings this period is clearly still particularly attractive to him (although as yet this statement is speculative assertion rather than empirically sustained). Moreover, I don't doubt that his long interest in Laurence Sterne derives from the continuing seventeenth-century resonances in his writings.

But, what is particularly meant by this appeal to the seventeenth century? That century is particularly interesting because much of the scientific thinking in this period was particularly concerned with breaking out from the cloying limitations of medieval systems of thought. This is especially pointed up in Newton's image of picking up pebbles from the beach. But of course Newton, too, shared many of the difficulties of thinkers of his age, with one foot still planted in medieval systems-thinking and the tinges of mysticism and magic seemingly associated with this.

What resonances the seventeenth-century breakout towards recognizably scientific modes of thinking must have had for Merton as he struggled to shape a model of selectively cumulative scientific advance for sociology in the twentieth century! Merton, too, saw sociology (lagging natural science by some centuries as he has several times stressed) as needing to break out from the limitations of "closed" comprehensive systems of thought. He repeatedly insists on the need to disaggregate systems (for instance, those of Comte, Marx, Spencer, or Freud) into their constituent elements, and then select only the more empirically viable parts. Indeed, Merton's strictures on general theory are often misunderstood, as they are in fact not dismissive of general theory but, rather, attacks on grand systems of thought.

Thus, while there is systematicity in Merton's thought, it is unlikely to be found in the model of nineteenth-century systems of thought. It is more subtle and more intrinsic to his mode of analysis, and is derived more from a seventeenth-century "middle-range" approach than from some nineteenth-century systems frameworks.

My attempt to shift Sztompka's image raises two types of question:

1. The first needs the approach of a Foucault, or a Kuhn, a Lakatos, or a Mary Douglas (or a Merton): what are the philosophical and theoretical questions that arise from the contrast between "closed systems" with their particular concern for fitting in evidence into a prearranged grand order and their emphasis on *taxonomy,* and "open systems" with their emphasis on *cumulation* outwards from a secure base, and their concern for *explanation*? Their emphasis on *solutions* rather than *problems*?
2. The second concerns the historical conditions under which these quite contrasting modes of organizing knowledge are produced. Why did the seventeenth century see the "dawn" of the middle-range theorizing that characterizes an open-ended system of knowledge? (My source for this is, of course, Merton himself; see *Social Theory and Social Structure,* 1968: 56–62). Why did the nineteenth century again usher in closed systems of thought? Might we reformulate (or add to) the "Merton thesis" that a crucial mechanism was the carrying across of Luther's middle-range *theological* theorizing into the *scientific* middle-range theorizing of the Baconian program? Is the nineteenth-century closed-system dominance related particularly to Teutonic approaches to scholarship and thus more dominant in nineteenth-century science because of the then dominance, as Ben-David (1971) has told us, of German science in that period. The necessary lack of qualifications in my briefly expressed speculations appalls me: I hope they might withstand some of the attacks they should rightly draw. Again, there is a range of more detailed points it is not appropriate to develop in a short comment. But I also hope that my comments will help push forward studies of Merton's thinking and its role in contemporary sociology, and will fruitfully complement Sztompka's work.

References

Ben-David, J. 1971. *The Scientist's Role in Society.* Englewood Cliffs, NJ: Prentice-Hall.
Merton, R.K. 1968. *Social Theory and Social Structure.* New York: Free Press.
Sztompka, P. 1986. *Robert K. Merton: An Intellectual Portrait.* New York: St. Martin's Press.

Afterword

Unanticipated Consequences and Kindred Sociological Ideas: A Personal Gloss

Robert K. Merton

One of the themes singled out for attention in this volume—most directly, in the chapters by Arnold Zingerle and Peter Gerlich—centers on the unanticipated consequences of social action. Emphatically introduced as a core theme in the 1930s, at a time when it was far from being a focus of sociological thinking, it continued to appear in various specified forms in my theoretical and empirical studies since. It is a sociological idea central to my first published monograph, *Science, Technology and Society in Seventeenth-Century England* (1938), which derived from a doctoral dissertation in what would emerge as the historical sociology of science. In that work it is proposed that Puritanism, and ascetic Protestantism generally, had inadvertently helped to legitimatize the newly emerging science, even though the contemporary charismatic religious leaders—Luther, Calvin, and Melanchthon chief among them—had attacked certain scientific discoveries and cosmological doctrines as pernicious. The sociological analysis of that specific historical case was based upon a generic theoretical analysis set forth in a paper with the encapsulating title, "The Unanticipated Consequences of Purposive Social Action" (Merton 1936).

The paper begins by taking note of the historically recurring rather than enduring interest in the phenomenon of unanticipated and unin-

295

tended consequences from at least the time of Machiavelli. Among the others who had variously directed their attention to one or another aspect of the phenomenon were "Vico, Adam Smith (and some later classical economists), Marx, Engels, Wundt, Pareto and Max Weber," to expand the list no further. It was further observed that the concept "has been related to such heterogeneous subjects as: the problem of evil (theodicy), moral responsibility, free will, predestination, deism, teleology, fatalism, logical, illogical and non-logical behavior, social prediction, planning and control, social cycles, the pleasure and reality principles, and historical 'accidents.'" The terms by which the whole or selected aspects of the phenomenon have been known were no less polymorphous: "Providence (incidental or transcendental), Moira, *Paradoxie der Folgen*, *Schicksal*, social forces, heterogony of ends, immanent causation, dialectical movement, principle of emergence and creative synthesis." Central to this variegated scatter, it was proposed, is the theoretical conundrum: How does the phenomenon of unintended and unanticipated consequences come about? How are we to think about its recurrence in every domain of society, culture, and civilization?

In view of discussions elsewhere in this volume, I need provide only the barest of summaries of the analysis set out in that paper. Various fundamental social and sociopsychological processes are held to make for unanticipated consequences. Ignorance and error are treated as transparently evident sources of "unexpected consequences," holding theoretical interest only insofar as they are socially or psychologically shaped. A third typal source is "the imperious immediacy of interests": "where the actor's paramount concern with the foreseen immediate consequences excludes consideration of further or other consequences of the same act." The fourth type, giving rise to paradoxical feedback, is one in which "a system of basic values enjoins certain *specific* actions, and adherents are concerned not with the objective consequence of these actions but with the subjective satisfaction of duty well performed." In this dynamic of social and cultural change—variously recognized by Hegel, Marx, Wundt, and others—"activities oriented toward certain values release processes that so react as to change the very scale of values which precipitated them."

Throughout, it is argued that the interdependence of social structure makes for "ramified" unforeseen consequences. Thus, "*precisely because a particular action is not carried out in a psychological or social vacuum, its effects will ramify into other spheres of value and interest."* It is the composites of aggregated and socially patterned actions that generate various kinds of unanticipated consequences for individuals, groups, society, culture, and civilization. The paper concludes by focusing on "self-defeating predictions" as a special type of unanticipated consequences holding methodological as well as sociological interest—but about this, more, much more, later.

In accord with the autobiographic account asked of me, I turn from that brief substantive summary to a personal gloss on my enduring interest in the sociological idea of unanticipated, unintended, and unrecognized consequences of purposive social action. That calls, of course, for the sort of contextual information about experienced continuities, discontinuities, and ramifications of a continuing idea that is ordinarily screened out of learned papers by the conventionalized editorial constraints on their contents. As I had occasion to remark at about the time I was writing the paper on unanticipated consequences, scientific work is "presented in a rigorously logical and 'scientific' fashion (in accordance with the rules of evidence current at the time) and *not* in the order in which the theory or law was derived" (Merton [1938] 1970: 220). Or as I reiterated decades later in quite another context, "Typically, the scientific paper or monograph presents an immaculate appearance which reproduces little or nothing of the intuitive leaps, false starts, mistakes, loose ends, and happy accidents that actually cluttered up the inquiry" (Merton 1968: 4). In short, the etiquette governing the writing of scientific (or scholarly) papers requires them to be works of vast expurgation, stripping the complex events that culminated in the published reports of everything except their delimited cognitive substance. We should perhaps note that this economic and efficient editorial norm might lead cumulatively to certain side-effects—or, one might say, to certain unanticipated consequences. For it invites a misleading imagery of scientists and scholars moving coolly, methodically, and unerringly to their reported ideas and findings.

That was surely not the case with my decades-long work on the core idea of unanticipated consequences and its derivative ideas. Difficulties are intimated in the first, 1936, paper. For in an early footnote, the author of that *Jugendwerk* had the innocent temerity to announce that a monograph devoted "to the history and analysis" of the central idea of unanticipated consequences and kindred ideas was in progress.

And indeed it was. But that footnote may turn out to be the most prolonged and periodically renewed promissory note in the recent history of sociological scholarship. For although the thematics of unanticipated consequences and related ideas have remained an enduring element in my work ever since, that promised full-scale monograph is still in intermittent preparation–a mere half-century later.

In slight extenuation, it should be said that aperiodic installments have been paid on that ancient promissory note. One of these, setting out the concepts and implications of latent functions and latent dysfunctions, directs us to theoretically fundamental types of unintended and unrecognized consequences. To me, the most theoretically interesting kind of latent function is that which loses its effectiveness as the intentions of participants and the consequences of the actions rise to the surface and become manifest. In the 1946 monograph, *Mass Persuasion*, focussed on a case of the mass sale of war bonds (as they were known), I identified and analyzed a prime specimen of this type in the form of *pseudo-Gemeinschaft*: the feigning of personal concern and intimacy with others in order to manipulate them the better and to bend them to one's own purposes. Once the tactic has been identified by those to whom it is applied—as, to take a massive present-day instance, in the use of word processors for seemingly personal letters that are actually mass mailings—it loses its efficacy. The more general theoretical problem remains: in cases not involving deliberate manipulation, how is it that once effective latent functions no longer operate as they become broadly manifest?

As for the concept of latent dysfunction, this has its own problematics. Persistent latent dysfunctions give rise to unwanted social conditions. Produced by purposive actions directed toward prized interests and values, these are conditions which are at odds with other declared interests and values of groups and strata in the society but are not widely recognized as being so by those engaged in inadvertently perpetuating those conditions. As I have had occasion to observe in this connection regarding the often murky notions of "value-free" and "value-laden" sociological ideas,

Sociologists do not impose their values upon others when they undertake to supply knowledge about latent problems that makes them generally manifest. Thus, when demographers . . . try to identify the social, economic, and cultural consequences of various rates of population growth, they in effect call the advocates of differing population policies to account for the results of putting one or another policy into practice. The demonstrated consequences of uncontrolled birth rates, for example, can then be seen as the aggregated result of people acting in accord with some of their values to produce outcomes that conflict with some of their other values.

This kind of latent social problem constitutes an important special case of the generic pattern of the unanticipated consequences of (individual or collective) social action. Total commitments to values of every kind–whether they be the value set on rapid economic expansion ("growth"), or rapid technological advance ("progress"), or rule-free communities or the value set on that full expression of self in which anything goes (analyzed by Lionel Trilling in the notion of "Authenticity")–have cumulative consequences that, if not counteracted, in due course undercut the originating values themselves.[1]

The Self-Fulfilling Prophecy

Another installment of that theoretical monograph on unanticipated consequences and kindred ideas appeared in the literary journal, *The Antioch Review*, Summer 1948, under the title, "The Self-Fulfilling Prophecy." Again, I follow the editors' suggestion to provide a personal gloss on the emergence and fate of ideas treated in these papers. I had deliberately decided to publish that paper in a journal for the general reader rather than in an academic journal. For I thought then, precisely forty years ago, as I still do now, that the concept of the self-fulfilling prophecy held direct and significant implications for the conduct of social life; I wanted to have it become more quickly and widely known than is ordinarily the case with the diffusion of technical sociological ideas into the public consciousness. And that is what seems to have happened. The article was often reprinted. In the English-speaking world, the concept-and-phrase, "the self-fulfilling prophecy," has made its way, often with uncritical ease, into everyday vernacular with its tacitly sociological thinking. Most reverberatively, it has become diffused through all the media of mass communication, principally newspapers and magazines but radio and television as well. Not least, the concept has been put to use (and abuse) in the halls of the American Congress and in presidential documents. Again, not always with discriminating judgement. I recall, for one example, the ambivalence with which I read in President Nixon's budget message of 1971 that he counted on his optimistic forecast for the economy becoming—the language is his—"a self-fulfilling prophecy." Like many another American, I preferred the prophesied outcome to a recession but was minded to inform the president that prophecies by publicly significant individuals become self-fulfilling, apart from other special conditions, only when the prophet has acquired widespread credibility.

Nor, of course, had that White-House usage of the concept recognized that the core pattern of the self-fulfilling prophecy is one in which an initially false but widely accepted prediction, expectation, or belief is fulfilled in social reality not because it was at the outset true, but because enough people in the given social system, large or small, took it to be true and, by acting accordingly, produced the outcome that would otherwise not have occurred. So it was that, back in the Great Depression of the 1930s, before federal deposit insurance was instituted by President Roosevelt, rumors of insolvency could produce runs on banks through which the rumors brought about their own fulfillment. The apparent but only specious "pragmatically confirmed" prophecy thus perpetuates a reign of error since the prophet(s) will cite the actual course of events as proof of having been right from the start. This form of the self-fulfilling prophecy, it also seemed to me then and still does now, is especially pernicious in the discriminatory treatment, throughout the human world, of racial, ethnic, class, sex, and other minorities (who are, of course, often in the great numerical majority). Thus, it was noted in that early paper, that the widespread hostility of white trade-unionists in the United States toward black workers after the close of the First World War was ostensibly based on blacks having been brought into industry by employers in the role of strike-breakers. The stereotype of the "inferior black," reinforced by the hostility directed against strike-breakers of any kind, continued to keep blacks out of the unions, thus limiting their routes to employment. But as the basic assumption that blacks were variously not deserving of membership in trade unions eroded and largely broke down, black workers with an enlarged though still far from equitable range of opportunities no longer found it necessary to enter industry through doors held open by strikebound employers. Appropriate institutional policy broke through the tragic and self-perpetuating circle of the self-fulfilling prophecy.

Diffusion of the concept has been widespread in various domains. Hundreds of papers in sociology, social psychology, psychology, economics, philosophy, political science, public administration, anthropology, and especially educational research have made basic use of the concept of self-fulfilling prophecy (and, in some instances, of its counterpart concept, the self-defeating prophecy). But it is not to these many papers and occasional books that I refer in these notes. Rather, I refer to the widespread drift of the concept-and-phrase into the public consciousness. As frequent news stories in the mass media testify, the concept has evidently provided a pragmatic and sometimes effective analytic tool for organizations and individuals dedicated to a counter-attack on discrimination visited upon various kinds of minorities and to the enlarging of equity for them.

That the concept-and-term has entered into the language is registered further by its having become a standard entry in most English dictionaries. A typical entry reads: "self-fulfilling: brought to fulfillment chiefly as an effect of having been expected or predicted [a *self-fulfilling* prophecy]." As a lifelong admirer of the grandest English dictionary of them all—I refer to *The Oxford English Dictionary*, of course—it meant much to me to have the editor of the grand *OED Supplement*, Robert Butterfield, hand me varied evidence, handwritten as well as printed, that, along with other concept-and-word coinages of mine, the "self-fulfilling prophecy" had been enshrined and perhaps canonized in the four-volume *Supplement*.

So much by way of a brief gloss on the *diffusion* of the idea of the self-fulfilling prophecy; now an account of its *origin and vicissitudes* before the originating paper by that title found its way into print. (It might be noted that I could not have put this account together from possibly undependable memory traces; it derives instead from letters and other personal documents drawn from old files).

The Self-Defeating Prophecy

The germ of the notion of the self-fulfilling prophecy is found in the closing pages of the 1936 paper on unanticipated consequences of social action. Those pages deal with what turned out to be the counterpart concept of the self-defeating prediction or prophecy. Thus, it is observed that

> Public predictions of future social developments are frequently not sustained precisely because the prediction has become a new element in the concrete situation thus tending to change the initial course of developments. This is not true of prediction in fields that do not pertain to human conduct. Thus, the prediction of Halley's comet does not in any way influence the orbit of that comet [as we have since seen from its having come into earthly sight once again in 1986, just as the seventeenth-century Halley had predicted it would]; but, to take a concrete social example, Marx's prediction of the progressive concentration of wealth and increas-

ing misery of the masses did influence [I believe that this would better read: may have influenced] the very process predicted.

The paper then concludes by observing that the self-defeating prediction holds a double interest for social science. It is not only a phenomenon which social scientists want to investigate in the experience of others but also one that introduces acute methodological problems in social science inquiry, sometimes making the empirical testing of predictions and forecasts formidable (if not, in principle, impossible).[2]

Perhaps of particular interest here is the concluding footnote of the paper which cites Corrado Gini, *Prime linee di patologia economica* (1935: 72–75) on the possibly self-defeating consequences of Marx's doctrinal forecast. That calls for further biographic contexts. It happens that Gini had spent the academic year 1935–36 as a visiting professor at Harvard, preliminary to receiving an honorary degree at the grand Tercentenary of the University. It happens also that, as a graduate student there in the spring of 1935, I was *commanded* by the chairman of the Department of Sociology, Professor Pitirim A. Sorokin, to acquire a firm reading knowledge of Italian by the autumn. The reason? Starting that fall, I would be the year-long teaching and research assistant of Professor Gini. (Even the masterful and sometimes imperious Sorokin did not demand that I also acquire a fluent speaking knowledge of the language). Obeying his command, I translated, during that year, a number of Gini's papers for presentation in classroom and in print. That, no doubt, is how I happened to come upon Gini's observations on the fate of Marx's work; I was evidently reading intensively in the opera of my newfound institutional master.

But it was not so much Gini's specific remarks about Marx that set me to thinking further about self-defeating predictions as a generic phenomenon related to the central idea of unanticipated consequences of action. For the theme of unintended consequences—only later differentiated from unanticipated and unrecognized consequences—had pervaded my doctoral dissertation on seventeenth-century English science which had been almost completed before my first encounter with Gini in the fall of 1935. Rather, having identified the self-defeating prediction as an element in "social movements developing in utterly unanticipated directions," I resonated at once to a passage in a book by the inventive nineteenth-century logician, John Venn—of "Venn diagram" fame. For, as I put it in that same footnote which cites Gini, "John Venn uses the picturesque term 'suicidal prophecies' to refer to this process [of the previously identified self-defeating prediction] and properly observes that it represents a class of considerations which have been much neglected by the various sciences of human conduct. See his *Logic of Chance* (London, 1888), pp. 225–26." So far as I know to this day, no one had previously resonated in public to this splendid passage of Venn's, suggesting to me now that my response to it may have been yet another specimen of what I would later identify as "the retroactive effect" in science and scholarship (Merton 1968: 35–38): *new* knowledge, personal or collective, "has a retroactive effect in helping us to recognize anticipations and adumbrations in earlier work" which have been passed by until the new idea or knowledge sensitizes us to the import of that belatedly discovered earlier work. In that pattern, there appear

> citations to classical writings that come about when the reader, stocked with his own ideas, finds in the earlier book precisely what he already had in mind. The idea, *still hidden from other readers, is* noted precisely because it is congenial to the reader who had developed it himself. It is often assumed that to cite an earlier source *necessarily* means that the idea or finding in that citation first came to mind upon the reading of it. Yet the evidence often indicates that the earlier passage is noted only because it agrees with what the reader has already developed on his own. What we find here is that unlikely sounding event: a dialogue between the dead and the living. These do not differ much from dialogues between contemporary scientists in which each is delighted as he discovers that the other agrees with what was until then an idea held in solitude and perhaps even suspect. Ideas take on new [probabilities of] validity when they are independently expressed by another, either in print or in conversation. The only advantage of coming upon it in print is that one knows there has been no inadvertent contagion between the book or article and one's own prior formulation of the same idea. (Merton 1968: 36)

Venn's clear-headed passage on the "suicidal prophecy" evidently set me thinking about the more general problem of other types of unanticipated consequences. Upon leaving Harvard in 1939, I gave my good friend and former colleague, the then dean of American social psychology, Gordon W. Allport, a batch of offprints of my work, including one of the article on unanticipated consequences. In a letter of response (dated 22 September 1939), Allport included these words of encouragement:

> Please continue your work along this direction. For one thing, I should like to see you develop still further the concept of self-defeating predictions. If I recall cor-

rectly, this is a favourite idea of W.E. Hocking. It has a good deal of practical
bearing on our present society which is so highly developed in its communications
and issuing of statements and predictions.

Thus far, this phase of an evolving sociological idea provides an
instructive specimen of the way in which a conceptual framework can
inhibit as well as facilitate an enlarged and deepened understanding of
phenomena under scrutiny. There we were—the overlooked Venn,
now a precise century ago, and a half-century later, Gini, Allport,
presumably Hocking, and definitely myself—all focusing, with differing degrees of awareness and generality upon one phenomenon: the
self-*defeating* prediction or suicidal prophecy. But none of us, at those
given times, managing to conceptualize this more broadly. No explicit
notice that this might be only one of a wider set of patterns in which
predictions, beliefs, or expectations might variously affect objective
outcomes of action.

Despite Allport's urging and for reasons not at all clear to me now,
for I have no further documents at this point, I elected not to continue
work on the delimited problem of self-*defeating* predictions. Instead,
my attention shifted to other social and sociopsychological phenomena that could be identified in the large conceptual class of unanticipated or unintended or unrecognized consequences of patterned social
action. So it was, then, during the decade after the 1936 paper, that I
began to turn from a focus on self-*negating* consequences of socially
patterned action—as in the special case of self-defeating predictions—
to a focus on self-*maintaining*, self-*fulfilling*, and self-*augmenting* consequences and processes.

Manifest and Latent Functions

The first of this latter set was initially identified in my Harvard
lectures of the late 1930s which centered on "latent" as distinct from
"manifest" consequences. Latent functions of designated social structures or socially patterned action referred to those unintended consequences for a specified unit (group, social stratum, social or cultural
system) which contribute to its adaptation, to its persistence and evolutionary change. Unlike manifest functions, latent functions are not
the result of plan or design but of social evolution. It will be noticed
that this pair of concepts presupposes a systematic distinction between
such subjective categories as intent, purpose, motive, or plan and ob-

jective categories of varying kinds of actual consequence. Too often even now, let alone back then in the 1930s, that basic distinction has been lost to view in sociological analyses that confuse subjective purpose and objective consequence—as, for example, in questioning that the family can have the *function* of socialization or the training of the young since "people marry *because* they are in love, or for other less romantic but no less personal *reasons*" or motives.

When introducing the sociological idea of latent and manifest functions half a century ago, I evidently began a personal pattern of inquiry which for the most part has continued ever since. The originating idea was largely developed over an extended period in the form of "oral publication" before being put into print.[3] It evolved in the course of the lectures at Harvard and at other centers of learning; in seminars, local and mobile; at conferences and meetings of learned societies, national and international. This continued for a dozen years before the nth "edition" of the evolving idea was finally put in print, this in the first edition of *Social Theory and Social Structure* (1949).

Vicissitudes of the Paper: Self-Fulfilling Prophecy

The same dozen years saw much the same pattern of a slowly evolving development in the case of that other offshoot of the mid-1930s paper on unanticipated consequences: the self-fulfilling prophecy. It was largely through oral publication that, as previously noted, the self-*fulfilling* prophecy emerged as the positive processual counterpart to the self-*defeating* prophecy. As I now find from various documents, soon to be quoted, it was not until 1947 that a compact paper on the central idea of the self-fulfilling prophecy seemed to me ready for publication in print.

As I have also noted, it seemed to me that this sociological idea might possibly become of valued pragmatic application if it were to become widely known and understood. For one example, it promised an enlarged understanding of the social process of racial and ethnic discrimination in which, as was observed in the published article, "the victim is punished for the crime." It was for such reasons that I wanted the article to appear in a widely circulating magazine for the informed general reader rather than, as had been the case for all my previous articles, appearing in a scientific or scholarly journal. I thereupon resolved to submit it to *Harper's Magazine*, one of the most esteemed

306 Robert K. Merton and Contemporary Sociology

and consequential of those journals of informed opinion. Since this was my first excursion of this sort, I turned for counsel, editorial opinion, and guidance to two friends, James M. Reid and John McCallum, both senior editors at the distinguished book-publishing house, Harcourt Brace and Company (where I had become the external advisory editor in sociology as I still am for its descendant firm, Harcourt Brace Jovanovich, forty years later). Their valuable advice proved to be prelude to a short, swift series of vicissitudes encountered by the manuscript and its author.

My knowing colleagues at Harcourt Brace summarized their forthright editorial suggestions at the outset of their more detailed running comments on the manuscript in these words:

> Dear Bob: October 17, 1947
>   Both John McCallum and I have read your piece, "The Self-Fulfilling Prophecy" with great care and the greatest interest. We are agreed on the following points:
>
> 1. If Harper's doesn't take it they are damn fools.
> 2. You should throw away the first two pages which are really very unpleasant reading, and start with a bang as the following detailed suggestions indicate.
> 3. Some of your sentences are more tortuous than they need be.
> 4. Some of the technical terms and sociological jargon can well be eliminated.
> 5. Your final paragraph should not be quite so cryptic.
>
> [Then begin two pages of "Detailed Suggestions," the first of which elucidates their injunction to "throw away" the opening pages of the manuscript as follows:]
>
> We beg of you to chuck out the first two pages. They comprise an unwarranted self-abnegation and don't prepare the reader for what follows. Forget entirely the physical scientists. Begin with section II on page 3 . . .
> [The letter concludes with] One other suggestion: I should think you might well consider an agent to handle your magazine material. I'll have a couple of suggestions of top agents if you want to do this . . .
>
> Sincerely,
> Jimmie [James M. Reid]

I follow most of these excellent editorial suggestions, send the manuscript off to *Harper's*, and, unlike scientific journals known to me, receive an immediate response from its editor which reads in its entirety thus:

Dear Dr. Merton: November 10, 1947
I'm afraid your piece, THE SELF-FULFILLING PROPHECY, just isn't for *Harper's*
Magazine. All of us who read it liked your thesis very much, but we
believe it is too specialized and too technical for us to use. It would
certainly be a wonderful article for one of the technical journals. Thanks a
lot for letting us see it; I wish it suited our magazine better.
Sincerely,
John Fischer
The manuscript is enclosed herewith.

Discomfited but still determined to have the paper appear in a magazine for the presumably informed general reader, I follow the further
suggestion of my editor friends at Harcourt Brace and get the manuscript to the then leading literary agents, Brandt & Brandt. Within a
matter of days, I receive a note from Bernice Baumgartner of the
agency advising me that the article is "not right for popular magazines." Frustrated, I decide to send it on to another magazine for the
general reader, this one, however, associated with a college, *The Antioch
Review*. Oddly enough, my ancient files of that time do not include
what must have been a swift letter of acceptance since the article did
appear just months later in the Summer 1948 issue of that *Review*.
Vicissitude soon turned into victory. For, as I have told in speaking of
the diffusion of the self-fulfilling prophecy as a consequential and
operative sociological idea, the paper was often reprinted—not least in
The Antioch Review Anthology—and thus experienced a multiplier
effect in cumulative circulation.

Yet another turn in the history of this sociological idea took place
while I was reading proofs of the article which had retained its title
throughout these vicissitudinous ups-and-downs: "The Self-Fulfilling
Prophecy." Receiving a copy of his newest book, *The More Perfect
Union* (New York: Macmillan, 1948), from my Columbia colleague,
the distinguished sociologist and political scientist, Robert M. MacIver,
I found that it dealt with the concept of the "self-fulfilling postulate,"
an idea plainly akin to the idea of the self-fulfilling prophecy. Luckily,
the timing of publication allowed me to insert a reference to the book
in the proofs of my article. Evidently, here was yet another case of a
multiple independent "discovery," a phenomenon in the history of
thought which, as I shall soon indicate, had held my interest from my
earliest work in the sociology of science in the 1930s.

It might be asked how this could qualify as an *independently* conceived idea since Robert MacIver and I had been colleagues since 1941. How could it be that a colleague would not know that the idea of the self-fulfilling prophecy had been gestating for a decade and more ever since my 1936 paper on unanticipated consequences with its concluding focus on the self-defeating or suicidal prophecy? Or, correlatively, how could it be that I would not know that he was at work on yet another book which would include discussion of the self-fulfilling postulate? The answer is found, I believe, in the nature of the amiable relationship between us. For, in strong contrast to another Columbia colleague, Paul F. Lazarsfeld, Robert MacIver never discussed his ongoing work with me—and, so far as I know, with other colleagues. The first that either Robert or I knew what the other was up to in his current or recent work would be through the exchange of books or offprints of articles as soon as they had found their way into print. Since Robert did not of course attend my lectures and since we had no joint seminars, he could not know of my oral publications on the self-fulfilling prophecy. And since his daily stint of writing was most reclusive—as I believe he reports in his autobiography—Robert did not discuss the substance of his work-in-progress with me—nor, I believe, with any other Columbia colleagues. Ours was an amiable rather than fully collegial relationship. When it came to the exchange of ideas, Robert MacIver and I might just as well have been colleagues-at-a-transcontinental-distance periodically exchanging offprints rather than [being] colleagues in the same department of sociology on Morningside Heights.

All this goes to show the need for fine-grained analysis of social interaction and social relationships by sociologists of science engaged in the study of multiple independent discovery and other patterns of intellectual development.[4] For such marked independence of ideas among local colleagues could not possibly have occurred between Paul Lazarsfeld and myself. We were not only colleagues and friends, but close collaborators, teaching joint seminars, working together in the Bureau of Applied Social Research and, above all, engaging in what retrospectively seems almost interminable talk—talk about every aspect and detail of our separate work-in-progress and work-in-prospect, talk about newly emerging ideas and long-developing ones, talk about students in their various phases of development, much anguished talk about the University administration with its dedicated failure to understand the need for supporting a laboratory of sociological research. We spent hours each day in talk, occasionally within the precincts of the Department and regularly and more intensely at the Bureau, he as its founding director, I as its co-opted associate director. (Paul tells the story in his detached and beautifully analytical paper, "Working with Merton," in the volume edited by Coser (1975: 35–66). More by way of context is set forth in the true-to-life memoir of Paul F. Lazarsfeld, written by David L. Sills for the National Academy of Sciences, pp. 251–82 of the 1987 *Biographical Memoirs*, vol. 56.)

Since I have embarked on this reminiscent digression, I continue a bit more with it, in what has plainly become a distinctly personal gloss on the contexts as well as the intellectual continuities and discontinuities of some related sociological ideas. I once made a back-of-the-envelope, order-of-magnitude estimate of the cumulative number of hours Paul Lazarsfeld and I spent in intensive talk over the span of some thirty-five years of close collaboration. It goes something like this: once I had been brought into the Bureau, soon after arriving at Columbia in 1941, we surely spent an average of two or three hours a day in talk. In his published paper, Paul estimates three. Adopting Paul's probably more accurate estimate of three hours a day for five—often six and sometimes seven—days a week, we arrive at an average of at least fifteen hours weekly. Assuming a conservative average of forty weeks a year of our interaction in the Bureau and the Department, that gives us 600 hours of talk a year over a shared collegial span of thirty years (more nearly thirty-five but I allow for Paul's years away from Columbia, teaching at the Sorbonne, establishing research bureaus in Norway and Austria, and advancing sundry other good causes). That gives us a grand total of some 18,000 hours or, stated in terms of reasonable units of ten-hour-workdays, a cumulative talkfest of about five years of incessant *tête-à-tête* conversation. It will be understood, then, why Paul Lazarsfeld and I could not arrive at fully independent formulations of the same sociological (or any other) idea, just as it will be understood why I wish Paul were here to vet these figures and the rest of this retrospective paper.

Multiple Discoveries, Priority Disputes, and the Reward System of Science

A retrospective paper that now turns to a conception in the sociology of science that is also governed by the enduring interest in unanticipated consequences. This is the conception of a distinctive reward system in science—one which, with its enormous emphasis upon the value of originality, has potentially pathogenic elements making for deviant behaviors of scientists. This conception derived ultimately from observations on the well-known phenomenon of simultaneous independent discoveries in the history of science over the centuries which, as I've said, first attracted my interest while I was writing my dissertation. What seemed to me most in point, however, was not so much the phenomenon of coincidental discoveries as the disputes over priority that often attended them.

As I found only some thirty years later, the historical *fact* of such independent multiple discoveries together with its implications for a theory of scientific development were self-exemplifying: they had been themselves independently noted and set down in print. Beginning at least with the nineteenth-century English historian and statesman, Thomas Babington Macaulay, in 1828 and concluding arbitrarily with the formulation by William F. Ogburn and Dorothy S. Thomas that is best known to sociologists (which, appropriately enough, was independently stated in that same year of 1922, though of course in far less detail, by the historian of science, Abel Rey, in France, and by the then leading exponent of Marxist theory in the Soviet Union, Nicolai Bukharin, who having been purged later on has now been restored to a saving Soviet grace). During the century between Macaulay and Ogburn-Thomas,

> Working scientists, historians and sociologists of science, biographers, inventors, lawyers, engineers, anthropologists, Marxists and anti-Marxists, Comteans and anti-Comteans have time and again, though with varying degrees of perceptiveness, called attention both to the fact of multiples [my abbreviated term for "multiple independent discoveries and inventions"] and to some of its implications. (Merton 1961: 476)

But if the phenomenon of multiples had been repeatedly noted and pondered, not so with the frequent attendant phenomenon of priority-conflicts which had then and for sometime since been ignored, for systematic study. Only now, in this personal gloss, do I note in the monograph deriving from my dissertation that I had identified the phenomenon of priority-conflicts in science as potentially a strategic research site:

> The frequency of disputes concerning priority which, to my knowledge, first becomes marked in the sixteenth century, constitutes an interesting problem for

further research. It implies a lofty estimation of "originality" and of competition; values which were largely foreign to the medieval mind which commonly sought to cloak the original under the tradition of earlier periods. The entire question is bound up with the rise of the concepts of plagiarism, patents, copy-rights and other institutional modes of regulating "intellectual property." (Merton [1938] 1970: 169n)

The phenomenon of conflicts of priority and the light its analysis could shed on science as a social institution and on the institutionally patterned motivations of scientists remained unexamined until 1957 when I elected to make it the focus of my exceedingly long presidential address to the American Sociological Society. There it was proposed that the phenomenon of acute priority-conflicts, often regarded as merely disagreeable and unworthy expressions of scientists' flawed personalities and temperaments by historians of science, provided strategic research materials for identifying the reward system of the institution of science. The sociological analysis of that system, one in which peer recognition of original scientific work provided the basic social and psychic income, led one to find that an overemphasis upon assessed originality could be pathogenic. It invited such pathologies as the concocting of fraudulent data, plagiary, and the misdemeanors of hoarding one's own data while making free use of others' data, as well as violating the mores of science by failing to make suitable acknowledgement of intellectual debts to predecessors. As I have lately come to indicate (Merton 1987: 21–23), this early focus on "fraud in science"—recently became a widespread concern of science practitioners and observers of science—derived theoretically from anomie-and-opportunity-structure theory and empirically from the identifying of priority-conflicts as a potentially strategic research site. In this way, one could begin to understand how the slowly identified components and processes of the reward system of science could produce such unanticipated consequences, such dysfunctions, as these deviant behaviors of scientists.

The Serendipity Pattern in Science

The other offshoot of the theme of unanticipated consequences in the domain of science found its way into print much sooner—in the 1940s. Here, the focus was on methodological and theoretical practices in scientific inquiry seen from a sociological perspective. What, in actual practice, rather than in textbooks on the so-called scientific method, were the modes of interplay between theory and empirical inquiry? The papers on that interplay deal with various pointed questions which I do not undertake to reexamine here; I refer only to the focus on what is described as "the serendipity pattern" in scientific inquiry: one in which observation of an "unanticipated, anomalous and strategic datum exerts pressure for initiating [new] theory" (Merton 1948). For here, once again, but now in the sphere of scientific practice, the theme of unanticipated consequences is renewed.

In the serendipity pattern, the unexpected occurs twice over. An unanticipated observation yields an unanticipated kind of knowledge. Or, as this was put back then in the 1940s, "The datum is, first of all, unanticipated. A research directed toward the test of one hypothesis yields a fortuitous by-product, an unexpected observation which bears upon theories not in question when the research was begun. Secondly, the observation is anomalous, surprising, either because it seems inconsistent with prevailing theory or with other established facts. In either case, the seeming inconsistency provokes curiosity; it stimulates the investigator to 'make sense of the datum,' to fit it into a broader frame of knowledge."

Along with these two components of the unexpected in the serendipity pattern is a third component having to do with the scientist who finds the datum evocative: "in noting that the unexpected fact must be strategic, i.e., that it must permit implications which bear upon generalized theory, we are, of course, referring rather to what the observer brings to the datum rather than to the datum itself. For it obviously requires a theoretically sensitized observer to detect the universal in the particular." In short, the unanticipated, anomalous and strategic datum is not simply "out there," but is in part (but only in part) a function of its observer's construction.

Given my continuing interest in the unanticipated, it is not at all surprising that, in examining scientific practices and methodology, my attention should have been drawn to the variously unexpected components of what was identified as "the serendipity pattern." The phenomenon of the "accidental" or "lucky" discovery in science had of course been noted times without end by practicing scientists and historians of science. And there had been astute observations on that phenomenon by both practitioners and historians. One inevitably recalls Pasteur's incisive aphorism that "Chance only favors the prepared mind."

Since the phenomenon of "accidental discovery" plainly linked up with the ongoing theme of the unanticipated in society and culture, it was bound to evoke that effort of mine to analyze its social and cognitive character. But that same circumstance was not at all bound to evoke the term "serendipity." For in 1945, when I first made use of it, "serendipity" was far from being the much abused vogue word it has since become. Back then, I made much of the thesis that "fruitful empirical research not only tests theoretically derived hypotheses; it also originates new hypotheses." And then went on to say that "This might be termed the 'serendipity' component of research, i.e., the discovery, by chance or sagacity [that should plainly read: by chance *and* sagacity], of valid results which were not sought for" (Merton 1945). When I elucidated this bare statement in a paper printed three years later, I could still write:

> Interestingly enough, the same outlandish [N.B.] term "serendipity" which has had little currency since it was coined by Horace Walpole in 1754 has also been used to refer to this component of research by the physiologist Walter B. Cannon. See his *The Way of an Investigator* (New York: W.W. Norton, 1945), chapter 6, in which he sets forth numerous instances of serendipity in several fields of science. (Merton 1968: 157)

And thereby hangs a serendipitous terminological tale. A tale not told before in print since only a personal gloss made up of contexts, continuities, and discontinuities allows for telling of that kind of episode. One might infer from the foregoing passage quoted in a paper published in 1948 that I had learned the "outlandish term 'serendipity'" from the superb autobiography by the imaginative Harvard physiologist, Walter B. Cannon, published in 1945. But it was not so. After all, I had had occasion in the paper on sociological theory which also appeared in 1945 to refer to "the 'serendipity' component of research," and to follow that with an appositive defining clause, "the discovery, by chance or sagacity, of valid results which were not sought for." Plainly, the paper appearing midway through the same year as Cannon's book must have been written some time before (as one recalls the long interval between the submission of a manuscript to an academic journal and its actual appearance in print).

I first came upon the word "serendipity" in quite another way. Indeed, as I have intimated, my coming upon "serendipity" was itself an instance of serendipity. While in search of the history of a word beginning with the letters *se*—it just may have been the word "sequestration" but I don't truly remember—I was riffling the pages of volume 9 of the incomparable *Oxford English Dictionary* organized on historical principles (to which I have made admiring reference) when my eye happened upon the strange-looking but euphonious word "serendipity." Strange-looking, since its etymology was far from obvious. Perhaps it was that etymological obscurity that led me to pause and read the entry in detail. As is typical for the *OED*, it quoted the originating sentence in which the word first appeared, this in a long unpublished letter by the eighteenth-century man of letters, Horace Walpole. At once, the word "serendipity" became a part of my working vocabulary.[5] I cannot put a date on this serendipitous moment, since one doesn't ordinarily record such an episode for future reference, particularly when one fails to keep a journal or a diary. But, as the inadvertent documentary evidence of the 1945 paper indicates, it must have been some time before.

Thus it was that my first coming upon the word "serendipity" was an altogether self-exemplifying episode.[6] I had stumbled upon the word at a time when it would resonate to my apparent fixation on the theme of the unanticipated and unexpected in social life and in social thought. More particularly, at a time when I was reflecting on actual rather than prescribed or idealized patterns of interplay between theoretical orientations and empirical data in scientific inquiry. Furthermore, like many another student of the history (as well as the historiography) of science, I was aware of the many recorded cases of significant scientific discovery that have been attributed to "chance," "luck," or "accident." Within that context, it scarcely required much "sagacity" to find the word altogether apt and to focus anew on the phenomenon itself in an effort to analyze its ingredients and workings. All that was required, under those circumstances, was my encountering the word by chance, luck, or accident in the pages of a favorite dictionary—favored enough, I might add, to have me invest a sizeable portion of my fellowship stipend during my third year of graduate study to purchase the set of a dozen-or-so volumes, in order to have ready and, as it happened, enduring access to its rich contents powerfully organized on historical principles.

So it is that the grand *Oxford English Dictionary* has entered twice into this gloss: once, as of the early 1940s in this episode of the serendipitous discovery (rather than invention) of the word "serendipity," and again, in the mid-1980s when, as I have told, its four-volume *Supplement* included entries on two forms of unanticipated consequences, latent functions and the self-fulfilling prophecy. It is not at all strange that the *OED* should have turned up in this account. For as new ideas emerge in any sphere of learning, they often require newly coined terms to designate them compactly. That is why every learned discipline and every field of practice develops a distinctive vocabulary. To those outside the given field, that special idiom will often be described as jargon, gibberish, or unintelligible patois (at times, justifiably so). As new terms pass muster in the discipline, they will be recorded first in its technical dictionaries and then, to a smaller extent, in the great unabridged dictionaries. This latter phase of diffusion occurs especially with technical terms which have begun to find their way into everyday language. In this way, the great dictionaries register the emergence of new ideas and their drift into the public consciousness.

This brief gloss has sketched out the origins and fate of several concepts linked with the core idea of unanticipated consequences, later differentiated into unanticipated, unintended, and unrecognized consequences—such concepts as latent functions and dysfunctions, the self-defeating and the self-fulfilling prophecy, the serendipity and self-exemplification patterns in scholarly inquiry. Perhaps this personal gloss can be taken as another small installment on that large promissory note of a half-century ago.

Excursus on Oral Publication

The term "oral publication" may seem to some an oxymoron, a compound of contradictory elements. When so regarded, that is because secondary meanings of the words "publish" and "publications" have been made primary to refer only to printed matter. But, of course, in English as in the originating Latin, "to publish" (*publicare*) means in the first instance "to make publicly known." The form in which that is done varies, historically and within the same culture in any given time. Publication may be in print but it surely was not so in European cultures before Guttenberg's fifteenth-century movable type. Moreover, various techniques and technologies of publication, old and new, tend to co-exist, though in differing proportions, as we learn for one period in illuminating detail from Elizabeth L. Eisenstein's splendid two-volume monograph, *The Printing Press as an Agent of Change: Communications and Cultural Transformations in Early-Modern Europe* (Cambridge University Press, 1979).

Not only in a nonliterate or oral culture but in the scribal culture as in the print culture and now in the electronic culture as well, oral publication is a major medium for the transmission of knowledge. There continue to be face-to-face (and now, at-a-distance) lectures, seminars, conferences, symposia, and workshops, to say nothing of the give-and-take in talk occurring in laboratories and other workplaces. Good, old-fashioned or new-fashioned talk. The sort of thing that was abundantly evident in this Amalfi conference.

Although it is transparently obvious, I dwell on this matter for two reasons. The first in response to several friendly critics who have taxed me with having perpetrated a contradictory idea in speaking of "oral publication" (in the opening chapter of *Sociological Traditions from Generation to Generation: Glimpses of the American Experience* [Norwood, NJ: Ablex Publishing Corp., 1980], edited by Matilda White Riley and myself). But that would scarcely be reason enough to append this excursus here.

The other reason became rather more in point once I found myself embarked on this distinctly personal gloss. For it turns out that much of what I have put in print during the past four decades or so was typically begun and then developed in the form of oral publications. As I have noted, that was the case, early on, with the monographic piece, "Manifest and Latent Functions." Set out in lectures and seminars, local and mobile, the successive versions amounted to an ongoing series of "editions" of an oral publication. For, more often than not, each successive exposition of a central sociological idea led to further revision and extended formulations. That is, of course, a common experience for many of us. Nevertheless, it seems widely and tacitly assumed that while books can have new editions, oral publications or even printed articles, cannot. I have never thought so. Instead, I have rather consistently provided for a period of oral publication, thus allowing for revised editions, before venturing to put a paper into print. It was only recently, however, that an interview by Caroline Hodges Persell led to an estimate of the interval between my first formulation of a sociological idea and its appearance in print (Persell 1984). Excluding the first decade of publication in print during the

1930s and early-1940s, the modal duration of that interval proves to be about a dozen years. That, as I have said, has been the case for most of the sociological ideas critically examined in these papers. An ample basis for concluding that I have been a flagrant procrastinator over the years when it comes to publishing in print.

Notes

1. This passage, designed to integrate the concepts of agent (whether individual, corporate, or aggregated), socially distributed values and interests, structural constraints, and objective unanticipated consequences, is drawn for convenience from my *Sociological Ambivalence*, pp. 173–74.
2. I say no more about the generic methodological issues here, for these have received much attention from Adolf Grünbaum, Herbert A. Simon, and many another scholar during the last two decades or so. Some brief comments on the matter appear in *Social Theory and Social Structure*, pp. 182–84.
3. A short excursus on "oral publication" is appended to this piece.
4. I have elucidated this and related points in "Multiple Discoveries as a Strategic Research Site" (1963) and other papers on the phenomenon of "multiples" in Merton 1973: 371–82, passim.
5. As it has for countless others after they first encountered it. The diffusion of the word into various social circles is the subject of a still unpublished monograph, the title page of which reads: *The Travels & Adventures of Serendipity: A Study in Historical Semantics*, by Robert K. Merton and Elinor Barber, 1958. [Some forty years later this monograph is now in press: *I viaggi e l'avventure della "Serendipity."* Bologna: Il Mulino.]
6. I do not digress yet again, this time to elucidate the idea of "self-exemplification" in thought although it is a theme briefly examined in some of these papers. It is enough to note that I have long maintained that the sociology of science in particular has a "strongly self-exemplifying character: its own history and behavior exemplify sociological ideas and findings . . . Nor is this an occasion for surprise. Were the sociology of science not self-exemplifying, then either the general ideas and findings would have to be thought unsound or the field itself is nothing like the scientific speciality it is commonly supposed to be." See Merton 1979: 4. More on the pattern of self-exemplification is indexed in Merton 1973 and in Merton [1965] 1985.

References

Coser, L.A. 1975. *The Idea of Social Structure.* New York: Harcourt Brace Jovanovich.

Gini, C. 1935. *Prime linee di patologia economica.* Milan: Giuffré.

Merton, R.K. [1936] 1976. "The Unanticipated Consequences of Purposive Social Action." *American Sociological Review* 1: 894–904. Reprinted in *Sociological Ambivalence*, 145–55. New York: Free Press.

———. [1938] 1970. *Science, Technology and Society in Seventh-Century England.* New York: Howard Fertig, Inc.

———. [1945] 1968. "Sociological Theory." *American Journal of Sociology* 50: 462–73. Reprinted in *Social Theory and Social Structure*.

————. [1948] 1968. "The Bearing of Empirical Research upon the Development of Sociological Theory." *American Sociological Review* 13: 505–15. Reprinted in *Social Theory and Social Structure*.

————. [1961] 1973. "Singletons and Multiples in-Scientific Discovery: A Chapter in the Sociology of Science." *Proceedings of the American Philosophical Society* 105 (October): 470–486. Reprinted in *The Sociology of Science*.

————. [1965] 1985. *On the Shoulders of Giants*. San Diego and New York: Harcourt Brace Jovanovich.

————. [1949, 1957] 1968. *Social Theory and Social Structure*. New York: Free Press.

————. 1973. *The Sociology of Science*. Chicago: University of Chicago Press.

————. 1979. *The Sociology of Science: An Episodic Memoir*. Carbondale: Southern Illinois University Press.

————. 1987. "Three Fragments from a Sociologist's Notebooks: Establishing the Phenomenon, Specified Ignorance, and Strategic Research Materials." *Annual Review of Sociology* 13: 1–28.

Persell, C.H. 1984. "An Interview with Robert K. Merton." *Teaching Sociology* 11: 355–86.

Contributors

Paolo Almondo teaches general sociology in the Social Sciences Department, Faculty of Political Science at the University of Turin. He is the author of the monograph *Razionalità e volontarismo in Talcott Parsons* (1984), and the essays *Parsons lecteur des règles de la méthode sociologique* (1995) and *Dalla scienza alla coscienza: a proposito della competenza operativa nelle scienze sociali* (1990), a study of the problems of professionalization of sociologists outside the university.

Paolo Ammassari (1931–1991), was professor of methodology of social research and later of sociology at the University of Rome, "La Sapienza." He was director of the post-doctoral School of Sociology and Social Research and president of the Institut International de Sociologie (1989–1991). His main publications include: *Worker Satisfaction and Occupational Life: A Study of the Automobile Worker in Italy* ([1964] 1970); *Classi e ceti nella società italiana* (1977); *Classes and Class Relationships in Italian Contemporary Society* in *Il Politico* (1979); *I fondamentali problemi di metodologia della ricerca sociale* in *Studi di Sociologia* (1985); "Validità e legittimità dell'analisi causale/ Gültigkeit und Legitimität der Kausalanalyse" in *Annali di Sociologia/ Soziologisches Jahrbuch* (1985); "L'analisi causale della ricerca sociale in Ricerca Sociologica," in *Informatica e Società Italiana* (1986); "Vecchi e nuovi contesti strutturali e culturali della stratificazione sociale" in *Tendenze della stratificazione sociale* (1993); and, *Saggi metodologici*, edited by Angelo Saporiti (1995).

Filippo Barbano has contributed to the rebirth of Italian sociology since just after the Second World War. He became professor of sociology in the Faculty of Political Science at the University of Turin in 1968, having taught in the newly created Faculty of Sociology in Trento in 1964. Author of numerous works on theory and research, he is currently finishing the *Storia della Sociologia in Italia (1945–1990).*

Elena Besozzi is associate professor in sociology of cultural and communicative processes at the Catholic University of the Sacred Heart in Milan. She teaches sociology of education and of deviancy. Among her published essays is "La circolarità, teorie e ricerca empirica: il contributo di R.K. Merton" in *Studi di Sociologia* (1985). Her recent books include: *Tra somiglianza e differenza: Teoria sociologica e modelli di differenziazione sociale* (1990); and, *Elementi di sociologia dell'educazione* (1993).

Rocco Caporale is professor of sociology at St. John's University. Born in Italy, he has taught at the University of California at Berkeley, the Claremont Colleges, and Manhattanville College. He is the author of several volumes in both English and Italian on the sociology of religion and on the sociology of natural disasters. He is also editor of a series of volumes on development in Southern Italy (*Mezzogiorno Revisited*). He conducted a number of research projects in the United States, South America, Asia, and Europe, the most notable of which is a ten-year study of the reconstruction after the 1980 earthquake in Southern Italy. In 1965 he received his Ph.D. in sociology from Columbia University as part of a cohort of students who, under the mentorship of Robert K. Merton, wrote their dissertation on world leaders in science, business, religion, and politics; they completed their degree in the record time of under five years.

Alessandro Cavalli is professor of sociology at the University of Pavia. He was educated at L. Bocconi University in Milan, Yale, and the University of California at Berkeley. He has served as visiting professor at Heidelberg (1989) and Louvain-la-Neuve (1994), and Fellow Collegium Budapest at the Institute for Advanced Study (1995). He is editor of *Enciclopedia delle Scienze Sociali* and director of *Il Mulino* (Journal for Politics and Culture). His fields of interest include: German social thought at the turn of the century, sociology of youth, time and education. He is currently researching patterns of collective memory, family and educational choices, and changes in value orientations of young people.

Charles Crothers is professor of sociology in the Department of Sociology at the University of Natal Durban, South Africa. He was junior lecturer at Victoria University of Wellington (where he received his Ph.D.) and senior lecturer at the University of Auckland until 1995.

He also served as president of the Sociological Association of Aotearo, New Zealand (1993–1995). His published works include a monograph on Merton's work for the Tavistock-Routledge series, *Key Ideas* (1987), as well as *Social Structure* (1996). He has been researching "sociology of sociology" topics, including studies of the "Columbia tradition" in sociology, trends and patterns in publication content, and natural sociologies. He is also interested in theoretical issues pertaining to social structure and more generally the social structures of post-colonial societies.

Pierpaolo Donati is professor of advanced sociology and director of the Study Center on Social Policy at the University of Bologna. He serves as president of the Italian Sociological Association and has been widely published (14 books, 250 essays and research reports, and 44 volumes in collaboration with others). His most recent works include: *La cittadinanza societaria* (1993); *Teoria relazionale della società* (1994); and, *Quarto Rapporto Cisf sulla famiglia in Italia* (1995).

Peter Gerlich is dean of the Faculty of Social Science at the University of Vienna and a department head at the Institute of Advanced Studies. He has been published in the field of comparative political studies.

Giuliano Giorio has the chair in sociological institutions in the Faculty of Political Science at the University of Trieste where he runs the "Science of Man" Department. He served as vice president of the Italian Sociology Association (1992–1995) and is the author of over a hundred essays and articles, among them *Strutture e sistemi sociali nell'attuale dinamica valoriale* ([1991] 1995), *Società e sistemi sociali* (1985), and *Aspetti e problemi della socializzazione oggi* (1979).

Alberto Izzo has the chair in history of sociology at the University of Rome, "La Sapienza." His major interests are the sociology of knowledge and the history of sociological theories. His publications include: *Karl Mannheim: Una introduzione* (1988); *Storia del pensiero sociologico* ([1991] 1995); and, *I percorsi della ragione: Il tema della razionalità nella storia del pensiero sociologico* (1995).

Maria Luisa Maniscalco is associate professor of sociology in the Faculty of Political Sciences at the University in Rome, III. She has written essays and research papers on the history of sociology, and on aspects and problems of contemporary society. Her recent publications include: *Spirito di setta e società* (1992) and *La sociologia di Vilfredo Pareto e il senso della modernità* (1994).

Volker Meja is professor of sociology at the Memorial University of Newfoundland in St. John's, Canada. His recent books include: *Modern German Sociology* (1987); *Politisches Wissen* (1989); *Knowledge and Politics* (1990); *Karl Mannheim* (1994), with David Kettler and Nico Stehr; and, *Karl Mannheim and the Crisis of Liberalism* (1995). He collaborated on editions of Mannheim's *Structures of Thinking* (1982) and *Conservatism* (1986), and is currently coauthoring a book with Nico Stehr entitled *The Foundations of the Modern Economy* to be published in 1997.

Carlo Mongardini has the chair in sociology in the Faculty of Political Sciences in the University of Rome, "La Sapienza." For many years he was coordinator of the Theory Section of the Italian Sociology Association. He is founder of the European Amalfi Prize for Sociology and the Social Sciences. His recent books include: *Il futuro della politica* (1990); *La cultura del presente: Tempo e storia nella tarda moderni* (1993); *Cultura moderna e comunicazione di massa* (1993); and, *Forme e formule della rappresentanza politica* (1994).

Birgitta Nedelmann is professor of sociology at the Johannes Gutenberg-University in Mainz, Germany. She has taught at the University of Lund, Sweden, Cologne, Freiburg im Breisgau, and at the European University Institute in Florence. She was a Fellow at the Wissenschaftskolleg in Berlin (1990–91) and is a current member of both the Academia Europaea and the Scientific Committee of the Premio Europeo Amalfi. Her main fields of research include political sociology (party systems, comparative politics, institutional change) and general theory of sociology (especially Georg Simmel). Her publications include *Rentenpolitik in Schweden* (1982) and *Sociology in Europe:In Search of Identity*, coedited with Piotr Sztompka (1993). She is also the editor of *Politische Institutionen im Wandel* (1995).

Gianni Statera has the chair in methodology and social research technique and is dean of the Faculty of Sociology in the University of Rome, "La Sapienza." His most recent works include: *La Politica Spettacolo* (1986); *Metodologia e tecniche della ricerca sociale* (3d ed., 1990); *Come votano gli italiani* (1993); *Logica dell'indagine scientifico-sociale* (1994); and, *Manuale di sociologia scientifica* (1996).

Nico Stehr is professor at the Peter Wall Institute for Advanced Studies and Green College, University of British Columbia in Vancouver. He is a Fellow of the Royal Society of Canada and editor of the *Canadian Journal of Sociology*. He coedited *Knowledge and Politics* (1990) with Volker Meja and *The Knowledge Society* (1986) with Gernot Böhme. He coauthored of *Political Knowledge* (1992), with David Kettler and Volker Meja and is the coeditor of several previously unpublished manuscripts by Karl Mannheim. His current research interests are reflected in *Practical Knowledge* (1992), *Knowledge Societies: Labour, Property and Knowledge* (1994), and *The Culture and Power of Knowledge: Inquiries into Contemporary Societies*, with Richard V. Ericson (1992). He is currently working on a book with Volker Meja entitled *The Fragility of Modern Society* to be published in 1997.

Piotr Sztompka is professor of sociology at the Jagiellonian University of Krakow in Poland and is a regular visiting professor at the University of California at Los Angeles. A member of the Academia Europaea (London) and the Polish Academy of Sciences (PAN), he serves on the Executive Committee of the International Sociological Association (ISA). His books include: *R.K. Merton: An Intellectual Profile* (1986); *Rethinking Progress* (1990), with Jeffrey Alexander; *European Sociology* (1993); *Society in Action* (1991); *The Sociology of Social Change* (1993); and, *Agency and Structure* (1994). He is currently editing a collection of Merton's work for the University of Chicago Press' Heritage of Sociology series, to be published in 1997.

Simonetta Tabboni is professore a contratto in General Sociology at the University of Political Science in Milan and chargée de conférences at the École des Hautes Études en Sciences Sociales in Paris. Her recent publications include: *Vicinanza e lontananza: Modelli e figure dello straniero come categoria sociologica* (1986); *La rappresentazione sociale del tempo* (1988); and, *Norbert Elias: Un ritratto intellettuale* (1993).

Arnold Zingerle is professor of sociology at the University of Bayreuth in Germany and co-director of the bilingual review *Annali di Sociologia/*

Soziologisches Jahrbuch published by the University of Trento, Italy. He has published works on the history of sociology between 1880 and 1920 (especially Max Weber) and on charisma, magic, honor, and other topics of the sociology of culture and religion.

Harriet Zuckerman, now vice president of the Andrew W. Mellon Foundation and Professor Emerita, was a member of the Department of Sociology at Columbia University between 1965 and 1992. She is the author of *Scientific Elite* ([1977] 1996), a study of Nobel Laureates in the sciences and has edited three volumes, most recently, *The Outer Circle: Women in the Scientific Community* (1991). Her papers have addressed a variety of subjects including the sociology of the reward system of science, intellectual property rights, the careers of men and women scientists and their research strategies, "postmature" discoveries in science, peer review, and the emergence of scientific specialties.

Index of Names

(Italicized pages refer to names cited in the notes or the bibliography)

Abel, Theodore, *137*
Abrams, Philip, 269, *270*
Adams, Henry, 185
Agassi, Joseph, 56
Alexander, Jeffrey C., 29, *40*
Allison, Paul, 149, 152, *158*, *160*
Allport, Gordon W., *156*, 303–304
Alvarez, Rodolfo, *161*
Ammassari, Paolo, 2, *59*
Anderson, Theodore, 241, 243
Andrews, William G., *196*
Archibald, Kathleen A., *237*
Archilochus, 5
Archimedes, *283*
Armeno, Cristoforo, 275, *283*
Aron, Raymond, 22, *40*
Asch, Solomon F., 242
Auden, W. H., 187
Axelrod, Julius, *156*

Bachelard, Gaston, 88
Bacon, Francis, 182, *185*, 202
Bagnasco, Arnaldo, 83
Baldamus, V., *38*, *40*
Bales, Robert F., 242
Bankowska, Anna, *136*
Barbano, Filippo, 2, 5, 16, 27, *40*, *58*, 96, 98, 207, 221–222, *238*, 252, 254, *255*, 285, *287*
Barber, Bernard, 202
Barber, Elinor G., 8, *20*, 21, 66, 70, *75*, *119–120*, 275, *284*, 317
Barker, John, 62

Barnes, S. B., 73
Barser, Bernhard, *40*
Barton, Allen, 241
Bateson, Gregory, 9, *20*, 113, *119*
Battaglini, Orsi, 136–137
Bauman, Zygmunt, xiii
Baumgartner, Bernice, 307
Beavin, Janet H., *20*
Becker, Howard, 202, 253
Beethoven, Ludwig van, *18*
Ben-David, Joseph, 70, 237, 294
Bendix, Reinhard, 22, *40*
Bensman, Stephen J., 153, *158*
Berger, Morroe, *137*
Bergstrasser, Arnold, 22, *40*
Berlin, Sir Isaiah, 5
Bernal, John D., 62–63, *75*
Bernstein, Richard J., *39–40*
Besozzi, Elena, *59–60*
Bierstedt, Robert, 16, *20*, *35*, *40*, *43*, 55, *60*
Blashfield, Robert K., *158*
Blau, Judith R., *158*, 202, 208
Blau, Peter M., *42*, 151–152, *158*
Blok, A., 194, *195*
Bloor, David, 73
Bluhm, William T., 190, *195*
Blume, Stuart, 67
Boeckmann, Margaret E., *158*, *160*
Bok, Sissela, *195*
Boudon, Raymond, *19–20*, 101, *119*, 179–180, *185*, 205, 227, 287
Bovone, Laura, 286, *287*

Brahms, Johannes, *18*
Bramson, Leon, 22, *40*
Bratina, Darko, 83
Brodbeck, May, 52, *60*
Broughton, Walter, 153, 155, *158*
Bruckmuller, Ernst, 193, *195*
Bukharin, Nikolai, 310
Burke, Kenneth, 56, 259, 261, 268, *270*
Busse, Thomas V., *158*
Butterfield, Robert, 301

Calvin, 295
Campbell, Colin, 229, *238*
Campbell, Norman R., 51, *59–60*
Cancian, Francesca, 231, *238*
Cannavò, Leonardo, 74, *75*
Cannon, Walter, 313
Capecchi, Vittorio, 82, 87
Caplovitz, David, 34, *40*
Caporale, Rocco, 14
Cavalli, Alessandro, *136*, *269*, *270*
Cavalli, Luciano, 83
Ceri, Paolo, 83
Chapin, F.Stuart, *185*, 236
Chiarelli, Brunetto, 122, 124–125, 127,
    129, 132–134, *136–137*
Christie, Richard, 241
Chubin, Daryl E., 73–74, *76*, 149, 152,
    158, *160–161*
Claessens, Dieter, *185*
Clark, Burton R., *161*
Clark, Shirley M., 152, 156, *159*
Clinard, Marshall, *174–175*, *210*
Cole, Jonathan R., 149, 151–152, 156,
    156–159, *161–162*, 205
Cole, Stephen, *39–40*, 149, 151–152, *156–
    158*, *159*, *161*, 163, *174*, 206, *210*
Coleman, James S., 179, *185*
Collins, Harry M., 73
Compton, Arthur, *158*
Comte, Auguste, 50, *185*, 202, 293
Cooley, Charles H., *185*
Corcoran, Mary, 153, 156, *159*
Coser, Lewis A., 5–6, 11, *18–20*, 21, 25,
    35, *38*, *39–40*, *43*, 89, *174–175*, *210*,
    251, *255*, 258, *270*, *282–284*, 309, 318
Coser, Rose Laub, 258, *270*
Critto, Adolpho, 244
Crothers, Charles, *36*, *40*, *159*, 200, 204,
    210, *282–283*
Cullen, Frank T., 164, *174*, *210*

Dahrendorf, Ralf, 26, *38*, *40*, *58*, *60*, 166,
    174, *210*
Dannefer, Dale, 153, *159*
Darwin, Charles, 64
Davis, Esther, 241
Davis, Kingsley, 27, *40*, 163, *175*, 202
De Finis, Giorgio, XIII, *137*
Demarchi, Franco, 255
Demerath, Nicholas J., *41–42*
De Mita, Ciriaco, 133
De Paulo, Bella M., *120*
Dewey, John, 50
Diamond, Sigmund, 241
Di Lellio, Anna, 89, 226, *238*, 258
Dix, Linda S., *137*, *161*
Donati, Pierpaolo, 3, *119*, 121, 225, 230,
    247, 255
Douglas, Mary, 294
Dri, Pietro, 275, *283*
Dumont, Louis, xiii
Duncan, Otis, *158*
Duncan, Simon S., 149, 151–152, *159*
Durkheim, Emile, 11, *18–19*, 29, *40*, 104,
    106, 109, 116–117, *119*, 123, 163, 165,
    167, 171, 173, 178, *185*, 202–203, 242,
    257–258, 260–261, 267, *270*, 287

Eisenstein, Elizabeth L., 316
Elias, Norbert, XIII, 21, 34, *40*, 180, *185*,
    262, 267, *269–270*
Elster, Jon, 205
Engels, Friedrich, *185*, 202, 296
Etzioni, Amitai, 205, 241, 244
Euclid, 56
Eulau, Heinz, 188, *195–196*

Faia, Michael A., *159*
Fanfani, Amintore, 133
Farley, Reynolds, 156, *159*
Featherman, David, 152
Ferguson, Adam, *185*
Fermi, Enrico, 33
Ferrarotti, Franco, 85, 87
Feyerabend, Paul, 74
Fischer, John, 307
Fleck, Ludwik, xv
Foner, Anne, *162*
Fornari, Franco, 118, *119*
Foucault, Michel, 294
Fox, Mary Frank, 152, *159*
Fraisse, Paul, *269–270*

Freud, Sigmund, *38*, 102, 202, 293
Friedrich, Carl J., 194, *196*
Friedrichs, Robert W., 21, *40*

Gallino, Luciano, 82
Galtung, Johan, 231
Garfield, Eugene, *18*, *20*, 34, *40*
Gaston, Jerry, 86, 152, *156*, *159*
Gerlich, Peter, 3, 188–194, *195–196*, 295
Gerth, Hans H., *34*, *41*
Giddens, Anthony, 29, *37*, *39*, *41*
Gieryn, Tom F., *20*, *40*, 131, *137*, 175, *210*
Giglioli, Pier Paolo, *19–20*
Gini, Corrado, *185*, 302–304, 318
Giorio, Giuliano, 251, 253, *255*
Goethe, Johann Wolfgang von, *21*, 183
Goffman, Erving, 10, *20*, 197
Goldstone, Jack A., 152, *159*
Goode, William J., 241, 243–244
Gouldner, Alvin W., 24, 28–29, *37–38*, *41*, 202
Gramsci, Antonio, 81
Grande E., 193, *196*
Guala, Chito, 83
Gursey, S., *160*
Gurvitch, Georges, *60*
Guttenberg, Johann, 316

Habermas, Jurgen, 87, 91, 110–111, 113
Hagstrom, Warren, 65–66, 70, *76*
Halacy, D.S., Jr., *283*
Hargens, Lowell L., 152, *159*, 161
Hecht, Pamela K., *159*
Hegel, G.F.W., 296
Henning, Eike, *37*, *41*
Hessen Boris, 62
Hiero, *283*
Hinkle, Gisela N., 21, *41*
Hinkle, Roscoe L., 21, *41*
Hobbes, Thomas, 242
Hocking, William Ernest, 304
Hoffman-Nowotny, Hans-Joachim, *185*
Hofstadter, Richard, 21, *41*
Hogben, Richard, 62
Homans, George, 24
Honolka, Harro, 28, *41*
Horkheimer, Max, *36*, *41*
Horowitz, Irving Louis, xiii, 25, *37–38*, *41*
Hubby, J.L., *157*, *160*

Hubert, Henri, 257
Hung, S.S., *156*, *161*
Hunt, Morton M., *36*, *41*
Husserl, Edmund, 213
Hyman, Herbert, 62, 241

Izzo, Alberto, 3, *20*, 83

Jackson, Don D., *20*
James, William, *269–270*
Jauss, Hans Robert, 95, *98*
Johnson, Marilyn, *162*
Jokisch, R., *185*
Jonas, Friedrich, *255–256*

Kantor, Paul B., *159*
Karabel, Jerome, 153, 155–156, *161*
Kecskemeti, Paul, 214, *219*
Kirk, Stuart A., *159*
Kistiakowsky, Vera, 153, *159*
Klausner, Samuel, 241
Klineberg, Otto, 241
Kluckhohn, Clyde, 252
Knorr-Cetina, Karin D., *76*, 152, *159–160*
Köcher, Renate, *195–196*
Köchler, Hans, *196*
Koschaker, Paul, 96–97, *98*,
Koselleck, Reinhart, 264–265, 267, *270*
Kramer, Helmut, 188–189, *196*
Krauze, Tad K., 152, *158*
Kuhn, Thomas, 67–72, 74, *76*, 148, 202, 294

Lakatos, Imre, 57, 294
Latour, Bruno, 74
Laudan, Saul, *41*
Lawani, Stephen M., *159*
Lazarsfeld, Paul F., *36*, 80–83, 87, 90–91, 131–132, *137*, 188, 202–203, 241, 243, 308–309
Lenk, Kurt, *37*
Lepenies, Wolf, 95, *98*
Lepsius, Rainer M., xiii
Lerner, Daniel, 236, *238*
Levi-Montalcini, Rita, 122, *136*
Levine, Donald N., 121–122, 128, *137*
Levine, Eugene, 241
Levy, Emanuel, 62, 153, 155, *159*
Lewis, G. N., 33
Lewontin, Richard, *157*, *160*
Linz, Juan, 241, 243

Lipset, Seymour Martin, 22, *35*, *41–42*
Liquori, Alfonso Maria, *136*
Loewenberg, Gerhard, 189, *196*
Long, J. Scott, 152, *158*, *160*
Loomis, Charles P., 27, *41*
Loomis, Zona, 27, *41*
Luckmann, Thomas, 85
Luhmann, Niklas, *38*, *41*, 87, 110–111, 113, 118, 221, *237–238*, 255, *256*, 267
Luther, Martin, 294–295
Lutterman, Kenneth G., *161*
Lynd, Robert S., 106

Macaulay, Thomas Babington, 310
Machiavelli, Niccolo, 185, 295
MacIver, Robert M., 202, 307–308
MacKenzie, Donald A., 73
Malinowski, Bronislaw, xvi, 27, *41*, 202–203, 252
Maniscalco, Maria Luisa, 273–284
Mannheim, Karl, 21, *34–35*, *41*, 202, 204, 213–219, *219*
Mansfield, Richard S., *158*
March, James G., 205
Marcson, Simon, 69
Marletti, Carlo, 82, 222, *238*
Martindale, Don, *255–256*, 285, *287*
Marvick, Dwaine, 69
Marx, Karl, 29, *40*, 50, 63, 109, *185*, 202–204, 293, 296, 302
Matthes, Joachim, *186*
Matthew, 31–33, 145, 147, 153, *156–157*, *159–161*, 178, 240, 282
Mauss, Marcel, 257
Mayntz, Renate, 123, 131, *137*
McCallum, John, 306
McGinnis, Robert, 152, *160*
McKee, James B., 21, 41
McPherson, Michael S., 160
Mead, George H., 92, 242
Mead, Margaret, 241
Meja, Volker, 2, *40*, 152, *160*, 251
Melanchthon, 295
Menger, Carl, 180, *185*
Mennel, Stephen, *39*, *41*
Merton, Vanessa, *119–120*
Merz, Peter Ulrich, *185*
Michels, Roberto, 78, 180
Mills, Edgar W., 153, 155, *158*
Mills, C. Wright, *35*, *37–38*, *39–42*, 46, *60*, 83

Misgeld, Dieter, *40*
Mittermeier, Roland, 152, *159–160*
Mommsen, Wolfang J., xiii
Mongardini, Carlo, 17, *20*, 108, *120*, *160*, 193, *195–196*, *238*, 255, *256*, *269–270*, *283–284*
Montesquieu, *185*, 242
Moore, Kathryn, 153, 156, *160*
Moore, Wilbert E., 27, *40*, *60*, 163, *175*, 258, *270*
Mosca, Gaetano, 78
Moscovici, Serge, xiii
Mozart, *18*
Mulkay, Michael J., *38*, *42*, 76, 152, *160*
Muller, W. C., 193, *196*
Mullins, Nicholas C., 152, *159*, 206

Nagel, Ernest, *38*, *42*, 51, *60*
Natta, Alessandro, 133
Nedelmann, Birgitta, 3, 123, 125, 131, *137*, 247
Needham, Joseph, 62
Newton, Isaac, 56, 62, 279, *283*, 292
Nietzsche, Friedrich, ix
Nisbet, Robert A., *283–284*
Nixon, Richard, 299
Noelle-Neumann, Elisabeth, *195–196*

O'Dea, Thomas, 241, 244
Ogburn, William F., 310
Oppenheimer, Franz, 26
O'Rand, Angela, 152, *160*
Ortega y Gasset, José, *161*

Pagani, Angelo, 83
Paganini, Niccolo, *18*
Page, Charles H., *137*
Pareto, Vilfredo, 78, *156*, *160*, *185*, 249, 278, 296
Park, Robert E., 107
Parsons, Talcott, 6, *18–19*, 24–26, 28–29, 31, 34, *35–37*, *39*, *42–43*, 48–50, 54, 56, *58*, *60*, 80–85, 90–91, 103, 109–110, 128, 202–204, 207, 222–224, 226, 230, 233, *237–238*, 242–243, 253
Pasteur, Louis, 313
Pauling, Linus, 33
Pavese, Cesare, 81
Pelinka, Anton, 192, *196*
Pepitone, Albert, 242
Persell, Caroline Hodges, 317–318

Peterson, Richard A., *41–42*
Piaget, Jean, *269–270*
Pinch, 73
Plasser, Fritz, *196*
Plato, 56
Plessner, Helmut, 34, *42*
Poggi, Gianfranco, 82
Polanyi Michael, 62, 71, *76*
Popper, Karl, 55, 57, *59–60*
Porter, Alan L., *158, 160*
Powell, Walter W., *18, 20*, 281, *283–284*
Price, Derek J. de Solla, 149, 152, *156–157, 160*

Radcliffe-Brown, A. R., 252
Rammstaedt, O., 267, *269–270*
Rampling, Charlotte, 124, 136
Reid, James M., 306
Reskin, Barbara F., 152, *160–161*
Restivo, Sal, 73–74, *76*
Rey, Abel, 310
Reynolds, Janice M., *41*
Reynolds, Larry T., *41*
Rice, Stuart A., *41*
Riley, Matilda White, *162*, 316
Ringel, E., *195–196*
Robbins, Richard, *18, 20*, 281, *283–284*
Roberts, Royston M., *283–284*
Robertson, Evie, xiii
Roche, Thomas, *161*
Roosevelt, F. D., 300
Rose, Hilary, 67
Rose, Steve, 67
Rosenblatt, Aaron, 152, *159, 175, 210*
Ross, Edward A., 236
Rossi, Paolo, 87
Roth, Guenther, *185*
Ryan, Alan, *38, 42*
Rubin, Leonard, *158–159*
Rudner, Richard S., *38, 42*
Russell, Bertrand, 63

Saage, Richard, *37, 41*
Samuelson, Paul, *157*
Sarton, George, 63, 203, *238*, 239
Savage, Stephen P., *36, 39, 43*
Scheler, Max, *42*, 202, 213
Schizzerotto, Antonio, 83
Schneider, Louis, 7–9, *20*
Schuker, Eleanor, 153, 155, *161*
Schutz, Alfred, 85, 185

Scott, Robert A., *35, 43*
Selznick, Philip, 205
Sewell, William H., 152
Shapin, Steven, 73
Sherif, Muzafer 242
Shils, Edward A., *36, 43*
Shore, Arnold R., *35, 43*
Sills, David L., 205, 309
Simmel, Georg, xi, 9–10, 121, 123–124, 137, 202–204, 250
Simmons, Anthony, 24, *43*
Simon, Herbert A., 7, *156 , 161*, 205, 317
Simonton, Dean K., 152, *161*
Smelser, Neil J., 21, *35, 41–43*, 286, *287*
Smith, David L., *161*, 180, *185*
Snizek, William E., *40, 161*
Socrates, 214
Sola, Giorgio, 83
Sormano, Andrea, 93, *98*
Sorokin, Pitirim, 5–6, *18, 20, 35, 43*, 109, *185*, 202–204, 226, 236, 257–258, 260, 267–268, *269–271*, 302
Spencer, Herbert, 50, 77, 293
Stark, Werner, 180, *186*
Statera, Gianni, 2, 61, 75, *76*, 86
Stehr, Nico, 2, 24, *38, 40, 43*, 152, *160*, 251
Steinberg, Ronnie, *157, 161*
Sterne, Laurence, 293
Stewart, John, 149, *158*
Stinchcombe, Arthur, 6, *20*, 29, *43*, *174–175*, 200, 208, *210*
Storer, Norman W., 65–66, *76*, 86, *175, 210*
Strykowski, B.F., *156, 161*
Sumner, William Graham, 242
Sztompka, Piotr, 6–9, 11–12, 17, *19–20*, 29, *36, 38, 43*, 45, 55, 58, *60, 161*, 164, *174–175*, 203–204, 208, *210*, 222–223, 228, *237–238*, 261, *271, 282, 284*, 289–294

Tabboni, Simonetta, xii, 9, *20, 160, 238*
Talos, Emmerich, *196*
Taylor, Ian, *39, 41, 43*
Taylor, Patricia A., 153, 155–156, *161*
Tellia, Bruno, 83
Tenbruck, Friedrich, 80, *120*
Tentori, Tullio, 239
Thomas, Dorothy S., 310
Thomas, W. I., 253–254, 286

Tilly, Charles, xiii
Tiryakian, Edward A., *20*
Tocqueville, Alexis de, *185*
Toulmin, Stephen, 74
Toynbee, Arnold J., *255–256*
Toynbee, Philip, *284*
Trilling, Lionel, 299
Trow, Martin, 153, 155, *161*
Tsai, Shiow-ling, 155, *161*
Turner, Stephen P., 149, *161*
Tyree, Andrea, *157–158*

Ucakar, Karl, 188, *196*
Ullmann-Margalit, Edna, 180, *186*
Unger, Rhoda Kesler, *161*
Useem, Michael, 153, 155–156, *161*
Vaccarini, Italo, *237–238*, *255–256*

Vallier, Ivan, 241, 244
Vanberg, V., *185*
Venn, John, 303–304
Vico, Gianbattista, *185*
Vijh, Ashok K., *161*
Vittorini, Elio, 81
Von Schelting, Alexander, *185*
Von Wiese, Leopold, 253
Young, Jack, *39, 43*

Wagner, Helmut R. 255–256
Walberg, Herbert J., 153, 155, *156, 161*
Waldheim, Kurt, 191

Wallace, Alfred Russel, *19–20*
Wallace, Walter L., *37, 43*
Wallas, Graham, *185*
Walpole, Horace, 275, *283–284*, 313–314
Walton, Paul, *39, 43*
Watkins, John, *59–60*
Watson, Goodwin, 241
Watzlawick, Paul, 9, *20*
Weber, Alfred, 181, *185–186*
Weber, Max, 25, *42*, 80–81, 85, 91, 109, 123, 178–180, 183–184, *185–186*, 202–204, 250, 287, 296
Weingart, Peter, 67, 73, *76*
Weisskopf, Victor F., 33
Whitehead, Alfred North, , 75, 202
Whitley, Richard, 67, 72, *76*
Wippler, Reinhard, *185–186*
Wittich, Claus, *185*
Wolf, Alison, *19–20*
Wolff, Kurt H., 213–214, 218, *220*
Woolgar, Steve, 74
Wundt, Wilhelm, 180–181, *185–186*, 296

Zetterberg, Hans L., *41*, 205, 241
Zerubavel, Eviatar, 258, 267, *271*
Zingerle, Arnold, 3, 221, 225, *238*, 295
Zipf, George Kingsley, *156, 161*
Znaniecki, Florian, 202–203, 253
Zuckerman, Harriet, 3, *137*, 140–141, 143, 149–151, 156, *156–157, 161–162*, 202, 205, 209, 244